Hidden Generalizations

Hidden Generalizations

Phonological Opacity in Optimality Theory

John J. McCarthy

LONDON OAKVILLE

Published by
UK: Equinox Publishing Ltd., Unit 6, The Village, 101 Amies St.,
London SW11 2JW
USA: DBBC, 28 Main Street, Oakville, CT 06779
www.equinoxpub.com

First published 2007

British Library Cataloguing-in-Publication Data
A catalogue record for this book is available from the British Library.

ISBN-10   1845530519   (hardback)
             1845530527   (paperback)

ISBN-13   9781845530518   (hardback)
             9781845530525   (paperback)

Library of Congress Cataloging-in-Publication Data
McCarthy, John J., 1953-
  Hidden generalizations : phonological opacity in optimality theory /
John J. McCarthy.
      p. cm. -- (Advances in optimality theory)
  Includes bibliographical references and index.
  ISBN 1-84553-051-9 (hb) -- ISBN 1-84553-052-7 (pb) 1. Grammar,
Comparative and general--Phonology. 2. Opacity (Linguistics) 3.
Optimality theory (Linguistics) I. Title. II. Series.
  P217.3.M39 2006
  414--dc22

                         2006009195

Typeset by Catchline, Milton Keynes (www.catchline.com)
Printed and bound in Great Britain by Antony Rowe Ltd, Chippenham

Contents

Acknowledgements

My colleagues and students at the University of Massachusetts were the first audience for this work and its predecessors, and they have given me much assistance along the way. I wish therefore to offer special thanks to Leah Bateman, Michael Becker, Tim Beechey, Della Chambless, Andries Coetzee, Paul de Lacy, Kathryn Flack, Maria Gouskova, Shigeto Kawahara, Mike Key, John Kingston, Elliott Moreton, Steve Parker, Joe Pater, Lisa Selkirk, Jen Smith, Anne-Michelle Tessier, Adam Werle, and Matt Wolf. I also had an opportunity to present this material in a short course at the University of Southern California. I am grateful to my hosts, Ania Łubowicz and Rachel Walker, to other participants from USC, and to Eric Bakovic, Bruce Hayes, Nicole Nelson, Jason Riggle, Colin Wilson, and Kie Zuraw. Their questions and comments were most valuable. In addition, I gave a lecture about this research at the Second Old World Conference in Phonology in Tromsø, Norway. For this opportunity and for much useful feedback, I thank the organizer, Curt Rice, and the other participants. Hamza Al-Mozainy could be counted on for speedy responses to my many emailed questions about Bedouin Arabic. Over the years, I have had many fruitful discussions of opacity and related topics with Alan Prince.

In addition to her other contributions, Kathryn Flack read the entire manuscript, pointing out weaknesses in the argumentation or exposition, correcting many inaccuracies, and generally making this work much better than it would otherwise have been.

I gratefully acknowledge the support of Armin Mester and Ellen Woolford, the editors of Advances in Optimality Theory. I am happy that this volume is the first of what will no doubt be a long line of works appearing in that series.

Readers are urged to consult my homepage, http://people.umass.edu/jjmccart, for any errata or additions to this text that came too late to make it into print.

This book is dedicated to the memory of my mother, Joan T. (Condon) McCarthy (June 9, 1928–November 17, 2005). 'For now we see as through a glass, darkly, but then face to face. Now I know in part, but then I will know even as I am known.'

1 Overview of the issues and the results

1.1 What is phonological opacity and why is it important?

The sound systems of languages are precisely that — systems. This means
that they exhibit various regularities of structure. If phonology only dealt with
those regularities that express categorical truths, however, it would not be a
very interesting enterprise. In reality, phonological research and theory are to a
great extent engaged with generalizations that fall short of categorical truth.

Some generalizations have lexical exceptions. Other generalizations are
outmatched by requirements with higher priority. (See §2.3 for an example
and discussion.) This book is about generalizations that are not quite true for a
different reason: the truths they state are hidden by other aspects of the system.
When a generalization is partially obscured in this way, it is said to be *opaque*.
(The origin of this term is explained in §2.2.)

Since this book includes plenty of examples, a couple will suffice for now.
In English, the past tense suffix is pronounced as [-əd] after [t] or [d]: *planted*,
braided. This generalization is sometimes hidden, though, because [t] can be
deleted after a nasal consonant: *planted* is pronounced carefully as [plæntəd]
but more usually as [plænəd]. Even when the [t] is absent, the suffix is still
pronounced as [-əd], so *planted* never merges with *planned*. Another example:
some English dialects add a rising off-glide between [æ] and tautosyllabic
[ŋ]: [bæe̯ŋ] *bang*. But when [ŋ] is derived by place assimilation from /n/, the
generalization is hidden and does not seem to hold: [mæŋkɑjnd], *[mæe̯ŋkɑjnd]
mankind.[1]

In these cases and others like them, generalizations of seemingly unques-
tionable validity turn out to be superficially invalid. I say 'superficially' because
these generalizations are only invalid as naïve statements about surface structure: in the surface form [plænəd] *planted*, the past tense suffix is pronounced
as [-əd] even though no [t] or [d] precedes, and in the surface form [mæŋkɑjnd]
the [æ] has no off-glide even though [ŋ] follows. In a deeper sense, though,
the generalizations really are valid, or at least they are invalid for principled
reasons. The [ə] in [plænəd] is somehow a response to the underlying /t/ of

plant, and the missing off-glide in [mæŋkɑjnd] is somehow a reflection of the /n/ that underlies [ŋ]. Furthermore, it is clear that these opaque generalizations are interacting with and being influenced by other regularities of the language, such as the loss of /t/ after /n/ in *planted* and the assimilation of /n/ to a following [k] in *mankind*.

A great deal of phonological research, ancient and modern, is devoted to understanding opacity. The earliest and most successful theory of opacity is the *derivation*. If the rule inserting [ə] before the English past tense suffix /-d/ precedes the rule deleting [t], then the [ə] rule sees a representation where the underlying /t/ is still present: /plænt-d/ $\rightarrow_{\text{ə-insertion}}$ [plæntəd] $\rightarrow_{t\text{-deletion}}$ [plænəd]. Likewise, if the rule inserting an off-glide between [æ] and [ŋ] is ordered before nasal place assimilation, then the glide-insertion rule sees a representation where the underlying /n/ is still present: [mænkɑjnd] $\rightarrow_{\textit{ʁ-epen}}$ *no change* $\rightarrow_{n\text{-assim}}$ [mæŋkɑjnd]. More recent work has explored alternatives to derivations, such as enrichments to phonological structure. This body of research is reviewed in §2.2 and §2.3.

It is not an exaggeration to say that the analysis of opacity has been one of the central themes of generative phonology. Although he does not frame it in these terms, opacity is the crux of Chomsky's (1964: 75ff.) argument against structuralist phonemics. He cites Joos's (1942) famous example from Canadian English, where the distinction between [ɹʌjɾəɹ] *writer* and [ɹɑjɾəɹ] *rider* is the result of derivational ordering: the rule that raises the /ɑj/ nucleus to [ʌj] before voiceless [t] is ordered before the rule that merges /t/ and /d/ into the voiced flap [ɾ] before an unstressed syllable. Opacity is also the main topic of the large and varied literature on rule ordering in generative phonology dating from about 1968 through 1980 (see §2.2). And opacity was at the heart of the controversy during that same period about the abstractness of underlying representations (see Kenstowicz and Kisseberth 1977: Chapter 1, 1979: Chapter 6). Abstract underlying forms only make sense when the rules that operate on them are opaque, since opaque rules are the only way for the abstract part of an underlying form to affect surface structure. In recent years, opacity has reemerged as an important challenge for phonological theories that rely primarily or exclusively on surface structure constraints, since opaque processes refer to conditions that are not visible in surface structure.

One reason for opacity's durability as an object of phonological research is that the alternatives to taking opacity seriously have proven to be unsatisfactory. Classical structuralist phonology was based on the premise that all authentic phonological generalizations are categorically true statements about the distribution of allophones. Chomsky's argument against structuralism therefore cites examples of generalizations that are not true in this sense, echoing concerns that the structuralists themselves had already expressed (see, for example, many of the contributions to Joos 1957). Later work, in reaction to Chomsky and Halle (1968), took the position that phonological rules must state surface-true generalizations and must be unordered (see §2.2.3). If this were correct, then opaque processes would be nothing more than the lexicalized residue of sound changes that are no longer productive. It is difficult to accept that the productive, variable, low-level processes of English cited above are not part of speakers' active phonological competence, even though they are opaque. (Further evidence that processes can be productive but opaque is presented in §2.2.3 and §4.3.3.) The idea that phonological knowledge is reducible to surface-true generalizations has turned out to be an intellectual dead end. Phonological generalizations, whether they are formulated as rules or constraints, can be active and productive aspects of linguistic knowledge even if they are opaque.

All serious approaches to opacity are attempts to answer a single question: when not all phonological generalizations *can* be true, which ones *are* true and which are not? Derivations are one answer to this question: generalizations that hold of later stages in the derivation take precedence, truth-wise, over generalizations that obtain earlier in the derivation. For instance, the generalization that [ʌj] occurs before voiceless obstruents and [ɑj] before voiced ones is true early in the derivation, but not later on when /t/ and /d/ merge to the flap [ɾ] before an unstressed syllable. The early generalization about [ʌj] is not surface true, but the late generalization about [ɾ] is. Another example of an early generalization that ceases to be true because of a later one is the requirement that there be an off-glide between [æ] and tautosyllabic [ŋ]. Derivations, then, allow generalizations to state temporary truths. Phonological theories that require all generalizations to state durable truths, such as structuralism and Natural Generative Phonology, are unable to analyze opacity. Optimality Theory (Prince and Smolensky 2004) does not require generalizations to be surface true, and it deals with competition among generalizations through ranking. Ranking supplies a partial theory of opacity and perhaps, with the changes proposed in this book, a complete one.

1.2   What does this book have to say about opacity?

This book's principal thesis is that the best theory of opacity — and of phonology generally — is a synthesis of Optimality Theory (hereafter OT) with derivations. I argue that a candidate in OT includes not just a surface form but also a series of intermediate forms, each of which is minimally different from the form that immediately precedes it. A candidate, then, supplies information about the sequence of operations needed to link the underlying and surface forms. In the *planted* example, for instance, the winning candidate is the ordered *n*-tuple <plænt-d, plæntəd, plænəd>, and among its competitors is *<plænt-d, plænd>. In the *mankind* example, the winning candidate is <mænkɑjnd, mæŋkɑjnd>, and its most important competitor is *<mænkɑjnd, mæŋkɑjnd, mæẽ̯ŋkɑjnd>. These ordered *n*-tuples are called *candidate chains*. This theory is referred to as *OT with candidate chains*, or *OT-CC* for short. (On the antecedents of OT-CC, see §3.2.3.)

Candidate chains are subject to three well-formedness conditions, the details of which will be explained more fully in §3. First, all chains are *faithfully initiated*. This means that the first form in a chain is identical with the underlying representation, except for syllabification and the like.

Second, chains are *gradually divergent*. This condition has already been hinted at: the successive forms in a chain are minimally different from their neighbors, so the path from input to output proceeds in small steps.

Third, chains are *harmonically improving*. Every form in a chain is more harmonic than its predecessor, relative to the constraint hierarchy of the language in question. Because of the gradualness requirement a form's successor in a chain may not be the ultimate surface form, but it must be more harmonic.

The evaluation of a candidate chain by the grammar has some familiar properties: markedness constraints assess the last form in the chain, which is the chain's output; and faithfulness constraints measure discrepancies between the first and last forms in the chain. A novel type of constraint, PREC (for 'precedence'), specifies the preferred order of faithfulness violations in a chain. For example, the winning chain from the input /mænkɑjnd/ is opaque <mænkɑjnd, mæŋkɑjnd>. Its transparent competitor *<mænkɑjnd, mæŋkɑjnd, mæẽ̯ŋkɑjnd> loses because of the constraint PREC(DEP, IDENT(Place)), which says that the IDENT(Place)-violating mapping of /n/ to [ŋ] cannot precede the DEP-violating insertion of the off-glide [e̯].

This proposal raises two fundamental questions: Why analyze opacity by incorporating derivations into *OT*? Why analyze opacity by incorporating *derivations* into OT? These questions and the issues they raise merit serious consideration.

Why OT? Opacity figures prominently in critiques of OT by proponents of rule-based phonology (see §2.3). These critiques suffer from selective vision, however, seeing only OT's opacity problem and ignoring the very real problems that typically afflict rule-based phonology, such as dearth of explanation and absence of typological predictions. A central failing of rule-based phonology in the tradition of Chomsky and Halle (1968) is that it promotes descriptive completeness over all other goals of linguistic theory, a miscasting of priorities that means that the theory with the richest descriptive resources inevitably wins.

OT's very real advantages in explaining phonological systems and limiting their typological possibilities need not be reviewed here. (Readers who need convincing might want to consult McCarthy 2002b.) Since OT has many strengths, if opacity is OT's principal weakness, then it makes sense to explore ways of remedying this weakness instead of giving up on the enterprise.

Why derivations? There have been many proposals for accommodating opacity in OT, and I argue in §2.3 that most of them share a common characteristic: they rely on a third level of representation, neither underlying nor surface, as a crucial part of the analysis of opaque alternations. The defining property of a derivation, in the sense I am employing here, is the presence of this third (or fourth or fifth) level of representation. It is therefore not inaccurate to say that derivations or something like them have already been shown to play a necessary role in any reasonably complete approach to opacity in OT. But these more limited proposals for incorporating derivations into OT turn out to be insufficient when the full range of opaque alternations is considered, and so I argue in §3 that a richer theory of derivations, candidate chains, is required in OT.

If candidate chains are to be a welcome addition to OT, then they should offer more than just a way out of the opacity jam — and they do. For one thing, the well-formedness requirements on candidate chains have the effect of severely limiting the size of the candidate set. Because there is no natural limit on the number of epenthesis operations that GEN can perform, classic OT[2] imposes no upper bound on the length of a candidate and therefore no bound on the size of the candidate set for any input. But the harmonic improvement requirement ensures that candidate chains are of bounded length, for all inputs and for all constraint hierarchies (see §3.2.2).

For another, the harmonic improvement and gradualness requirements operate in concert to impose limitations on what kinds of mappings from underlying to surface representation are possible. In classic OT, a necessary and sufficient condition for the mapping /A/ → [B] in a language L is that [B] is more harmonic, according to L's constraint hierarchy, than any other candidate derived from /A/. With chains, this condition is still necessary but it is no longer sufficient: for [B] to be a possible output from /A/, there must be a well-formed chain connecting /A/ with [B]. Suppose that the chain must contain the intermediate form [C] because of the gradualness requirement: <A, C, B>. Then [C] must be more harmonic than [A] and less harmonic than [B] according to L's hierarchy. Sometimes this means that L's hierarchy must rank constraints that would be nonconflicting and therefore unrankable in classic OT. More importantly, sometimes it means that the /A/ → [B] mapping will be impossible in L. In this way, candidate chain theory restricts OT's power to perform certain global optimizations. This is also a major point of difference between chain theory and standard derivational models, which have no analogous notion of improvement or progress in their derivations (see §3.2.4.3).

The final chapter of this book presents case studies of two languages with significant amounts of opaque phonology. Because of my background and knowledge, both of the languages are varieties of Arabic, but I believe that they are fully representative of the kinds of opaque interactions that can be found in other, unrelated languages. Furthermore, most of the processes that are discussed are independent innovations rather than the legacies of a common ancestor. These case studies are a necessary adjunct to the theoretical proposal because many of the more complex issues in studying opacity only arise in analyses of sufficient depth to show more than two processes interacting (cf. Cathey and Demers 1970).

1.3   How should this book be read?

Readers who are new to OT are advised not to start with this book and to begin instead with a textbook introduction like Kager (1999a) or an overview like McCarthy (2002b). Either of those works will provide more than enough background to understand and critically evaluate the contents of the following chapters. The majority of readers will probably want to proceed linearly through §2 and §3, and then sample the extended analyses in §4. Those who are familiar with previous work on opacity before and since OT could skim rather than read §2. Readers who prefer praxis to theory may want to try reading §4 on the basis of just the brief introduction to candidate chains in §1.2, but I would not recommend it.

Notes

1   The *mankind* example comes from Donegan and Stampe (1979: 148–149). They also describe many other opaque interactions in English casual speech and dialect variation.

2   Throughout, I use the expression 'classic OT' as shorthand for the approach that has become a *de facto* standard, a synthesis of Prince and Smolensky's (2004) original proposals with correspondence-based faithfulness (McCarthy and Prince 1995, 1999). Among the characteristics of classic OT is a universal, finite constraint component Con that is limited to markedness and faithfulness constraints, and a single Eval that evaluates fully formed output candidates that show the effects of all phonological processes in parallel.

2 Opacity, derivations, and Optimality Theory

2.1 Overview

This chapter begins (§2.2) by explaining what opacity is and how it is analyzed in rule-based phonology. The discussion then turns (§2.3) to a description of 'classic' Optimality Theory, the problems that opacity presents for classic OT, and various ideas about how to modify the classic theory to accommodate it. The conclusion I draw (§2.4) is that there is something fundamentally correct about rule-based phonology's serial derivation, leading to the proposal in §3 for an analogue of the serial derivation in a framework that retains all of classic OT's essential elements.

2.2 Opacity and derivations

2.2.1 Levels of representation

The theory of generative phonology recognizes two principal levels of representation, underlying and surface. At the underlying level, every morpheme has a unique representation. For example, the three principal surface alternants of the English plural suffix — [-z], [-s], and [-əz] — are derived by phonological rules from a single underlying representation, such as /-z/. Only suppletive or allomorphic alternants of morphemes require distinct underlying representations, such as the plural allomorphs /-ən/ of *children* and /-iː-/ of *geese*.

When a morpheme alternates nonsuppletively, its underlying representation must be discovered by the analyst and by the learner. In paradigms like German [bʊnt]/[bʊntə] 'multicolored/pl.' and [bʊnt]/[bʊndə] 'federation/pl.', distinct underlying representations are required because there are distinct patterns of voicing alternation: /bʊnt/ 'multi-colored' is voiceless throughout its paradigm and /bʊnd/ 'federation' alternates between voiced and voiceless. In theory and in actual practice, the relationship between the hypothesized underlying representation and the observed surface paradigm is sometimes less transparent than this.

Some recent research explores alternatives to positing an underlying level of representation. These approaches are monostratal in the sense that they recognize only a single level of representation, the surface form. In Declarative Phonology (Scobbie, Coleman, and Bird 1996), the work of underlying representations is done by constraints that describe morphemes. These descriptions are crucially incomplete in the case of alternating morphemes: e.g., for German [bʊnt]/[bʊndə], a constraint requires a final alveolar stop in 'federation' but says nothing about its voicing. Another monostratal approach seeks to express phonological generalizations purely in terms of relations between surface forms (e.g., Albright 2002, Burzio 2002).

In this context, it is worth reviewing the reasons why generative phonology posits an underlying level of representation (see Kenstowicz and Kisseberth 1979: chapter 6 for an overview of the evidence). The main argument comes from paradigms where the relationships among surface forms make sense only when mediated by an underlying form that is distinct from all of the surface forms. Schane's (1974) Palauan example in (2-1) is a well-known case. Because unstressed vowels reduce to [ə] and there is only one stress per word, disyllabic roots like 'cover an opening' and 'pull out' never show up with more than one surface nonschwa vowel. The hypothesized underlying representations /daŋob/ and /teʔib/ record the quality of the vowels as they appear when stressed in different members of the paradigm. These underlying representations incorporate all of the unpredictable phonological information about these morphemes. In generative phonology, the underlying representation of a root is the nexus of a set of related words, so it must contain sufficient information to allow the surface forms of all of those words to be derived by the grammar of the language. (See §4.3.3 for detailed argumentation in support of underlying representations in a case similar to Palauan.)

(2-1)   Palauan Vowel Reduction

Underlying	Present Middle	Future Participle	
/daŋob/	mə-ˈdaŋəb	dəˈŋob-l	'cover an opening'
/teʔib/	mə-ˈteʔəb	təˈʔib-l	'pull out'

Generative phonology in the tradition of *The Sound Pattern of English* (SPE — Chomsky and Halle 1968) also allows for any number of levels intermediate between the underlying and surface levels. These intermediate levels are the result of sequential application of phonological rules. If a language has *n* rules in its grammar, it has *n*–1 intermediate representations, each of which is a potentially distinct way of representing the linguistic form that is being derived.

In Palauan, for example, the *SPE* theory requires an intermediate level at which stress has been assigned but vowel reduction has not yet applied: /daŋob-l/ →$_{stress}$ [da'ŋobl] →$_{reduction}$ [də'ŋobl]. Indeed, *SPE* requires rules to apply sequentially even when simultaneous application would produce the same result.

2.2.2　Derivations

Any mapping from the underlying to the surface level of representation is a derivation. In this sense, any multistratal theory of phonology is derivational, including classic OT. The various multistratal theories differ significantly, however, in the complexity and internal organization of the derivations they posit.

The *SPE* approach to derivations retains considerable currency because it is often assumed even in contemporary research that has moved far beyond *SPE*'s other hypotheses about rules and representations (see §2.2.6). In *SPE*, the grammar consists of an ordered list of rules. The rules are applied in a strict sequence, with the output of rule i supplying the input to rule $i+1$. The output of each rule (except the last) is therefore a level of representation intermediate between the underlying and surface levels.

An important insight, due originally to Kiparsky (1968), is that rules may have different functional relationships to one another. In the least interesting case, a pair of rules may not interact at all — an example would be word-initial vowel epenthesis and word-final obstruent devoicing. When rules do interact, however, the functional relationship between them can often be classified as feeding or bleeding.

Rule A is said to *feed* rule B if A can create additional inputs to B. If A in fact precedes B, then A and B are in feeding order. (If B precedes A, then they are in counterfeeding order, which will be explained in §2.2.3.) An example of feeding order is the interaction between vowel and consonant epenthesis in Classical Arabic. Words that begin with consonant clusters receive prothetic [ʔi] (or [ʔu], if the next vowel is also [u]). As the derivation in (2-2) shows, prothesis of [ʔi] is the result of a feeding interaction between [i] epenthesis before word-initial clusters (= rule A) and [ʔ] epenthesis before word-initial vowels (= rule B).

(2-2)　Feeding order in Classical Arabic

Underlying	/dˤrib/	'beat (m. sg.)!'
Vowel epenthesis	idˤrib	
[ʔ] epenthesis	ʔidˤrib	
Surface	[ʔidˤrib]	

Rule A is said to *bleed* rule B if A can eliminate potential inputs to B. If A in fact precedes B, then A and B are in bleeding order. (If B precedes A, then they are in counterbleeding order, which will also be explained in §2.2.3.) For example, in a southern Palestinian variety of Arabic, progressive assimilation of pharyngealization (= rule B) is blocked by high front segments, among them [i]. When the vowel [i] is epenthesized into triconsonantal clusters (= rule A), it also blocks assimilation, as shown in (2-3) (Davis 1995).

(2-3)   Bleeding order in southern Palestinian Arabic
      Underlying   /batˤn-ha/ 'her stomach'
      Vowel epenthesis   batˤinha
      Progressive assimilation   *Blocked*
      Regressive assimilation   bˤaˤtˤinha
      Surface   [bˤaˤtˤinha]

Feeding and bleeding orders have something in common: when rules apply in feeding or bleeding order, those structures that are derived by rules are treated exactly the same as similar structures that were already present in underlying representation. For example, the process of [ʔ]-epenthesis in Classical Arabic applies to words with an underlying initial vowel, /al-walad-u/ → [ʔalwaladu] 'the boy (nominative)', and also to words with a derived initial vowel, such as the intermediate representation [idˤrib] in (2-2). Likewise, epenthetic and nonepenthetic [i] equally block progressive assimilation in Palestinian Arabic, as shown by (2-3) and /sˤiħħa/ → [sˤiħħa], *[sˤiˤħˤħˤaˤ] 'health'. In feeding and bleeding interactions, what you see is what you get: when derived and underived structures are identical, they exhibit identical phonological behavior. This is emphatically not the case with counterfeeding and counterbleeding interactions.

2.2.3   Opacity in derivations

If rule A feeds rule B and they are applied in the order B precedes A, then these rules are said to be in *counterfeeding* order. For example, in a Bedouin Arabic dialect (see §4.3.3), there are processes raising short /a/ to a high vowel in a nonfinal open syllable (= rule A) and deleting short high vowels in nonfinal open syllables (= rule B). These processes are in a feeding relationship, since raising has the potential to create new inputs to deletion. But their order is actually counterfeeding, as shown in (2-4). High vowels derived by raising are treated differently from underlying high vowels; only the underlying high vowels are subject to deletion. When rules apply in feeding order, derived and underlying structures behave alike, but when they apply in counterfeeding order, derived and underlying structures behave differently.

(2-4) Counterfeeding order in Bedouin Arabic[1]

Underlying	a. /dafaʕ/ 'he pushed'	b. /ʃarib-at/ 'she drank'
Deletion	—	ʃarbat
Raising	difaʕ	—
Surface	[difaʕ]	[ʃarbat]

The same is true of *counterbleeding* order, where rule A bleeds rule B but they are applied with B preceding A. In this same Arabic dialect, there is also a process palatalizing velars when they precede front vowels (see §3.3.3). Deletion (= rule A) bleeds palatalization (= rule B), since deletion can remove a high front vowel that would condition velar palatalization. But their order is counterbleeding, as shown in (2-5). High front vowels, even when they are absent from surface forms, induce adjoining velars to palatalize. Effects like this are typical with counterbleeding order.

(2-5) Counterbleeding order in Bedouin Arabic

Underlying	a. /ħaːkim-iːn/	b. /t-ħakum-in/
Palatalization	ħaːkʲimiːn	—
Deletion	ħaːkʲmiːn	tħakmin
Surface	[ħaːkʲmiːn]	[tħakmin]
	'ruling (masculine plural)'	'they (feminine) rule'

The result of counterfeeding and counterbleeding interactions is phonological opacity. Kiparsky's (1973: 79, 1976: 178–179) definition of opacity appears in (2-6). Clause (c) of this definition describes all processes of neutralization and so it is not relevant to our concerns here. We will therefore focus on clauses (a) and (b).

(2-6) Opacity

A phonological rule P of the form $A \rightarrow B \mathbin{/} C\underline{\quad}D$ is *opaque* if there are surface structures with any of the following characteristics:

   a. instances of A in the environment $C\underline{\quad}D$,
   b. instances of B derived by P that occur in environments other than $C\underline{\quad}D$,
or   c. instances of B not derived by P that occur in the environment $C\underline{\quad}D$.

In the derivation /dafaʕ/ $\rightarrow$ [difaʕ] in (2-4), the high-vowel deletion rule is opaque under clause (a) of this definition: [difaʕ] has [i] (= A) in an open syllable (= $C\underline{\quad}D$). Rules applied in counterfeeding order produce opacity of the clause (a) type, in which surface forms contain phonological structures that look like they should have undergone some process but in fact did not.[2]

   In the derivation /ħaːkim-iːn/ $\rightarrow$ [ħaːkʲmiːn] in (2-5), the palatalization rule is opaque under clause (b) of this definition: [ħaːkʲmiːn] has [kʲ] (= B) derived by palatalization (= *P*), but [kʲ] is not adjacent to a front vowel (= *C__D*). Rules applied in counterbleeding order produce opacity of this type, in which surface forms contain derived phonological structures without the context that shows how they were derived.

Counterfeeding and counterbleeding interactions supply the best — arguably, the only — evidence for language-particular rule ordering. It is not surprising, then, that skepticism about stipulated, language-particular ordering stimulated efforts to deny that opaque interactions involve living phonological processes (cf. §1.1). According to the proponents of Natural Generative Phonology (NGP), authentic phonological rules must state surface-true generalizations and they must be unordered (Hooper [Bybee] 1976, 1979, Vennemann 1972, 1974). NGP therefore maintains that opaque processes are merely the lexicalized residue of sound changes that are no longer productive — opaque rules were said to be 'not psychologically real'. (Recent work advocating similar views in an OT context includes Green (2004), Mielke, Hume, and Armstrong (2003), and Sanders (2002, 2003).) In fact, much if not all of the abstractness controversy of the 1970's, which dealt with proposed limits on the degree of disparity between underlying and surface representations (see Kenstowicz and Kisseberth 1977: Chapter 1, 1979: Chapter 6), was really an argument about opacity, since abstract underlying forms can influence the output only if opaque rules apply to them.

Certainly, there have been dubious analyses based on opaque rules and excessively abstract underlying forms, but outright denial of all opaque interactions is an empirically unsupportable overreaction. The example of Bedouin Arabic is instructive. (See §4.3.3 for detailed discussion.) Al-Mozainy (1981) presents several arguments that the opaque processes in this language are alive and productive. First, they are active in borrowed words. Second, high vowel deletion, even though it is opaque, applies productively in external sandhi, as shown in (2-7). If a process applies in external sandhi, it cannot be lexicalized, since it is impossible to list the infinite number of word collocations that the syntax provides.[3]

(2-7)   Phrase-level deletion in Bedouin Arabic (Al-Mozainy 1981: 50–51)

/kaːtib al-ʒawaːb/	kaːt.bal.ʒu.waːb	'writing the letter'
	*kaː.ti.bal.ʒu.waːb	
/tiʕtˤuːnih al-museːʕiːdi/	tiʕ.tˤuːn.hal.m.seː.ʕiː.di	'you give it to the one
	*tiʕ.tˤuː.ni.hal.m.seː.ʕiː.di	from the clan of
		Musaiʕīd'

Third, the most compelling evidence that raising is productive comes from a kind of play language. Although raising usually affects any short /a/ in a nonfinal open syllable, there are phonological conditions under which raising regularly fails to apply: after a guttural consonant ([ʔ], [h], [ʕ], [ħ], [χ], [ʁ]), or before a guttural consonant or coronal sonorant ([l], [r], [n]) that is itself followed by [a]. Bedouin Arabic has a secret language that permutes the consonants of the root, and this will sometimes affect the position of gutturals or coronal sonorants relative to the potentially raised vowel. When that happens, the vowel raises or fails to raise in exact conformity with these generalizations, as (2-8) shows. Other secret language data show that palatalization is also productive, even though it is opaque (see §3.3.3). In sum, the opaque phonology of Bedouin Arabic is also its living, productive phonology. (For further examples of processes that are productive yet opaque, see Donegan and Stampe (1979).)

(2-8)   Raising alternations in a secret language
  /dafaʕ/ Underlying representation
  difaʕ Unpermuted form
  fidaʕ Raising as expected
  daʕaf No raising before guttural + [a]
  faʕad   "
  ʕadaf No raising after guttural
  ʕafad   "

Although this sort of evidence shows that opacity is a fact of phonological life, certain types of opacity have received and deserve a skeptical reception. A famous example is *SPE*'s /ɹixt/ → [ɹɑjt] *right*. The point is that a few dubious analyses are not grounds to reject a theoretical construct, particularly when it is strongly supported by sound analyses, as it is in Bedouin Arabic.

A type of opacity that received particular attention in the 1970's is the Duke-of-York derivation (Hogg 1978, Pullum 1976). Like the eponymous Duke of the nursery rhyme,[4] underlying /A/ is changed by a rule to intermediate [B], but a later rule changes [B] back into [A]. Unlike the Duke's peregrinations, this activity is not as pointless as it seems: during the temporary [B] stage, erstwhile /A/ may opaquely escape an A-affecting process or cause a B-triggered one. More often, though, Duke-of-York derivations are simply an artifact of the commitment to sequential rule application. We will return to this topic, with exemplification, in §2.3.2.

2.2.4   Simultaneous application

Discussions of rule ordering often overlook an important alternative to the sequential derivation: simultaneous application. In many cases, rules could be applied simultaneously with no loss of generality, and so it is worth exploring which phenomena are and are not consistent with simultaneous application (for discussion, see Anderson 1974: 64–67, Donegan and Stampe 1979: 150, Hyman 1993: 204ff., Koutsoudas 1976, Koutsoudas, Sanders, and Noll 1974: 5–8).

Since simultaneous application is a somewhat unfamiliar notion, we should first get clear on what it means in rule-based phonology. A phonological rule describes a configuration that must be met in the rule's input — the rule's structural description — and a change that is to be effected in the rule's output — its structural change. If two rules are applied simultaneously, then their structural descriptions are analyzing exactly the same representation. It follows, then, that neither rule has access to any information that is contributed by the other rule's structural change. In sequential application, by contrast, the later rule always has access to information contributed by the earlier rule's structural change.

Opaque interactions are often compatible with simultaneous application, but transparent interactions require sequential application. The counterbleeding derivation /ħaːkim-iːn/ → [ħaːkʲmiːn] in (2-5), for example, would also work if the rules of palatalization and deletion were applied simultaneously. The structural description of the palatalization rule analyzes an input that contains [k] before [i], and so [k] is palatalized with complete indifference to the fact that the deletion rule is analyzing that same input toward the goal of deleting [i]. The important thing in this opaque derivation is that deletion must not precede palatalization; that desideratum could in principle be fulfilled by ordering palatalization before deletion, as in (2-5), or by requiring them to apply simultaneously.

Similarly, the counterfeeding derivation /dafaʕ/ → [difaʕ] in (2-4) is possible if deletion of high vowels and raising of low vowels apply simultaneously. The structural description of the high-vowel deletion rule is not met by /dafaʕ/, but the raising rule's structural description is met, so only raising actually applies. The important thing in this opaque derivation is that deletion should not apply to the output of raising; that desideratum could in principle be fulfilled by ordering raising before deletion, as in (2-4), or by requiring them to apply simultaneously.

Feeding and bleeding interactions, however, are incompatible with simultaneous application. In the feeding derivation /dˤrib/ → [ʔidˤrib] (2-2), for instance, the structural description of [ʔ] epenthesis is not met until after vowel epenthesis has applied, so sequential application is necessary. In the bleeding derivation /batˤn-ha/ → [bˤaˤtˤinha] (2-3), simultaneous application of vowel epenthesis and progressive assimilation would produce the result *[bˤaˤtˤinˤhˤaˤ], in which the epenthetic vowel is neither subject to nor a blocker of assimilation.

It is interesting that simultaneous application of rules typically produces opaque interactions but not transparent ones (unless the rules do not interact at all). Classic OT, though it evaluates candidates in which the effects of several processes are felt simultaneously, can model transparent interactions but not opaque ones (see §2.3.3). The reason for this difference is that rules and OT markedness constraints analyze different levels of representation. The structural description of a rule is met by the rule's *input*, which is sometimes identical to the underlying representation. The structural description of an OT markedness constraint is met in the ultimate *output*, the surface representation. Opacity requires reference to conditions obtaining in presurface representations, whereas transparency requires reference to conditions obtaining in surface representations.

2.2.5   Theories of rule ordering

In *SPE*, the order in which the rules are applied is *extrinsic*, which means that it is imposed on the rules by the language-particular grammar and cannot usually be predicted from rule form or function. From about 1969 through 1980, a voluminous literature developed around the question of whether some or even all aspects of rule ordering could be predicted. (See Anderson (1979: 15–18) and Iverson (1995) for brief surveys or Anderson (1974) and Kenstowicz and Kisseberth (1977: chapters 4, 6) for more extensive discussion.)

An *SPE*-style phonology of Classical Arabic must include a statement to the effect that vowel epenthesis precedes [ʔ] epenthesis to ensure that these rules apply in the order observed in (2-2). In some revisions of that model (e.g., Anderson 1974, Koutsoudas, Sanders, and Noll 1974), this ordering statement was dismissed as superfluous on the grounds that feeding order is unmarked or natural. In what sense is feeding order natural? If rules are allowed to apply freely at any point in the derivation when their structural descriptions are met, then the result will be the same as (2-2). Feeding orders maximize rule applicability. As was noted in §2.2.2, feeding orders also help to ensure that rules enforce true generalizations about surface structure: in Arabic, no word starts with a vowel because [ʔ] epenthesis is ordered after and thereby fed by vowel epenthesis. In the terminology of Donegan and Stampe (1979: 157), counterfeeding order of vowel epenthesis and [ʔ] epenthesis would act as a 'constraint' on the latter, preventing it from acting on derived representations and so rendering the [ʔ]-epenthesis generalization not categorically true.

Although feeding order was generally seen as natural and a second natural order was believed to exist, there is disagreement in the literature of that era over the question of whether the other natural rule order is bleeding or coun-terbleeding. In the earliest work on this topic, Kiparsky (1968) argued that historical change tends to maximize feeding and minimize bleeding orders. On the assumption the languages are attracted toward natural rule orders, this would mean that feeding and counterbleeding orders are natural. Anderson (1974) integrates this idea into his theory of local ordering, according to which feeding and counterbleeding order constitute a default case that can only be overridden by language-particular stipulation. Anderson's evidence includes analyses, none of them uncontroversial, in which maintaining the natural interaction between a pair of rules can cause them to apply in different orders within a single language. (This is the sense in which ordering is 'local': the theory comprehends ordering as a local relation between a pair of rules rather than a global list of ordered rules in the *SPE* fashion. Cf. §3.2.3.) Koutsoudas, Sanders, and Noll (1974) also argue for the naturalness of counterbleeding order.

Another body of work took the position that bleeding rather than counterbleeding order is natural (Iverson 1974, Kenstowicz and Kisseberth 1971, Kiparsky 1971). Apart from disagreements about analyses, the dispute is really one about the principle that determines the natural orders. If feeding and counterbleeding orders are natural, then what makes them natural is a principle that favors maximizing rule applicability: if A feeds B, then A supplies additional opportunities for rules to apply; and if A is not allowed to bleed B, then A cannot steal away some of B's opportunities to apply. If feeding and bleeding orders are natural, then what makes them natural is a principle that favors maximizing rule transparency: counterfeeding and counterbleeding orders produce opacity, whereas feeding and bleeding orders produce transparency, in which the effects of phonological generalizations are visible at surface structure.

In the course of research during the 1970's, these and other ordering principles were discussed, and there were even proposals about priority relationships among them (Anderson 1974: 217–218, Iverson 1976). The ultimate goal of the research program, according to some (e.g., Koutsoudas, Sanders, and Noll 1974), was the elimination of all language-particular ordering statements in favor of universal principles of applicational precedence. Supposedly *prima facie* arguments against this position have been adduced, such as two Canadian English dialects that differ solely in rule order (Bromberger and Halle 1989, Joos 1942), but in reality the argument is not that easy to make (Iverson 1995: 612–613). There never was a knock-down argument in support of language-particular ordering, nor was there general agreement on rule-ordering principles. Instead, the decade ended with a tacit consensus that research on universals of rule ordering had gone about as far as it could go.

2.2.6   Later developments

Interest in the topic of rule ordering waned around 1980. (An important exception is Goldsmith (1993b).) As the focus of phonological research moved elsewhere, however, matters of rule ordering and interaction sometimes reemerged in new contexts.

The development of nonlinear phonology and underspecification theory, beginning with works like Goldsmith (1976a), Kahn (1976), Liberman (1975), Liberman and Prince (1977), Clements and Ford (1979), McCarthy (1981), Prince (1983), and Archangeli (1984), took some of the analytic pressure off of phonological rules and shifted it to well-formedness constraints on phonological representations. In principle, an enriched theory of representations might lead to a reduction in the need for language-particular rule ordering, but in actual practice this line of research received little attention.

Satisfaction of representational constraints, however, required a new class of persistent rules that apply automatically at any point in the derivation when they are required (Chafe 1968, Myers 1991a). For example, when a consonant becomes unsyllabified in the course of a derivation, a persistent rule immediately adjoins it to a nearby syllable: /patika/ $\rightarrow$ *[pa]$_\sigma$ [ti]$_\sigma$ [ka]$_\sigma$* $\rightarrow_{\text{syncope}}$ *[pa]$_\sigma$ t [ka]$_\sigma$* $\rightarrow_{\text{persistent}}$ *[pat]$_\sigma$ [ka]$_\sigma$*. An important role of persistent rules, then, is to repair violations of well-formedness conditions, thereby ensuring that these conditions are respected not only at the beginning or end of the derivation but also in the middle. The free (re-)applicability of persistent rules is, of course, consistent with the principle favoring maximal rule application that was mentioned at the end of §2.2.5.

Another relevant post-1980 development is the theory of Lexical Phonology (Kaisse and Hargus 1993b, Kaisse and Shaw 1985, Kiparsky 1982, 1985, Mohanan 1982, among many others). Lexical Phonology is an extension of *SPE*'s theory of cyclic rule application. Certain rules may be designated as cyclic — in *SPE*, these are the English stress rules — and this causes them to apply repeatedly to successively larger morphological or syntactic constituents. The cycle accounts for transderivational similarities like the following:[5]

(i) Monomorphemic words like ˌ*Kalama'zoo* and ˌ*Winnepe'saukee* exhibit the normal English stress pattern when three light syllables precede the main stress. Derived words like *acˌcredi'tation* and *iˌmagi'nation* deviate from this pattern under the influence of *ac'credit* and *i'magine*.

(ii) A closed, sonorant-final syllable is normally unstressed in prestress position: ˌ*seren'dipity*, ˌ*gorgon'zola*, ˌ*Pennsyl'vania*. But the same kind of syllable may be stressed in the derived words ˌ*auˌthen'ticity* and ˌ*conˌdem'nation* under the influence of ˌ*au'thentic* and *con'demn*.

In *SPE*, the aberrant stress of derived words is explained by their bracketing and cyclic application of stress. The stress rules first apply on the inner constituents of [*accredit*]*ation* or [*authentic*]*ity* and then on the outer constituents. The primary stress assigned on the first cycle becomes a secondary stress on the second cycle, when the stress rule reapplies and a new primary stress is assigned further to the right. Monomorphemic *Kalamazoo* and *serendipity* have no inner cycle, so they show the effects of just a single pass through the stress rules.

Lexical Phonology departs from *SPE* in regarding cyclic application as the norm rather than the exception for certain phonological rules. In addition, Lexical Phonology imposes further structure on the grammar, dividing the phonology up into separate components, called strata. At a minimum, there are two such strata, lexical and postlexical. The input to the lexical stratum is the underlying representation; the output of the lexical stratum is the input to the postlexical stratum; and the output of the postlexical stratum is the surface representation. Each stratum is a separate phonological grammar, though specific overlap requirements have sometimes been imposed (Borowsky 1986, Kiparsky 1984: 141–143, Myers 1991b) (see §2.3.4.2). It is usually assumed that the lexical stratum actually consists of several strata, and at each lexical stratum a different set of morphological and phonological processes may be in effect. For example, English suffixes like *-ity* are affixed in the first lexical stratum, and that is also where the stress assignment rules apply. Suffixes like *-ness* are not attached until the second lexical stratum, at which point the stress assignment rules are no longer active. That is why suffixes like *-ity* are stress-determining and suffixes like *-ness* are stress-neutral. It is sometimes also assumed that rules apply cyclically within each lexical stratum, as each affix of that stratum is added: e.g., /period/ → 'period → peri'odic → perio'dicity, all within the first lexical stratum.

Lexical Phonology retains *SPE*'s assumption that the rules within a grammar (= a stratum) are in a strict linear order. Despite this within-grammar strict ordering, the same rule can be observed to reapply at different points in the course of an entire derivation. As in *SPE*, the cycle offers one opportunity: a rule can reapply in the same stratum as multiple affixes are added. But even without any affixation at all, a rule can reapply if it is assigned to more than one stratum. (This situation is not unusual.) If a rule is included in the grammar of more than one stratum, it will simply reapply when the later stratum is reached. Lexical Phonology is thereby able to reanalyze some (perhaps all) of the evidence that had earlier been adduced in favor of a principle of unmarked feeding order or maximizing rule application. An example is Kiparsky's (1984) reanalysis of the interaction of Icelandic *u*-umlaut and syncope, which had previously been cited by Anderson (1974) as evidence for local ordering. Instead of allowing *u*-umlaut and syncope to apply in either order, whichever produces a feeding relationship, the Lexical Phonology approach fixes the within-stratum order as *u*-umlaut precedes syncope, but then allows *u*-umlaut to follow syncope by reapplying in a later stratum.

Assignment of rules to different strata offers a way of imposing extrinsic ordering on them: if rule A applies only in stratum 1 and rule B applies only in stratum 2, then A necessarily precedes B. Therefore, assignment of rules to strata could be used to reproduce some of the effects of *SPE*-style extrinsic ordering. This leads to some questions: Is extrinsic ordering within strata truly necessary? Could all rules in the same stratum apply simultaneously or in a universally predictable order? These questions were not asked, much less answered, in mainstream work on Lexical Phonology, though they were discussed in work that is not usually identified with the Lexical Phonology research program (Goldsmith 1993a, Lakoff 1993). In any case, the questions persist to this day, as we will see in §2.3.4.2.

Apart from these developments, the common consensus about rule ordering and opacity did not change very much in the period after 1980. Most phonologists, perhaps more from a lack of interest than strong conviction, continued to assume something like the *SPE* model of rule interaction.

2.3   Opacity in Optimality Theory

2.3.1   Properties of classic OT

This section is not intended as an introduction to or comprehensive overview of OT (for the former see Kager (1999a), and for the latter see Prince and Smolensky (2004) or McCarthy (2002b)). Rather, the goal is to review those aspects of OT that assume particular significance in the analysis of opacity.

In OT, a grammar of a language is a ranking of constraints. Ranking differs from language to language, so the ranking relation between any given pair of constraints is not generally predictable. Because language-particular ranking offers a way of accounting for language differences, it is reasonable (though not strictly necessary) to adopt the null hypothesis that the constraints themselves are universal and so are drawn from a universal constraint component, called CON. If CON is indeed universal, as is standardly assumed in classic OT, then it is fair to say that OT is an inherently typological theory of language. In other words, OT and a specific hypothesis about CON combine to predict all and only the possible grammars of human languages.

In classic OT, the constraints in CON are limited to two types: markedness constraints evaluate output forms, favoring some over others; and faithfulness constraints evaluate input-output mappings, favoring those mappings that maintain identity. Classic OT, in the sense employed here, also incorporates the assumption that the faithfulness constraints are formalized in terms of a correspondence relation between input and output forms (McCarthy and Prince 1995, 1999). Because the substantive properties of CON, particularly the markedness constraints, are largely unknown, empirical research in OT is mostly focused on developing a detailed picture of CON. Some of this research has led to proposals for constraint types that are neither markedness nor faithfulness, such as antifaithfulness (Alderete 2001a, 2001b) or morpheme realization (Kurisu 2001), but these ideas go well beyond the limits of what I am calling classic OT.

OT is inherently comparative. In the simplest case, the evaluative component EVAL applies a language-particular constraint hierarchy to the task of comparing two possible outputs derived from a common input. Of these two outputs, called candidates, the more harmonic one is that which performs better on the highest-ranking constraint on which they differ.[6] The most harmonic or optimal candidate is the one that is more harmonic, in this sense, than any of its competitors.

Moreton (2003) has shown that classic OT entails a requirement of *harmonic improvement*. Assume that every candidate set contains at least one candidate that is fully faithful by virtue of obeying all of the faithfulness constraints in CON.[7] If the output of an OT grammar is not this fully faithful candidate, then it must be a candidate that is less marked than the fully faithful candidate relative to the language's constraint hierarchy. Moreton provides a formal proof of this result, but the intuition behind it is also clear: since a classic OT grammar has only markedness and faithfulness constraints, the only reason to violate a faithfulness constraint is satisfaction of a higher-ranking markedness constraint. Informally, you can stay the same or get better, but you can't get worse.

2.3.2   Process interaction in classic OT

Except for digressions in chapter 2 of Prince and Smolensky (2004) and in the appendix of McCarthy and Prince (1993b), classic OT has usually included an assumption of *parallelism*. This means that the candidates under evaluation can show the effects of several phonological processes simultaneously — that is, the effects of processes are evaluated in parallel. Classic OT is therefore a bistratal theory: it recognizes two levels of representation, input and output, but nothing in between. This is obviously very different from *SPE*, which has nearly as many intermediate levels of representation as there are rules (see §2.2.1).

In general, transparent interaction of processes is fully compatible with parallelism. Consider first a feeding interaction like (2-2), where underlying /dˤrib/ becomes surface [ʔidˤrib], showing the effects of two processes, vowel epenthesis and [ʔ] epenthesis. Taken separately, each process involves, *inter alia*, a basic markedness-dominates-faithfulness ranking, as shown in (2-9) and (2-10).[8] Faithful syllabification of the initial cluster in /dˤrib/ is impossible because of *COMPLEX-ONSET and other markedness constraints. Violation of the lower-ranking antiepenthesis constraint DEP is the chosen alternative. Faithful syllabification of a word-initial vowel is a breach of ONSET, which also ranks above DEP. The feeding interaction between the two types of epenthesis is simply the result of satisfying both *COMPLEX-ONSET and ONSET simultaneously. Among the candidates derived from /dˤrib/ is one in which both vowel and [ʔ] epenthesis have occurred. This candidate is favored by both of the high-ranking constraints, as tableau (2-11) illustrates.

(2-9)　　*COMPLEX-ONSET >> DEP

/dˤrib/	*COMP-ONS	DEP
→ ʔidˤrib		2
dˤrib	W₁	L

(2-10)　　ONSET >> DEP

/al-walad-u/	ONSET	DEP
→ ʔalwaladu		1
alwaladu	W₁	L

(2-11)　　Feeding interaction

/dˤrib/	ONSET	*COMP-ONS	DEP
→ ʔidˤrib			2
dˤrib		W₁	L
idˤrib	W₁		L₁

I noted in §2.2.4 that transparent interactions are incompatible with simultaneous application of phonological rules. That is because a rule's structural description analyzes that rule's input, and the fed rule's structural description cannot be met until after the feeding rule has applied. In OT, however, the structural descriptions of markedness constraints analyze outputs, and feeding interactions are simply a consequence of satisfying such constraints. This is the sense in which classic OT exhibits parallelism: high-ranking markedness constraints can favor a candidate that differs from the input by the simultaneous effects of two or more processes, as in (2-11).

The situation is the same with the other type of transparent interaction, bleeding. The difference is that bleeding interactions may involve conflict between markedness constraints. For instance, the mapping /batˤn-ha/ → [bˤaˤtˤinha] in (2-3) shows that the markedness constraint responsible for progressive assimilation of pharyngealization is crucially dominated by two other markedness constraints, one forbidding pharyngealization of [i] and the other ruling out medial triconsonantal clusters (and thereby demanding [i] epenthesis). In this way, the output [bˤaˤtˤinha] is favored over alternatives like *[bˤaˤtˤiˤnˤhˤaˤ], with pharyngealized [i], and *[bˤaˤtˤnˤhˤaˤ], with a triconsonantal cluster.

Parallel evaluation in classic OT also eliminates the need for certain kinds of Duke-of-York derivations (see §2.2.3). An example comes from Nuuchahnulth, formerly known as Nootka (Campbell 1973, Kenstowicz and Kisseberth 1977: 171ff., McCarthy 2003c, Sapir and Swadesh 1978).[9] This language has a process that rounds velars and uvulars when they follow round vowels (2-12), as well as a process that unrounds velars and uvulars at the end of a syllable (2-13). (Syllable boundaries are shown by a period/full stop.) These two processes are in a mutual feeding relationship: when a velar or uvular follows a round vowel, as in (2-14), rounding creates inputs to unrounding and unrounding creates inputs to rounding. In the *SPE* tradition, this kind of conflict can only be resolved by rule ordering, and indeed mutual feeding relationships presented special challenges to those seeking to predict rule ordering (§2.2.5). The stipulated ordering is given in (2-14). Because unrounding gets its hands on the form later in the derivation, it states the surface-true generalization that syllable-final consonants are unrounded. The truth of the rounding generalization consequently suffers: there exist some nonrounded velars and uvulars that are preceded by a round vowel.

(2-12) Rounding in Nuuchahnulth

Underlying	/ħaju-qi/	'ten on top'
Rounding	ħa.ju.qʷi	
Surface	[ħa.ju.qʷi]	(cf. [ħi.ta.qi] 'on top')

(2-13) Unrounding

Underlying	/ɬaːkʷ-ʃitɬ/	'to take pity on'
Unrounding	ɬaːk.ʃitɬ	
Surface	[ɬaːk.ʃitɬ]	(cf. [ɬaː.kʷiq.nak] 'pitiful')

(2-14) Duke-of-York derivation

Underlying	/mʔuːq/	'throwing off sparks'
Rounding	mʔuːqʷ	
Unrounding	mʔuːq	
Surface	[mʔuːq]	(cf. [mʔo.qʷak] 'phosphorescent')

In OT, deriving [mʔuːq] from /mʔuːq/ does not require passing through the intermediate step [mʔuːqʷ]. Rather, this is a matter of conflict between markedness constraints, and it is resolved, as are all constraint conflicts, by ranking the conflicting constraints. In (2-15), I introduce two ad hoc markedness constraints and show how the higher-ranking constraint is the one that favors nonround consonants syllable-finally. Both are ranked above the faithfulness constraint IDENT(round), to account for the predictability of consonant rounding in this context.

(2-15) *Kʷ]$_\sigma$ >> *uK >> IDENT(round)

/mʔuːq/	*Kʷ]$_\sigma$	*uK	ID(round)
→ mʔuːq		1	
mʔuːqʷ	W₁	L	W₁

It is useful to compare the *SPE*-style analysis in (2-14) with the OT analysis in (2-15). The comparison shows why parallelism is and should be the null hypothesis for OT. In the *SPE* model, ordering is a way of establishing priority relationships among rules, and in a case like Nuuchahnulth it is the last rule that has priority in the sense that it states a surface-true generalization, even though the earlier rule does not. In OT, priority relationships among constraints are established by ranking them, and this example shows that ranking can replace at least some applications of rule ordering. The null hypothesis, then, is that OT can dispense with ordering and all of its trappings, including intermediate derivational steps. In its place, OT has constraint ranking, which is required independently. This very strong claim is certainly not uncontroversial, and opacity presents the main challenge.

Before we go on to look at opacity in OT, however, it is appropriate to examine some conceptual arguments that have been advanced against parallelism and in favor of *SPE*-style serial derivations. One of these conceptual arguments holds that sequential rules accurately model a system of mental computation (Bromberger and Halle 1997). The failure of the Derivational Theory of Complexity showed that this idea is very far off the mark, at least in syntax (Fodor, Bever, and Garrett 1974); the same is true in phonology (Goldsmith 1993b). Indeed, if the goal of generative grammar is to construct competence models (Chomsky 1965), then it is a category mistake to ask whether these models faithfully replicate mental computation.

Another argument offered in favor of sequential rule application is that it makes sense in terms of language history (Bromberger and Halle 1989): the ordering of synchronic rules matches the chronology of diachronic sound changes. The principal problem with this view is that it misconceives language change. If language learners in generation Y innovate a sound change, they do not simply add a rule onto the end of generation X's phonological grammar — they cannot, since generation Y does not have direct access to generation X's internalized grammar. Generation Y's learning is informed exclusively by X's actual productions, as filtered through Y's perceptual system. X's productions offer only indirect evidence of X's grammar, subject to well-known limitations like the absence of negative evidence. From this perspective, we neither expect nor do we necessarily observe that grammars change by accreting rules at the end of the ordering.

2.3.3   Opacity in classic OT[10]

Classic OT recognizes just two types of constraints, markedness and faithfulness, and just two levels of representation, underlying and surface. Markedness constraints can refer to only one of those levels of representation, surface structure. Faithfulness constraints refer to both levels, but they can only do one thing: require identity. The standard derivational approach to opacity relies on having intermediate levels of representation (see §2.2.3), but classic OT has none. Furthermore, the limitation of markedness constraints to evaluating surface structure has unwelcome consequences for the analysis of counterbleeding opacity.

In counterbleeding opacity, a phonological process occurs even though the conditioning environment is not present in surface structure. In the Bedouin Arabic example (2-5), for instance, /k/ palatalizes even though it is not followed by a front vowel in the surface form: /haːkim-iːn/ → [haːkʲmiːn]. In other words, the /k/ → [kʲ] unfaithful mapping is a response to phonological conditions that are not visible in the output form, though they are visible in the input. Because markedness constraints are limited to evaluating outputs, the markedness preference for [kʲ] over [k] before front vowels cannot be invoked to explain why /k/ is palatalized before a vowel that is no longer present. The problem is apparent from tableau (2-16), which shows that [ħaːkʲmiːn] is harmonically bounded by *[ħaːkmiːn].

(2-16) Counterbleeding opacity in classic OT[11]

/ħaːkim-iːn/	*iCV	Max	*ki	Id(back)
→ ħaːkʲmiːn		1		1
a. ħaːkmiːn		1		L
b. ħaːkʲimiːn	W₁	L		1
c. ħaːkimiːn	W₁	L	W₁	L

Row (a) in (2-16) contains no W's and one L, so the candidate in (a) harmonically bounds the intended winner. Moreover, since this candidate is more faithful and less marked than the intended winner, no other classic OT faithfulness or markedness constraint could be introduced to break this harmonic bounding. (On an alternative analysis with coalescence, see §2.3.4.1. For the OT-CC analysis of palatalization, see §3.3.3, and for the analysis of syncope — minus the ad hoc constraint *iCV — see §4.3.3.)

In this and other cases of counterbleeding opacity, an unfaithful mapping occurs for reasons that cannot be explained with classic OT markedness constraints because the conditions that encourage the unfaithful mapping are no longer apparent in surface structure. Although analyses of particular instances of counterbleeding opacity (including this one) have been proposed, there is no general solution that remains within the strictures of classic OT.

In contrast to counterbleeding opacity, counterfeeding opacity can in principle be accommodated in classic OT. Consider the Bedouin Arabic example in (2-4), in which underlying /i/ deletes (/ʃarib-at/ → [ʃarbat]) but [i] derived from /a/ does not (/dafaʕ/ → [difaʕ], *[dfaʕ]). As above, let *iCV stand for the constraint that favors [ʃarbat] over faithful [ʃaribat]; it dominates Max. Let *aCV stand for the constraint that favors [difaʕ] over faithful [dafaʕ]; it dominates Ident(+low). Tableau (2-17) shows that the desired output [difaʕ] is unattainable with just these four constraints. To circumvent this paradox, we require a constraint that favors the desired winner in (2-17) over the loser in (a). This constraint, which can be called MAX-A, forbids the /a/ → Ø mapping. MAX-A meets the formal requirements for faithfulness constraints: it requires identity between underlying and surface structure. Ranked above *iCV, MAX-A correctly favors [difaʕ], as shown in (2-18). Furthermore, MAX-A does not interfere with the analysis of high vowel syncope in forms like /ʃarib-at/. (See §4.3.3 for the full analysis.)

(2-17) Impossibility of [difaʕ] without MAX-A

/dafaʕ/	*aCV	ID(low)	*iCV	MAX
→ difaʕ		1	1	
a. dfaʕ		L	L	W$_1$
b. dafaʕ	W$_1$	L	L	

(2-18) Counterfeeding opacity in classic OT

/dafaʕ/	MAX-A	*aCV	*iCV	ID(low)	MAX
→ difaʕ			1	1	
a. dfaʕ	W$_1$		L	L	W$_1$
b. dafaʕ		W$_1$	L	L	

In theory, this mode of analysis could be generalized to all instances of counterfeeding opacity, thereby providing classic OT with a ready-made solution to this half of the opacity problem. In practice, though, that would not be a good idea. Dealing with the full range of counterfeeding interactions will require a very rich faithfulness theory, undoubtedly much richer than we want or would otherwise need. Another counterfeeding interaction in Bedouin Arabic illustrates. Raising of /a/ to [i] in an open syllable is not fed by a process of epenthesis that breaks up final consonant clusters: /gabr/ → [gabur], *[gibur] 'grave'. To analyze this phenomenon in the same manner as (2-18), we would need a faithfulness constraint with the following definition: 'Assign a violation mark for every instance of a surface high vowel that stands in correspondence with an underlying low vowel, provided that this surface high vowel is followed in the next syllable by a vowel that has no underlying correspondent.' In other words, the counterfeeding interaction in [gabur] requires a version of IDENT(+low) that is applicable only if the vowel in the next syllable is epenthetic. Constraints like this are necessarily embedded in a faithfulness theory that makes unattested and implausible typological predictions. Rather than demonstrate this now, I return to the matter in §2.3.4.1 when I discuss a theory of faithfulness that countenances such constraints, local conjunction.

Classic OT has an inherent bias toward transparent interactions (§2.3.2). Counterfeeding opacity requires undesirable enrichment of faithfulness theory, and counterbleeding opacity is usually intractable. Since opacity appears to be an authentic property of phonological systems, classic OT needs to be modified. The question is how.

2.3.4   Previous approaches to opacity in classic OT

More than a few different proposals have been made about how to integrate the analysis opacity into OT. Some are recent or short-lived; others date back to the earliest work in the theory. For discussion purposes, they can be grouped into four broad categories:

i) Changes in substantive properties of phonological representation or the constraint component CON (§2.3.4.1). The goal is to analyze some or all cases of opacity by enriching representations or creating new constraints. (The approach discussed at the end of the previous section is an example.)

ii) Introduction of intermediate derivational stages and something like rule ordering to OT (§2.3.4.2).

iii) Introduction of an equivalent of intermediate derivational stages, but without any direct counterpart to rule ordering (§2.3.4.3).

iv) Reinterpretation of opacity as a mechanism for preserving underlying contrasts (§2.3.4.4).

2.3.4.1   Opacity via novel substantive assumptions

This section describes approaches to opacity that place the main analytic burden on assumptions about substantive matters. Three lines of attack will be discussed in turn: *representational approaches*, which enrich surface structure in ways that allow opaque processes to be reanalyzed as transparent; reanalysis of counterbleeding opacity as a type of *segmental coalescence*; and reanalysis of counterfeeding opacity as a faithfulness effect using *local constraint conjunction.*

Representational approaches to opacity. Opacity issues arose in the very first work on OT, Prince and Smolensky (2004). The topic comes up in the context of two analyses, Lardil (pp. 145, 148) and Fula (p. 255).

In Lardil nominative case forms, final vowels are deleted (Hale 1973): /jilijili/ → [jilijil] 'oyster species (nominative)' (cf. the nonfuture accusative [jilijili-n], with suffix /-n/ and no truncation). When this apocope process exposes a final consonant that is not allowed syllable-finally (Wilkinson 1988), the consonant deletes as well: /ŋawuŋawu/ → [ŋawuŋa] 'termite'. Apocope therefore feeds consonant deletion. Crucially, apocope must not be fed by consonant deletion; if it were, then we would expect to find apocope and consonant deletion chewing through words until a licit coda is found (as in *[murkun] from /murkunima/ 'nullah') or the bimoraic word minimum is reached (as in *[kuru] from /kurumpuwa/ 'tata-spear'). This is an example of counterfeeding opacity.

Fula has two processes that refer to geminate consonants. One process shortens a geminate after a long vowel, and the other hardens geminate continuants into stops (Paradis 1988). They interact in counterbleeding fashion, with an underlying geminate continuant undergoing hardening even if it is also shortened: /laːwːi/ → [laːbi] 'roads'.

The analytic strategy that Prince and Smolensky apply to both of these cases is closely connected with their implementation of faithfulness constraints. Faithfulness is essential to OT, since without faithfulness markedness runs amok, driving every input down to some least marked output like [ba] (cf. Chomsky 1995: 380fn.). The idea of faithfulness is thus a key insight without which OT would be a failed enterprise. The implementational details are much less central, though relevant to the analysis of opacity. The implementation adopted in Prince and Smolensky (2004) is based on a principle dubbed Containment in McCarthy and Prince (1993b): all of the phonological material in the underlying representation must be preserved in every candidate output form.

Containment therefore entails that there are no literal deletion processes. Instead, the effects of deletion are obtained from the joint action of three additional assumptions, all with precedents elsewhere:

(i)   Underlying representations lack prosodic structure, particularly syllabification.

(ii) Phonological material may remain unincorporated into prosodic structure.

(iii) Unincorporated phonological material receives no phonetic interpretation.

Thus, a deleted segment like the final /i/ of [jilijil] is present in the output form but syllabically unparsed: [ji]$_\sigma$ [li]$_\sigma$ [jil]$_\sigma$ i, or more compactly [jilijil<i>]. With a shortening process like /laːwːi/ → [laːbi], an underlying mora is preserved in the output but also syllabically unparsed. Both situations violate constraints from the PARSE family, which require segments, moras, and other structural elements to be incorporated into prosodic structure. Some theories of syntactic deletion are a close parallel (e.g., Chomsky 1995).

Containment supplies an analytic strategy for many cases of opacity. For example, in Prince and Smolensky's analysis of Lardil, apocope is the result of satisfying the constraint FREE-V 'Word-final vowels must not be parsed (in the nominative)' (p. 123). In [ŋawuŋa<wu>], the word-final vowel is unparsed, as requested, and the preceding [w] is unparsed because it is not a licit syllable coda. Nonparsing of the preceding [a], however, would violate PARSE for no reason — if 'word-final' means 'rightmost segment, parsed or not', then the word-final vowel is [u], and [a] has no claim to word-final status. Apocope cannot feed itself, then, because apocope can only affect a vowel that is word-final in underlying representation. (This also explains why the last but not word-final vowel of /wuŋkunuŋ/ does not apocopate: [wuŋkunu<ŋ>] 'queen-fish'.)

In Fula, we need to explain how a mapping with hardening and degemination of geminate continuants (/laːwːi/ → [laːbi]) can be more harmonic than a mapping with degemination alone (/laːwːi/ → *[laːwi]). Since *[laːwi] is not pronounced with a geminate, it should not lose to the hardened former geminate in [laːbi]. Prince and Smolensky's solution (p. 255) again relies on Containment. The two skeletal positions linked to geminate /w/ in /laːwːi/ can never be literally deleted; rather, both are present but one is syllabically unparsed in candidates with degemination like [laːbi] and *[laːwi]. The markedness constraint against geminate continuants defines a 'geminate' as a consonant linked to two skeletal positions, regardless of whether the skeletal positions are syllabified. This markedness constraint, then, is sensitive to the representation and not the pronunciation, and the representation of *[laːwi] contains a 'geminate' continuant because it is derived from /laːwːi/ under Containment. Once a geminate, always a geminate, as far as this constraint is concerned.

This theory of opacity requires no changes in OT proper, and that makes it attractive. It has empirical problems of two types, however: there are observed opaque interactions that it cannot easily accommodate; and there are transparent interactions that ought to be opaque if this theory is right. We will examine each in turn. (For related discussion, also see the critique of Containment in McCarthy and Prince (1995, 1999).)

A basic prediction of the Containment model is that syllabification always interacts transparently with processes because syllabification is present only in the output. With syllabification though not with segmental structure, the pronunciation and the representation are true to one another. Cases like the Bedouin Arabic /gabr/ → [gabur] example (§2.3.3) are therefore problematic: /a/ raises to [i] in an open syllable, and [ga.bur] has an open syllable. There is no earlier stage of syllabification to refer to opaquely, in which /a/ is in a closed syllable. Another example along the same general lines can be found in Levantine Arabic (see §4.2). When a final cluster is resolved by epenthesis, stress is assigned to the erstwhile final syllable, in conformity with the general pattern for words ending in such 'superheavy' syllables: /katab-t/ → [ka'tabit] 'I wrote'. Forms with the same surface syllable structure but without epenthesis are stressed differently: /katab-it/ → ['katabit] 'she wrote'. Since syllabification is necessarily transparent under Containment, this opaque interaction between stress and syllabification/epenthesis is inexpressible.

The other problem is that many transparent processes, which should be unremarkable, end up tripping over the unparsed remnants of deletion (cf. Beckman 1997: 27–31). In Maltese, for example, there is a completely transparent process of regressive voicing assimilation in obstruent clusters (Borg 1997). Because it is completely transparent, this process also affects consonant clusters that are created by syncope: /ni-ktib-u/ → ['nigdbu] 'we write'. Under Containment, syncope does not affect string-adjacency relations among segments because no segment is literally deleted. Therefore, voicing assimilation affects a sequence of noncontiguous consonants: ['nigd<i>bu]. This is a surprising result, since voicing assimilation has never been observed to traverse a pronounced vowel in any language. This problem could be avoided by adopting a more sophisticated theory of locality that reckons segments as adjacent if no parsed segment appears between them, but this move would be inconsistent with the Containment-based analysis of Lardil, where unparsed segments do count in determining whether a vowel is final or not.

A usual (though not essential) accompaniment to Containment is the assumption that epenthesis is not literal segmental insertion but rather prosodic overparsing (after Broselow 1982, Ito 1986, 1989, Lowenstamm and Kaye 1986, Piggott and Singh 1985, Selkirk 1981b and others). In overparsing, syllables are created with empty structural positions. The phonetic content of these empty positions is determined extrasystemically — that is, outside the phonological grammar proper. Those positions that are devoid of segmental content violate faithfulness constraints from the Fɪʟʟ family, which militate against such mismatches between segmental and prosodic structure. An example: the phonological output corresponding to Classical Arabic [ʔidˤrib] is [ONdˤrib], where O and N stand for an unfilled onset and nucleus, respectively. The spell-out of O as [ʔ] and N as [i] happens in some later module that interprets the output structures derived by the OT phonological grammar.

Because the phonetic identity of epenthetic segments is supplied extraphonologically, processes of segmental phonology should treat them opaquely, as if they were not present, whereas syllable-sensitive processes should treat epenthesis transparently, for reasons already given. There are indeed some cases where epenthesis interacts opaquely with segmental phonology. For example, Herzallah (1990: 109–110) reports for her northern Palestinian Arabic dialect that the vowel [i] causes a preceding pharyngealized /rˤ/ to lose its pharyngealization: [ʔafrˤaz] ~ [jifriz] 'he classified ~ he classifies'. Epenthetic [i] does not have this effect, however: /farˤm/ → [farˤim] 'cutting'. This observation is consistent with the claim that information about the quality of epenthetic vowels is determined after the phonological grammar has done its work. On the other hand, the example in (2-3) shows for a southern Palestinian dialect that epenthetic [i] blocks the spread of pharyngealization, acting just like non-epenthetic [i] in this respect. So epenthesis does not show consistent opaque interaction with segmental processes. Rather, interaction may be transparent or opaque on a language-specific basis. This is contrary to the predictions of the FILL-based model of epenthesis.

The Containment theory of faithfulness is, as we have seen, also a theory of opacity, but not an entirely successful one. Two main problems have been identified. Under Containment, deleted segments should be consistently visible to processes that are conditioned purely by segmental adjacency but consistently invisible to processes that are conditioned by syllable structure. This predicts opaque interactions in the former case and transparent interactions in the latter, but there are counterexamples to both predictions. Under the empty-node theory of epenthesis, epenthetic segments should be consistently invisible to processes that are conditioned by segmental adjacency but consistently visible to processes that are conditioned purely by syllable structure. This predicts opaque interactions in the former case and transparent interactions in the latter, but again there are counterexamples to both predictions. The inherent simplicity and consequent attractiveness of this theory of opacity yields to its empirical inadequacies.

There is some later work exploring enhancements of this theory of opacity to grant it greater descriptive power (Goldrick 2000, Goldrick and Smolensky 1998). The key idea of this approach, called Turbidity, is that the symmetric *is associated with* relation between prosodic and segmental structure is divided into two asymmetric relations: segments *project* prosodic structure, and prosodic structure *is pronounced as* segments. Usually, these two relations operate in tandem, with segment *s* projecting prosody *p* if and only if *p* is pronounced as *s*.

The hallmark of opacity in Turbidity theory is a mismatch between the Project and Pronounce relations. Compensatory lengthening presents a typical example.[12] Compensatory lengthening is a type of counterbleeding opacity: a deleted segment projects a mora, but that mora is pronounced with a different segment, thereby lengthening it. In Turkish, for example, coda /h/ is optionally deleted before a continuant or nasal, in which case the preceding vowel lengthens (Sezer 1985: 230): [kahve] ~ [kaːve] 'coffee'. The representation of [kaːve] is shown in (2-19), with upward and downward arrows standing for the Project and Pronounce relations, respectively. In this representation, the segments [a] and [h] each project a mora (upward arrows), but the mora projected by [h] is pronounced as [a] (diagonal downward arrow).

(2-19) Compensatory lengthening in Turbidity theory

$$\begin{array}{ccc} \mu\,\mu & & \mu \\ \updownarrow\!\!\nwarrow\uparrow & & \updownarrow \\ \text{k a h} & & \text{v e} \end{array}$$

In Turbidity theory, markedness constraints are defined in terms of the Project and Pronounce relations. One constraint requires coda consonants, such as [h] in (2-19), to project a mora. This constraint is indifferent to whether the [h] is pronounced with its projected mora. Another markedness constraint requires that every mora be pronounced with some segment. This constraint is indifferent to whether the mora is pronounced with the segment that projects it. Though such mismatches between Project and Pronounce are possible — and (2-19) is an example — they are marked, violating a constraint called RECIPROCITY. This, in outline, is how opaque analyses are constructed in this theory.

What would it take to extend Turbidity theory to deal with the full range of opaque interactions? Very likely, it will require two coexistent phonological representations, the pronounced one and the projected one. These two representations are folded together in (2-19), but (2-19) is not representative of the full range of opaque interactions. An instructive example is Bedouin Arabic /gabr/ → [gabur], where /a/ is not raised in a derived open syllable. In Turbidity terms, this means that [gabur] must be represented with two coexistent syllabic parses, one where [b] projects as the coda of the syllable [gab] and one where it is pronounced as the onset of the syllable [bur]. Phenomena like Palestinian Arabic /farˁm/ → [farˁim] require extending the Project/Pronounce distinction to linear order relations among segments. Epenthetic [i] is pronounced as the successor to [rˁ] in the segmental string, but [m] is projected as [rˁ]'s successor. In short, there can be Project/Pronounce mismatches in all of the ways that phonological elements relate to one another. This means that there are two complete phonological representations, with two sets of markedness constraints. RECIPROCITY maintains a check on divergence between the two representations, and violation of RECIPROCITY is the source of opacity.

Looked at in this way, Turbidity has much in common with those theories of opacity that posit a single additional level of representation besides underlying and surface structure. It also shares some of the limitations of these theories. We will examine those limitations in §2.3.4.2.

Segmental coalescence. Segmental coalescence may sound like a peculiar theory of opacity, but it plays such a role in much of the OT literature. It has been applied to one rather common form of counterbleeding opacity, in which a segment is observed to assimilate to another nearby segment that has deleted. The palatalization/syncope interaction in (2-5) is typical: /ħaːkim-iːn/ → [ħaːkʲmiːn]. Although this derivation is opaque under the assumption that palatalization is the result of assimilation, it can be analyzed as transparent under the assumption that palatalization and syncope are united into a single process of segmental coalescence. The underlying $/k_1 i_2/$ sequence fuses into the single output segment $[k^j_{1,2}]$. There is no literal deletion, no failure of input-output correspondence, so MAX is satisfied. The resulting segment is palatalized because $[k^j_{1,2}]$ is faithful to the color features of one of its underlying correspondents, $/i_2/$. Another alternative: when /i/ deletes, it leaves behind the feature specification [–back], which reassociates autosegmentally to the preceding /k/. In this case, although MAX is violated, the feature-specific constraint MAX(–back) is not. Analyses along these general lines can be found in Causley (1997), Gnanadesikan (1997, 2004), Lamontagne and Rice (1995), McCarthy and Prince (1995), and Pater (1996), among others.

These alternatives to opacity have their merits, but they also have their problems. A parochial concern is that palatalization in Bedouin Arabic is not limited to deleted /i/. Overt front vowels also cause palatalization, so palatalization must not be inextricably linked with deletion of the triggering segment, as both the coalescence and autosegmental analyses imply. A broader worry is that observed counterbleeding interactions are not conveniently limited to situations that can plausibly be regarded as coalescence. For example, Donegan and Stampe (1979: 153) point out that there is a counterbleeding interaction in English between intervocalic /t/-flapping and optional desyllabification of prevocalic liquids: /ʃætɹɪŋ/ →_{t-flapping} [ʃærɹɪŋ] →_{optional} [ʃærɹɪŋ] *shattering*. There is no way of reanalyzing this opaque interaction as a single coalescence process. Another example, this time from Kenstowicz and Kisseberth (1979: 292–294): in Tunica (Gulf, Louisiana), a sequence $/V_1 ʔa/$ is altered by assimilating /a/ to the color of $/V_1/$ and by deleting $/V_1/$ if it is unstressed. The result is a counterbleeding interaction in cases like /ˈhipu-ʔaki/ → [ˈhipʔɔki] 'she dances', with /a/ assimilating to the deleted vowel. The deletion + assimilation combination is unlikely to be reducible to a single process of coalescence for three reasons: (i) Deletion occurs independently of assimilation in cases like /ˈhɑrɑ-ʔuhki/ → [ˈhɑrʔuhki] 'he dances'; (ii) Assimilation occurs independently of deletion in cases like /ˈtʃu-ʔɑki/ → [ˈtʃuʔɔki] 'she takes'; and (iii) Coalescence of nonadjacent segments is probably unattested and very likely impossible (see §3.2.4.3).

Local constraint conjunction. As I noted in §2.3.3, counterfeeding opacity can be accommodated in classic OT if the theory of faithfulness constraints is sufficiently rich. (There is no comparable way of dealing with counterbleeding opacity.) It has been proposed that *local conjunction* of faithfulness constraints is the proper mechanism for incorporating this richer theory of faithfulness into Con (Ito and Mester 2003c, Kirchner 1996, Moreton and Smolensky 2002).

Local constraint conjunction is proposed by Smolensky (1995) as a theory of the internal structure of Con. Complex constraints are built by conjoining simpler constraints. (The simpler constraints may be irreducible, or they may themselves be the product of local conjunction.) The local conjunction of constraints A and B, $[A\&B]_\delta$, is defined as a constraint that is violated once for each instance of the domain δ in which both A and B are violated. Conjunction of markedness constraints supplies the most persuasive examples. Codas are marked by the constraint No-Coda and voiced obstruents are marked by the constraint No-Vcd-Obst. The local conjunction of these constraints within the domain of a segment, $[\text{No-Coda} \ \& \ \text{No-Vcd-Obst}]_{Seg}$, militates against the combination of these two marked properties, a voiced obstruent in coda position. In general, local conjunction of markedness constraints forbids the cooccurrence of marked structures in near proximity to one another.

In counterfeeding opacity, unfaithful mappings cannot occur in close proximity to one another. For instance, the counterfeeding interaction in Bedouin Arabic /gabr/ → [gabur] requires the local conjunction of Ident(low) and Dep in the domain of adjacent syllables: $[\text{Ident(low)}\&\text{Dep}]_{Adj-\sigma}$. By ranking $[\text{Ident(low)}\&\text{Dep}]_{Adj-\sigma}$ above the markedness constraint responsible for the open-syllable raising process (*aCV in (2-20)), we ensure that opaque [gabur], which satisfies this constraint, is more harmonic than transparent *[gibur], which violates it.

(2-20) Counterfeeding opacity with local conjunction[13]

/gabr/	$[\text{Id(low)}\&\text{Dep}]_{Adj-\sigma}$	*Comp-Coda	*aCV	Dep	Id(low)
→ gabur				1	1
a. gibur	W₁		L	1	W₁
b. gabr		W₁	L	L	

This is a particularly elegant theory of counterfeeding opacity, but it cannot account for the full range of opacity phenomena, and it predicts a kind of pseudo-opacity that does not seem to exist (McCarthy 1999: 365–366, 2002a, 2003a, Padgett 2002). The reasons for both of these problems go right to the core of the local-conjunction theory: real counterfeeding opacity is a matter of forbidden process *interaction*, but local conjunction regulates process *proximity*. Interaction and proximity are two very different things, and it is a mistake to confound them.

The Bedouin Arabic example illustrates this mistake. The [gabur] example shows that raising is blocked when the epenthetic vowel *follows* the syllable with the potentially raised vowel. On the other hand, (2-21) shows that raising is not blocked when the (italicized) epenthetic vowel *precedes* the (boldface) raised vowel. The conjoined constraint [IDENT(low)&DEP]$_{\text{Adj-}\sigma}$ is unable to make this distinction, since it forbids raising and epenthesis in adjacent syllables, regardless of their linear order.

(2-21)   Adjacent epenthesis and raising in Bedouin Arabic
         /tˤarad ʁanam-ih/   [tˤa.ra.d*ɪ*ʁ.ni.mih]   'he pursued his sheep'

This is not a mere technical glitch, to be solved with a more sophisticated theory of the domains of conjunction. Rather, it is a basic failure of principle. It is not an accident that raising is prohibited *before* an epenthetic vowel but allowed *after* one. When the epenthetic vowel follows, epenthesis interacts with raising, since following epenthesis puts the potentially raised vowel into an open syllable. When the epenthetic vowel precedes, however, epenthesis does not interact with raising, since preceding epenthesis has no effect on whether the potentially raised vowel is in an open syllable. Local conjunction uses proximity — the adjacent-syllables domain — as a proxy for interaction, and interaction is the real basis for opacity. Because phonological processes are usually locally conditioned, proximity is often successful as a proxy for opacity, but examples like this one decouple the effects of proximity and interaction, showing that interaction, not proximity, is what really matters.

Another way of grasping the problem with local conjunction's proximity = interaction equation is to look at the effects of locally conjoining faithfulness constraints in inappropriate domains. For example, the constraint [IDENT(low)&DEP]$_{\text{Wd}}$ — identical to Bedouin Arabic, except that the domain is larger — will block raising if a vowel has been epenthesized anywhere in the same word. If Bedouin Arabic were to have such a constraint, underlying /samiʕ-t-k/ 'I heard you (masculine singular)' would map to [samiʕtak] instead of the expected [simiʕtak]. No known language exhibits this sort of hyperopacity, in which counterfeeding behavior is extended from a local, interacting context to a distant, noninteracting context. Yet the local conjunction theory of counterfeeding opacity would seem to predict exactly this, since the domain of conjunction is stipulated independently of the conjoined constraint (Alderete 1997, Ito and Mester 2003a: 105ff.).

Similar problems arise when inappropriate constraint combinations are assembled by local conjunction. Imagine a language that is identical to Bedouin Arabic except that it also has final devoicing of obstruents. The conjoined constraint [IDENT(low)&IDENT(voice)]$_{\text{Adj-}\sigma}$ could block raising whenever an adjoining syllable contains a devoiced obstruent: /katab/ → [**kata p**]. This sort of hyperopacity is never attested — that is, we never find that one process blocks another if the two processes by their very nature cannot interact.

There have been efforts to impose restrictions on local conjunction to address some of these problems (Bakovic 1999, Fukazawa and Miglio 1998, Hewitt and Crowhurst 1996, Ito and Mester 2003a: 102ff., 2003c, Łubowicz 2002, 2006). Typically, these proposals rely on the shared formal properties of two constraints to determine whether they are conjoinable or, if conjoined, what their domain is. None of these proposals has been fully successful in addressing the problems described here and elsewhere (McCarthy 1999, 2002a, 2003a, Padgett 2002). The reason for this failure is not far to seek: counterfeeding opacity is a matter of forbidden process interaction, and process interaction is not something that can be determined solely by looking at the formal properties of faithfulness constraints.[14] Whether and under what conditions two processes will interact is something that depends on the circumstances that obtain in a particular language. We require a theory of opacity that is sensitive to these circumstances. Rule ordering is an example of such a theory, but others will be discussed here and in later chapters.

2.3.4.2   Analogues to serial derivations and rule ordering

Since rule-based phonology uses serial derivations to account for opacity, it is natural to ask whether derivations and the effects of rule-ordering can be reconstructed in OT, which is a theory without rules. A multi-step serial derivation can be obtained simply by assuming that the output of an OT grammar is not the surface form but instead is the input to another OT grammar. Actual implementations differ in whether or not the second grammar is the same as the first one. The approaches to be discussed are: single-grammar serial OT, which is known as harmonic serialism; multi-grammar serial OT, which is sometimes known as Stratal OT; and output-output faithfulness, often referred to as OO correspondence.

Harmonic serialism. In harmonic serialism, the output of an OT grammar is returned as the input to that same grammar (McCarthy 2000a, 2002b: 159–163, 2007a, Prince and Smolensky 2004: 6–7, 94–95). This process continues until 'convergence', when the output of a pass through the grammar is identical to the output of the previous pass. (Convergence in a finite number of passes is guaranteed for reasons discussed by Moreton (2003).)

Harmonic serialism in its simplest form turns out to be surprisingly ineffective in dealing with opacity. It is no better off than classic OT in dealing with counterbleeding opacity. In (2-16), we saw that classic OT stumbles on a case of counterbleeding opacity like /ħaːkim-iːn/ → [ħaːkʲmiːn] because there is no visible motive in surface structure for palatalization of the /k/. Harmonic serialism does no better. On the first pass through the grammar, there is nothing to prevent the transparent mapping /ħaːkim-iːn/ → *[ħaːkmiːn], just like (2-16). In general, wherever classic OT has a problem with counterbleeding opacity, harmonic serialism will too, since harmonic serialism is just classic OT, iterated.

Harmonic serialism actually does worse than classic OT on some kinds of counterfeeding opacity. Recall from (2-18) that classic OT can accommodate counterfeeding interactions by positing the right faithfulness constraints. In Bedouin Arabic, because /i/ deletes in the same environment where /a/ changes to [i], what is needed is a constraint that specifically militates against deleting /a/, MAX-A. But MAX-A is useless under the harmonic serialism regime. The first pass through the grammar, which is shown in tableau (2-22), maps /dafaʕ/ to [difaʕ]. The output of the first pass becomes the input to the second pass, shown in tableau (2-23), and [difaʕ] *qua* pass-two input is mapped to *[dfaʕ]. On the third pass, [dfaʕ] *qua* pass-three input maps to itself, and there is convergence — on the wrong output.

(2-22)   Harmonic serialism: first pass through grammar

/dafaʕ/	MAX-A	*aCV	*iCV	ID(low)	MAX
→ difaʕ			1	1	
a. dfaʕ	W₁		L	L	W₁
b. dafaʕ		W₁	L	L	

(2-23) Harmonic serialism: second pass through grammar

[difaʕ]	Max-A	*aCV	*iCV	Id(low)	Max
→ dfaʕ					1
a. difaʕ			W$_1$		L
b. dafaʕ		W$_1$		W$_1$	L

The problem in (2-23) is this: with [difaʕ] as the input, Max-A no longer protects the vowel in the first syllable from deletion. When the second and subsequent passes through the grammar come around, information about the original input is no longer available to Eval. For this reason, counterfeeding opacity in general cannot be analyzed using harmonic serialism. (See Norton 2003: 247ff. for related discussion.)

These failures of harmonic serialism show that a single-grammar implementation of serial OT is of no value in analyzing opacity. We will see in §3.2.3, however, that harmonic serialism has some significant connections with OT-CC.

Multi-grammar serial OT. The principal thesis of the theory of Lexical Phonology is that the phonological system of a language consists of a series of separate modules, called levels or strata, each of which is an *SPE* grammar in its own right (see §2.2.6). Strata are usually associated with different morphological subsystems in the lexicon or with the difference between word-internal and phrasal phonology. There is an ordering among the strata, and the output of one stratum is the input to the next. The output of the last or postlexical stratum is the actual surface form.

It seems like a small step to go from assuming that strata are *SPE* grammars to assuming that they are OT grammars, and so this move has been advocated almost since the beginning of OT. Although implementational details differ, this idea of linking OT grammars serially is common to all of the approaches that go under names like LP/OT, Derivational OT, or Stratal OT. Throughout, I will use the name Stratal OT to refer to any theory that incorporates these basic assumptions.[15]

Stratal OT uses the ordering of strata to reproduce the effects of opaque ordering in rule-based phonology. If rule A precedes rule B in counterfeeding order in a rule-based analysis, then the Stratal OT reanalysis posits two strata. The grammar of the first stratum effects mappings equivalent to rule A, and the grammar of the second stratum effects mappings equivalent to rule B. The output of the first stratum is the input to the second stratum just as the output of rule A is the input to rule B. Because of the assumed correlation between strata and morphological subsystems, the Stratal OT hypothesis about opacity is somewhat stronger than the rule-based hypothesis, which establishes no linkage between morphology and opacity.

Each stratum is an OT grammar, so within-stratum interactions are necessarily transparent just as they are in classic OT. The different strata are moreover *different* OT grammars from one another — that is, they are different permutations of the universal constraint set CON. This assumption is essential to Stratal OT's theory of opacity. Without it, Stratal OT would be another version of harmonic serialism, and we have already seen that harmonic serialism is a failed theory of opacity.

Stratal OT's central analytic strategy for opacity, then, is to isolate the opaquely interacting processes into different strata, with the ordering of the strata supplying the counterbleeding or counterfeeding order of the processes. For instance, the counterbleeding order between Bedouin Arabic palatalization and syncope in /ħaːkim-iːn/ →$_{\text{palatalization}}$ [ħaːkʲim-iːn] →$_{\text{syncope}}$ [ħaːkʲmiːn] shows that the stratum where palatalization occurs must be ordered before the stratum where syncope occurs. Because strata correlate with morphological subsystems or the lexical/postlexical distinction, it will sometimes be possible to use other evidence to determine exactly which strata are involved. Since syncope occurs in phrases as well as words (see (2-7)), it must occur in the postlexical stratum. For palatalization to precede syncope in counterfeeding order, palatalization must occur in some earlier, therefore lexical stratum. The OT grammar of the lexical stratum, shown in (2-24), takes the input /ħaːkim-iːn/ and maps it to [ħaːkʲimiːn], with palatalization but no syncope. The grammar of the postlexical stratum in (2-25) then takes [ħaːkʲimiːn] as input and maps it to [ħaːkʲmiːn], with syncope. Observe that the two strata are inconsistent in how they rank MAX and *iCV; they are, in every sense, different OT grammars.

(2-24) Lexical stratum

/ħaːkim-iːn/	MAX	*ki	*iCV	ID(back)
→ ħaːkʲimiːn			1	1
a. ħaːkmiːn	W$_1$		L	L
b. ħaːkʲmiːn	W$_1$		L	1
c. ħaːkimiːn		W$_1$	1	L

(2-25) Postlexical stratum

/ħaːkʲimiːn/	*iCV	*ki	Max	Id(back)
→ ħaːkʲmiːn			1	
a. ħaːkmiːn			1	W₁
b. ħaːkʲimiːn	W₁		L	
c. ħaːkimiːn	W₁	W₁	L	W₁

There are two main problems with Stratal OT as a theory of opacity. First, Stratal OT is not powerful enough to deal with the full range of observed opaque interactions. Second, Stratal OT is also too powerful, since it massively overpredicts phonological systems that are never observed and seem impossible. There is, then, a two-way mismatch between the predictions of Stratal OT and the typology of known opaque interactions.

The argument that Stratal OT has insufficient power was foreshadowed at the end of §2.2.6. Like Stratal OT, rule-based Lexical Phonology allows for the possibility of between-stratum opaque orderings. But since each rule-based Lexical Phonology stratum is an *SPE* grammar, within-stratum opaque ordering is also possible. In general, the Lexical Phonology research program never sought to eliminate within-stratum rule ordering, including opaque ordering. In light of the extensive pre-Lexical Phonology literature arguing for the elimination of extrinsic ordering, this failure to pursue an obvious hypothesis might seem surprising, at least until one realizes the reason for it:[16] the hypothesis was self-evidently wrong. That is, research on rule-based Lexical Phonology never progressed in the direction of eliminating within-stratum opaque ordering because there was no shortage of Lexical Phonology analyses that crucially relied on such ordering, such as Kiparsky's (1984) analysis of Icelandic or Kiparsky's (1985) analyses of Catalan and Russian.

In Catalan, for example, there is a counterbleeding relationship between nasal place assimilation and final cluster simplification. According to Kiparsky, cluster simplification must be assigned to the lexical stratum because clusters cannot be rescued by postlexical resyllabification before vowel-initial words: *pont antic* 'old bridge' is pronounced as [ˌpo.nən.'tik] and not *[ˌpɔn.tən.'tik]. Since nasal place assimilation precedes cluster simplification, as shown in (2–26), nasal place assimilation must also apply in the lexical stratum. The result in this case, as in so many other Lexical Phonology analyses, is a within-stratum opaque (counterbleeding) order.

(2-26) Counterbleeding order in Catalan (Kiparsky 1985:96–97)

Underlying	/bɛn-k/
Place assimilation	[bɛŋk]
Cluster simplification	[bɛŋ]
Surface	['bɛŋ]
	'I sell'

Bedouin Arabic supplies another example of the insufficiency of between-stratum ordering as a theory of opaque rule ordering. (See §4.3.3 for details.) In a rule-based analysis, deletion of high vowels must precede raising of low vowels in counterfeeding order: /dafaʕ/ $\rightarrow_{\text{deletion}}$ DNA^{17} $\rightarrow_{\text{raising}}$ [difaʕ] (see (2-4)). We know from (2-7) that deletion is a process of the phrasal phonology, so it must occur as late as the postlexical stratum. Raising, on the other hand, is not a phrasal process — it only applies within words and never when its open-syllable context arises by resyllabification across word juncture. Therefore, raising cannot occur later than the last lexical stratum. Since raising is lexical and deletion is postlexical, these processes are intrinsically ordered by virtue of their stratal assignments, and so raising *must* precede deletion. But this is exactly the wrong conclusion, since it puts them in feeding order rather than counterfeeding order. Because raising is lexical, the lexical stratum maps /dafaʕ/ to [difaʕ], and because deletion is postlexical, the postlexical stratum goes on to map [difaʕ] to *[dfaʕ] (just as it maps /difiʕ/ 'was pushed' to [dfiʕ]).

There is more to be said about this example. As I showed in (2-18), classic OT can analyze this counterfeeding interaction if it has a constraint MAX-A. This constraint prevents deletion of any underlying /a/, even if its surface realization is something other than [a]. MAX-A is of no help in the stratal account, however. The problem is that the lexical stratum output [difaʕ] is the postlexical stratum input, and so the postlexical phonology sees an input [i] in the first syllable of this word. MAX-A does not protect input [i]s from deletion. In Stratal OT, faithfulness constraints are local to each stratum: they require identity between that stratum's input and its output, and they have no way of accessing the original underlying representation /dafaʕ/. The information that the first vowel of [difaʕ] is an erstwhile /a/ has been lost irretrievably by the time the postlexical stratum comes along, and so neither MAX-A nor any other constraint can account for the counterfeeding interaction between these two processes whose stratal assignments place them in feeding order. With respect to this example, then, Stratal OT is actually worse off than classic OT.

The Catalan and Arabic examples reveal some general properties of theories that seek to reduce opaque interactions to between-stratum orderings. If rule A precedes rule B in counterbleeding order, then A must apply on some stratum that is earlier than the stratum where B first applies. A may continue to apply on later strata, but A's earliest application must precede B's earliest application. If rule A precedes rule B in counterfeeding order, then A must apply on some stratum that is earlier than the stratum where B first applies, and A must not apply on B's earliest stratum or any subsequent stratum. These entailments of Stratal OT tell us what situations would constitute *prima facie* counterexamples to this theory of opacity, such as counterbleeding order with B in the earliest stratum or counterfeeding order with A in the last stratum. A specific prediction: postlexical processes like syncope in Bedouin Arabic are never opaque. See §4.3 for various demonstrations that this process is indeed opaque.

From the examples discussed, it appears that Stratal OT's premises are insufficient to account for the full range of observed opaque interactions (see also Noyer 1997: 515, Paradis 1997: 542, Roca 1997b: 14ff., Rubach 1997: 578 for similar remarks). The literature in support of Stratal OT and its variants has mostly focused on exhibiting between-stratum opaque interactions and arguing against other approaches to opacity in OT, such as sympathy theory (§2.3.4.3). I am not aware of comparable work arguing that Stratal OT is sufficient to account for the full range of observed opaque interactions. The evidence described here and in the Lexical Phonology literature challenges this claim.

Stratal OT is also an overly powerful theory because it imposes no limits on differences among strata within a single language. There is a profound but mostly unacknowledged difference between rule-based Lexical Phonology and Stratal OT on exactly this point. Each Lexical Phonology stratum is an *SPE* grammar and each Stratal OT stratum is an OT grammar. This seeming parallelism is misleading, however, because the literature on rule-based Lexical Phonology was highly attentive to the problem of constraining between-stratum differences. There are serious and well-argued (though not uncontroversial) proposals about how to do this. The earliest proposals took the form of principles for separating lexical and postlexical processes (e.g., Kaisse and Hargus 1993a: 16–17, Kiparsky 1983, Mohanan 1982): lexical rules are structure-preserving (i.e., neutralizing or nonallophonic); lexical rules are word-bounded; lexical rules apply only in derived environments; lexical rules apply only to the lexical categories noun, verb, and adjective; only lexical rules may have exceptions; only lexical rules are sensitive to word-internal morphological structure; and lexical rules are categorical, never gradient. This body of work culminated in the Strong Domain Hypothesis (Borowsky 1986, Kiparsky 1984, Myers 1991b, Selkirk 1982b): all strata, lexical and postlexical, share a single *SPE*-type grammar. The observed differences between strata are obtained from a combination of universal principles like structure preservation, which can prevent some rules from applying in lexical strata, and language-particular stipulations about when certain rules stop applying. An approach like this is clearly far more restrictive than the original Lexical Phonology thesis that each stratum is a separate *SPE* grammar.

This restrictive version of Lexical Phonology cannot be reconstructed in Stratal OT, however. Structure preservation, for example, is the cornerstone of the Strong Domain Hypothesis, but there is no hope of developing an analogue to structure preservation in Stratal OT. The principle of structure preservation says that rule application in lexical strata cannot create segments or structures that are not already present in underlying representations. In other words, the well-formedness conditions on underlying representations persist as conditions on rule application throughout the lexical strata, although they may be relaxed or turned off in the postlexical stratum.

Structure preservation has no OT analogue for two reasons:

First, the hypothesis that grammars differ only in constraint ranking entails that there can be no language-particular conditions on underlying representation (McCarthy 2002b: 70–71, Prince and Smolensky 2004). This requirement is called richness of the base (ROTB) (see also §3.5.2). Under ROTB, the grammar itself, unaided by restrictions on its inputs, is responsible for observed phonotactic patterns. Since there are no restrictions on inputs, it would make no sense to speak of such restrictions persisting in their effects through the lexical strata.

Second, OT offers no way of reconstructing rule-based Lexical Phonology's notion that some lexical constraints are turned off in later strata. The naïve supposition is that turning-off effects can be simulated by demoting markedness constraints or promoting faithfulness constraints. In reality, though, OT offers no simple equivalence between demotion or promotion and deactivation. Even low-ranking markedness constraints may be active in situations where the faithfulness constraints ranked above them are not relevant. Thus, the specific effects of markedness demotion or faithfulness promotion cannot be predicted without meticulous examination of the entire constraint hierarchy and array of inputs. Prince and Smolensky (2004: 27ff.) emphasize this point for faithfulness constraints; reduplicative emergence of the unmarked illustrates the same point for markedness constraints (Alderete *et al.* 1999, McCarthy and Prince 1994). Known conditions of literal deactivation of a constraint, such as Panini's Theorem (Prince and Smolensky 2004: 97–99), have such specific conditions that they are of little value in characterizing permitted differences between strata.

It follows, then, that the restrictive theory of differences between strata that was developed in rule-based Lexical Phonology does not and presumably cannot inform our understanding of such differences in Stratal OT. This problem is not unknown to proponents of Stratal OT, and they have attempted to develop simple principles for relating the constraint hierarchies of different strata within a language. An example: Kiparsky (1997: 17) proposes that the ranking of markedness constraints is constant across all of the strata of a language, so between-stratum differences are limited to promotions and demotions of faithfulness constraints. Another example: Koontz-Garboden (2003), citing a personal communication from Kiparsky, proposes that between-stratum reranking is limited to promoting constraints to undominated status in later strata (that is, stratum $n+1$ is identical to stratum n except that some lower-ranking constraint(s) in n are undominated in $n+1$). It is not hard to find counterexamples to these hypotheses in the Stratal OT literature. For example, Ito and Mester (2001: 274–276) argue that the lexical and postlexical strata in German differ in markedness ranking, contrary to the first hypothesis. The second hypothesis is inconsistent with Kiparsky's (2003) analysis of syncope in colloquial Arabic. In that analysis, syncope is the result of satisfying a constraint against light syllables. This constraint is promoted to a higher rank in the word stratum than in the earlier, stem stratum. But this promotion cannot be to undominated status; the constraint against light syllables must be dominated since the language has some light syllables that escape the effects of syncope. If it were undominated, then the language could have no light syllables whatsoever.

In summary, Stratal OT has not and probably cannot recapture Lexical Phonology's restrictive theory of between-stratum differences, nor does it yet have a workable substitute. Absent such restrictions, Stratal OT allows the strata of a single language to differ by as much as one language differs from another. A stratum is just a ranking of CON, with no obligations to the rankings of CON in other strata of the same language. From the perspective of language typology and learnability, this is an unwelcome conclusion.

Output-output faithfulness. The theory of output-output correspondence posits faithfulness relations among morphologically related output forms (Benua 1997, Kenstowicz 1996a, Pater 2000, and many others). Information flows via faithfulness constraints from an output form called the 'base' to other forms derived from it by affixation. OO correspondence can be applied to phonological opacity, as in Kager (1999b). If the base transparently undergoes or fails to undergo the potentially opaque process, then OO faithfulness constraints can transmit this information by compelling related forms to resemble the base. For example, the opaquely palatalized velar in Bedouin Arabic /ħaːkim-iːn/ → [ħaːkʲmiːn] could be explained with reference to the unaffixed singular base form [ħaːkʲim], where palatalization is transparent.

This is accomplished formally by deploying the output-output faithfulness constraint OO-IDENT(back), ranking it higher than its input-output counterpart IO-IDENT(back) (which is referred to as just IDENT(back) in tableau (2-16)). In this way, the phonologically unremarkable velar palatalization in [ħaːkʲim] is transmitted to the rest of the paradigm, even to forms where the triggering front vowel is absent from surface structure.

OO faithfulness does not suffice as a theory of opacity, however. There are three main arguments against it (also see Benua 1997, Booij 1996, 1997, Ito and Mester 1997b, Karvonen and Sherman [Ussishkin] 1998, McCarthy 1999: 385–387, Noyer 1997, Paradis 1997, Rubach 1997).

First, it is impossible to use OO faithfulness as a comprehensive theory of opacity and also have a principled theory of what can be the base of an OO correspondence relation. The [ħaːkʲmiːn] example is attractive because the morphologically basic form is the one where the process is transparent and the forms derived from it are the ones where the process is opaque. In the Bedouin Arabic counterfeeding case /gabr/ → [gabur], however, there is no word that is morphologically more basic than [gabur] 'grave'. The only paradigm members where the lack of raising can be explained transparently are the derived forms, such as [gabri] 'my grave'. Clearly, it is unreasonable to insist that [gabur] 'grave' is derived from [gabri] 'my grave', but that is exactly what would be required to account for [gabur]'s unraised vowel using OO faithfulness.

Another argument against OO faithfulness as a theory of opacity is the existence of cases where the (non-)application of a process is transparent in *no* member of the paradigm. The analysis of Tiberian Hebrew epenthesis in McCarthy (1999) is an example. Alternations like those in (2-27) show that surface [ˈpɛlɛ] is derived from an underlying form with a final glottal stop, /pɛlʔ/. In a rule-based analysis (Malone 1993: 59–60, 93–94, Prince 1975: 37ff.), this mapping is the result of three processes applied in the opaque order shown in (2-28).[18] Epenthesis renders stress opaque, and deletion of [ʔ] renders epenthesis opaque.

(2-27)   Alternations of underlying /pɛlʔ/

/pɛlʔ/	ˈpɛlɛ	'a wonder' (Exodus 15, verse 11)
/pɛlʔ-akaː/	pilʔăˈxaː	'your wonder' (Psalms 89, verse 6)
/pɛlʔ-iːm/	pəlaːˈʔiːm	'wonders' (Lamentations 1, verse 9)

(2-28)   Tiberian Hebrew /pɛlʔ/ → [ˈpɛlɛ] derivation

Underlying	/pɛlʔ/
Stress final closed syllable	ˈpɛlʔ
Epenthesis in final cluster	ˈpɛlɛʔ
Deletion of final [ʔ]	ˈpɛlɛ
Surface	[ˈpɛlɛ]

To analyze opaque stress and epenthesis using OO faithfulness, at a minimum we would need to find paradigm members where stress on [pɛ] and epenthesis between [l] and [ʔ] are occurring transparently. There are none. The rest of the paradigm consists of words with vowel-initial suffixes. Because of these suffixes, stress is never retracted as far as [pɛ] and epenthesis is unnecessary. Therefore, neither of these opaque phenomena can be obtained with OO correspondence constraints.

The same problem for OO faithfulness — transparency nowhere in the paradigm — arises whenever an underlying phonological contrast undergoes absolute neutralization. For example, the underlying pharyngeal /ʕ/ in Maltese appears to condition a number of phonological processes, though it is always deleted at the surface (Borg 1997, Brame 1972). One such process lowers vowels next to pharyngeal consonants: /nimsiħ/ → [nimsaħ] 'I wipe'. This process is conditioned opaquely by the deleted /ʕ/: /nismiʕ/ → [nisma] 'I hear'. Nowhere in the paradigm of /smiʕ/ or, indeed, any other word of standard Maltese is the /ʕ/ preserved on the surface, to condition lowering transparently.

The Hebrew and Maltese critiques of OO faithfulness as a theory of opacity apply with equal force to approaches based on paradigm uniformity (see Downing, Hall, and Raffelsiefen (eds), (2005)). Paradigm uniformity allows information to flow in any direction among paradigm members, so a morphologically complex form can affect a simple form. This greater freedom is useless, however, in analyzing opacity when no member of the paradigm meets the transparency requirement.

A final argument against OO faithfulness as a theory of opacity is the existence of cases where OO faithfulness overpredicts opaque behavior. In Levantine Arabic (see §4.2), stress and epenthesis interact opaquely, leading to surface contrasts like ['katabit] 'she wrote' (from /katab-it/) vs. [ka'tabit] 'I wrote' (from /katab-t/). Stress is assigned transparently in /katab-it/ → ['katabit], but stress is assigned opaquely in /katab-t/ → [ka'tabit], as if the epenthetic vowel were not present. To account for the opaque stress of [ka'tabit] 'I wrote' in OO faithfulness terms, we would need to explain why this form is taking its cues, stress-wise, from paradigm members like [ka'tabna] 'we wrote' and not from ['katabit] 'she wrote' or ['katab] 'he wrote'. Furthermore, we would need to explain why a high-ranking OO faithfulness or paradigm uniformity constraint affects only [ka'tabit], the form that just happens to contain an epenthetic vowel. Any OO faithfulness constraint that would affect [ka'tabit] would surely resist all stress alternations throughout the paradigm, so we would expect consistent stress on the second syllable: *[ka'tabit] for 'she wrote', *[ka'tab] for 'he wrote', and so on. An OO faithfulness analysis of these facts seems quite hopeless.

OO faithfulness's inadequacy as a theory of opacity is not entirely unexpected. OO faithfulness is a reasonable theory of phonological similarity among morphologically related forms, but this is a far cry from opacity's hidden generalizations.

2.3.4.3 Analogues to intermediate derivational forms

Sympathy (McCarthy 1999, 2003c), targeted constraints (Wilson 2000), enriched inputs (Sprouse 1997, 1998), and comparative markedness (McCarthy 2003a, 2003d) are four theories of opacity in OT that share a commitment to using a third form, neither input nor output, in candidate evaluation. Since sympathy theory has been examined more extensively than the other approaches, the discussion here will focus on it exclusively.[19]

In sympathy theory, the third form is called the sympathetic candidate. The sympathetic candidate is just that, a candidate, so it is a kind of output form, though different from the actual output. The sympathetic form differs from the actual output by virtue of satisfying some faithfulness constraint that the actual output violates. This faithfulness constraint is called the selector. Apart from obeying the selector, the sympathetic candidate is as harmonic as possible; it is, in short, the most harmonic candidate among those that obey the selector. For example, in the Bedouin Arabic palatalization/syncope interaction (2-5), the selector constraint is MAX, so the sympathetic candidate does not have syncope, though the actual output does. But because the sympathetic candidate is maximally harmonic in all other respects, it shows the effects of all of the other (transparent) phonology of the language. Therefore, the sympathetic candidate from input /ħaːkim-iːn/ is [ħaːkʲimiːn], without syncope but with palatalization, since palatalization of velars is required before front vowels.

The sympathetic candidate influences the choice of the actual output form by way of sympathy constraints. Sympathy constraints look like faithfulness constraints, but they evaluate resemblance to the sympathetic candidate rather than resemblance to the input. With the right ranking, as shown in (2-29), the sympathy constraint favors opaque [ħaːkʲmiːn], whose palatalization matches sympathetic [ħaːkʲimiːn], over the transparent form [ħaːkmiːn], which has no palatalization. Two candidates in (2-29) obey the selector constraint MAX, (b) and (c). Of these, (b) is more harmonic by virtue of satisfying *ki, so it is the sympathetic candidate. (To avoid circularity, the sympathy constraint itself must be ignored in determining the sympathetic candidate.) The sympathy constraint IDENT(back)$_{Sym}$ is satisfied by candidates that match the palatalization in the sympathetic candidate, thereby ruling out (a). Recall from (2-16) that (a) harmonically bounds the intended winner in classic OT. The sympathy constraint breaks this harmonic bounding.

(2-29) Counterbleeding opacity with sympathy

/ħaːkim-iːn/	ID(back)$_{Sym}$ (sympathy)	*iCV	*ki	MAX (selector)	ID(back)
→ ħaːkʲmiːn				1	1
a. ħaːkmiːn	W$_1$			1	L
b. ħaːkʲimiːn (sympathetic cand.)		W$_1$		L	1
c. ħaːkimiːn	W$_1$	W$_1$	W$_1$	L	L

The sympathetic candidate [ħaːkʲimiːn] is identical with the intermediate stage of the serial derivation (2-5). This is no accident. The changes that sympathy theory requires in classic OT are not so different from the changes that are required in a derivational approach like Stratal OT. The selection of the sympathetic candidate requires a separate harmonic evaluation in which a single faithfulness constraint, the selector, is promoted to undominated status. Except for the more limited reranking possibilities, this is not unlike the grammars of different strata in Stratal OT. Furthermore, there is a fundamental asymmetry between the sympathetic candidate and real output candidates: the sympathetic candidate influences the choice of the actual output, but the actual output is not allowed to influence the choice of the sympathetic candidate. This asymmetry is a necessary property of serial derivations: the early stages of the derivation influence the later stages, and not vice-versa.

Various objections have been raised against sympathy theory (Bye 2001, Idsardi 1997, Ito and Mester 2001, Kiparsky 2000, McMahon 2000), but the biggest problem may be the analysis of multiple interacting opaque processes. The most famous example of multiple interaction is Yawelmani Yokuts. (References on this language include Archangeli 1985, Archangeli and Suzuki 1996, 1997, Cole and Kisseberth 1995, Dell 1973, Goldsmith 1993a, Hockett 1973, Kenstowicz and Kisseberth 1977, 1979, Kisseberth 1969, Kuroda 1967, Lakoff 1993, Newman 1944 (the original source), Noske 1984, Prince 1987, Steriade 1986, Wheeler and Touretzky 1993, Zoll 1993.)

Yawelmani has three processes that interact opaquely:

a) *Height-stratified rounding harmony:* a suffix vowel takes on the rounding of the preceding vowel if they agree in height. E.g., the high-voweled nonfuture suffix /-hin/ alternates as follows: [dubhun] 'lead by the hand' vs. [bokʔhin] 'find'; cf. [xathin] 'eat', [xilhin] 'tangle'. In contrast, the nonhigh-voweled dubitative suffix /-al/ alternates like this: [kˀoʔol] 'throw' vs. [hud**a**l] 'recognize'; cf. [maxal] 'procure', [gijˀal] 'touch'.

b) *Long-vowel lowering:* underlying long high vowels become mid. E.g., /ʔiliː-hin/ → [ʔil**eː**hin] 'fan', /cˀujuː-hin/ → [cˀuj**oː**hun] 'urinate'.

c) *Closed syllable shortening:* long vowels are shortened in medial and final closed syllables. E.g., /ṣaːp-hin/ → [ṣ**a**phin] 'burn', /panaː-al/ → [pan**a**l] 'arrive'.

In a rule-based analysis or its Stratal OT counterpart (Kiparsky 2001), these three processes must apply in the order shown in (2-30). (For a different analysis of Yawelmani, see §3.3.5.) No other order of application will do. If the order of rounding harmony and lowering were reversed, then the high suffix vowel would not harmonize with an originally high root vowel that has been lowered because of its length: /ʔuːṭ-hin/ →$_{lowering}$ [ʔo̞ːṭ-hin] →$_{harmony}$ *DNA* →$_{shortening}$ *[ʔo̞ṭhin]. And if the order of lowering and closed syllable shortening were reversed, then the derived short vowel would fail to lower: /ʔuːṭ-hin/ →$_{harmony}$ [ʔuːṭh**u**n] →$_{shortening}$ [ʔuṭhun] →$_{lowering}$ *DNA* →$_{surface}$ *[ʔuṭhun].

(2-30)   Rule-based or Stratal OT derivation for Yawelmani

Underlying	/ʔuːṭ-hin/	'steal'
Rounding harmony	ʔuːṭhun	
Long-vowel lowering	ʔo̞ːṭhun	
Closed syllable shortening	ʔo̞ṭhun	
Surface	[ʔo̞ṭhun]	

Unsurprisingly, Yawelmani's multiple opaque interactions cannot be analyzed with a single selector constraint choosing a single sympathetic candidate. Two selector constraints, two sympathetic candidates, and two sympathy constraints are required. One of the selectors is the antishortening constraint MAX-μ, and from the input /ʔuːṭ-hin/ it favors the sympathetic candidate [ʔo̞ːṭhin]. The other selector is IDENT(high), and it favors the sympathetic candidate [ʔuṭhun]. Each sympathetic candidate has its own sympathy constraint. The role of the sympathetic candidate [ʔo̞ːṭhin] is to determine the height of the actual output [ʔo̞ṭhun]'s root vowel. It does this by way of a sympathy constraint called IDENT(high)$_{\text{MAX-μ}}$. (The MAX-μ subscript is there to index this sympathy constraint to the selector of its sympathetic candidate.) The other sympathetic candidate, [ʔuṭhun], determines the rounding of [ʔo̞ṭhun]'s suffix vowel. It does this by way of the sympathy constraint IDENT(round)$_{\text{IDENT(high)}}$. In sum, the output's vowel height is taken from the sympathetic candidate selected by

Max-μ, whereas the output's rounding comes from the sympathetic candidate selected by Ident(high).

Once sympathy theory is provided with these additional analytic resources to handle multiple opacity, however, it is in serious danger of overgeneration. Kiparsky (2001) presents a simple but striking example. Assume that Con has only the markedness constraint No-Coda and consonant- and vowel-specific versions of the faithfulness constraints Dep and Max. As shown in (2-31), Dep-V and Max-C can each act as a selector. Given the input /pam/ and a ranking where No-Coda dominates both Dep-V and Max-C, Dep-V selects the sympathetic candidate [pa], which deals with the potential coda by deletion, and Max-C selects the sympathetic candidate [pamə], which deals with the potential coda by epenthesis. The sympathy constraints favor outputs that resemble these two sympathetic candidates in specific ways. The sympathy constraint Dep-C$_{\text{Dep-V}}$ favors any candidate that has no consonants that are not present in the Dep-V-selected sympathetic candidate [pa]. This means that Dep-C$_{\text{Dep-V}}$ favors forms that replicate [pa]'s consonant deletion. Similarly, the sympathy constraint Max-V$_{\text{Max-C}}$ favors any candidate that has all of the vowels that are present in the Max-C-selected sympathetic candidate [pamə]. This means that Max-V$_{\text{Max-C}}$ favors forms that replicate [pamə]'s vowel epenthesis. The net result is that the winner is [paə], a form that reproduces both [pa]'s consonant deletion and [pamə]'s vowel epenthesis.

(2-31) An unwelcome result of sympathy

/pam/	Dep-C$_{\text{Dep-V}}$ (sympathy)	Max-V$_{\text{Max-C}}$ (sympathy)	No-Coda	Dep-V (selector)	Max-C (selector)
→ paə				1	1
a. pam	W$_1$	W$_1$	W$_1$	L	L
b. pamə (sympathetic via Max-C)	W$_1$			1	L
c. pa (sympathetic via Dep-V)		W$_1$		L	1

The problem with (2-31) is that this sort of opaque interaction is unattested and no doubt impossible. The sympathetic candidates reflect two different ways of satisfying No-Coda, epenthesis and deletion. The sympathy constraints force the winner to reproduce the effects of *both* ways of satisfying No-Coda, both epenthesizing and deleting when either one alone would be enough. Obviously, additional constraints could be introduced to rule out [paə], but this sort of local fix misses the broader point. This is simply not an attested opaque interaction; it is gratuitous unfaithfulness, a kind of hyperopacity. It would seem, then, that giving sympathy the power to deal with multiple opacity also gives it the power to produce such unlikely results as (2-31).

A final remark about sympathy. Bye (2001, 2003), Jun (1999), and Odden (1997) introduce variations on sympathy theory that make the sympathetic form part of the candidate that is evaluated. One way of implementing this idea is to assume that a candidate is not a single form but rather an ordered pair: (*sympathetic-form, output-form*). In Bedouin Arabic, for example, the winning candidate would be ([ħaːkʲimiːn], [ħaːkʲmiːn]), and it competes against alternatives like those listed in (2-32). There are various ways of constructing a system of constraints for evaluating candidates like these; the comments at the right in (2-32) give a sense of what the constraints will need to be sensitive to. As we will see in §3, candidate chains are a somewhat similar idea.

(2-32)   Candidates as (*sympathetic-form, output-form*)
     ([ħaːkʲimiːn], [ħaːkʲmiːn])   Winner.
     ([ħaːkʲimiːn], [ħaːkmiːn])   Palatalization mismatch.
     ([ħaːkimiːn], [ħaːkmiːn])   No palatalization in the sympathetic form.
     ([ħaːkmiːn], [ħaːkmiːn])   Syncope in the sympathetic form.

2.3.4.4 *Opacity as a mechanism for preserving contrasts*

Donegan and Stampe (1979), Kaye (1974, 1975), Kisseberth (1976), and Gussmann (1976) propose that opaque rule ordering has a functional explanation. The general idea is that opacity preserves phonemic contrasts, avoiding neutralizations that would occur if the rules applied in transparent order.

Kaye (1974) looks at counterbleeding orders like the one in (2-33), which comes from Ojibwa (Algonquian, US and Canada). This is a counterbleeding order because, if the rules were applied in the opposite order, cluster simplification would deprive place assimilation of an opportunity to apply, yielding *[takoʃʃin] instead (cf. Catalan). Kaye observes that the opaque order makes sense functionally: to a listener hearing the surface form, '… it is immediately apparent that the underlying representation ends in *k*, given the rules cited above and the fact that ŋ is not part of the inventory of underlying segments. … The only possible source of ŋ is as a result of the assimilation of a nasal to a following velar stop' (Kaye 1974: 144). Kaye uses the term 'recoverability' to describe this functional motivation for opacity.

(2-33) Counterbleeding order in Ojibwa (Kaye 1974: 140)

Underlying	/takossin-k/	
Place assimilation	takossiŋk	
Cluster simplification	takossiŋ	
Surface	[takoʃʃiŋ]	'(if) he arrives'

Donegan and Stampe (1979: 145–151) make a somewhat similar point about counterfeeding order. They see phonology as the result of conflict between phonetic (articulatory) and phonological (perceptual) aims. Transparent interaction of processes is phonetically motivated, since it presumably maximizes articulatory ease. Opaque interactions of the non-surface-true variety are phonologically motivated, in their sense, because opacity 'bring[s] speech closer to its phonological intentions' (p. 147). As an example, Donegan and Stampe cite nasal deletion and intervocalic flapping in English *plant it*. For some speakers, they interact opaquely, as shown in (2-34). (Compare [plæt ɪt] with [plæ̃ɾ ɪ̃t], which other speakers produce from transparent interaction of the same processes.) In Donegan and Stampe's view, this and other instances of counterfeeding order 'prevent the merger of phonologically distinct representations' (p. 147), such as *plant it* and *plan it*. The desire to avoid merger must be weighed against the cost of opaque [plæt ɪt]'s greater articulatory difficulty in comparison with transparent [plæ̃ɾ ɪ̃t].

(2-34) Counterfeeding order in English *plant it*

Underlying	/plænt ɪt/
[nasal] assimilation	plæ̃nt ɪt
[t] flapping	*Inapplicable because [t] is not intervocalic*
Nasal deletion	plæ̃t ɪt
Surface	[plæ̃t ɪt]

Łubowicz (2003) develops an Optimality-Theoretic system, called PC theory (for 'preserve contrast'), in which these ideas about opacity's functional motivation are given a formal basis. With Flemming (1995), Padgett (2003), and others, she assumes that the objects of phonological evaluation are systems of contrasts, which she calls scenarios, rather than individual forms. (E.g., a scenario for German /bʊnd/ 'federation' might include all of its logically possible minimal pairs, including /bʊnt/.) This move allows CON to include constraints against neutralization, which can favor opaque interactions precisely when they help to preserve a contrast that would otherwise be lost.

Łubowicz applies PC theory to, among other things, counterfeeding opacity. Take an example like Bedouin Arabic /gabr/ → [gabur] (see (2-20)). Because the output contains an unraised vowel in an open syllable, it offers a hint that the openness of the syllable is not original. PC theory expresses this intuition formally by introducing constraints on scenarios, among which is one called $PC_{IN}(V/Ø)$. This constraint is violated by any output scenario that neutralizes a contrast between a vowel and zero that obtains in the input scenario. Importantly, $PC_{IN}(V/Ø)$ does not say *how* the contrast is to be preserved; it can be preserved as-is, or it can be transferred to some other segment, depending on interaction with other constraints. Thus, if /pat/ and /pati/ both map to [pati], $PC_{IN}(V/Ø)$ is violated, but it is not violated if /pat/ maps to [pati] and /pati/ maps to [padi].

In the Arabic case, $PC_{IN}(V/Ø)$ evaluates scenarios like those in (2-35). (Underlying /gabur/ is hypothetical; the scenarios deal with possible rather than actual words.) To block raising and thereby favor the opaque scenario, $PC_{IN}(V/Ø)$ must crucially dominate the markedness constraint that favors raising, *aCV. The effect of the ranking $[PC_{IN}(V/Ø) \gg {}$*aCV$]$ in (2-36) is that the underlying contrast between a vowel and zero, which epenthesis threatens to neutralize, is transferred to the quality of the vowel of the preceding syllable. This brief analysis glosses over some important issues, but it is sufficient to get a sense of how PC theory works and how it can account for opacity.

(2-35) Arabic scenarios in PC theory

    a. Transparent

       /gabur/ → [gibur]

       /gabr/   → [gibur]

    b. Opaque

       /gabur/ → [gibur]

       /gabr/   → [gabur]

(2-36) Counterfeeding opacity in PC theory

	/gabur/ /gabr/	$PC_{IN}(V/Ø)$	*Comp-Coda	*aCV	Dep	Id(low)
→	/gabur/ → [gibur] /gabr/ → [gabur]			1	1	1
a.	/gabur/ → [gibur] /gabr/ → [gibur]	W₁		L	1	W₂
b.	/gabur/ → [gibur] /gabr/ → [gabr]		W₁	L	L	1

Łubowicz does not discuss counterbleeding opacity, but PC theory also seems applicable to cases like Kaye's Ojibwa example. Two of the relevant scenarios are given in (2-37). The transparent scenario is clearly less marked and more faithful, yet the opaque one wins. For this to happen, $PC_{IN}(C/\varnothing)$ must be ranked above the markedness and faithfulness constraints that favor the transparent scenario. This ranking argument is shown in (2-38). The idea is that the contrast between /k/ and $\varnothing$ is preserved by being transferred onto the preceding consonant.

(2-37) Ojibwa scenarios in PC theory

a. Transparent

/…in/ → […in]
/…ink/ → […in]

b. Opaque

/…in/ → […in]
/…ink/ → […iŋ]

(2-38) Counterbleeding opacity in PC theory

/…in/ /…ink/	$PC_{IN}(C/\varnothing)$	*Comp-Coda	*ŋ	Id(coronal)
→ /…in/ → […in] /…ink/ → […iŋ]			1	1
a. /…in/ → […in] /…ink/ → […in]	W₁		L	L
b. /…in/ → […in] /…ink/ → […ink]		W₁	L	L

PC theory is by far the most original theory of opacity among those we have seen, since it offers a radical restatement of the entire rationale for opaque interactions. But it is not without its problems, the most serious of which can be illustrated with the Ojibwa example in (2-38). The constraint $PC_{IN}(C/\varnothing)$ chooses the opaque winner over its transparent competitor in (a). That may seem unexceptionable, but in a way the PC constraint works *too* well. The victory of the opaque scenario in (2-38) is unrelated to the fact that Ojibwa independently has a process of nasal place assimilation (e.g., [takoʃʃiŋkipan] '(if) he arrived then'). In (2-38), the winner manages to beat (a) without reference to any markedness constraint that favors [ŋk] over [nk]. The analysis in (2-38) therefore makes no connection between how contrast is preserved and the independent existence of a nasal place assimilation process in the language.

This means that, without significant modifications, PC theory allows contrasts to be preserved in ways that are fundamentally unnatural, since they do not depend on markedness constraints for their motivation (Łubowicz 2003: 148–153). For example, the contrast between /k/ and Ø in Ojibwa could in principle be preserved by rounding the preceding vowel: /…in/ → […in], /…ink/ → […yn]. This outcome is made possible by ranking PC_{IN}(C/Ø) above *y and IDENT(round), even though neither Ojibwa nor any other language is likely to have a process that transparently maps /…ink/ to […ynk].

Attested cases of opacity are not like this. The opaque process in Ojibwa is not different in kind from the transparent processes in other languages. The opaque processes that we actually find in languages are natural. In OT terms, this means that those processes should devolve from standard markedness-over-faithfulness rankings, since such rankings, combined with the universality of CON, are the only means within this theory for explaining phonological naturalness. This result establishes a strong precondition for the adequacy of any theory of opacity in OT.

2.4   What have we learned?

Perhaps the most striking result of this review of previous work on opacity is the central role played by structure that is not present in either underlying or surface representations. With the exception of contrast preservation (§2.3.4.4), all reasonably complete theories of opacity make crucial reference, via rules or constraints, to some nonunderlying, nonsurface representation. In *SPE* (§2.2.3), it is the intermediate step of a serial derivation with ordered rules. In Stratal OT (§2.3.4.2), it is the output of one stratum that is also the input to the next stratum. In sympathy, targeted constraints, and comparative markedness (§2.3.4.3), it is a more faithful candidate than the actual output form. And in Containment or Turbidity (§2.3.4.1), the counterpart to the intermediate derivational step is not exactly a level of representation, but it is nonetheless present as coexistent, unpronounced structure in the output form.

The discussion of local conjunction (§2.3.4.1) and contrast preservation (§2.3.4.4) emphasizes another point: opacity is a result of process interaction. Our understanding of opacity cannot be separated from our understanding of what 'process' means in OT, nor can it be separated from our understanding of how different processes may make inconsistent demands on phonological mappings. Opacity is deeply connected with the phonology of a language, and any adequate theory of opacity must recognize this.

From all this, I conclude that there is some fundamental truth to the derivational view of opacity. But OT denies the existence of rules and therefore of rule ordering, for some very good reasons (McCarthy 2002b: chapter 3, Prince and Smolensky 2004: chapters 2–5, 9). We have also seen that previous attempts to meld OT with serial derivations or their analogues have not been fully successful (§2.3.4.1–§2.3.4.3). The challenge, then, is to make use of the derivational insight without losing hold of OT's essential properties and basic results. The next chapter presents a proposal intended to do exactly that.

Notes

1   The derivation in (2-4) also includes a bleeding interaction: deletion bleeds raising in the derivation of [ʃarbat].

2   Lexical exceptions will also look like they should have undergone a process but did not. Kiparsky's definition of opacity is limited to the effects of process interaction and not exceptionality. See Laferriere (1975) for a useful distinction between 'internal' opacity (exceptionality) and 'external' opacity (2-6).

3   Hayes's (1990) notion of 'precompilation' provides a way of lexically listing morphologized alternations that occur in external sandhi. Precompilation is therefore intended for phenomena like morphological mutation. It is by intent and by design inappropriate for examples like high-vowel deletion in Bedouin Arabic, where there are no morphological or grammatical conditions.

4   Oh, the grand old Duke of York, / He had ten thousand men; / He marched them up the hill, / And he marched them down again.

5   See Pater (2000) for an analysis of these data in OT using output-output correspondence.

6   This formulation is due to Jane Grimshaw.

7   The qualification 'at least' implies that there may be more than one fully faithful candidate from a given input. This is possible if there are dimensions along which candidates may differ that are not protected by faithfulness constraints. Syllabification is the standard example. For further discussion, see McCarthy (2002a, 2003c) and §3.2.4.1.

8   Throughout, I follow Prince (2002) in using comparative tableaux. The winning candidate appears to the right of the arrow, and losers are in the rows below it. Subscripted integers stand for the number of violation marks incurred by a candidate, replacing the familiar strings of asterisks. In loser rows, the effects of the constraints are indicated by W and L, W if the constraint favors the winner and L if it favors the loser. These annotations are much more useful and perspicuous than the exclamation point and shading that they replace. For example, the sufficiency of any tableau can be easily checked: every L must be outranked by ($\approx$ to the right of) some W in the same row, and every loser row must contain at least one W.

9   I am grateful to Adam Werle for help with the Nuuchahnulth data.

10   There is a great deal of previous literature discussing the challenges that opacity presents to classic OT, including Archangeli and Suzuki (1996, 1997), Black (1993), Booij (1997), Cho (1995), Clements (1997), Chomsky (1995), Goldsmith (1996), Halle and Idsardi (1997), Idsardi (1998), Jensen (1995), Kager (1997, 1999b), McCarthy (1996, 1999), McCarthy and Prince (1993b), Noyer (1997), Paradis (1997), Prince and Smolensky (2004), Roca (1997b), Rubach (1997), and various contributions to Hermans and van Oostendorp (eds) (1999).

11   The double vertical line in the middle of tableau (2-16) is used to separate blocks of constraints that cannot be ranked on the basis of the information provided. That is, no ranking relations are asserted across this double line.

12   On compensatory lengthening, see among others Hayes (1989) and Wetzels and Sezer (eds) (1986).

13   The constraint *Complex-Coda* (*Comp-Coda*) is violated by any tautosyllabic syllable-final cluster.

14   The problems of constraint conjoinability and domains arise regardless of whether we regard conjoined constraints as literally present in universal Con or merely immanent in it (see Ito and Mester 2003a: 24 on this distinction). Either way, linguistic theory is obliged to explain why certain logical possibilities do not occur.

15   Modular, serial implementations of OT along the lines of the theory of Lexical Phonology have been proposed or discussed in the following works, among others: Bermúdez-Otero (1999, forthcoming), Cohn and McCarthy (1994/1998), Hale and Kissock (1998), Hale, Kissock, and Reiss (1998), Ito and Mester (2001, 2003b, 2003c), Kenstowicz (1995), Kiparsky (2003, to appear), McCarthy (2000b), McCarthy and Prince (1993b), Orgun (1996b), Potter (1994), Rubach (2000), and many of the contributions to Hermans and van Oostendorp (eds) (1999) and Roca (ed.) (1997a).

16   The hypothesis that strata can eliminate the need for extrinsic ordering is pursued in a somewhat different theoretical context by Goldsmith (1993a) and Lakoff (1993). Their theories are distinct from both LP, because they do not allow within-stratum ordering, and from Stratal OT, because they employ 'two-level' rules that can refer to input environments. (Stratal OT's markedness constraints, like classic OT markedness constraints, can only refer to output environments.)

17   *DNA* stands for 'does not apply'.

18   The processes in (2-28), though opaque, are nearly exceptionless. I know of no lexical exceptions to stressing of final closed syllables or deletion of final [ʔ]. The only lexical exceptions to epenthesis in final clusters are the words [neːrd] 'nard' (Canticles 4, verse 14), a borrowing from Persian, and [qoʃtˤ] 'truth' (Proverbs 22, verse 21), a *hapax legomenon*.

19   There is a fairly extensive literature on sympathy theory and its applications (Bakovic 2000, Davis 1997a, 1997b, de Lacy 1998, Dinnsen *et al.* 1998, Fukazawa 1999, Harrikari 1999, Ito and Mester 1997a, 1997b, 1998, Jun 1999, Karvonen and Sherman [Ussishkin] 1997, 1998, Katayama 1998, Kikuchi 1999, Lee 1999, McGarrity 1999, Merchant 1997, Odden 1997, Parker 1998, Sanders 1997, Walker 1998, 2003, Wilbur 1998).

3   Candidate chains and phonological opacity

3.1   Introduction

In Optimality Theory, all phonological alternations are the result of well-formedness conditions on surface structure. This claim follows from the basic structure of OT: alternations involve unfaithfulness to underlying representations, and any unfaithfulness must be compelled by a markedness constraint. A markedness constraint is precisely a condition on the well-formedness of surface structure.

The evidence discussed in §2 suggests that the universal quantifier at the beginning of the preceding paragraph is too strong. In counterbleeding opacity, alternations occur for reasons that are not visible in surface structure. In counterfeeding opacity, an expected alternation fails to occur for reasons that are not visible in surface structure and not reasonably attributable to faithfulness. The existence of solid phonological analyses that involve opacity is therefore a challenge to some of the premises of classic OT.

In rule-based generative phonology, phonological opacity is attributed to derivations. In a derivation, rules produce and affect levels of representation intermediate between underlying and surface structure. The most successful approaches to opacity in OT have something in common: they also incorporate derivations or something similar into the system (see §2.3.4).

It seems that some sort of derivational approach to opacity is unavoidable. If so, then what is the best way of incorporating the derivational insight into OT? The resulting revision of OT ought to have sufficient analytic resources to deal with well-attested and well-understood types of opaque interaction. Ideally, the revised theory will also impose interesting and plausible limits on opacity. Certainly it should not abandon OT's central results about conspiracies, language typology, learning, and other matters, since otherwise the exercise would be pointless.

In this chapter, I develop a modification of classic OT that achieves these desiderata. The central point of difference is a change in the definition of candidates: instead of being single output forms, candidates are chains of forms that link the input and output by minimal phonological differences. Candidate chains approximate — but also differ crucially from — the steps in a derivation in classic generative phonology. This modification of OT will be referred to as OT-CC (for OT with candidate chains).

This chapter is organized as follows. The theory of chains is laid out in §3.2. That section does not discuss opacity, focusing instead on establishing the formal properties of chains and some interesting results and predictions that are unrelated to opacity. The theory of chains is applied to the opacity problem in §3.3. That section introduces PREC constraints, which regulate the order of unfaithful mappings in a chain. The theory is illustrated with examples of counterbleeding and counterfeeding opacity abstracted from the fuller analyses in §4, and with the multiple opaque interactions of Yawelmani. Learning problems are briefly discussed in §3.4, and some ways in which faithfulness is involved in opacity are the topic of §3.5. Finally, §3.6 compares OT-CC with the various alternative approaches to opacity, inside and outside OT, that were discussed in §2.

3.2   The theory of chains

3.2.1   The basics

In OT-CC, a candidate is a chain of forms rather than a single form. (This statement is not precisely true; we will see in §3.3.2 that the actual candidates are reduced versions of chains that discard all but the essential information.) A chain is an ordered n-tuple that connects the input with the output through a sequence of intermediate forms, each of which differs minimally from the forms that immediately precede and follow it. The last member of the chain is its output, and the output of a chain has exactly the same status as the output form in classic OT. Since chains are ordered n-tuples, I will use vector notation to represent them: e.g., <pat, pati, patʃi> is a chain representing a transparent interaction of coda-relieving [i]-epenthesis and palatalization triggered by [i].

There are three conditions on chain well-formedness: (i) The first member of any chain must be *fully faithful* to the input. (ii) The successive forms in a chain must accumulate differences from the input *gradually*. (iii) The forms in a chain are *locally optimal*. The following paragraphs and subsequent sections of this chapter explain these statements in detail and consider alternative formulations.

(i) **Faithful first member** (§3.2.4.1). The first member of every candidate chain based on the input /in/ is a *fully faithful parse* of /in/.[1] A fully faithful parse of /in/ is any analysis of /in/ that violates no faithfulness constraints. The fully faithful parse can therefore differ from /in/ in any phonological property that is not protected by faithfulness constraints. There can be more than one fully faithful parse of /in/; the one that actually initiates a chain is determined by the principle of local optimality in (iii).

(ii) **Gradualness** (§3.2.4.2). A single violation of a basic faithfulness constraint[2] in a specific location in a form is a *localized unfaithful mapping*, or LUM. Gradualness embodies two related requirements: the successive forms in a candidate chain are required to accumulate all of their predecessors' LUMs; and a form adds exactly one LUM to those of its immediate predecessor. For example, while <pat.ka, pa.tə.ka, pa.də.ka> can be a valid chain from the input /patka/, **<pat.ka, pa.də.ka> cannot, since the mapping /patka/ → [pa.də.ka] cannot be accomplished with a single LUM. (I will use double asterisks to mark chains that are invalid, reserving single asterisks for chains that are valid but nonoptimal.) In short, chains are characterized by monotonically increasing unfaithfulness relative to the original input, and the slope of the line is one LUM for every link in the chain.

(iii) **Local optimality** (§3.2.4.3). In OT-CC, unlike classic OT, the candidates derived from a particular input can differ from language to language. The source of this difference is the local optimality requirement, which has two aspects:

(a) The initial form of a chain is the fully faithful parse of the input that is most harmonic according to the constraint hierarchy of the language in question. In other words, it is locally optimal among all faithful parses.

(b) Every noninitial form in a chain is more harmonic than its predecessor (= harmonic improvement). It is also more harmonic than every other form that can be derived by violating the same basic faithfulness constraint (= best violation). For example, for <…, pat.ka, pa.tə.ka, …> to be a valid chain in a language with the constraint hierarchy ℋ, [pa.tə.ka] must be more harmonic according to ℋ than its predecessor [pat.ka] (harmonic improvement). Furthermore, because [pa.tə.ka] is produced by an epenthetic LUM, it must also be more harmonic according to ℋ than all the forms with alternative epenthesis sites, such as [ə.pat.ka], [pə.at.ka], [pat.ə.ka], etc. (best violation).

Local optimality has two consequences for noninitial members of chains. First, it ensures harmonic improvement: each form in a chain is more harmonic than its predecessors. Since we know from the gradualness requirement (ii) that a form is always less faithful than its predecessors in the chain, it must by local optimality be less marked relative to $\mathcal{H}$ than its predecessors, since a less faithful form can be more harmonic only if it is less marked (see Moreton (2003) and §2.3.1). Second, local optimality chooses the best way of violating a particular faithfulness constraint when several harmonically improving possibilities for violating the same constraint might present themselves. For further discussion of local optimality and its role in defining chains, see §4.2.3.

These three requirements on chains are summarized and slightly rearranged in (3-1).

(3-1) Definition: Candidate Chain

A candidate chain associated with an input /in/ in a language with the constraint hierarchy $\mathcal{H}$ is an ordered *n*-tuple of forms $C = <f_0, f_1, ..., f_n>$ that meets the following conditions:

a. Initial form: f_0 is the faithful parse of /in/ that is most harmonic according to $\mathcal{H}$.

b. Gradualness: In every pair of immediately successive forms in C, $<..., f_i, f_{i+1}, ...>$ $(0 \leq i < n)$, f_{i+1} has all of f_i's localized unfaithful mappings relative to /in/, plus one more.

c. Local optimality (harmonic improvement + best violation): For every pair of immediately successive forms in C, $<..., f_i, f_{i+1}, ...>$ $(0 \leq i < n)$, where F is the basic faithfulness constraint violated by the LUM that distinguishes f_{i+1} from f_i, f_{i+1} is more harmonic according to $\mathcal{H}$ than f_i and every other form that differs from f_i by a different F-violating LUM.

For example, assume there is a language with the constraint hierarchy in (3-2). Among the valid chains derived from the input /pap/ are those in (3-3); they include a chain consisting only of the most harmonic faithful parse of /pap/, and also other chains that extend this singleton chain by epenthesis, deletion, or epenthesis and intervocalic voicing. (Observe that, according to the definition in (3-1), <pap, pa.pə> and <pap, pa> are both valid chains, even though MAX dominates DEP.) The chains in (3-4), on the other hand, are not valid because they deviate from one or more of the requirements in (3-1).

(3-2) A hypothetical constraint hierarchy

No-Coda >> Max >> Dep >> $*VC_{VCLS}V$ >> Id(voice)

(3-3) Some valid chains for input /pap/ under (3-2)

<pap>   Faithful parse.

<pap, pa.pə>   Harmonically improving because No-Coda >> Dep.

<pap, pa>   Harmonically improving because No-Coda >> Max.

<pap, pa.pə, pa.bə>   Harmonically improving because <pap, papə> is
                           harmonically improving and $*VC_{Vcls}V$ >> Id(voice).

(3-4) Some invalid chains for input /pap/ under (3-2)

**<pap, pab>   Final voicing is not harmonically improving
                               under ℋ.

**<pap, pab, pa.bə>   Contains nonchain <pap, pab> (see §3.2.2).

**<pa.pə, pa.bə>   Not initiated by faithful candidate.

**<pap, pa.bə>   Adds more than one LUM at a time.

**<pap, pap>   Adds no LUMs.

**<pap, pa.pə, pa.bə, pab> Subtracts a LUM.

The local optimality requirement requires interaction between Gen and Eval,
and this necessitates a revision of OT's basic architecture along the lines of
(3-5).[3] As the double-headed arrow indicates, information flows back and
forth between Gen and Eval, since Gen must consult Eval to determine which
faithful parse of the input is most harmonic, whether the addition of a particular
LUM to a chain results in harmonic improvement, and which LUM violating a
particular faithfulness constraint leads to the most harmonic result. As we will
see in §3.2.2, it is a fairly straightforward matter to give a recursive procedure
for chain construction based on local optimization.

(3-5) Basic architecture of OT-CC

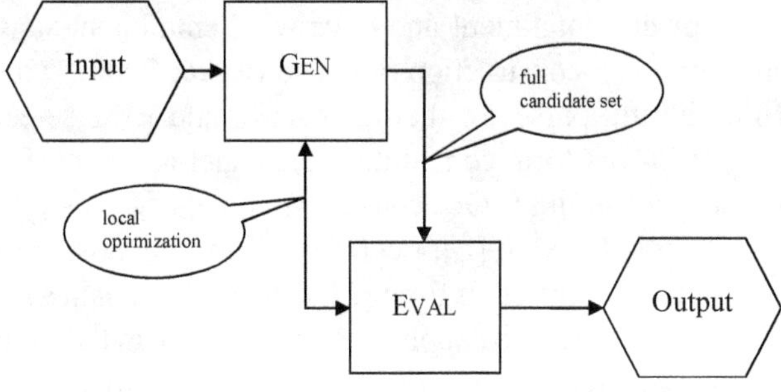

3.2.2   Some properties of candidate chains

The definition in (3-1) requires certain relationships between chains and their subchains. When combined with the harmonic improvement property of classic OT, it also imposes limits on the size and number of valid candidate chains for a given input.

Chain/subchain relationships. Definition (3-1) implies an *upward entailment* requirement on chains: no valid chain can contain an invalid left-aligned subchain. That is, if $**\langle f_0, f_1, ..., f_m \rangle$ is not a valid chain for input /in/ under constraint hierarchy $\mathcal{H}$, then $**\langle f_0, f_1, ..., f_m, ..., \mathbf{f_n} \rangle$ is also invalid. Merely adding forms onto the end of an invalid chain, while holding all else equal, will never make it valid. This result follows from (3-1) because any of the possible explanations for why $**\langle f_0, f_1, ..., f_m \rangle$ is not a valid chain must also hold of $**\langle f_0, f_1, ..., f_m, ..., f_n \rangle$: f_0 is not the most harmonic faithful parse of /in/; or some form in $**\langle f_0, f_1, ..., f_m \rangle$ fails to add exactly one LUM to its immediate predecessor's LUM set; or some form in $**\langle f_0, f_1, ..., f_m \rangle$ is not locally optimal in the sense of clause (c) of (3-1).

   This definition also imposes a *downward entailment* requirement on chains: all of the left-aligned subchains of a valid chain are also valid chains. That is, if $\langle f_0, f_1, ..., f_n \rangle$ is a valid chain for input /i/ under hierarchy $\mathcal{H}$, then so are all of its left-aligned subchains $\langle f_0, f_1, ..., f_m \rangle$, where $m<n$. This statement follows from (3-1) because, if $\langle f_0, f_1, ..., f_m, ..., f_n \rangle$ is a valid chain, then all of the desiderata of valid chains must also hold for $\langle f_0, f_1, ..., f_m \rangle$: f_0 is the most harmonic faithful parse of /in/; and every form in $\langle f_0, f_1, ..., f_m \rangle$ adds exactly one LUM to its immediate predecessor's LUM set; and every form in $\langle f_0, f_1, ..., f_m \rangle$ is locally optimal in the sense of clause (c) of (3-1).

   Taken together, upward entailment and downward entailment suggest a recursive procedure for chain construction (see also Becker 2006).[4] GEN first constructs all of the faithful parses of the input form, and EVAL selects the most harmonic one, $[f_0]$. This form constitutes the singleton chain $\langle f_0 \rangle$. For every basic faithfulness constraint F, GEN constructs the set of forms $\{_F f^i\}$ that add exactly one F-violating LUM to $[f_0]$. Let $[h]$ stand for the most harmonic member of $\{_F f^i\} \cup \{f_0\}$. If $[h]$ is different from $[f_0]$, then add the chain $\langle f_0, h \rangle$ to the candidate set. Proceed recursively, applying GEN and EVAL to the rightmost member of every newly added chain. The recursion terminates when no chains can be added because further harmonic improvement is impossible. Termination is guaranteed by basic properties of OT — see below.

   The relation between a chain and its left-aligned subchains is also relevant to the opacity/transparency distinction. In transparent phonology, $\langle f_0, f_1, ..., f_m, ..., f_n \rangle$ consistently beats $\langle f_0, f_1, ..., f_m \rangle$, since for these chains to be valid

f_n must be more harmonic than f_m. In counterfeeding opacity, however, the winner can be the shorter chain, $<f_0, f_1, ..., f_m>$. For example, transparent *$<$gabr, ga.bur, gi.bur$>$ loses to opaque $<$gabr, ga.bur$>$ in Bedouin Arabic, even though *[gi.bur] is less marked than [ga.bur]. PREC constraints, which evaluate chains, are responsible for such opaque outcomes; see §3.3.

Length and number of chains. The classic OT candidate set is standardly described as infinite. It is infinite because GEN includes unrestricted structure-building operations, of which epenthesis is the most obvious example. With unrestricted epenthesis in GEN, there is no upper bound on the length of a candidate. Epenthesis is unrestricted in classic OT's GEN for reasons of theoretical parsimony: all observed limits on epenthesis are adequately explained by factorial typology. Excessive epenthesis brings additional faithfulness violations with no concomitant improvement in markedness performance, so there is no need for a GEN-internal restriction on iterated epenthesis.

In OT-CC, however, the candidate set is finite. As diagram (3-5) makes clear, chain construction requires two-way communication between GEN and EVAL. Chain validity depends upon, among other things, harmonic improvement relative to the language-particular constraint hierarchy. If a form has undergone epenthesis with no concomitant improvement in markedness, then it cannot be added to a chain. Infinitely iterated epenthesis is an impossibility in OT-CC because the basic EVAL-mediated economy of epenthesis affects what GEN is allowed to do. There can be no chain $<$pa, pa.ə, pa.ə.ə, pa.ə.ə.ə, ...$>$ unless CON includes markedness constraints that favor [pa.ə.ə] over [pa.ə], [pa.ə.ə.ə] over [pa.ə.ə], and so on. Since CON is finite, and since markedness constraints evaluate output forms without reference to the input, there must come a point where further epenthesis yields no further harmonic improvement and the chain can grow no longer.[5] Hence, chains are bounded and the candidate set is finite. This result harks back to Tesar's (1995b) syllabic parsing model, which proceeds directionally rather than derivationally but with the same basic idea.

A somewhat more formal statement of this result can be derived from Moreton's (2003) Characterization Theorem. This theorem states that any classic OT grammar is *eventually idempotent.* A function f is idempotent if and only if $f(a) = f \circ f(a)$ for any a — that is, if the result of applying f to a is the same as the result of applying f to the result of applying f to a. Any generative grammar, including an OT grammar, is a function $G(/in/) \rightarrow [out]$. This function G is *eventually* idempotent if and only if, for any input, there comes a point when repeated application of G to its own output yields no further changes. That is, $\forall /in/ \ \exists n$ such that $G^n(/in/) = G^{n+1}(/in/)$. To say that every classic OT grammar is eventually idempotent is therefore to say that there is always an upper bound on harmonic improvement for any input under any grammar; if the grammar is repeatedly given its own output as input, there will always come a point when the output is identical to the input because no further harmonic improvement is possible.

This result about classic OT grammars is directly relevant to OT-CC. Chains are subject to a harmonic improvement requirement: if $<..., f_i, f_{i+1}, ...>$ is a valid chain, then f_{i+1} is more harmonic than f_i. That is the same as saying that a classic OT grammar, when presented with f_i and f_{i+1} as the only candidates, will choose f_{i+1} as optimal. With the Characterization Theorem, we know for certain that every chain will eventually reach a point where no form is more harmonic than the current chain-final form, so further growth in chain length is impossible. That is, for any input and any constraint hierarchy $\mathcal{H}$, there is some n such that $[f_n] \succ [f_{n+1}]$ for all $[f_{n+1}]$ that can be obtained by adding a single LUM to f_n. (For the symbol $\succ$, read 'is more harmonic than'.) Therefore, the length of valid chains is bounded.

This result about candidate chains gives OT-CC a decidedly finitistic cast, but by itself it is not enough to ensure that all evaluations are finite. Because of the local optimality requirement on the forms in chains, there are other evaluations that take place in the course of chain construction: the chain initiator is the most harmonic faithful parse of the input, and adding an F-violating LUM to a chain requires that there be no more harmonic way of violating F.

In both of these evaluations, the threat of the infinite comes from those properties of phonological representation that can be introduced or changed at no cost in faithfulness. For concreteness, suppose that syllabification is such a property (cf. §3.2.4.1). It may seem that there are only a few ways of syllabifying the input /pa/, such as $[pa]_\sigma$ and $[p]_\sigma [a]_\sigma$. But if GEN is free, at no cost in faithfulness, to create syllables without segmental content, then the number of possibilities is infinite — not just $[pa]_\sigma$ but also $[pa]_\sigma [\ ]_\sigma$ or $[pa]_\sigma [\ ]_\sigma$, $[\ ]_\sigma$, and so on. The same thing goes if GEN is free to recurse syllables, such as $[[pa]_\sigma]_\sigma$ and $[[[pa]_\sigma]_\sigma]_\sigma$. To ensure that the chain-building evaluations are finite, then, it is necessary to rule out these structural possibilities by imposing certain inviolable restrictions on GEN. First, GEN must be barred from positing headless syllables. Rather, every syllable must have an overt segmental nucleus. Second, GEN must also be forbidden to posit recursive prosodic structure. The first of these restrictions is a natural one, given the ubiquity of the notion 'head' in linguistic theory (since Harris 1946) and the replacement of the empty-node approach to epenthesis by correspondence theory (cf. §2.3.4.1). But a GEN-internal ban on recursion of prosodic structure seems more problematic in light of work arguing that the nonrecursiveness of the prosodic hierarchy is a consequence of violable constraints (Selkirk 1996), as well as Grimshaw's

(1994) and Gouskova's (2003) results about EVAL-based structural economy. Still, it is notable that the only solid case for prosodic recursion involves the phonological word node; recursion of syllables and feet appears to be unnecessary and may even be problematic.

The finiteness of the candidate set in OT-CC should not be seen as a major result.[6] It is the responsibility of linguistic theory to define the function G that maps inputs to outputs. The responsibility to offer a well-defined G is entirely separate from the question of whether G is efficiently computable, a point that has often been emphasized by Chomsky (e.g., 1965: 9, 1968: 117). If we choose to address this entirely separate question of computability, then we must do so using the theories and methods of computation. The 'challenge' of the infinite candidate set comes from assuming that the computational model looks just like the competence model, struggling with the Sisyphean task of sorting an infinite set into harmonic order. Serious work in computation does not use such brute force methods, as we can see in Tesar (1995a, 1995b). Furthermore, if the size of the candidate set matters at all, then there is unlikely to be much of a difference between infinite and big-but-finite. After all, if an ill-conceived computational model can do no better than sorting the candidate set into harmonic order, it does not matter whether there are infinitely many candidates or only a million candidates — either way, the model is too slow to be a reasonable theory of language processing. More important than the finiteness of OT-CC's candidate sets is the fact that they are *small* (Becker 2006).

In summary, the theory of candidate chains defined in (3-1) leads to an attractive result about the size of the candidate set. This result is not without some cost in expressive power, however. As we will see in §3.2.4.3, some /in/ → [out] mappings that are possible in classic OT are impossible in OT-CC. The reason: while classic OT requires that [out] be more harmonic than [in], OT-CC also requires that there be a monotonic path of gradually increasing unfaithfulness and improving harmony from /in/ to [out]. The requirement that unfaithfulness increase only *gradually*, one LUM at a time, is the nexus of this difference.

3.2.3   Intellectual precursors to candidate chains

There is an obvious resemblance between a candidate chain and the sequence of forms that appear in a phonological derivation: both involve intermediate representations that describe a path between the underlying and surface levels of representation. But there are important differences as well (also see §3.4).

The principal difference is that most derivational approaches do not — and by their nature cannot — impose a harmonic improvement requirement on derivations. In OT-CC, the links in a candidate chain must show steady harmonic improvement relative to the constraint hierarchy $\mathcal{H}$. A candidate chain $<f_0, f_1, ..., f_n>$ is harmonically improving only if $[f_1] \succ [f_0]$ according to $\mathcal{H}$, $[f_2] \succ [f_1]$ according to that same $\mathcal{H}$, and so on. Neither of the two most prominent derivational models, rule-based phonology (§2.2.2) and Stratal OT (§2.3.4.2), can sensibly demand that derivations have this harmonic-improvement property.

In Stratal OT, if $/f_0/ \rightarrow [f_1]$ in stratum 1, then $[f_1]$ is more harmonic than the faithful output $[f_0]$ and every other candidate, according to the stratum-1 constraint hierarchy $\mathcal{H}_1$. If $/f_1/ \rightarrow [f_2]$ in stratum 2, then the output $[f_2]$ is more harmonic than $[f_1]$ and every other candidate according to the stratum-2 constraint hierarchy $\mathcal{H}_2$, and so on. The central, defining hypothesis of Stratal OT is that different strata have different, partially contradictory rankings of the same universal constraint set. Therefore, it is possible for $\mathcal{H}_1$ to assert $[f_i] \succ [f_j]$ and for $\mathcal{H}_2$ to assert $[f_j] \succ [f_i]$ *in the same language*. That is a reason why Stratal OT can produce Duke-of-York derivations (cf. McCarthy 2003c, Pullum 1976): A $\rightarrow$ B $\rightarrow$ A (see §2.2.3 and §2.3.2). For an example of a Stratal OT Duke-of-York derivation, see Ito & Mester's (2001, 2003b) analysis of Japanese [g]~[ŋ] alternations, discussed in McCarthy (2005b) and below in §3.5.

The reason why Stratal OT has this analytic richness is that there are no known restrictions on constraint reranking across strata, various proposed restrictions having failed to hold up under empirical scrutiny (see §2.3.4.2). Therefore $\mathcal{H}_1$ and $\mathcal{H}_2$ in a single language can in principle vary as much as the constraint hierarchies of two entirely different languages. The upshot is that Stratal OT derivations are not and could not reasonably be required to be harmonically improving relative to a single constraint hierarchy.

A notion like harmonic improvement is even more alien to rule-based phonology, which has no notions like 'harmony' or 'improvement'. To facilitate comparison, though, we can think of rule-based phonology as a special case of Stratal OT with no limit on the number of strata. The effects of a single phonological rule R could be approximated with some ranking of CON, which I'll call $\mathcal{H}_R$. The effects of a sequence of phonological rules (R1, R2, R3, ...) could then be duplicated with a series of strata applied in sequence (cf. Black 1993): $\mathcal{H}_{R1} \rightarrow \mathcal{H}_{R2} \rightarrow \mathcal{H}_{R3}$ ... Therefore, a harmonic improvement requirement on derivations is very distant from the assumptions of rule-based phonology.

Another source of differences between candidate chains and derivations is the requirement of monotonically increasing unfaithfulness: each member of a valid chain adds exactly one LUM to the form that immediately precedes it. In Chomsky and Halle's (1968) theory of rule formulation, phonological rules are not limited to a single small change at a time, though there have been efforts in the autosegmental and metrical literature to limit rules to certain elementary operations (e.g., Prince's (1983) 'Move *x*' or Archangeli and Pulleyblank's (1994) 'Insert Path'). In Stratal OT, a single stratum can require any number of unfaithful mappings simultaneously, since the grammar of a stratum is nothing but a classic OT grammar, and classic OT grammars can require several unfaithful mappings simultaneously. Rules and strata can also produce nonmonotonicity of unfaithfulness relative to the input, of which Duke-of-York derivations are the classic example. The chains of OT-CC are required to have monotonically increasing unfaithfulness, and this excludes some Duke-of-York interactions.

OT-CC is closer to harmonic serialism than to any other variant architecture for OT (see §2.3.4.2). In harmonic serialism, GEN takes the input /in/ and derives from it the candidate set *cand-set$_0$*, which is submitted to EVAL. The most harmonic member of *cand-set$_0$*, as determined by EVAL, is [out$_1$]. It is not necessarily the final output, however; [out$_1$] is returned to GEN for further processing as a new input. This process continues, looping back and forth, until there is convergence, when the output of pass *n* is identical to the output of pass *n–1*. (As I noted previously in a different context, convergence in finitely many passes is guaranteed by Moreton's (2003) Characterization Theorem for classic OT grammars.) When there is convergence, what we have is the final output of the grammar.

Prince and Smolensky (2004: 94–95) link their discussion of harmonic serialism with a restriction on GEN (see also McCarthy 2000a):

> Universal grammar must provide a function Gen that admits the candidates to be evaluated. In the discussion in chapter 2 we have entertained two different conceptions of Gen. The first, closer to standard generative theory, is based on serial or derivational processing: some general procedure (Do-α) is allowed to make a certain single modification to the input, producing the candidate set of all possible outcomes of such modification. This is then evaluated; and the process continues with the output so determined. In this serial version of grammar, the theory of rules is narrowly circumscribed, but it is inaccurate to think of it as trivial. There are constraints inherent in the limitation to a single operation and in the requirement that each individual operation in the sequence improve Harmony. (An example that springs to mind is the Move-x theory of rhythmic adjustments in Prince (1983); it is argued for precisely on the basis of entailments that follow from these two conditions, pp. 31–43.)

In other words, on each pass GEN is limited to doing approximately what a single rule is usually called on to do: deleting, adding, or changing a segment, for example. In the terminology introduced here, GEN emits one candidate for each single LUM that can be imposed on its input (plus the faithful candidate, of course).

OT-CC's GEN was inspired by harmonic serialism. They have important similarities: gradualness in OT-CC is related to the 'certain single modification' that produces the candidate set in harmonic serialism; and evaluation of this restricted candidate set in harmonic serialism is similar to local optimization in OT-CC. But there are two important differences between harmonic serialism and OT-CC that directly impact the analysis of opacity.

First, harmonic serialism allows different single modifications of the input to compete with one another, whereas OT-CC's GEN does not. In other words, harmonic serialism picks the best of all forms that deviate from the input by one violation of *any* faithfulness constraint, whereas OT-CC's GEN picks the best of those forms that deviate by a violation of a *specific* faithfulness constraint, and then it does the same for all of the other basic faithfulness constraints.

In counterbleeding opacity, the first step in the winning chain is not necessarily the most harmonic form among those that deviate from the input by any single LUM; it is merely more harmonic than the faithful form. For instance, in a harmonic serialist analysis of the Bedouin Arabic example (2-4), the candidate set on the first pass through EVAL will include both [ħaːkʲimiːn] and [ħaːkmiːn]. To get the correct (opaque) result, [ħaːkʲimiːn] needs to win on this pass, with syncope occurring on the next pass. But, as (2-16) shows, [ħaːkmiːn] harmonically bounds [ħaːkʲimiːn], so [ħaːkʲimiːn] cannot possibly win if these two forms are compared directly.

The situation is different in OT-CC: [ħaːkmiːn] and [ħaːkʲimiːn] do not compete with each other in chain generation since they violate different faithfulness constraints. Both opaque <ħaː.ki.miːn, ħaː.kʲi.miːn, ħaːkʲ.miːn> and transparent <ħaː.ki.miːn, ħaːk.miːn> are valid members of the candidate set; a PREC constraint on chains (§3.3.2) can then favor the opaque chain over its transparent competitor.

Second, harmonic serialism has problems with counterfeeding opacity, as we saw in §2.3.4.2. The problem is that harmonic serialism takes each intermediate input to be a new output, and so it loses sight of the original input. This means that harmonic serialism cannot analyze chain-shift mappings. In a language where /æ/ → [e] and /e/ → [i] occur in the same context, the original input /æ/ maps to [e] after the first pass through GEN and EVAL, and then [e] becomes a new input which must map to [i] on the second pass. There is no way of preventing the unwanted /æ/ → [i] mapping within the assumptions of harmonic serialism because the original input /æ/ is no longer accessible by the time that the second pass rolls around. The situation in OT-CC is different, however, because faithfulness is always reckoned in relation to the original input. This chain shift is then a matter of choosing between the candidate chains <æ, e> and <æ, e, i>, both of which include the original input /æ/.

A more distant precedent for OT-CC is an analysis in Chen (1999).[7] Chen is dealing with a system of tone sandhi, and he seeks a way of expressing the following generalization (p. 109): 'By default, rules apply from left to right — unless such a mode of application produces an ill-formed output, in which case reverse the direction of operation.' He accomplishes this by using a tableau to compare two derivations, one obtained by left-to-right rule application and the other obtained by right-to-left application. One constraint favors left-to-right application, but it is dominated by a markedness constraint, so right-to-left application is sometimes favored. In short, an OT-like system chooses between derivations, somewhat like OT-CC, but the derivations themselves are the result of conventional rule application, quite unlike OT-CC.

There are many other distant precedents for OT-CC. The approaches to opacity in OT that posit nonderivational analogues to the intermediate forms in derivations have obvious connections with the idea of candidates as chains (§2.3.4.3). The idea that a candidate can be more complex than a single output form has many fathers and mothers, including those who have worked on contrast preservation (§2.3.4.4), on alternative formalizations of sympathy theory (§2.3.4.3), and on candidates consisting of entire morphological paradigms (see the contributions to Downing, Hall, and Raffelsiefen (eds) 2005 and references cited there). Many of the approaches to opacity in OT that were described in §2.3.4.3 are also precedents for OT-CC.

It is clear from this brief survey that OT-CC, though it has resemblances to earlier proposals, is significantly different from all of them. The candidate chain is not unlike a derivation, but it is also distinct from a derivation in important characteristics.

3.2.4   Further details of the theory of chains

The definition of a candidate chain in (3-1) specifies three requirements: the properties of the initial form in a chain, gradualness, and local optimization/harmonic improvement. The following subsections discuss each of these points in greater detail, explaining their rationale, further defining the theory of LUMs (§3.2.4.2), and deriving some empirical results that are independent of opacity (§3.2.4.3).

3.2.4.1 *The initial form in a chain*

Some aspects of phonological representation are not protected by faithfulness constraints but can differ from language to language. The standard example is syllabification. Languages differ in whether they syllabify a form like /tabla/ as [tab.la] (Arabic) or [ta.bla] (English, Spanish), but no known language has a contrast between monomorphemic [tab.la] and [ta.bla] (Blevins 1995: 221, Clements 1986: 318, Hayes 1989: 260, McCarthy 2003c: 60–62). One could exclude syllabification from underlying representations by fiat, but it is closer to the spirit of OT to assume that no constraints in Con demand faithfulness to syllabification, thereby guaranteeing that no information about syllabification can ever be transmitted from underlying representations to surface forms.

The initial form in every candidate chain is, by hypothesis, a fully faithful parse of the input. For the reason just given, though, this principle will not necessarily identify a unique form. For example, the faithful parses of /tabla/ are quite diverse, including not only [tab.la] and [ta.bla] but also more outlandish possibilities like [tabl.a], with a complex coda and an onsetless syllable.

According to clause (a) of (3-1), this range of possible chain initiators is brought under control by harmonic evaluation: all chains from a given input are initiated by whichever faithful parse is most harmonic according to the constraint hierarchy of the language in question. Since all of the candidates for the most harmonic faithful parse are equally (and perfectly) faithful, this choice will be determined exclusively by the ranking of markedness constraints. For example, the candidate chains for input /tabla/ will be initiated by [tab.la] if the highest ranking constraint that distinguishes [tab.la] from [ta.bla] is *Complex-Onset or something like it.

There is a theory-internal reason for assuming that the chain initiator is the *most harmonic* faithful form. The gradualness requirement (clause (b) of (3-1)) says that each step in the chain must introduce a new unfaithful mapping. This means that a valid chain cannot contain a step that does nothing except resyllabify, with no effect on faithfulness. Now consider a language where /tabla/ maps faithfully to [tab.la]. If the chain were initiated by [ta.bla], contrary to the hypothesis that every chain begins with the most harmonic faithful form, then there would be no way to get to the desired winner [tab.la]. The problem is that **<ta.bla, tab.la> is not a valid chain under gradualness. In sum, every chain must be initiated by the most harmonic faithful form because sometimes a chain with no unfaithful mappings is optimal. (On the weakness of the premise underlying this theory-internal argument, see the next section.)

An alternative is to include in the candidate set all of the valid chains initiated by *every* faithful parse. This would mean that GEN supplies a set of candidate chains that includes <ta.bla, …>, <tab.la, …>, and even <tabl.a, …> for the input /tabla/. The problem lies with chains like <tabl.a, …>, where the initial form is harmonically bounded. If a harmonically bounded parse were to start a chain, it would have many possible successors, since any non-harmonically-bounded form is a harmonic improvement over one that is harmonically bounded. I have not succeeded in constructing an example where the possibility of harmonically-bounded chain initiators leads to outright failure, but it certainly seems like a needless complication.

A final reason to assume that chains are initiated by the most harmonic faithful parse comes from a problem in positional faithfulness theory. Beckman (1998: 36fn.), citing a personal communication from Rolf Noyer, observes that the positional faithfulness constraint IDENT$_{\text{ONS}}$(voice) and the markedness constraint No-Vcd-Obst can jointly coerce an underlying voiced obstruent into coda position in order to devoice it: /pada/ → [pat.a]. All that is required is to rank these two constraints above ONSET, as shown in (3-6). Since the same grammar maps underlying /pata/ to [pa.ta], the resulting language ends up with a surface contrast in syllabification: [pat.a] from /pada/ versus [pa.ta] from /pata/. As I have already noted, contrastive syllabification of tautomorphemic sequences is unattested. This example shows that IDENT$_{\text{ONS}}$ constraints can produce this unwanted contrast even without constraints on faithfulness to syllabification.

(3-6)   An unwanted effect of IDENT$_{\text{ONS}}$(voice) >> No-Vcd-Obst >> ONSET, IDENT(voice)

		ID$_{\text{ONS}}$(voice)	No-Vcd-Obst	ONSET	ID(voice)
/pada/					
→	pat.a			1	1
a.	pa.da		W$_1$	L	L
b.	pa.ta	W$_1$		L	1
/pata/					
→	pa.ta				
c.	pat.a			W$_1$	

The source of this problem is the assumption that IDENT$_{\text{ONS}}$(voice) refers to a consonant's onset status in *surface* structure. Since classic OT recognizes only two levels of representation, surface and underlying, the only other logical possibility in classic OT is to require IDENT$_{\text{ONS}}$ and other positional faithfulness constraints to refer to underlying form. This causes other problems, however. If a segment's underlying syllabification is what matters, then underlying /ag.pa/ will map to [ak.pa], as desired. Under richness of the base (§3.5.2), however, we cannot limit our attention to inputs like /ag.pa/ whose syllabification conveniently matches the canons of output syllabification. The grammar must also successfully contend with 'wrongly' syllabified inputs like /a.gpa/, which will map to [ag.pa] if IDENT$_{\text{ONS}}$ is sensitive to underlying syllabification (see (3-7)). The underlying difference in syllabification is lost, but it is converted into a surface difference in voicing. In consequence, the basic phonotactics of German become unanalyzeable: if IDENT$_{\text{ONS}}$(voice) refers to the syllabification of underlying representations, then there is no way of using this constraint to describe a system where all surface codas are voiceless.

(3-7)   An unwanted result if IDENT$_{\text{ONS}}$(voice) refers to underlying syllabification

/a.gpa/	ID$_{\text{ONS}}$(voice)	No-Vcd-Obst	ID(voice)
→ ag.pa		1	
ak.pa	W$_1$	L	W$_1$

OT-CC offers an alternative that is not available in classic OT: IDENT$_{\text{ONS}}$(voice) can refer to the syllabification of the chain-initial form. This is similar to referring to underlying syllabification, but there is a crucial difference. The problem with referring to underlying syllabification is its untrustworthiness: as in (3-7), a consonant with the wrong underlying syllabification undermines the effect of IDENT$_{\text{ONS}}$(voice) and other positional faithfulness constraints. But the syllabification of the chain-initial form is under the control of the grammar, since the chain-initial form is the most harmonic faithful parse. If positional faithfulness constraints refer to prosodic positions as they are present in the chain-initial form, then we have none of the problems of allowing positional faithfulness to refer to underlying or surface syllabification.

To solve the Beckman-Noyer problem in this light, we need to explain why the grammar (3-6) cannot perform the unattested and unwanted mapping /pada/ → [pat.a]. All chains derived from input /pada/ will begin with <pa.da, ...>, since no other syllabification is more harmonic (Prince and Smolensky 2004). The grammar in (3-6) has an undominated positional faithfulness constraint, IDENT$_{\text{ONS}}$(voice). The novel hypothesis is that IDENT$_{\text{ONS}}$(voice) refers to a consonant's status as an onset in the *chain-initial* form, and in chain-initial <pa.da, ...> the [d] is an onset. This means that it is subject to IDENT$_{\text{ONS}}$(voice) no matter how it ends up being syllabified in surface structure. Therefore, the unwanted output [pat.a] is not a possible continuation of this chain because **<pa.da, pat.a> is not harmonically improving under the grammar in (3-6). The problem with **<pa.da, pat.a> is that it violates top-ranked IDENT$_{ONS}$(voice), since it devoices a consonant that is in onset position in the chain-initial form, and the chain-initial form is what matters for positional faithfulness.[8]

This proposal leads to the general prediction that IDENT$_{ONS}$ and other sylla-ble-sensitive positional faithfulness constraints can never *affect* syllabification; they can only *respond to* syllabification that is given to them at the outset of the chain. This prediction seems to be correct. It also entails that these constraints cannot refer to surface syllabification even when it differs from faithful syl-labification. For example, in /padima/ → [pad.ma], [d] is subject to IDENT$_{ONS}$ if the faithful syllabification is [pa.di.ma]. This prediction needs closer study and may turn out to be incorrect.[9]

Choosing the most harmonic faithful parse raises some issues, and ranking is one of them. It may happen that every faithful parse of the input violates at least one markedness constraint that is unviolated in surface forms of the language. For example, Yawelmani (§3.3.5) has a process of closed syllable shortening: /ṣaːp-hin/ → [ṣaphin] 'burn'. Phonological theory offers several ways of faithfully parsing the initial CVːC sequence: a trimoraic CVːC syllable, a CVːC syllable with a nonmoraic appendix, a CVː syllable followed by a word appendix, or a CVː syllable plus a complex onset. Let M* stand for the set of markedness constraints that these various parses violate. In classic OT, only one ranking inference is possible: all of the M* constraints dominate faithfulness to vowel length, because all of the faithful parses fail to surface. Nothing can be inferred about the ranking relations among the M* constraints, since all are unviolated in surface forms of Yawelmani.

The situation is different in OT-CC, however. The choice of the chain initiator will depend on the ranking relations among the various M* constraints. Phenomena like positional faithfulness or opacity may provide indirect evi-dence for this ranking, but in the limiting case there may be no evidence of ranking. Then the choice of the chain initiator may be somewhat arbitrary, at least for the analyst.

Strictly speaking, the ranking in OT-CC is no more arbitrary than classic OT. In both classic OT and OT-CC, a constraint hierarchy is a total ordering of CON (Prince and Smolensky 2004). Therefore, the M* constraints must be placed in some order even in classic OT and even when there is no evidence for their ranking. Whether this order is entirely arbitrary depends on the details of the ranking biases that learners are endowed with.

Any arbitrariness in selecting the chain initiator should not lead to bad results. The reason is that no properties of the chain-initiating faithful parse have any durability. LUMs are enduring commitments: once a LUM has been added to a chain, it cannot be withdrawn (see clause (b) of (3-1)). But a faithful parse, by definition, contributes no LUMs. Syllabification and other properties that are not protected by faithfulness constraints can be and are freely altered in subsequent forms of the chain. (E.g., once the vowel of /ṣaːp-hin/ has been shortened, the [p] becomes a coda, and it does not matter whether it was previously parsed as a moraic coda, as a nonmoraic appendix, or in a complex onset.) For this reason, any uncertainty that may attend the selection of the most harmonic faithful parse should not lead to problems in the analysis.

The choice of the most harmonic faithful parse also raises a substantive issue: which aspects of phonological representation can be assigned in a faithful parse? A comprehensive answer to this question requires a complete theory of the faithfulness constraints in Con and of the atoms of phonological representation (e.g., segments) and their attributes (e.g., features). The problem is framed in this way because a faithful parse can assign or alter anything in the atom and attribute inventory that has no protective faithfulness constraint. OT-CC *per se* requires no particular stance on the faithfulness constraints or the representational system, but analysis in OT-CC cannot be conducted without at least a partial answer to the question that introduces this paragraph.

I have assumed throughout that syllabic parsing is not subject to faithfulness and therefore that syllables may be freely assigned and reassigned in chains. Metrical parsing, or at least the location of prominence, is subject to faithfulness, however, since there are languages with lexical stress (e.g., English and Russian). For this reason, stress assignment must constitute a LUM, and information about stress will be absent from chain-initial forms unless it is inherited from the input (see §4.2.2 for further discussion). Deletion and insertion of phonological elements like segments and tones are also unfaithful mappings, as are changes in the attributes of these elements (i.e., Ident violations). All of these transformations clearly violate faithfulness constraints, so their LUM status is not in doubt.

Moras have always had a somewhat difficult status in faithfulness theory. The problem lies in the fact that moras have two main functions: they mark the distinctions between long and short and between syllabic and nonsyllabic segments; and they 'make position', designating some CVC syllables as heavy. Quantity and syllabicity are matters of faithfulness, since they are both contrastive in some languages,[10] but weight by position is probably not, since the weight of codas never seems to be contrastive within a language (though see Elfner 2006). It follows that changing a segment's quantity or syllabicity is a LUM, but, say, resyllabifying a moraic coda as a nonmoraic onset is not. For my purposes, this matter is most simply resolved by assuming that moras can be freely added or removed at no cost in faithfulness, but changes in quantity and syllabicity violate IDENT constraints. This assumption is not a necessary one, however, and the analyses developed here should be equally compatible with an approach that defines the MAX(μ) and DEP(μ) constraints more elaborately, as proposed by Bermúdez-Otero (2001) and Campos-Astorkiza (2004), or an approach that treats geminates like all other clusters and does not rely on moras as the sole indicator of gemination (Beechey 2006).

3.2.4.2 Gradualness and the theory of LUMS

This section discusses two interlocking issues: the proper formulation of the gradualness requirement ((b) in (3-1)), and the proper definition of the localized unfaithful mapping (LUM). The following section also discusses some related matters that arise in the context of the local optimality requirement on chains.

The gradualness requirement says that the successive forms in a chain must monotonically increase in unfaithfulness relative to the input. The monotonic increase has a slope of one LUM per form in the chain. This succinct, formally attractive statement of the gradualness requirement embodies three distinct restrictions on chains. Of these, the first is clearly necessary for the smooth functioning of OT-CC, but the latter two may not be.

First, gradualness entails that chains are limited to adding LUMs one at a time. For instance, **<pap, pa.bə> is an invalid chain because it has combined vowel epenthesis and intervocalic voicing in a single step. Gradualness demands that these operations be separated, as in the chain <pap, pa.pə, pa.bə>. This consequence of the gradualness requirement is essential to analyzing counterfeeding opacity, as I will show in detail in §3.3.4.

Second, as I noted in the previous section, gradualness prohibits chains with steps that contribute no LUMs at all, such as pure resyllabification with no concomitant changes in other aspects of phonological structure: **<..., tab.la, ta.bla, ...>. This effect of gradualness is not really necessary, however, since it is already guaranteed by the independently necessary local optimality requirement ((c) in (3-1)). In any valid chain of the form <..., tab.la, ta.bla, ...>, [ta.bla] must be more harmonic than [tab.la]. But if [ta.bla] and [tab.la] are equally faithful, as assumed, then under the local optimality requirement they directly compete with each other as the proper successor to the '<...,' part of the chain. And if [ta.bla] is more harmonic than [tab.la], then it is the only proper successor. That is because local optimality says that only the most harmonic among several equally faithful forms is a proper continuation of a chain. In sum, a restriction on chains that prohibits steps involving purely faithful mappings, such as resyllabification, is unnecessary because local optimality gets it right the first time. (See McCarthy (2007a) for exploration of a variant of OT-CC that does not impose this restriction.)

Third, a putative chain like **<pap, pa.pə, pa.bə, pab> is invalid under the gradualness requirement because it adds and then withdraws a DEP-violating LUM, so its path of increasing unfaithfulness is nonmonotonic. Monotonicity entails steady accumulation of LUMs with greater distance from the input, thereby ruling out this sort of advance and retreat. Chains of this type can, at least in principle, be harmonically improving, so nothing else in the theory rules them out. In §4.3.2, I describe an empirical result that follows from this aspect of monotonicity, though it is not inconceivable that the same result could be obtained under other assumptions.

In sum, monotonically increasing unfaithfulness is a simple and therefore appealing formulation of the gradualness requirement. Nonetheless, it says rather more about chain validity than we might want to say, and so it is an area where further research may lead to some modifications in OT-CC.

We turn now to the topic of LUMs. (The LUM notion was first introduced in the context of a different theory of opacity in McCarthy (2003c).) LUMs are the unit by which the gradualness requirement on chains is measured. Intuitively, a LUM is a change that brings a single violation of a single faithfulness constraint. But this intuition is not precise enough, because some individual changes can bring single violations of several faithfulness constraints at once. This occurs because faithfulness constraints may overlap in their assessments. One situation where this happens is when two faithfulness constraints are in a stringency relationship (de Lacy 2002, Prince 1997).[11] For example, IDENT(voice) and its positional version IDENT$_{\text{ONS}}$(voice) are in such a relationship, and the mapping /pata/ → [pa.da] violates both of these constraints. Obviously, we would not like our theory of LUMs to imply that <pa.ta, pa.da> is a universally invalid chain, since some languages actually have intervocalic voicing. Furthermore, faithfulness constraints that are not in a formal stringency relationship can overlap in their effects — e.g., the constraint I-CONTIG prohibits *internal* deletion and metathesis (Kenstowicz 1994, McCarthy and Prince 1995, 1999), so it overlaps in its effects with MAX or LINEARITY, which respectively prohibit *all* deletion and *all* metathesis.[12] If a LUM were limited to literally one faithfulness violation at a time, then chains with internal syncope, such as <pa.tə.ka, pat.ka>, would be universally invalid under the gradualness criterion. This would also be an unwelcome result, since internal syncope occurs in some languages.

A more discriminating theory of LUMs can be obtained from correspondence theory (McCarthy and Prince 1995, 1999), which, at least implicitly, treats certain faithfulness constraints as basic. The *basic faithfulness constraints* are limited to the following: MAX(x) and DEP(x) constraints, which militate against deletion and insertion of elements of type x that stand in correspondence; IDENT(f) (abbreviated ID(f)) constraints, which forbid changing particular attributes f of these elements; and perhaps one or two others, such as LINEARITY (see §3.2.4.3). These particular faithfulness constraints are basic or primitive in the sense that they cover the full range of unfaithful mappings but they do not overlap with one another — e.g., segmental deletion violates MAX but not IDENT. A LUM is a mapping that brings exactly one violation of exactly one basic faithfulness constraint.

LUMs have another property: they are *localized*. An unfaithful mapping is localized in a form if it includes sufficient information to apply unambiguously to that form. There is a difference, for example, between epenthesizing a [ə] after the [t] versus after the [k] of /patrakla/, just as there is a difference between inserting a [ə] or a [ɨ] after the [t]. Therefore, DEP-violating LUMs must include information about which segment is inserted and where it is inserted. Similarly, MAX-violating LUMs must indicate which segment is deleted, and IDENT-violating LUMs must specify the affected segment and the changed feature-value. A LINEARITY-violating LUM is localized by reference to the segments whose linear-ordering relations have been altered.

To sum up, a LUM in a candidate chain is the smallest possible step in an unfaithful direction. It is the smallest because it is limited to a single instance of violation of one of the basic faithfulness constraints. It is in an unfaithful direction, away from the input and the fully faithful candidate, because it contributes a single basic faithfulness violation to those that the chain has already accrued. A LUM is also unambiguously applicable; starting from a fully faithful candidate and applying a sequence of LUMs with local optimization (§3.2.4.3), the output is completely determined in all of its details.

Before leaving this topic, it is appropriate to take note of a variant of OT-CC suggested by Matt Wolf. Suppose that affixation or other morphological processes are treated as single LUMs. The resulting theory will share characteristics of *SPE*'s cycles. For instance, cyclic stress in Levantine Arabic (see §4.2.5) could be analyzed with a chain where stress assignment both precedes and follows affixation: <simiʕ, 'simiʕ, 'simiʕkum, ˌsi'miʕkum> 'he heard you (pl.)'. This interesting idea, which remains to be explored in detail, is representative of the range of novel possibilities that OT-CC opens up.

3.2.4.3 *Local optimality*

According to clause (c) in (3-1), a form $[f_{i+1}]$ can be the immediate successor to $[f_i]$ in a valid chain only if it is locally optimal in the following two senses: $[f_{i+1}]$ is more harmonic than $[f_i]$ (= harmonic improvement); and, if the difference between $[f_i]$ and $[f_{i+1}]$ is the result of a LUM that violates the faithfulness constraint F, then $[f_{i+1}]$ must be the most harmonic form among those that can be derived from $[f_i]$ by virtue of an F-violating LUM (= best violation).

The roles of the harmonic improvement and best violation requirements in the analysis of opacity will be discussed in §3.3 and §4.2.3, respectively. The goal of the current section is to examine some of the consequences of local optimality, particularly harmonic improvement, for phenomena that are unrelated to opacity. It will emerge that, taken together, the harmonic improvement and gradualness requirements impose limits on OT-CC's capacity to do optimizations where two or more unfaithful mappings are necessary to realize any markedness improvement. I argue that these limits give OT-CC an advantage over classic OT.

We will approach this topic somewhat indirectly by first looking at how the basis for ranking arguments is expanded in OT-CC. The requirement that chains improve harmonically can motivate ranking arguments that are not possible in classic OT. Prince and Smolensky's (2004: 141) analysis of augmentation in Lardil supplies an example. As shown in (3-8), unaffixed monomoraic roots are augmented with paragogic [Ca], where C is a stop that is homorganic with the preceding consonant. Augmentation is a response to the requirement that feet be bimoraic, FtBin (4–10), which dominates Dep. But FtBin would be satisfied if /ṛil/ were augmented to just *[ṛi.la], so another constraint is required to force epenthesis of the [C] part of the [Ca] augment. In Prince and Smolensky's analysis (slightly updated here), this constraint is Align-R(root, σ), which is satisfied only if the root-final segment is also syllable-final. Align-R(root, σ) must also dominate Dep, as (3-9) demonstrates.

(3-8) Lardil augmentation (Hale 1973, Klokeid 1976, Wilkinson 1988)

Root	Nominative /-Ø/	Locative /-e/	
/ṛil/	ṛilta	ṛile	'neck'
/ṭal/	ṭalta	ṭale	'vulva'
/maṛ/	maṛta	maṛe	'hand'
/kaŋ/	kaŋka	kaŋe	'speech'

(3-9)   FᴛBɪɴ, Aʟɪɢɴ-R(root, σ) >> Dᴇᴘ

/ɽil/	FᴛBɪɴ	Aʟɪɢɴ-R(root, σ)	Dᴇᴘ
→ ɽil.ta			2
a. ɽi.la		W$_1$	L$_1$
b. ɽil	W$_1$		L

In classic OT, the /ɽil/ → [ɽilta] mapping does not supply evidence about how FᴛBɪɴ and Aʟɪɢɴ-R(root, σ) are ranked with respect to one another; since [ɽilta] obeys both of these constraints, they are not in conflict. In OT-CC, though, this mapping is not possible unless FᴛBɪɴ dominates Aʟɪɢɴ-R(root, σ). The putative one-step chain **<ɽil, ɽil.ta> is invalid because of the gradualness requirement, since it conflates two Dᴇᴘ-violating LUMs into a single step. For gradualness reasons, then, epenthesis of [t] and [a] must be done in separate steps, either <ɽil, ɽilt, ɽil.ta> or <ɽil, ɽi.la, ɽil.ta>. The first of these putative chains, **<ɽil, ɽilt, ɽil.ta>, is invalid because its first step is not harmonically improving: [ɽilt] violates Dᴇᴘ without purchasing better performance on either of the markedness constraints Aʟɪɢɴ-R(root, σ) or FᴛBɪɴ. (Codas are never moraic in Lardil.) The winning candidate chain must therefore be <ɽil, ɽi.la, ɽil.ta>. But for this chain to be harmonically improving, it is necessary to rank FᴛBɪɴ above Aʟɪɢɴ-R(root, σ), since faithful [ɽil] is well-aligned but nonbinary and [ɽi.la] improves on FᴛBɪɴ but introduces a violation of Aʟɪɢɴ-R(root, σ). As shown in (3-10), chain validity can serve as the basis for inferences about ranking in OT-CC.

(3-10)   Ranking from chain validity: FᴛBɪɴ >> Aʟɪɢɴ-R(root, σ)

/ɽil/	FᴛBɪɴ	Aʟɪɢɴ-R(root, σ)
→ ɽi.la		1
ɽil	W$_1$	L

Tableau (3-10) is representative of a type of ranking argument that is possible (and necessary) in OT-CC but not classic OT. Because of the gradualness requirement on chains, the route from input /A/ to output [B] may involve one or more intermediate forms. These intermediate forms must improve harmonically over their predecessors, and this may require constraint rankings that cannot be demonstrated with conventional ranking argumentation. Conventional ranking arguments involve comparison of losers with the ultimate output form. OT-CC in addition has ranking arguments that involve comparison of an intermediate form in a chain with its immediate predecessor, if that chain leads to the ultimate output.

The ranking [FTBIN >> ALIGN-R(root, σ)] that is required for chain validity has independent support from conventional ranking argumentation. The [C] part of the [Ca] augment is omitted when the result would be an illicit cluster: /jak/ → [ja.ka], *[jakka] 'fish' because geminates are prohibited; /teɾ/ → [te.ɾa], *[teɾ.ta] 'thigh' because [ɾt] clusters are prohibited. Because vowel epenthesis adversely affects alignment, FTBIN must dominate ALIGN-R(root, σ) if misaligned [teɾa] is to beat subminimal but well-aligned *[teɾ] (see (3-11)).

(3-11)   Ranking from conventional argument: FTBIN >> ALIGN-R(root, σ)

/teɾ/		*ɾt	FTBIN	ALIGN-R(root, σ)	DEP
→	te.ɾa			1	1
a.	teɾ.ta	W₁		L	W₂
b.	teɾ		W₁	L	L

In Lardil, these two types of ranking argumentation converge. But it can also happen that chain validity will require a ranking that, while not contradicted by conventional ranking arguments, is also not supported by them. Augmentation in Axininca Campa (Arawakan, Peru) is an example (McCarthy and Prince 1993a, 1993b, Payne 1981, Spring 1990).[13] Under certain conditions, stems must be minimally bimoraic to satisfy FTBIN. Monomoraic roots like /tʰo/ augment to bimoraicity by epenthesizing the syllable [ta]: [tʰo.ta]. Augmentation of /tʰo/ presumes a chain <tʰo, tʰo.a, tʰo.ta>. This chain must be valid, since otherwise the desired output form [tʰota] would be unreachable.[14] By downward entailment (§3.2.2), the initial subchain of any valid chain is harmonically improving, so <tʰo, tʰo.a> must be harmonically improving according to the grammar of Axininca Campa. For <tʰo, tʰo.a> to be harmonically improving, however, FTBIN must dominate ONSET, since vowel epenthesis creates a syllable that is onsetless in the intermediate form [tʰo.a]. The ranking [FTBIN >> ONSET] is not contradicted by any of the Axininca Campa rankings supported by conventional argumentation in McCarthy and Prince (1993a, 1993b). But a conventional argument for [FTBIN >> ONSET] is impossible because FTBIN and ONSET never conflict over any actual output forms of this language.

Evidence of convergence — or at least consistency — between two sources of ranking information, one novel and the other familiar, suggests that we are on the right track. Since harmonic improvement in chains is measured against the same constraint hierarchy that selects the optimal output form, it is important that there be consistency between any rankings that are required for chain validity and any rankings that are motivated by conventional OT argumentation. Rankings derived from the two sources should agree, as in Lardil, or at least not contradict one another, as in Axininca Campa. If there is outright disagreement — a situation where chain validity requires [A >> B] and conventional argumentation requires [B >> A] — then something is fundamentally wrong with the analysis or perhaps even the theory. As in classic OT, consistency of ranking is an important check on the soundness of an analysis.

Before we continue, it should be noted that observations about harmonic ascent in chains depend not only on constraint ranking but also on assumptions about the basic faithfulness constraints that define the gradualness requirement. If the putative chain <ɻil, ɻil.ta> were somehow allowed under the gradualness requirement (for instance, if epenthesis of a string of segments were to count as a single DEP violation and therefore a single LUM), then the harmonic ascent requirement would supply no information about the ranking of FTBIN and ALIGN-R(root, σ). The ranking argument [FTBIN >> ALIGN-R(root, σ)] from harmonic ascent in chains is therefore dependent on the assumption that **<ɻil, ɻil.ta> is invalid because of gradualness — an assumption that is, in this case at least, uncontroversial. The point is that harmonic ascent, gradualness, and faithfulness are interlocked. We will return to this topic later in this section.

The most interesting consequence of the harmonic improvement requirement on chains is that some input-output mappings that are possible in classic OT are simply impossible in OT-CC under reasonable assumptions about the basic faithfulness constraints. (For related discussion, see McCarthy (2007a, 2007b).) The reasoning about impossible mappings goes like this. In classic OT, if a language with the constraint hierarchy ℋ maps /A/ unfaithfully to [B], then [B] must be less marked than [A] according to the markedness constraints in CON as they are ranked in ℋ. In other words, the <A, B> relation must be harmonically improving. Because of clause (c) of (3-1), however, OT-CC imposes a stricter requirement: if /A/ and [B] differ by more than a single LUM, then every LUM-sized step in the chain from /A/ to [B] must also be harmonically improving according to ℋ. This stronger requirement can prevent certain complex mappings that classic OT permits.

This aspect of OT-CC will first be illustrated with a hypothetical permutation of Lardil's ranking. In classic OT, changing the ranking from [FTBIN >> ALIGN-R(root, σ) >> DEP] to [ALIGN-R(root, σ) >> FTBIN >> DEP] predicts that augmentation will be blocked just in those cases where it is dealigning, as shown in (3-12) (cf. (3-11)). In this made-up language, augmentation of /teɻ/ fails entirely because there is no way of augmenting while maintaining good alignment and satisfying the prohibition on [rt] clusters. Augmentation still goes through in those forms like [ɻil.ta] where there is no problem with augmenting while still satisfying ALIGN-R(root, σ).

(3-12) Effect of ALIGN-R(root, σ) >> FTBIN >> DEP in classic OT

		*ɾt	ALIGN-R(root, σ)	FTBIN	DEP
/teɾ/					
→	teɾ				
a.	teɾ.ta	W$_1$		L	W$_2$
b.	te.ɾa		W$_1$	L	W$_1$
/ʈil/					
→	ʈil.ta				2
c.	ʈi.la		W$_1$		L$_1$
d.	ʈil			W$_1$	L

In OT-CC, however, this ranking blocks augmentation across the board, for all inputs: /ʈil/ → [ʈil] and /teɾ/ → [teɾ]. That is because neither of the putative chains leading to [ʈilta] is valid under this ranking. As we saw previously, **<ʈil, ʈilt, ʈil.ta> is invalid because its initial subchain **<ʈil, ʈilt> is not harmonically improving under this grammar. The same is true of **<ʈil, ʈi.la, ʈil.ta>: its initial subchain **<ʈil, ʈi.la> is not harmonically improving because ALIGN-R(root, σ) dominates FTBIN.

The upshot is that classic OT and OT-CC describe different languages under this ranking. In classic OT, the [a] part of [Ca] augmentation is blocked whenever the [C] part is blocked, but otherwise [Ca] augmentation occurs. In OT-CC, there is no augmentation anywhere, the same as if the ranking were [DEP >> FTBIN]. In short, classic OT predicts the possibility of a pseudo-Lardil language with /ʈil/ → [ʈil.ta] and /teɾ/ → [teɾ], while OT-CC denies that there could be such a language — keeping all the *cetera* exactly *paria*, of course.

In general, for the input-output mapping /A/ → [B] to be possible in OT-CC, this mapping must be possible in classic OT and, moreover, the LUMs that distinguish [B] from /A/ must be orderable in such a way that the chain <A, ..., B> is of monotonically decreasing faithfulness (by clause (b) of (3-1)) and of monotonically increasing harmony (by clause (c) of (3-1)). The pseudo-Lardil example shows that OT-CC's additional requirement on optimal mappings can make a difference empirically, at least in principle. We will now see that this requirement yields welcome results by reining in some of classic OT's excess capacity for global optimization. (The concept of global optimization will be explained below.)

The constraint FINAL-C requires that every phonological word end in a consonant (Gafos 1998, McCarthy 1993a, McCarthy and Prince 1994, Wiese 2001). When combined with a constraint CODA-COND that prohibits syllable-final obstruents (Ito 1989, Zec 1995), FINAL-C will favor words that end in sonorant consonants. If FINAL-C, CODA-COND, and DEP are ranked above MAX, then all words will be truncated after the rightmost sonorant consonant. (If the word contains no sonorant consonants, then there will be no truncation.) Tableau (3-13) shows how truncation occurs under this ranking.

(3-13) Effect of FINAL-C, CODA-COND, DEP >> MAX in classic OT

/palasanataka/	FINAL-C	CODA-COND	DEP	MAX
→ pa.la.san				$_5$
a. pa.la.sa.na.ta.ka	W$_1$			L
b. pa.la.sa.na.tak		W$_1$		L$_1$
c. pa.la.sa.na.ta	W$_1$			L$_2$
d. pa.la.sa.nat		W$_1$		L$_3$
e. pa.la.sa.na	W$_1$			L$_4$
f. pa.la.sa.na.ta.kan			W$_1$	L

Neither the constraints nor the individual rankings in (3-13) are at all unusual, but the result is very peculiar indeed. To my knowledge, no language has a truncation process that works like this, deleting unboundedly many segments until a satisfactory final segment is found.

Significantly, these constraints and this ranking will not produce this unattested pattern in OT-CC. Because of the gradualness requirement, the /palasanataka/ → [pa.la.san] mapping can only be obtained with a candidate chain that strips away one segment at a time, such as <pa.la.sa.na.ta.ka, pa.la.sa.na.tak, pa.la.sa.na.ta, pa.la.sa.nat, pa.la.sa.na, pa.la.san>. This putative chain is not valid, however, because it is not harmonically improving under the ranking in (3-13). The initial subchain <pa.la.sa.na.ta.ka, pa.la.sa.na.tak> is harmonically improving only if FINAL-C dominates CODA-COND. But the next link in the chain, [pa.la.sa.na.ta], is a harmonic improvement over its immediate predecessor [pa.la.sa.na.tak] only if CODA-COND dominates FINAL-C — an obvious contradiction. It follows, then, that this constraint set cannot produce the /palasanataka/ → [pa.la.san] mapping in OT-CC, even though the same constraint set can favor this mapping in classic OT.

To be perfectly clear, I am not claiming that wholesale truncation is impossible *in principle* in OT-CC. Rather, the claim is that FINAL-C and CODA-COND cannot compel it. Other markedness constraints could support truncation in a way that is consistent with OT-CC's gradualness and harmonic improvement requirements. For instance, a language that truncates words to a disyllabic foot shows the effect of PARSE-SYLL, which is defined as 'every syllable belongs to some foot' (McCarthy and Prince 1994). If PARSE-SYLL dominates *COMPLEX-CODA which itself dominates MAX, then there can be a valid, harmonically improving chain <…, (ka.pa)na.sa, (ka.pa)nas, (ka.pans), (ka.pan)>.[15] This chain eliminates syllables outside the foot by deleting their nuclei and cleaning up the remaining consonants. Each unfooted syllable that is eliminated also eliminates a violation of PARSE-SYLL, so monotonic harmonic improvement is assured. In general, OT-CC by itself does not make claims about which mappings are licit or illicit; like classic OT, most of OT-CC's predictions about possible and impossible mappings are obtained in conjunction with a specific theory of CON or in relation to a specific subset of CON.

The mapping /palasanataka/ → [pa.la.san] requires multiple phonological operations in pursuit of a distant goal: satisfaction of FINAL-C and CODA-COND. Taken individually, the operations offer no harmonic improvement; it is all or nothing. This all-or-nothing behavior is well within the analytic scope of classic OT, since the candidates that are evaluated may show the simultaneous effects of many processes. But, because of the gradualness requirement, OT-CC cannot elide the intermediate steps between /palasanataka/ and [pa.la.san]. OT-CC requires local harmonic improvement at each step in the chain, and /palasanataka/ → [pa.la.san] does not offer that under the grammar in (3-13).

In general, this point of difference between classic OT and OT-CC is the distinction between *global* and *local optimization*. In classic OT, the results of all unfaithful mappings are evaluated together, so the effects of the visibly active markedness constraints may be expressed globally in the overall structure of the form. In OT-CC, each successive unfaithful mapping is evaluated locally for harmonic improvement, so each individual unfaithful mapping must yield better markedness performance. Therefore, classic OT allows grammars to favor outcomes that are the net result of many unfaithful mappings, but OT-CC must also look at the immediate results of each of the individual mappings. This limits OT-CC's expressive capacity — and, if this example is typical, it limits that capacity in a way that conforms with observed language typology. (See McCarthy (2007a, 2007b) for further discussion.)

We will now look at several other examples that illustrate this difference between classic OT and OT-CC. As we will see, they support OT-CC's more restrictive predictions.

Metathesis processes are fertile ground for this investigation. By ranking ONSET or NO-CODA above the antimetathesis constraint LINEARITY, classic OT can produce a mapping with double metathesis: /apekto/ → [pa.ke.to]. This is double metathesis because two different transpositions are involved, /ap/ → [pa] and /ek/ → [ke]. Tableau (3-14) shows how this happens. (Candidates with long-distance metathesis, such as [ka.pe.to], will be discussed shortly.)

(3-14)   Double metathesis from ONSET *or* NO-CODA >> LINEARITY in classic OT

/apekto/	ONSET	NO-CODA	LINEARITY
→ pa.ke.to			2
a. a.pek.to	W$_1$	W$_1$	L
b. pa.ek.to	W$_1$	W$_1$	L$_1$
c. ap.ke.to	W$_1$	W$_1$	L$_1$

In OT-CC, however, this mapping is not possible. Each LINEARITY-violating LUM requires a separate step in a chain, so the only way to get from /apekto/ to [pa.ke.to] is via an intermediate form in which only one consonant has moved: <a.pek.to, pa.ek.to, pa.ke.to> or <a.pek.to, ap.ke.to, pa.ke.to>. Neither of these chains is valid, however, since neither is harmonically improving in its initial subchain. The subchain **<a.pek.to, pa.ek.to> is invalid because it merely swaps one ONSET violation for another. The subchain **<a.pek.to, ap.ke.to> is not harmonically improving because it just swaps one NO-CODA violation for another. Since double metathesis of the /apekto/ → [pa.ke.to] type has never been reported and seems quite improbable, OT-CC's more limited descriptive power is supported by this example.

Long-distance metathesis is another instructive example. If we assume that every pair of reordered segments brings another LINEARITY violation, as in Hume (1998), then distant metathesis requires a chain of local metatheses, each of which is a harmonic improvement over its predecessor. This is not easy to achieve with a reasonable theory of markedness — nor, in fact, do we want to achieve it, since synchronic long-distance metathesis is attested in only a few heavily morphologized processes (Carpenter 2002, Hume 2001: 7, Poser 1982).[16]

For example, obtaining the long-distance metathesis of /art/ → [tar] in classic OT requires that a CODA-COND constraint prohibiting obstruent codas (as in Zec 1995) dominate LINEARITY. This ranking result is shown in (3-15).

(3-15)   Long-distance metathesis in classic OT

/art/	CODA-COND	LINEARITY
→ tar		2
a. art	W$_1$	L
b. atr	W$_1$	L$_1$
c. rat	W$_1$	L$_1$

The situation in OT-CC is different, however. Because of the gradualness requirement, long-distance metathesis can only be obtained with a succession of local transpositions, each of which must be harmonically improving. Therefore, getting from /art/ to [tar] requires a chain of local transpositions <art, atr, tar>. This putative chain is not valid, however, because its initial subchain **<art, atr> is not harmonically improving under the ranking in (3-15). This unattested pattern of long-distance metathesis, though readily accommodated in classic OT, is predicted to be impossible in OT-CC.

A real-life example where long-distance metathesis must be avoided comes from Hume's (1998: 168ff.) analysis of Leti (Austronesian, Indonesia). In Leti, LINEARITY is dominated by both ONSET and a constraint forbidding phrase-final consonants. This engenders some difficulty in explaining why phrase-final /ukar/ 'finger, toe' becomes [uk.ra], with local metathesis, and not *[ru.ka], with distant metathesis. Hume proposes that a constraint requiring initial faithfulness blocks *[ru.ka]. Although this is a well-motivated proposal in the context of Leti's phonology, it does not address the broader typological problem: a mapping like /ukar/ → [ru.ka] is never attested in any language, so a solution based on a language-particular ranking is inappropriate. In OT-CC, on the other hand, this mapping would require that the putative chain <u.kar, uk.ra, ur.ka, ru.ka> be harmonically improving and that its output be more harmonic than the output of an obvious alternative like <u.kar, uk.ra, ku.ra>, with two local metatheses. Neither of these conditions is likely to obtain under any plausible theory of CON.

In general, although OT-CC does not prohibit long-distance metathesis categorically, it establishes relatively stringent conditions under which it can be possible. In classic OT, the unfaithful mapping /abc/ → [cab] requires that distantly metathetic [cab] be less marked than faithful [abc], locally metathetic [acb], and locally metathetic [bac]: [cab] ≻ [abc], [acb], [bac]. OT-CC imposes an additional requirement: the locally metathetic intermediate form [acb] must be less marked than faithful [abc] ([acb] ≻ [abc]). As metathesis gets more distant, the markedness requirements become even stricter, since every intermediate step must improve over its predecessors. As I noted above, long distance metathesis must be analyzable as a succession of harmonically improving local metatheses under the OT-CC regime.[17]

Coalescence processes have received a great deal of attention in the OT literature (Causley 1999, de Lacy 2002: Chapt. 8, Gnanadesikan 1997, 2004, Keer 1999, Lamontagne and Rice 1995, McCarthy 2000b, McCarthy and Prince 1995, Pater 1996, 1999). As coalescence is standardly analyzed in correspondence theory (and in Chomsky and Halle (1968: 358–364)), two underlying segments are fused into a single output segment: $/p_1a_2n_3/ \rightarrow [p_1\tilde{a}_{2,3}]$.

This many-to-one mapping violates the faithfulness constraint UNIFORMITY. Furthermore, an IDENT constraint is violated for each featural mismatch between the output segment and its input correspondents. In the example cited, there are violations of IDENT(–nasal), for the /a/ → [ã] part of the mapping, and of IDENT(+consonantal), IDENT(+coronal), and so on for the /n/ → [ã] part of the mapping. The relative contribution of each input segment to the output is determined by the ranking of IDENT constraints (Pater 1999): [IDENT(+nasal) >> IDENT(–nasal)], [IDENT(–consonantal) >> IDENT(+consonantal)], and so on.

There has always been a tension, however, between this fusional theory of coalescence and an assimilation + deletion theory. An example of the latter is Schane's (1968: 38) analysis of French: an assimilation rule nasalizes a vowel before a coda nasal, and then a deletion rule eliminates the coda nasal. This is an opaque, counterbleeding order, with an assimilation process applying before a deletion process. In OT-CC terms, the chain <pan, pãn, pã> is optimal.

As I suggested in §2.3.4.1, coalescence has gotten so much attention in the OT literature precisely because it offers a way of accommodating some cases of counterbleeding opacity within the strictures of classic OT. But if it is accepted that the general problem of opacity requires something like candidate chains, then the case for the assimilation + deletion theory should be reopened. Furthermore, the fusional theory of coalescence is difficult to reconcile with the gradualness requirement in OT-CC. As we just saw, a single instance of fusional coalescence introduces violations of several basic faithfulness constraints simultaneously, so segmental fusion is not a possible step in a candidate chain without considerable fiddling of the theory of LUMs.

The fusional theory regards coalescence as fundamentally *sui generis*: it involves a special correspondence relation and an atypical application of IDENT constraints. For that reason, it does not predict much about coalescence phenomena. In contrast, the assimilation + deletion theory is not really a theory of coalescence at all: 'coalescence' phenomena have to be explained in terms of the independently motivated theories of assimilation, deletion, and counterbleeding opacity. The assimilation + deletion theory therefore leads to more restrictive predictions: only features that are observed to assimilate cross-linguistically will survive 'coalescence'; only segments of the types and in the positions that encourage deletion will be affected; and the same locality conditions that affect assimilation generally will be operative in 'coalescence'. (On locality in assimilation, see Gafos (1999), Ní Chiosáin and Padgettt (2001), and Walker (1998), among others.) A further difference between the assimilation + deletion theory and the fusional theory is that the former is fundamentally asymmetrical — one segment deletes and one does not — and the latter is fundamentally symmetrical — two segments merge.

I have not done a typological survey of coalescence phenomena (though see Casali 1996: 71ff., de Haas 1988, de Lacy 2002), but my impression is that these predictions have some truth to them. For example, the assimilation + deletion theory predicts that the assimilating features and the contexts in which they assimilate will be the same in 'coalescence' as they are in transparent assimilation processes in other languages. The features that are preserved assimilatorily in coalescence are usually [voice], [nasal], [back] and [round], and the like, all of which are involved in assimilation processes cross-linguistically. Features that notoriously do not tend to participate in assimilation, such as [sonorant] and [consonantal], are not usually preserved assimilatorily in coalescence.

In many cases, the putative coalescence process is paralleled by transparent assimilation in the same language. For example, as I noted in §2.3.4.1, the supposed coalescence in Bedouin Arabic /haːkim-iːn/ → [haːkʲmiːn] is belied by the fact that velars palatalize before undeleted front vowels as well. In reality, there is just palatalization, which is sometimes rendered opaque by deletion of the triggering vowel in a typical counterbleeding interaction. What about French, though, where vowel nasalization is never transparent, since it is always accompanied by nasal deletion? This is hardly proof against the assimilation + deletion theory of coalescence. Nasalization of vowels before tautosyllabic nasals is a common phonological process, and so is deletion of coda nasals. That two common processes happen to cooccur in some language is not sufficient reason to conclude that they must be united into a single process with its own special correspondence mechanism.[18]

Finally, the assimilation + deletion approach to coalescence supplies a simple answer to a vexed question: why does coalescence (almost) never affect nonadjacent segments? The fusional approach has no ready answer. In the assimilation + deletion approach, the question simply evaporates. Coalescence only affects adjacent segments because, when assimilation and deletion interact opaquely on nonadjacent segments, phonologists do not call it 'coalescence'. For example, in the Maltese mapping /ni-rbot-u/ → [norbtu] 'I tie him' (Brame 1972), the prefix vowel assimilates to the stem vowel /o/, which itself deletes in a counterbleeding interaction. No analyst would call this coalescence, yet it is not different in kind from what is happening in /pan/ → [pã]. Under the assimilation + deletion approach, coalescence is subject to the same locality restrictions, whatever they may be, as assimilation.

Before leaving this topic, I need to address an argument against the assimilation + deletion approach that was developed by Stahlke (1976) and Pater (1999: 314). Clusters of a nasal plus a voiceless obstruent appear to coalesce in Indonesian and other languages: /məŋ-pilih/ → [məmilih] 'to choose'. Could this mapping be accomplished with an opaque derivation /məŋ-pilih/ → [məmpilih] → [məmilih], in which the coda nasal assimilates in place before the following voiceless obstruent deletes? The answer is evidently no, because deletion of a voiceless obstruent after a nasal is never observed cross-linguistically without concomitant assimilation of the nasal to the obstruent's place of articulation. A fusional approach couples assimilation and deletion into a single process, so it need not posit a free-standing process that deletes voiceless obstruents after nasals.

There is, however, an alternative assimilation + deletion analysis that is not vulnerable to this objection: /məŋ-pilih/ → [məŋmilih] → [məmilih]. In this account, the voiceless obstruent assimilates in nasality to the preceding nasal, which then deletes. Nasality assimilation of this type is attested as an independent process in the Austronesian language Konjo (Pater 1999: 323), and deletion of coda nasals is not uncommon cross-linguistically.

Flop is another process that violates two basic faithfulness constraints at once. In flop, a feature or tone is delinked from one host and relinked to another. Flop rules were introduced in the earliest work on autosegmental phonology (Goldsmith 1976b), and flop mappings can be found in various classic OT analyses. Esimbi (Niger-Congo, Cameroon) supplies a nice example (Clements 1991, Hyman 1988, Stallcup 1980, Walker 1997, 2001). In this language, the height of a prefix vowel is determined by the underlying height of the root vowel, and the root vowel neutralizes to [+high]. For example, as shown in (3-16), the infinitival prefix is a back rounded vowel that alternates among [u], [o], and [ɔ], depending on the following root. Hyman and Walker analyze this as a flop process: the height features of the root vowel are transferred to the prefix syllable, and the root vowel retains its original color but becomes high by default.

(3-16) Esimbi vowel alternations

Underlying root	Infinitive	
/ri/	u-ri	'to eat'
/zu/	u-zu	'to kill'
/se/	o-si	'to laugh'
/to/	o-tu	'to insult'
/d͡zə/	o-d͡zɨ	'to steal'
/rɛ/	ɔ-ri	'to daub'
/hɔ/	ɔ-hu	'to knead'
/ba/	ɔ-bɨ	'to come'

Flop cannot be accomplished in a single LUM because it introduces two violations of a basic faithfulness constraint: both the prefix vowel and the root vowel incur marks from IDENT(height) or some equivalent constraint. Therefore, OT-CC can analyze Esimbi only by decomposing flop into two LUMs. Flop can be analyzed as a combination of assimilation and neutralization in counterbleeding order: <u-se, o-se, o-si>. In this chain, the prefix assimilates to the height features of the root, and at the next step the root vowel neutralizes to high. This chain meets the gradualness requirement, unlike direct, one-step flop. Furthermore, it is harmonically improving, and therefore valid, with only a very slight tweak of Walker's classic OT analysis.

Walker argues that flop in Esimbi is a response to two markedness constraints. One of them, LICENSE(–high, $_{Wd}[\sigma]$), requires any token of a [–high] feature value to be licensed by (that is, linked to) a word-initial syllable (cf. Zoll 2004). The other, CRISP(σ, high), prohibits any token of the feature [high] from being linked to more than one syllable at a time (cf. Ito and Mester 1999). These constraints are ranked above IDENT(high), as shown in (3-17).

(3-17) Esimbi in Walker (2001)

/u-se/ 		 +h -h	LIC(–high, $_{Wd}[\sigma]$)	CRISP(σ, high)	ID(high)
→ o-si 		 -h +h			2
a. u-se 		 +h -h	W$_1$		L
b. o-se V -h		W$_1$	L$_1$

In the classic OT analysis (3-17), LIC(–high, $_{Wd}[\sigma]$) and CRISP(σ, high) are unrankable since both are obeyed by the winning candidate. In OT-CC, however, they are rankable by chain validity: LIC(–high, $_{Wd}[\sigma]$) must dominate CRISP(σ, height) to ensure the validity of <u-se, o-se, o-si> in its initial subchain (see (3-18)). This is a case where harmonic improvement in a chain requires ranking two constraints that do not conflict in surface forms of the language and for which no other classic OT ranking argument can be devised.[19]

(3-18) Ranking from chain validity

/u-se/ 		 +h -h	LIC(–high, $_{Wd}[\sigma]$)	CRISP(σ, [high])	ID(high)
→ o-se V -h		1	1
u-se 		 +h -h	W$_1$	L	L

This reanalysis of Esimbi implies the claim that all instances of flop are reducible to opaque interactions of assimilation and neutralization. If this is correct, then flop, like coalescence, should have properties that are similar to transparent assimilation processes in other languages. An example: in Emakhuwa (Bantu, Mozambique), dialects differ in whether a particular process involves tone spreading or tone flop (Cassimjee and Kisseberth 1999). Another example: in Rimi (Bantu, Tanzania), high tone flops exactly one syllable to the right: /rá-mu-ntu/ → [ramúntu] 'of a person'. To prevent the tone from moving any further, Myers (1997: 875–880) introduces a somewhat baroque faithfulness constraint requiring one edge of an output tone to match some edge of where the input tone would have been. Under the approach to flop advocated here, this ad hoc constraint is unnecessary: flop is local because the spreading process that underlies it is local. In general, all proposed locality restrictions on assimilation should be paralleled in flop phenomena, and there should be no instances of flop where assimilation would be universally impossible.

To sum up, the harmonic improvement requirement on candidate chains, when combined with a specific theory of LUMs and faithfulness, makes restrictive predictions about which phonological mappings are and are not possible. Essentially, OT-CC requires that complex mappings show local improvement on the way to global improvement. Classic OT, on the other hand, permits complex mappings that produce global harmonic improvement but are not decomposable into any chain of local improvements. This is an important difference, and it is likely to have implications that go well beyond the examples discussed here.[20] (See McCarthy (2007a, 2007b) for some preliminary exploration of these matters.)

3.3   Chains and opacity

3.3.1   The proposal in outline

In Bedouin Arabic, a velar is palatalized before a front vowel, even if the front vowel is deleted (see (2-5)): /ħaːkim-iːn/ → [ħaːkʲ.miːn]. From the perspective of OT-CC, this case of counterbleeding opacity reduces to the following question: why is the opaque chain <ħaː.ki.miːn, ħaːkʲi.miːn, ħaːkʲ.miːn> more harmonic than the transparent chain *<ħaː.ki.miːn, ħaːk.miːn>? The output form in the transparent chain, *[ħaːk.miːn], is both more faithful and less marked than the output form in the opaque chain, [ħaːkʲ.miːn], yet the opaque chain wins. The goal of this section is to explain why this is possible using a theory of constraints on the order of LUMs in candidate chains.

The transparent phonology of the language gives us its basic constraint ranking (see (2-16) for a schematization and §4.3 for the details). A constraint violated by short high vowels in open syllables — call it *iCV — dominates

MAX, and a constraint against sequences of a plain velar and a front vowel — call it **ki* — dominates IDENT(back). Given these rankings, all and only the candidate chains listed in (3-19) meet the harmonic improvement requirement on chain validity. (In lists of chains like (3-19), the intended winner is called out by the symbol ✓.) To analyze this case of counterbleeding opacity, it is necessary to explain why (d) is the winner, and that really comes down to explaining why (d) is more harmonic than (c), since (a) and (b) are ruled out anyway by **iCV*.

(3-19) Valid chains from /ħaːkim-iːn/ in Bedouin Arabic
   a. <ħaː.ki.miːn>
   b. <ħaː.ki.miːn, ħaː.kʲi.miːn>
   c. <ħaː.ki.miːn, ħaːk.miːn>
   d. <ħaː.ki.miːn, ħaː.kʲi.miːn, ħaːkʲ.miːn>✓

The crucial difference between (c) and (d) in (3-19) is disclosed by looking at the sequence of LUMs that defines these two chains. In (c), there is just a single LUM, a violation of MAX that affects the medial [i]. In the more harmonic chain (d), the MAX-violating LUM is preceded by an IDENT(back)-violating LUM. A PREC constraint, defined in §3.3.2, favors chains where any MAX-violating LUMs are preceded by some IDENT(back)-violating LUM. This constraint favors the LUM sequence in chain (d), thereby preferring the output form [ħaːkʲ.miːn], despite its poorer markedness and faithfulness performance.

PREC constraints are also involved in counterfeeding opacity. In the same variety of Arabic, raising of low vowels in open syllables is not fed by epenthesis into final clusters: /gabr/ → [ga.bur], *[gi.bur]. As in the preceding example, the transparent phonology of the language gives us the basic constraint ranking (see (2-20) for a schematization and §4.3 for the details). A constraint violated by low vowels in open syllables — call it **aCV* — dominates IDENT(low), and a constraint against final clusters — **COMPLEX-CODA* — dominates DEP. Given these rankings, all and only the candidate chains in (3-20) meet the harmonic improvement requirement. To analyze this example, it is necessary to explain why (b) is the winner, even though (c)'s output form performs better on high-ranking **aCV*.

(3-20) Valid chains from /gabr/ in Bedouin Arabic
    a. <gabr>
    b. <gabr, ga.bur>✓
    c. <gabr, ga.bur, gi.bur>

The crucial difference between (b) and (c) in (3-20) again comes from looking at the sequences of LUMs that define these two chains. In (b), there is only a Dᴇᴘ-violating LUM. Chain (c) begins with that same LUM, but then it continues with an Iᴅᴇɴᴛ(low) violation. A Pʀᴇᴄ constraint favors chain (b) over (c) because in (b) the LUM that violates Dᴇᴘ is not followed by a LUM that violates Iᴅᴇɴᴛ(low).

Candidate chains bear some resemblance to traditional phonological derivations, and Pʀᴇᴄ constraints bear some resemblance to statements about rule ordering. But there are also important differences, some of which emerge from OT's general properties and some of which derive from specific assumptions of OT-CC. Several of these differences were discussed in §3.2.3 and others will be explained in §3.4. But first the formal details of the proposal and its applications need to be seen.

3.3.2 Pʀᴇᴄ constraints and candidate evaluation

The phrase 'candidate chain', though not thoroughly misleading, is something of a misnomer, since chains *per se* are not evaluated. The reason is that chains contain too much information, information that is necessary in Gᴇɴ to ensure that the chains are valid, but unnecessary, and sometimes invidious, when Eᴠᴀʟ proper is applied.[21]

One respect in which chains contain too much information is the presence of nonoutput forms. In Eᴠᴀʟ proper, only the output form of the chain is evaluated by markedness constraints. (Markedness constraints are, of course, important in determining whether a chain meets the local optimality requirement (c) in (3-1), but I speak now of the evaluation of completed candidate chains rather than chain validity.) Because nonoutput forms in a chain are irrelevant to markedness in Eᴠᴀʟ, there is no reason to include them in the candidates. A chain can be reduced to just two pieces of essential information: the output form, which is no different from classic OT, and the sequence of LUMs that link this output form with its input.

A sequence of LUMs, or *LUMSeq*, is projected from a candidate chain. The singleton chain, consisting only of the faithful parse, has the empty LUMSeq < >. Longer chains have longer LUMSeqs, since each subsequent step in the chain involves a different LUM. Since a LUM is defined in terms of what it does and where it does it, a LUM can be referred to by the faithfulness constraint that it violates and an index to the locus of violation. For example, the LUM in the chain <a.bi.ta, ab.ta> can be referred to as Mᴀx@3, assuming that the fully faithful form is indexed as $[a_1 b_2 i_3 t_4 a_5]$. With this notation, the LUMSeq of the chain <haː.ki.miːn, haː.kʲi.miːn, haːkʲ.miːn> is <Iᴅ(back)@3, Mᴀx@4>. This notation may need to be refined to deal with epenthesis and with autosegmental operations, but it will suffice for now. Bear in mind that this notation is nothing but a convenience, and it does not supersede the theory of LUMs in §3.2.4.2. Often, the indices will be omitted unless it is necessary to distinguish between two LUMs that violate the same faithfulness constraint in different loci.

Chains also contain too much information whenever two or more of them have the same output form and differ only in the order in which their LUMs are applied. For example, in a language that nasalizes a vowel after a nasal consonant and also devoices final obstruents, the mapping /mad/ → [mãt] can be derived via two different chains: <mad, mãd, mãt> and <mad, mat, mãt>. The results and the LUMs are the same; only the order of the LUMs differs. Situations like this are not uncommon, arising whenever there is no interaction among processes. (In rule-based phonology, cases like this would be regarded as not probative on questions of rule ordering.)

For reasons that will be made clear in §3.3.3, candidate evaluation must not be sensitive to the spurious distinction between chains with such linguistically irrelevant differences in LUM ordering. OT-CC abstracts away from this distinction by treating *convergent chains* as if they were identical. Chains are convergent if they meet the requirements in (3-21): they have the same output form and the same LUMs, but in different orders. Chains that are convergent in this sense constitute a single candidate. As a result, distinctions in LUM ordering that have no effect on input-output mappings are not accessible in EVAL.

(3-21) Chain convergence

A nonempty set of chains $\mathbb{C}$ derived from input /in/ is convergent if and only if
(i)   there exists a form [out] such that, for any chain $c_i \in \mathbb{C}$, $c_i = $ <..., out>
and
(ii)   there exists a set of LUMs, L, such that, for any $c_i \in \mathbb{C}$, c_i is associated with a LUMSeq l_i that is an ordering of L.

Convergent chains are collapsed into a single candidate by merging their LUMSeqs, retaining all and only the LUM precedence relations that are common to the set of convergent chains. Intuitively, two or more orderings can be merged by retaining only the linear precedence relations that are common to them. For instance, the merger of <A, B, C> and <C, A, B> yields the properly partial order where A precedes B and C is unordered with respect to A and B. Formally, this is known as *intersection of total orders*, and it is usually defined for orders that are reflexive. A reflexive total order that has been represented here as <A, B, C> is expressed in set notation as {(A, A), (B, B), (C, C), (A, B), (A, C), (B, C)}. If this order is intersected with <C, A, B>, which has the set representation {(A, A), (B, B), (C, C), (A, B), (C, A), (C, B)}, the result is {(A, A), (B, B), (C, C), (A, B)}. This result is a properly partial order that includes the information that A precedes B but C is unordered with respect to A or B.

For notational compactness and expositional clarity, I will describe a partial order like {(A, A), (B, B), (C, C), (A, B)} with two formal objects. One of them, called the $\mathcal{L}$-set, is just a list of all the elements that enter into the ordering — that is, {A, B, C}. The $\mathcal{L}$-set, then, is simply a list of all the LUMs violated in a chain or set of convergent chains. The other object, called the rLUMSeq ('r' for 'reduced'), is a list of all the pairwise orders other than the reflexive ones — that is, {<A, B>}. This set may be empty, as in the /mad/ → [mãt] example. Often, unless greater precision is required, I will present rLUMSeqs as total orders like <X, Y, Z> rather than use the more cumbersome notation {<X, Y>, <X, Z>, <Y, X>}.

Referring back to diagram (3-5), we can identify the point where convergent chains are collapsed as the arrow from GEN to EVAL that is marked with the balloon 'full candidate set'. Once all of the valid chains have been identified, but before they are submitted to EVAL, all sets of chains that are convergent according to (3-21) are collapsed into partial orderings represented by the $\mathcal{L}$-set and rLUMSeq. Individually nonconvergent chains also have $\mathcal{L}$-sets and rLUMSeqs, of course, but the information they contain is not different from the original, totally ordered LUMSeq.

To sum up, a candidate in OT-CC contains four pieces of information, in accordance with the definition in (3-22). Three of the components of a candidate in OT-CC are essentially identical with the candidates of classic OT: *in* and *out* are unchanged, and the $\mathcal{L}$-set with its list of faithfulness violations contains information similar to the input-output correspondence relation $\mathfrak{R}_{IO}$. The only novelty is the rLUMSeq. It is a partial ordering of a subset of the $\mathcal{L}$-set — a total ordering of the $\mathcal{L}$-set when a chain has no convergent mates, and a properly partial order of the $\mathcal{L}$-set when two or more chains converge.

(3-22) Candidate in OT-CC
>   A candidate is an ordered 4-tuple (*in*, *out*, $\mathcal{L}$-set, rLUMSeq), where
>> *in* is a linguistic form, the input;
>> *out* is a linguistic form, the output;
>> $\mathcal{L}$-set is a set of LUMs on *in* → *out*;
>> and rLUMSeq is a partial ordering on a subset of $\mathcal{L}$-set.

The various components of an OT-CC candidate have their own constraint-types. Markedness constraints evaluate *out*, and faithfulness constraints evaluate the *in-out* relations encoded in the $\mathcal{L}$-set or its near-equivalent, the correspondence relation. Evaluation of rLUMSeqs is the responsibility of PREC constraints, which favor certain precedence relations among the constituent LUMs of an rLUMSeq and penalize others.

The general form of a Prec constraint is given in (3-23), where A and B are faithfulness constraints.[22]

(3-23) Prec(A, B)(*cand*)
  Let A′ and B′ stand for LUMs that violate the faithfulness constraints A and B, respectively.
  Let *cand* = (*in*, *out*, $\mathcal{L}$, rL).
    (i) $\forall$B′ $\in$ $\mathcal{L}$, if $\nexists$A′ $\in$ $\mathcal{L}$, where <A′, B′> $\in$ rL, assign a violation mark.
  and
    (ii) $\forall$B′ $\in$ $\mathcal{L}$, if $\exists$A′ $\in$ $\mathcal{L}$, where <B′, A′> $\in$ rL, assign a violation mark.

To paraphrase (3-23), Prec(A, B) demands that every B-violating LUM be preceded and not followed by an A-violating LUM in the rLUMSeq. There are, then, two situations where Prec(A, B) can assign a violation mark. First, if there is a B-violating LUM in $\mathcal{L}$, and this LUM is not preceded in the rLUMSeq by some A-violating LUM, then Prec(A, B) has been disobeyed. Second, if there is a B-violating LUM in $\mathcal{L}$ and it precedes some A-violating LUM, then a violation mark is also assigned. Thus, if the $\mathcal{L}$-set is {A′, B′, C′}, the rLUMSeq {<A′, C′>, <B′, C′>} would receive one mark from Prec(A, B), because the ordering <A′, B′> is not a member of this rLUMSeq. The rLUMSeq {<A′, C′>, <B′, C′>, <B′, A′>} would receive two marks, one under each clause of (3-23), because the ordering <A′, B′> is not a member of this rLUMSeq and the ordering <B′, A′> is a member of it.

Under certain rankings, Prec constraints favor opaque outcomes by preferring candidate chains with particular orderings of their LUMs. In general, transparent chains that compete with counterbleeding chains will be disfavored under clause (i) of (3-23), and transparent chains that compete with counterfeeding chains will be disfavored under clause (ii) of (3-23). (The two clauses of (3-23) should perhaps be assigned to separate constraints, but as yet I have seen no evidence for this slightly less parsimonious hypothesis.) Illustrative applications of this theory to counterbleeding and counterfeeding opacity are presented in §3.3.3 and §3.3.4, respectively. A more complex case is illustrated in §3.3.5, and of course the case studies in §4 supply additional examples.

Although Prec constraints, like all OT constraints, are ranked and violable, their ranking is not entirely free. A necessary condition for violation of Prec(A, B) is violation of the faithfulness constraint B, as the definition (3-23) makes clear. For reasons that will emerge shortly, Prec(A, B), though it obviously *depends on* whether B is violated, must never *affect* whether B is violated. In OT, the only way to ensure this is to require that Prec(A, B) never dominate B. This requirement is formalized as the ranking metaconstraint (3-24).

(3-24) Metaconstraint on the ranking of Prec constraints
B >> Prec(A, B)

Ranking metaconstraints were first introduced by Prince and Smolensky (2004) as a way of formalizing multi-tiered markedness hierarchies related to linguistic scales, such as sonority. They were later extended to pairs of constraints standing in a specific/general relationship, such as the requirement that the local conjunction of constraints A and B dominate both A and B (Bakovic 2000, Smolensky 1995) or that the positionally-restricted version of the faithfulness constraint F dominate unrestricted F (Beckman 1998: 35). The meaning of (3-24) is that B must always dominate Prec(A, B), for all faithfulness constraints A.

Because Prec constraints refer to the ℒ-set and rLUMSeq, they cannot be evaluated until the complete set of chains has been determined and tested for convergence. This means that Prec constraints are irrelevant to determining chain validity — they are vacuously satisfied by all forms, so they cannot bear on the question of whether or not a form is a harmonically improving addition to a chain. We can therefore safely ignore Prec constraints until the final evaluation of all candidates.[23]

3.3.3 Application to counterbleeding opacity

We return once again to counterbleeding opacity in Bedouin Arabic. The velar stops /k/ and /g/ are palatalized to [kʲ] and [gʲ] when adjacent to the front vowel [i]. The data in (3-25) illustrate transparent alternations between plain and palatalized velars in related words. Further evidence that palatalization is productive comes from the invented secret language that Al-Mozainy taught to his consultants (§4.3.3). The word [gʲibaːjil] 'tribes' becomes, in that secret language, [gaħarbaːjil], showing the expected alternation between a fronted velar in a palatalizing context and a plain velar in a nonpalatalizing context.

(3-25) Velar palatalization (Al-Mozainy 1981: 23ff.)

ruːg	'be calm'	rawwigʲ	'do not make noise!'
ðuːg	'taste'	ðawwigʲ	'make somebody taste!'
guːl	'say!'	gʲiːl	'it was said'
mamluːk	'owned'	jmallikʲ	'he makes someone own'
jaskut	'he becomes silent'	jsakʲkʲit	'he silences someone'
fukk	'let go'	fikʲkʲ	'it was let go'

Palatalization is also conditioned by the front alternants of the low vowel (Al-Mozainy 1981: 33ff.), but here we will focus on the effects of the high vowels, since that is where there is evidence of opacity. As the data in (3-26) show, palatalization occurs even when the conditioning high vowel is deleted.

(3-26) Opaque interaction of palatalization and syncope (Al-Mozainy 1981: 49f., 73ff.)[24]

/ħaːkim-iːn/	ħaːkʲmiːn	'ruling (m. pl.)'
		cf. [ħaːkʲim] 'ruling (m. sg.)'
/kitib-t/	kʲtibt	'you (m. sg.) were written'
		cf. [kʲitbaw] 'they (m.) were written'

The harmonically improving chains from input /ħaːkim-iːn/ were supplied in (3-19) and are repeated in (3-27), with their LUMSeqs added. Since no chains in (3-27) are convergent under definition (3-21), the translation from LUMSeqs to rLUMSeqs is straightforward: the rLUMSeq consists of all the nonreflexive pairwise orderings in the LUMSeq.[25] The candidates corresponding to these chains are given in (3-28).

(3-27) Harmonically improving chains from /ħaːkim-iːn/ and their LUMSeqs
  a. <ħaː.ki.miːn>   < >
  b. <ħaː.ki.miːn, ħaː.kʲi.miːn>   <ID(back)@3>
  c. <ħaː.ki.miːn, ħaːk.miːn>   <MAX@4>
  d. <ħaː.ki.miːn, ħaː.kʲi.miːn, ħaːkʲ.miːn>✓ <ID(back)@3, MAX@4>

(3-28) Candidates from (3-27) as (*in*, *out*, ℒ-set, rLUMSeq)
  a. (/ħaːkim-iːn/, ħaː.ki.miːn, Ø, Ø)
  b. (/ħaːkim-iːn/, ħaː.kʲi.miːn, {ID(back)@3}, Ø)
  c. (/ħaːkim-iːn/, ħaːk.miːn, {MAX@4}, Ø)
  d. (/ħaːkim-iːn/, ħaːkʲ.miːn, {ID(back)@3, MAX@4}, {<ID(back)@3, MAX@4>})✓

The intended winner is candidate (d) with output [ħaːkʲ.miːn], and its most challenging competitor is the transparent candidate (c) with output [ħaːk.miːn]. The difference between them is that (c) has a MAX-violating LUM in its ℒ-set, but no IDENT(back)-violating LUM precedes the MAX-violating LUM in the rLUMSeq. The constraint PREC(ID(back), MAX) makes the necessary distinction between these two candidates, if it is ranked above [ħaːkʲ.miːn]'s worst mark, its violation of IDENT(back). This ranking argument is shown in (3-29).

(3-29) Counterbleeding opacity in OT-CC[26]

/ħaːkim-iːn/	*_i_CV	*_ki_	Max	Prec(Id(back), Max)	Id(back)
d. → ħaːkʲ.miːn {Id(back)@3, Max@4} {<Id(back)@3, Max@4>}			1		1
a. ħaː.ki.miːn Ø Ø	W₁	W₁	L		L
b. ħaː.kʲi.miːn {Id(back)@3} Ø	W₁		L		1
c. ħaːk.miːn {Max@4} Ø			1	W₁	L

The ranking in tableau (3-29) presupposes the metaconstraint (3-24). The metaconstraint says that Prec(A, B) never dominates the faithfulness constraint B. This means that Prec(Id(back), Max) is necessarily and universally ranked below Max. To see why this metaconstraint is needed, we consider the effect of permuting the ranking in (3-29) in ways that violate the metaconstraint.

Suppose Prec(Id(bk), Max) were ranked above *_i_CV, the markedness constraint that encourages deletion of high vowels in open syllables. Since *_i_CV dominates Max, by transitivity Prec(Id(back), Max) will also dominate Max, in violation of metaconstraint (3-24). Under this permuted ranking, as (3-30) shows, high vowel deletion is blocked when there is no palatalization. With an input that contains no /ki/ sequences, such as /ʃarib-at/ 'he drank', there are no harmonically improving chains with palatalization, so none of the competing rLUMSeqs includes an Ident(back)-violating LUM. The only way to satisfy Prec(Id(back), Max) would be by not violating Max, so that Prec(Id(back), Max) is vacuously satisfied. This result is bizarre: expected syncope is blocked just in those cases where it is not accompanied by velar palatalization. Intuitively, this goes beyond anything encountered in attested opaque phonology; it is as if syncope were blocked unless palatalization applies opaquely. No real phonological system does or could work this way, so we need a language-independent explanation for why this never happens.

(3-30) Unwanted effect of violating the ranking metaconstraint (3-24)

/ʃarib-at/	PREC(ID(bk), MAX)	*ki	*iCV	MAX	ID(back)
→ *ʃa.ri.bat Ø Ø			1		
ʃar.bat {MAX@4} Ø	W₁		L	1	

The solution lies in imposing the universal condition in (3-24) on the ranking of PREC constraints. This ranking metaconstraint requires that MAX dominate PREC(ID(back), MAX), and that makes it impossible for PREC(ID(back), MAX) to have any effect on the vowel deletion process. The general import of (3-24) is that PREC(A, B) cannot in any way influence satisfaction of B, though it may and indeed does affect whether A is satisfied. Because of the way the definition in (3-23) is stated, PREC(A, B) cannot be violated except when B is violated. The metaconstraint ensures that PREC(A, B) can only evaluate the consequences of violating B when B violation is independently required.

The ranking metaconstraint (3-24) has another consequence: because B dominates PREC(A, B), any constraint that PREC(A, B) dominates is also dominated by B, and the phonology of the language as a whole must be compatible with this entailed ranking. In Bedouin Arabic, there is no other argument for ranking MAX above IDENT(back), so the fixed ranking required by PREC(ID(back), MAX) is not contradicted but also not confirmed by what the language says independently. In other cases, however, the rankings entailed by (3-24) can be confirmed by conventional ranking argumentation. Even when other evidence of ranking is lacking, there must never be a contradiction between these two sources of information about ranking.

Tableau (3-29) can also be used to demonstrate the need for the harmonic improvement requirement on candidate chains. Without the harmonic improvement requirement, there is a potential danger in positing constraints like PREC(ID(back), MAX). If chains need not be harmonically improving, then among the chains from input /t-ħakum-in/ 'they (f.) rule' is <ħa.ku.min, ħa.kʲu.min, ħakʲ.min>. This chain is not harmonically improving because it palatalizes /k/ in a nonpalatalizing environment, before /u/. With this chain in the candidate set, the intended winner <ħa.ku.min, ħak.min> is doomed. The problem can be seen in tableau (3-31). PREC(ID(back), MAX) favors the incorrect mapping /t-ħakum-in/ → *[ħakʲ.min] over the correct one, /t-ħakum-in/ → [ħak.min], because *[ħakʲ.min]'s LUMSeq has a violation of MAX that is preceded by a violation of IDENT(back), whereas *[ħak.min]'s LUMSeq does not.

(3-31) Unwanted effect of allowing non-harmonically-improving chains

/t-ħakum-in/		*iCV	*ki	Max	Prec(Id(bk), Max)	Id(back)
→	*ṭhakʲ.min {Id(back)@4, Max@5} {<Id(back)@4, Max@5>}			1		1
a.	tha.ku.min Ø Ø	W₁		L		
b.	thak.min {Max@5} Ø			1	W₁	L

In reality, there is no danger of Prec constraints ever having effects like this. The reason why is the harmonic improvement requirement on candidate chains. The chain **<tha.ku.min, tha.kʲu.min, thakʲ.min> is invalid because its initial subchain **<tha.ku.min, tha.kʲu.min> is not harmonically improving according to the constraint ranking in Bedouin Arabic — no markedness constraint compels violation of Ident(back) when a velar is followed by a back vowel. Therefore, *[thakʲ.min] and its LUMSeq <Id(back)@4, Max@5> are not among the candidates that Prec(Id(back), Max) evaluates, so this alleged winner does not belong in (3-31). In general, Prec constraints cannot compel unfaithful mappings unless those mappings are harmonically improving. The role of a Prec constraint in counterbleeding opacity is to favor a mapping that is permitted by harmonic improvement but not otherwise required by harmonic evaluation.

Finally, Bedouin Arabic palatalization can be recruited in an argument in support of chain convergence. Recall that candidate chains are convergent if they have the same output and if their LUMSeqs are permutations of one another (see (3-21)). Convergent chains fuse into a single candidate, and Prec constraints see only those aspects of the LUM ordering that are shared among all of the convergent chains.

Chain convergence is important when there is more than one potential locus of opacity in a form. Because this language's root cooccurrence restrictions disallow multiple velars, I have to use a hypothetical example modeled after Bedouin Arabic. An adequate theory of opacity needs to be able to handle inputs like /kætaki/, with two potential loci of palatalization since there are two /k/+front vowel sequences. The phonology should map this input to [kʲæ.takʲ], with transparent palatalization of the first [k] and opaque palatalization of the second. The potential problem comes from the competing output form *[kʲæ.tak], which can be derived with the chain *<kæ.ta.ki, kʲæ.ta.ki, kʲæ.tak>. Even though *[kʲæ.tak] has only transparent palatalization, its chain seems to satisfy Prec(Id(back), Max), since the syncopating LUM follows a palatalizing

LUM. The presence of transparent palatalization elsewhere in the word is fooling the Prec constraint. If the Prec constraint does not discriminate between opaque [kʲæ.takʲ] and transparent *[kʲæ.tak], the choice falls to lower-ranking constraints. Both markedness and faithfulness favor the wrong form, *[kʲæ.tak]. In general, it looks as if transparent application of a process anywhere in the word relieves the necessity for opaque application. Needless to say, real phonological systems do not behave like this.[27]

Chain convergence is OT-CC's answer to this potential problem. Prec constraints do not evaluate raw LUMSeqs. Rather, they evaluate the partial ordering that results from intersecting the LUMSeqs of convergent chains (see (3-21)). The output form *[kʲæ.tak] is produced by the two convergent chains in (3-32). Intuitively, the order in which the first /k/ is palatalized and the final /i/ is deleted does not matter, and that is why these chains converge. A candidate's performance on Prec constraints should not depend on LUM orderings that do not matter, and the theory of chain convergence eliminates these irrelevant orderings from the purview of the Prec constraints.

(3-32) Chains converging on *[kʲæ.tak] and their LUMSeqs
    <kæ.ta.ki, kʲæ.ta.ki, kʲæ.tak>   <Id(bk)@1, Max@6>
    <kæ.ta.ki, kæ.tak, kʲæ.tak>   <Max@6, Id(bk)@1>

When chains converge, as they do in (3-32), the LUMSeqs of all of the convergent chains are intersected. Although the LUMSeqs are total orders, their intersection is a properly partial order. The result of intersecting the LUMSeqs in (3-32) is a partial order that contains the LUMs Id(bk)@1 and Max@6 but asserts no ordering relation between them. I have chosen to represent these partial orders with two formal objects, the ℒ-set and the rLUMSeq. The ℒ-set and rLUMSeq of (3-32) are given in (3-33). The ℒ-set is a list of all elements that enter into the partial ordering. (A partial ordering may include elements that have no ordering relations at all.) The rLUMSeq is a set that lists all of the nonreflexive pairwise orders in the partial ordering. In (3-33), since there are only two LUMs in the ℒ-set and they appear in both orders in the convergent chains, the rLUMSeq is the empty set.

(3-33) ℒ-set and rLUMSeq for (3-32)
    ℒ = {Id(bk)@1, Max@6}
    rL = Ø

The problem I identified above is that the transparent chain *<kæ.ta.ki, kʲæ.ta.ki, kʲæ.tak> seems to perform too well on Prec(Id(back), Max). But this chain is never directly evaluated by any Prec constraint. Rather, the Prec constraints see only the result of merging convergent chains. When PREC(ID(back), MAX) evaluates the ℒ-set and rLUMSeq in (3-33), it assigns a violation mark since the ℒ-set contains a MAX-violating LUM and the rLUMSeq does not contain any ordering where the MAX-violating LUM is preceded by an ID(back)-violating LUM.

The situation is different with the intended output form [kʲæ.takʲ]. Three chains converge on this output, but all three share the LUM ordering <ID(bk)@5, MAX@6> (see (3-34)). This ordering really does satisfy PREC(ID(back), MAX) — as indeed it should, since [kʲæ.takʲ] is the expected and desired result of opaque interaction between velar palatalization and high vowel deletion.

(3-34)   Chains converging on [kʲætakʲ]

<kæ.ta.ki, kʲæ.ta.ki, kʲæ.ta.kʲi, kʲæ.takʲ>   <ID(bk)@1, ID(bk)@5, MAX@6>
<kæ.ta.ki, kæ.ta.kʲi, kʲæ.ta.kʲi, kʲæ.takʲ>   <ID(bk)@5, ID(bk)@1, MAX@6>
<kæ.ta.ki, kæ.ta.kʲi, kæ.takʲ, kʲæ.takʲ>   <ID(bk)@5, MAX@6, ID(bk)@1>
     ℒ = {ID(bk)@1, ID(bk)@5, MAX@6}
     rL = {<ID(bk)@5, MAX@6>}

Chain convergence is also applicable in situations where there are two separate loci of opaque interaction, such as hypothetical /kitaki/ → [kʲtakʲ]. The rLUMSeq for this mapping asserts only two orders: palatalization of the first /k/ precedes deletion of the first /i/, and palatalization of the second /k/ precedes deletion of the second /i/. This rLUMSeq satisfies PREC(ID(back), MAX) because every MAX-violating LUM is preceded in the rLUMSeq by an IDENT(back)-violating LUM.

Why does chain convergence work? Because it filters out the LUM orderings that do not affect the outcome and retains the LUM orderings that do affect the outcome. The two chains that lead to *[kʲæ.tak] in (3-32) have different orderings of their constituent LUMs, but the ordering does not matter. The reason: palatalization of the initial /k/ and deletion of /i/ after the final /k/ do not interact. The three chains that lead to [kʲæ.takʲ] in (3-34) are different in one important respect: they all crucially order palatalization of the final /k/ before deletion of the high vowel. The reason: these phonological operations crucially interact, since if the vowel were deleted first the final /k/ would not palatalize. Chain convergence successfully abstracts away from accidental LUM orderings and zeroes in on nonaccidental ones.

Chain convergence is a surprisingly simple yet powerful tool for distinguishing between interaction and noninteraction of processes. We will return to this topic in §3.6.3 when we compare OT-CC with theories of opacity based on constraint conjunction or contrast preservation.

3.3.4   Application to counterfeeding opacity

In one of Bedouin Arabic's counterfeeding interactions, raising of low vowels in open syllables does not occur when syllables are open by virtue of epenthesis: /gabr/ → [ga.bur], *[gi.bur]. The harmonically improving chains from input /gabr/ were supplied in (3-20) and are repeated in (3-35) with their LUMSeqs. Since no chains in (3-35) converge, the LUMSeqs and their associated rLUM-Seqs are identical except for the bookkeeping device of eliminating reflexive orderings. The candidates corresponding to these chains are given in (3-36). (The properties of the initial form in the chain will be discussed shortly. Further details are provided in §4.3.3 and §4.3.4.)

(3-35) Harmonically improving chains from /gabr/ and the LUMSeqs[28]
     a. <gabr>   < >
     b. <gabr, ga.bur>✓   <Dep@3>
     c. <gabr, ga.bur, gi.bur>   <Dep@3, Id(low)@2>

(3-36) Candidates from (3-35)
     a. (/gabr/, gabr, Ø, Ø)
     b. (/gabr/, ga.bur, {Dep@3}, Ø)✓
     c. (/gabr/, gi.bur, {Dep@3, Id(low)@2}, {<Dep@3, Id(low)@2>})

The intended opaque winner is [ga.bur] ((b) in (3-36)), and its most challenging competitor is the transparent candidate (c) [gi.bur]. The important difference between them is that (c) has a Dep-violating LUM with a following Ident(low)-violating LUM, but (b) has only the Dep-violating LUM. The constraint Prec(Id(low), Dep) makes the necessary distinction between these two candidates, if it is ranked above [ga.bur]'s worst mark (i.e., its highest ranking constraint violation), which is its violation of *aCV (cf. (2-20)). This ranking argument is shown in (3-37). Prec(Id(low), Dep) is ranked below Dep, as required by the ranking metaconstraint (3-24). This means that satisfaction of the Prec constraint cannot influence epenthesis, though it is obviously affected by the presence of epenthesis in a candidate.

    Tableau (3-37) shows a typical analysis of counterfeeding opacity in OT-CC. Prec(Id(low), Dep) is violated by both the opaque winner and its transparent competitor (c), but the winner violates it less. The winner's rLUMSeq <Dep@3> receives one violation mark from Prec(Id(low), Dep) because it contains a Dep-violating LUM without a preceding Ident(low)-violating LUM. The transparent competitor's rLUMSeq <Dep@3, Id(low)@2> is worse, however, because it not only has a Dep-violating LUM without a preceding IDENT(low)-violating LUM, but it also has a DEP-violating LUM with a *following* IDENT(low)-violating LUM. In other words, candidate (c) is in violation of both clauses (i) and (ii) of the PREC definition in (3-23). Therefore, (c) gets two violation marks from PREC(ID(low), DEP), while the winner (b) gets only one.

(3-37) Counterfeeding opacity in OT-CC

/gabr/		*COMP-CODA	DEP	PREC(ID(low), DEP)	*aCV	ID(low)
b. →	ga.bur {DEP@3} ∅		1	1	1	
a.	gabr ∅ ∅	W₁	L	L	L	
c.	gi.bur {DEP@3, ID(low)@2} {<DEP@3, ID(low)@2>}		1	W₂	L	W₁

This example of counterfeeding opacity, like the previous example of counter-bleeding opacity, can be used to argue for several of OT-CC's main premises: the ranking metaconstraint (3-24); the harmonic improvement requirement on chains; the requirement that the chain-initial form be optimal among all the faithful candidates; and the gradualness requirement.

The argument for the ranking metaconstraint, like the parallel argument in the previous section, is based on an undesirable effect of too-liberal ranking permutation. Suppose, contrary to the metaconstraint, that PREC(ID(low), DEP) and DEP were freely permutable. Then PREC(ID(low), DEP) could be ranked above *COMPLEX-CODA, which dominates DEP. This permuted ranking is shown in (3-38). PREC(ID(low), DEP) then blocks epenthesis, favoring faithful [gabr] over the alternatives. This is not so odd in itself, since there are certainly languages that have no epenthesis. But the reason why there is no epenthesis in (3-38) is very peculiar: PREC(ID(low), DEP) is blocking epenthesis to avoid the problematic interaction of epenthesis with raising. Because of the ranking metaconstraint, PREC constraints can never have effects like this. In general, the metaconstraint disallows any possibility of PREC(A, B) affecting satisfaction of B.

(3-38)   An unwelcome result if PREC(ID(low), DEP) >> *COMPLEX-CODA >> DEP

	/gabr/	PREC(ID(low), DEP)	*COMP-CODA	DEP	*aCV	ID(low)
b. →	gabr Ø Ø		1			
a.	ga.bur {DEP@3} Ø	W$_1$	L	W$_1$	W$_1$	
c.	gi.bur {DEP@3, ID(low)@2} {<DEP@3, ID(low)@2>}	W$_2$	L	W$_1$		W$_1$

Example (3-37) also confirms another of the points made in the preceding section: the need for a harmonic improvement requirement on candidate chains. Suppose there were a chain <gabr, gibr, gibur>, with raising in a closed syllable and subsequent epenthesis. This chain has the LUMSeq <ID(low)@2, DEP@3>, which perfectly satisfies PREC(ID(low), DEP). It therefore threatens the intended winner, which has one mark from this PREC constraint. In reality, though, **<gabr, gibr, gi.bur> is not a valid chain in this language: its initial subchain **<gabr, gibr> is invalid because it violates IDENT(low) with no improvement in performance on a higher-ranking markedness constraint. The taint of invalidity infects the whole chain by upward entailment.

This example is also relevant to the premise that the chain-initial form is the most harmonic of the faithful parses. It is crucial that the /gabr/ → [ga.bur] chain be initiated by a faithful parse with a closed syllable, either <gabr, ...>, with a complex coda, or <gab.r, ...> with an extrasyllabic appendix. If the chain were initiated by a parse with an open syllable, such as <ga.br, ...>, where both [b] and [r] are parsed as appendices, then the chain could continue with raising and then epenthesis: <ga.br, gi.br, gi.bur>.[29] And if <ga.br, gi.br, gi.bur> were a valid chain, then PREC(ID(low), DEP) would be useless for ruling out *[gi.bur], and the desired opaque outcome [ga.bur] would be unobtainable.

The reason why chains initiated by [ga.br] are invalid is that [ga.br] is not the most harmonic faithful parse of the input, and clause (a) of (3-1) requires that chains be initiated by the most harmonic faithful parse. In Bedouin Arabic, the syllabification constraints must be ranked so as to favor [gabr] over [ga.br] — for example, a constraint against syllable appendices must dominate *COMPLEX-CODA and NO-CODA. This conclusion is consistent with standard assumptions about how such words are parsed in Arabic — see §4.2.2 and §4.3. With this ranking, any chain beginning with [ga.br] is invalid; all valid chains from the input /gabr/ are initiated by [gabr] in this language.

Finally, this example can be adduced in support of the gradualness requirement on chains. If there were no gradualness requirement, then there could be a chain <gabr, gi.bur>, with raising and epenthesis occurring together in a single step. This chain is harmonically improving, and it ties with the intended winner by violating Prec(Id(low), Dep) once, since the Dep-violating mapping is not preceded by an Ident(low)-violating mapping. Since this putative chain's output form *[gi.bur] performs better than [ga.bur] on the markedness constraint *aCV, the intended winner is certainly threatened. In reality, though, **<gabr, gi.bur> is invalid because it conflates two LUMs into a single step. Without the gradualness restriction on chains, this and other examples of counterfeeding opacity would be intractable in OT-CC.

3.3.5   Application to multiple opacity

No discussion of opacity can be considered complete unless it includes an analysis of Yawelmani Yokuts,[30] a language in which three different processes interact opaquely. The three processes are these:

(i) *Rounding harmony* is height-stratified: a suffix vowel takes on the rounding of the preceding vowel if they agree in height. E.g., the high-voweled nonfuture suffix /-hin/ alternates as follows: [xathin] 'eat', [bokʔhin] 'find', [xilhin] 'tangle', but [dubhun] 'lead by the hand'. In contrast, the non-high-voweled dubitative suffix /-al/ alternates like this: [maxal] 'procure', [hudal] 'recognize', [gijʔal] 'touch', but [kʔoʔol] 'throw'.

(ii) *Lowering* changes underlying high long vowels into their nonhigh counterparts: /ʔiliː-hin/ → [ʔileːhin] 'fan', /cʔujuː-hin/ → [cʔujoːhun] 'urinate'.[31]

(iii) *Closed syllable shortening* affects long vowels in medial and final closed syllables: /ṣaːp-hin/ → [ṣap.hin] 'burn', /panaː-al/ → [panal] 'arrive'.

These processes interact opaquely in various ways. Closed syllable shortening has the potential to bleed lowering of long vowels, but in fact it does not: /miːkʔ-hin/ → [mekʔhin], *[mikʔhin] 'swallow'. This is a counterbleeding interaction. Rounding harmony only affects vowels that are of the same height class, but the underlying and not the surface height of a long vowel is what matters. Thus, a suffix with a high vowel harmonizes with a high-voweled root, even if the root vowel is lowered in surface structure because it is long: /cʔuːm-it/ → [cʔoːmut], *[cʔoːmit] 'destroy–passive aorist'. This is a counterbleeding interaction. And suffixes with nonhigh vowels do not harmonize with root vowels that are the result of lowering: /cʔuːm-al/ → [cʔoːmal], *[cʔoːmol]. This is a counterfeeding interaction. Some forms, such as /cʔuːm-hin/ → [cʔomhun], are doubly opaque, with counterbleeding interactions between shortening and lowering and between lowering and rounding harmony.

To understand Yawelmani's opaque phonology, it is first necessary to have a grasp of the transparent phonology. The basic elements of the analysis are set out in Archangeli and Suzuki (1997) and McCarthy (1999). Closed syllable shortening is the result of ranking a constraint against trimoraic syllables, *[μμμ]$_\sigma$, above faithfulness to moras, as (3-39) shows. (Classic OT ranking arguments like (3-39) are a legitimate shortcut in OT-CC when they deal with the effect of only one process at a time and they include the most harmonic faithful candidate. Tableau (3-39) is equivalent to asking whether the chain <ṣaːp.hin, ṣap.hin> is harmonically improving.)

(3-39) *[μμμ]$_\sigma$ >> IDENT(long) in Yawelmani

/ṣaːp-hin/	*[μμμ]$_\sigma$	ID(long)
→ ṣap.hin		1
ṣaːp.hin	W$_1$	L

Lowering of long vowels is an indication that a constraint against long high vowels, LONG/-HI, is ranked above IDENT(high). To foreclose the alternative of satisfying LONG/-HI by shortening rather than lowering, faithfulness to vowel length must also dominate IDENT(high). These ranking arguments are given in (3-40).

(3-40) LONG/-HI, IDENT(long) >> IDENT(high) in Yawelmani

/ʔiliː-hin/	ID(long)	LONG/-HI	ID(hi)
→ ʔileːhin			1
a. ʔiliːhin		W$_1$	L
b. ʔilihin	W$_1$		L

As for rounding harmony, Archangeli and Suzuki (1997: 207ff.) propose that it is the result of interaction among the three constraints listed in (3-41). The featural alignment constraint ALIGN(Color) in (b) induces harmony by dominating the faithfulness constraint IDENT(Color) in (c). But ALIGN(Color) is itself ranked below the constraint RD/αHI in (a), which demands that vowels sharing [round] also share [high]. This has the effect of limiting rounding harmony to vowels of the same height. The ranking arguments are provided in (3-42) and (3-43).

(3-41) Constraints active in rounding harmony

    a. Rᴅ/αHɪ

      Every path including [round$_i$] includes [αhigh].

        i.e., no token of [round] is linked to vowels of different heights.

    b. Aʟɪɢɴ(Color) (Aʟ(Col))

      Align(Color, R, Word, R)

        i.e., every token of Color ([back] and [round]) is final in some word.[32]

    c. Iᴅᴇɴᴛ(Color) (Iᴅ(Col))

      Segments standing in correspondence have identical values for [back] and [round].

(3-42) Aʟɪɢɴ-Cᴏʟᴏʀ >> Iᴅᴇɴᴛ(Color) in Yawelmani

/dub-hin/	Aʟ(Col)	Iᴅ(Col)
→ dubhun		1
dubhin	W$_1$	L

(3-43) Rᴅ/αHɪ >> Aʟɪɢɴ-Cᴏʟᴏʀ in Yawelmani

/hud-al/	Rᴅ/αHɪ	Aʟ(Col)
→ hudal		1
hudol	W$_1$	L

We are now ready to analyze Yawelmani's opaque interactions, starting with the lowering/shortening interaction. Underlying high long vowels are lowered even when they are also shortened in a closed syllable: /miːkʔ-hin/ → [mekʔ.hin]. The valid candidate chains from input /miːkʔ-hin/, together with their LUMSeqs, are given in (3-44). The winning chain is the one in (d), with the lowering LUM preceding the shortening LUM. Its main competitor is the transparent chain (c), with shortening only.

(3-44) Chains from /miːkʔ-hin/ and their LUMSeqs

    a. <miːkʔ.hin>   < >

    b. <miːkʔ.hin, meːkʔ.hin>   <Iᴅ(hi)@2>

    c. <miːkʔ.hin, mikʔ.hin>   <Iᴅ(long)@2>

    d. <miːkʔ.hin, meːkʔ.hin, mekʔ.hin>✓ <Iᴅ(hi)@2, Iᴅ(long)@2>

Since opaque [mekʔhin] in (d) is less faithful and no more marked than transparent [mikʔhin] in (c), some constraint other than markedness or faithfulness must be favoring (d). That constraint is Pʀᴇᴄ(Iᴅ(high), Iᴅ(long)), which requires that any Iᴅᴇɴᴛ(long)-violating LUM be preceded by an Iᴅᴇɴᴛ(high)-violating

LUM. If it is to favor opaque (d) over transparent (c), PREC(ID(high), ID(long)) must dominate (d)'s worst mark that is not shared with (c). Candidate (d)'s worst unshared mark is its violation of IDENT(high), the highest-ranking (and only) constraint that (d) violates and (c) does not. This ranking argument is certified by tableau (3-45).

(3-45) PREC(ID(high), ID(long)) >> IDENT(high)

/mi:k$^?$-hin/		*[μμμ]$_\sigma$	LONG/-HI	ID(long)	PREC(ID(hi), ID(long))	ID(hi)
d. →	mek$^?$.hin <ID(hi)@2, ID(long)@2>			1		1
a.	mi:k$^?$.hin < >	W$_1$	W$_1$	L		L
b.	me:k$^?$.hin <ID(hi)@2>	W$_1$		L		1
c.	mik$^?$.hin <ID(long)@2>			1	W$_1$	L

Beginning with tableau (3-45), I will be making a typographic simplification. Except when a candidate incorporates two or more convergent chains, I will give its LUMSeq rather than its £-set and rLUMSeq. When there are no convergent chains, the LUMSeq is an adequate substitute for the rLUMSeq. Bear in mind, however, that the actual definition of PREC in (3-23) refers to £-sets and rLUMSeqs, not LUMSeqs.

The ranking argument in tableau (3-45) completes a transitive ordering relation among constraints that is consistent with a ranking obtained by direct argumentation. The direct argument is in (3-40): IDENT(long) must dominate IDENT(high), since long high vowels in open syllables are lowered rather than shortened. The transitive ranking argument comes from a combination of a direct argument —PREC(ID(high), ID(long)) dominates IDENT(high) in (3-45) — and the ranking metaconstraint (3-24), which requires IDENT(long) to dominate PREC(ID(high), ID(long)). Therefore, two distinct sources of information about ranking converge in asserting that IDENT(long) dominates IDENT(high). Results like this are important because they highlight one of the ways in which OT-CC is falsifiable: the phonology of a language must be reducible to a single ranking of markedness, faithfulness, and PREC constraints. If not, and if the analysis is otherwise sound, then some premise(s) of OT-CC must be incorrect.

The other opaque interaction in Yawelmani is the relationship between long-vowel lowering and rounding harmony. Rounding harmony only occurs when the root and suffix vowel are both high or both nonhigh, and it is the vowels' underlying height that matters. High suffix vowels harmonize with erstwhile high root vowels — /c²uːm-it/ → [c²oːmut] — while nonhigh suffix vowels do not harmonize with them — /c²uːm-al/ → [c²oːmal].

The valid chains for /c²uːm-it/ are provided in (3-46). For (d) to win, the constraint PREC(ID(Color), ID(high)) has to dominate RD/αHI (see (3-47)). That is because RD/αHI normally prevents vowels of different height from agreeing in rounding, as it does in (d)'s transparent competitor (c). (Tableau (3-47) also shows IDENT(high) dominating PREC(ID(Color), ID(high)), as required by the ranking metaconstraint.)

(3-46) Chains from /c²uːm-it/ and their LUMSeqs
    a. <c²uː.mit>   <>
    b. <c²uː.mit, c²uː.mut>   <ID(Col)@4>
    c. <c²uː.mit, c²oː.mit>   <ID(hi)@2>
    d. <c²uː.mit, c²uː.mut, c²oː.mut>✓ <ID(Col)@4, ID(hi)@2>

(3-47) PREC(ID(Color), ID(high)) >> RD/αHI

	/c²uːm-it/	LG/-HI	ID(hi)	PREC(ID(Col), ID(hi))	RD/αHI	AL(Col)	ID(Col)
d. →	c²oː.mut <ID(Col)@4, ID(hi)@2>		1		1		1
a.	c²uː.mit <>	W₁	L		L	W₁	L
b.	c²uː.mut <ID(Col)@4>	W₁	L		L		1
c.	c²oː.mit <ID(hi)@2>		1	W₁	L	W₁	L

This example also illustrates convergence of different sources of ranking evidence. For the winning candidate chain <c²uː.mit, c²uː.mut, c²oː.mut> to be harmonically improving, and thus valid at all, LONG/-HI must dominate RD/αHI. That is because the last link in this chain eliminates a violation of LONG/-HI at the expense of introducing a violation of RD/αHI. This ranking is required independently by transitivity of the domination relation. LONG/-HI dominates IDENT(high) (see (3-40)) and IDENT(high) dominates PREC(ID(Color), ID(high)) because of the metaconstraint (3-24). The final step in the transitive sequence comes from tableau (3-47): PREC(ID(Color), ID(high)) dominates RD/αHI. The full sequence of these rankings is [LONG/-HI >> IDENT(high) >> PREC(ID(Color), ID(high)) >> RD/αHI], and it shows, as promised, that LONG/-HI dominates RD/αHI by transitivity. Thus, a ranking that is necessary to ensure chain validity is also required by a combination of conventional ranking arguments and a metaconstraint.

The unexpected failure of rounding harmony in opaque /cˀuːm-al/ → [cˀoːmal] has the same explanation as the unexpected success of harmony in opaque /cˀuːm-it/ → [cˀoːmut]. The winning candidate chain is <cˀuː.mal, cˀoː.mal>. Its LUMSeq <Iᴅ(hi)> is more harmonic according to Pʀᴇᴄ(Iᴅ(Col), Iᴅ(hi)) than the <Iᴅ(hi), Iᴅ(Col)> LUMSeq of the competing transparent chain <cˀuː.mal, cˀoː.mal, cˀoː.mol>. As usual in counterfeeding interactions, the opaque candidate and its main competitor both violate the Pʀᴇᴄ constraint, but the opaque chain incurs just one violation mark to the transparent competitor's two. The valid chains from /cˀuːm-al/ are supplied in (3-48) and the verificatory tableau is in (3-49).

(3-48) Chains from /cˀuːm-al/ and their LUMSeqs
  a. <cˀuː.mal>   <>
  b. <cˀuː.mal, cˀoː.mal>✓   <Iᴅ(hi)@2>
  c. <cˀuː.mal, cˀoː.mal, cˀoː.mol> <Iᴅ(hi)@2, Iᴅ(Col)@4>

(3-49) Pʀᴇᴄ(Iᴅ(Color), Iᴅ(high)) >> Aʟɪɢɴ(Color)

/cˀuːm-al/	Lɢ/-Hɪ	Iᴅ(hi)	Pʀᴇᴄ(Iᴅ(Col), Iᴅ(hi))	Aʟ(Col)	Iᴅ(Col)
b. → cˀoː.mal <Iᴅ(hi)@2>		1	1	1	
a. cˀuː.mal <>	W$_1$	L	L	1	
c. cˀoː.mol <Iᴅ(hi)@2, Iᴅ(Col)@4>		1	W$_2$	L	W$_1$

Tableau (3-49) shows by direct argument that Pʀᴇᴄ(Iᴅ(Color), Iᴅ(high)) must dominate Aʟɪɢɴ(Color), since [cˀoːmal] lacks the expected rounding harmony. The same ranking is independently required by transitivity of constraint domination, since Pʀᴇᴄ(Iᴅ(Color), Iᴅ(high)) dominates Rᴅ/αHɪ (3-47) and Rᴅ/αHɪ dominates Aʟɪɢɴ(Color) (3-43).

From the evidence considered so far, we obtain the constraint hierarchy in (3-50). The two undominated markedness constraints, *[μμμ]$_σ$ and Lᴏɴɢ/-Hɪ, bear primary responsibility for the shortening and lowering processes. The opaque interaction between shortening and lowering is a result of activity by Pʀᴇᴄ(Iᴅ(hi), Iᴅ(long)). Because it dominates Iᴅᴇɴᴛ(high), the Pʀᴇᴄ constraint is able to force the otherwise superfluous lowering in /miːkˀ-hin/ → [mekˀ.hin]. Height-stratified rounding harmony is a result of the three constraints at the

bottom of the hierarchy. Rounding harmony interacts opaquely with lowering because of PREC(ID(Col), ID(hi)), which induces harmony in /cʔuːm-it/ →
[cʔoːmut] and blocks it in /cʔuːm-al/ → [cʔoːmal].

(3-50) Yawelmani ranking summary

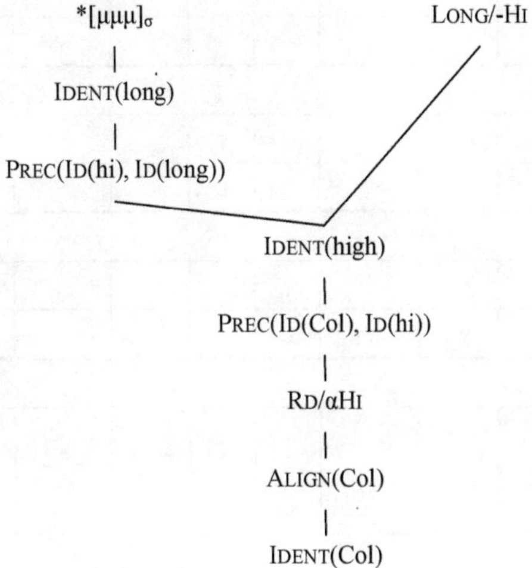

If the analysis is successful, then the ranking in (3-50) or one that is consistent
with it will also account for the double opacity in /cʔuːm-hin/ → [cʔom.hun].
The first step in the analysis is selection of the most harmonic faithful form as
the chain initiator. This is [cʔuːm.hin], which must be favored over alternatives
like [cʔuː.mhin] by syllabification constraints that need not detain us here.
Tableaux (3-51), (3-52), and (3-53) show how to determine the other valid
candidate chains.[33] These three tableaux are organized by the initial subchains.
For example, (3-51) considers the putative chains that begin with a violation of
IDENT(Color). The harmonic improvement requirement means that each chain
of length n must be compared with its initial subchain of length $n-1$. In some
cases, such as the <ID(high), ID(Color)> rows of (3-52), harmonic improvement is not obtained, so no chain with this LUMSeq is valid. In some cases,
such as row (b) of (3-52), a chain's validity depends on choosing the locus of
faithfulness violation that produces the most harmonic result ('best violation'
in clause (c) of (3-1)). Other putative chains with different loci of violation or
even multiple loci of violation could be adduced, but they would not change
the overall result. In sum, the valid chains of length greater than 1 are exactly
those that are preceded by a winner's arrow in (3-51), (3-52), and (3-53).[34]

(3-51) Valid chains of form <ID(Color), …>

/$c^{ʔ}$u:m-hin/	*[μμμ]$_σ$	LONG/-HI	ID(lg)	ID(hi)	RD/αHI	AL(Col)	ID(Col)
<ID(Col)>							
→ <$c^{ʔ}$u:m.hin, $c^{ʔ}$u:m.hun>	1	1					1
a. <$c^{ʔ}$u:m.hin>	1	1				W_1	L
<ID(Col), ID(hi)>							
→ <$c^{ʔ}$u:m.hin, $c^{ʔ}$u:m.hun, $c^{ʔ}$o:m.hun>	1			1	1		1
b. <$c^{ʔ}$u:m.hin, $c^{ʔ}$u:m.hun>	1	W_1		L	L		1
<ID(Col), ID(lg)>							
→ <$c^{ʔ}$u:m.hin, $c^{ʔ}$u:m.hun, $c^{ʔ}$um.hun>			1				1
c. <$c^{ʔ}$u:m.hin, $c^{ʔ}$u:m.hun>	W_1	W_1	L				1
<ID(Col), ID(hi), ID(lg)>							
→ <$c^{ʔ}$u:m.hin, $c^{ʔ}$u:m.hun, $c^{ʔ}$o:m.hun, $c^{ʔ}$om.hun>			1	1	1		1
d. <$c^{ʔ}$u:m.hin, $c^{ʔ}$u:m.hun, $c^{ʔ}$o:m.hun>	W_1		L	1	1		1

(3-52) Valid chains of form <ID(high), …>

/$c^{ʔ}$u:m-hin/	*[μμμ]$_σ$	LONG/-HI	ID(lg)	ID(hi)	RD/αHI	AL(Col)	ID(Col)
<ID(hi)>							
→ <$c^{ʔ}$u:m.hin, $c^{ʔ}$o:m.hin>	1			1		1	
a. <$c^{ʔ}$u:m.hin>	1	W_1		L		1	
b. <$c^{ʔ}$u:m.hin, $c^{ʔ}$u:m.hen>	1	W_1		1		1	
<ID(hi), ID(lg)>							
→ <$c^{ʔ}$u:m.hin, $c^{ʔ}$o:m.hin, $c^{ʔ}$om.hin>			1	1		1	
c. <$c^{ʔ}$u:m.hin, $c^{ʔ}$o:m.hin>	W_1		L	1		1	
**<ID(hi), ID(Col)>							
→ <$c^{ʔ}$u:m.hin, $c^{ʔ}$o:m.hin>	1			1		1	
d. <$c^{ʔ}$u:m.hin, $c^{ʔ}$o:m.hin, $c^{ʔ}$o:m.hun>	1			1	W_1	L	W_1
**<ID(hi), ID(lg), ID(Col)>							
→ <$c^{ʔ}$u:m.hin, $c^{ʔ}$o:m.hin, $c^{ʔ}$om.hin>			1	1		1	
e. <$c^{ʔ}$u:m.hin, $c^{ʔ}$o:m.hin, $c^{ʔ}$om.hin, $c^{ʔ}$om.hun>			1	1	W_1	L	W_1

(3-53) Valid chains of form <ID(long), …>

/cˀuːm-hin/	*[μμμ]σ	LONG/-HI	ID(lg)	ID(hi)	RD/αHI	AL(Col)	ID(Col)
<ID(lg)>							
→ <cˀuːm.hin, cˀum.hin>			1			1	
a. <cˀuːm.hin>	W₁	W₁	L			1	
<ID(lg), ID(Col)>							
→ <ĉ uːm.hin, ĉ um.hin, ĉ um.hun>			1				1
b. <ĉ uːm.hin, ĉ um.hin>			1			W₁	L
**<ID(lg), ID(hi)>							
→ <cˀuːm.hin, cˀum.hin>			1			1	
c. <cˀuːm.hin, cˀum.hin, cˀom.hin>			1	W₁		1	
**<ID(lg), ID(Col), ID(hi)>							
→ <cˀuːm.hin, cˀum.hin, cˀum.hun>			1				1
d. <cˀuːm.hin, cˀum.hin, cˀum.hun,cˀom.hun>			1	W₁	W₁	W₁	1

The valid chains collected from these three tableaux are assembled in (3-54). The two chains in (f) are convergent in the sense of (3-21): they have the same output and their LUMSeqs are permutations of one another, reflecting the fact that the sequencing of these two LUMs has no impact on the result. These convergent chains constitute a single candidate whose rLUMSeq consists of those orderings that are common to both chains (i.e., none at all).

(3-54) Chains from /cˀuːm-hin/ and their LUMSeqs
    a. <cˀuːm.hin>   < >
    b. <cˀuːm.hin, cˀuːm.hun>   <ID(Col)@5>
    c. <cˀuːm.hin, cˀoːm.hin>   <ID(hi)@2>
    d. <cˀuːm.hin, cˀum.hin>   <ID(long)@2>
    e. <cˀuːm.hin, cˀuːm.hun, cˀoːm.hun> <ID(Col)@5, ID(hi)@2>
    f. <cˀuːm.hin, cˀuːm.hun, cˀum.hun>   <ID(Col)@5, ID(long)@2>
      <cˀuːm.hin, cˀum.hin, cˀum.hun>   <ID(long)@2, ID(Col)@5>
    g. <cˀuːm.hin, cˀoːm.hin, cˀom.hin>   <ID(hi)@2, ID(long)@2>
    h. <cˀuːm.hin, cˀuːm.hun, cˀoːm.hun, cˀom.hun>✓ <ID(Col)@5, ID(hi)@2,
                                        ID(long)@2>

The analysis is completed with tableau (3-55), where the optimal, doubly opaque candidate (h) is selected. Pay particular attention to (d), (f), and (g). They are the transparent competitors that would win if not for the PREC constraints.

(3-55) Double opacity in Yawelmani

/c²uːm-hin/	*[μμμ]$_\sigma$	LG/-HI	ID(lg)	PREC (ID(hi), ID(lg))	ID(hi)	PREC (ID(Col), ID(hi))	RD/αHI	AL(Col)	ID(Col)
h. → c²om.hun <ID(Col)@5, ID(hi)@2, ID(lg)@2>			1		1		1		1
a. c²uːm.hin < >	W₁	W₁	L		L		L	W₁	L
b. c²uːm.hun <ID(Col)@5>	W₁	W₁	L		L		L		1
c. c²oːm.hin <ID(hi)@2>	W₁		L		1	W₁	L	W₁	L
d. c²um.hin <ID(lg)@2>			1	W₁	L		L	W₁	L
e. c²oːm.hun <ID(Col)@5, ID(hi)@2>	W₁		L		1		1		1
f. c²um.hun {ID(Col)@5, ID(lg)@2} ∅			1	W₁	L		L		1
g. c²omhin <ID(hi)@2, ID(lg)@2>			1		1	W₁	L	W₁	L

Apart from showing the success of the analysis in the most complex case Yawelmani has to offer, tableau (3-55) is useful because it allows us to quickly explore the effects of permuting the ranking of PREC constraints. Within this constraint hierarchy, the PREC constraints could not be ranked any higher than they are now, because of the ranking metaconstraint. Therefore, we need only look at the potential effects of ranking them lower. If PREC(ID(high), ID(long)) were any lower, it would not be visibly active over this candidate set. The only surviving candidates would be (d) and (f), neither of which is opaque. The same goes for PREC(ID(Color), ID(high)); merely demoting it below RD/αHI is enough to deprive it of visible activity over this candidate set.

This foray into the complexities of Yawelmani shows that OT-CC is capable of analyzing even relatively complex interlocking opacities. The case studies in §4 lend further support to this claim. Yawelmani also reveals some of OT-CC's predictive power: by deriving opacity from a single constraint ranking, OT-CC demands consistency of rankings obtained from multiple sources of evidence: direct ranking arguments, inferences about ranking from transitivity of the domination relation, the ranking metaconstraint (3-24), and the local optimality requirements on valid candidate chains. With ranking evidence from disparate sources converging on a consistent hierarchy, this analysis gains in plausibility.

3.4   Learning in OT-CC [35]

Are the PREC constraints universally present in CON, or are they constructed on the fly by language learners who face otherwise refractory data? This question is difficult to answer, and perhaps not very important in any case, because the range of logically possible PREC constraints is so narrow.

If there are n faithfulness constraints in CON, then there are $n*(n–1)$ logically possible PREC constraints.[36] It may be that some of these constraints are not and could not ever be visibly active in any language. For example, it is difficult to imagine a circumstance where there is crucial interaction between a glottalization process and rounding harmony, so there may be no use for PREC(ID(glottal), ID(round)) or PREC(ID(round), ID(glottal)). But this gap emerges from the accidents of the markedness constraints in CON — if they fail to make any sort of connection between rounding and glottalization — and not from some *a priori* limitations on PREC constraints. So it seems likely that all of the logical possibilities for PREC constraints are at least in principle available to the language learner. Whether these possibilities are already compiled in CON or computed as needed is a question of great subtlety. In theory, one might be able to distinguish between these two hypotheses by using emergence of the unmarked (McCarthy and Prince 1994): are there special circumstances, invisible to learners, where even unlearnable and therefore unlearned PREC constraints are visibly active? I do not know of any relevant cases.

If PREC constraints are universally present in grammars, then it is reasonable to assume that they are initially ranked at the bottom of the hierarchy, below even the faithfulness constraints. (*Inter alia*, this ensures that they are in conformity with the metaconstraint (3-24), which requires B to dominate PREC(A, B).) Learners will be moved to demote faithfulness and/or markedness constraints below some PREC constraint only when they encounter data that simply cannot be analyzed by permuting only faithfulness and markedness constraints.

Imagine, for example, a learner who has arrived at the Yawelmani Yokuts ranking in (3-56) based solely on transparent alternations and the assumption that PREC constraints start at the bottom of the hierarchy.

(3-56) Yokuts ranking (intermediate learning stage)

LONG/-HI >> ID(hi) >> RD/αHI >> ALIGN(Col) >> ID(Col) >> PREC(ID(Col), ID(hi))

The PREC constraint is tucked safely out of the way, where it has remained since the beginning of learning. Up to this point, the learner has had no reason to consult the LUMSeqs that are included in every candidate.

But then comes the confrontation with an opaque interaction, as in (3-57). Because candidate (c) has an undominated loser-favoring L, the current ranking favors this candidate over the intended winner. (Candidate (c) is the transparent result of height-stratified rounding harmony.) To get the right candidate to win, the learner has no option except to rank PREC(ID(Col), ID(high)) above RD/αHI, since no other constraint has the right favoring relations.[37]

(3-57) Opacity at intermediate learning stage in Yawelmani (cf. (3-47))

/cʔuːm-it/	LONG/-HI	ID(hi)	RD/αHI	AL(Col)	ID(Col)	PREC(ID(Col), ID(hi))
→ cʔoː.mut <ID(Col)@4, ID(hi)@2>		1	1		1	
a. cʔuː.mit < >	W₁	L	L	W₁	L	
b. cʔuː.mut <ID(Col)@4>	W₁	L	L		1	
c. cʔoː.mit <ID(hi)@2>		1	L	W₁	L	W₁

Little is known about the learning of morphophonemic alternations, and even less (i.e., next to nothing) is known about the learning of opaque morphophonemic alternations. Nonetheless, this seems like a fairly reasonable approach: to learn opaque alternations, learners must make use of a type of information, the LUMSeq, that was always available to them but was not needed previously.

3.5   Opacity and faithfulness

OT-CC is closely connected with the theory of faithfulness. Some of the implications of this connection for phenomena other than opacity were discussed in §3.2.4. We will now look at how the theory of faithfulness impacts the analysis of opacity. The discussion is organized under three rubrics: identical faithfulness violations entail identical opaque interactions; opacity as a result of allophonic alternations; and the proper allocation of responsibility for counterfeeding opacity between faithfulness constraints and PREC constraints.

3.5.1   Identical faithfulness violations entail identical opaque interactions

In OT-CC, if two notionally distinct processes produce identical faithfulness violations, then they cannot differ in their opaque interactions. This follows from the theory of candidate chains and PREC constraints. A 'process' has no independent existence in OT, so OT-CC must exercise its control over opacity via faithfulness violations rather than processes. PREC(A, B) is potentially active in all B-violating chains, regardless of which 'process' is responsible for the violations of B or A. To put the matter in a way that is truer to the letter and spirit of OT, PREC(A, B) is insensitive to differences in the markedness constraints that compel the A or B violations.

Because sympathy theory (§2.3.4.3) makes a similar claim, though for somewhat different reasons, this prediction has already received some attention in the literature. Yawelmani supplies a potential counterexample. Recall from §3.3.5 that Yawelmani has an opaque, counterbleeding interaction between lowering of long vowels and shortening of long vowels in closed syllables: /ʔiliː-kʔa/ → [ʔilekʔ] 'fan (him)!'. But before the future and absolutive suffixes, both of which are /-ʔ/, lowering and shortening seem to interact transparently (Bye 2001: 54–56, Kiparsky 2001: 15, Kisseberth 1973: 432, McCarthy 1999: 345, Newman 1944: 26): /ʔiliː-ʔ/ → [ʔiliʔ], *[ʔileʔ] 'will fan'. In a rule-based analysis like Kisseberth's, a derivation like (3-58) is required. There are two closed syllable shortening rules, one limited to long vowels before word-final [ʔ] and the other without this limitation. The more specific shortening rule is ordered before lowering, and the general one is ordered after lowering.

(3-58)   Rule sandwiching in Yawelmani

Underlying	/ʔiliː-kʔa/	/ʔiliː-ʔ/
Apocope	ʔiliː-kʔ	—
Pre-[ʔ]# closed syllable shortening	—	ʔiliʔ
Long-vowel lowering	ʔileːkʔ	—
General closed syllable shortening	ʔilekʔ	—
Surface	[ʔilekʔ]	[ʔiliʔ]

Bye (2001) and Levi (2000) introduce the term 'rule sandwiching' to describe cases like this, the idea being that one rule (here, lowering) is sandwiched between two other rules with similar effects. The filling of the sandwich, lowering, interacts transparently with the earlier rule of pre-[ʔ]# shortening and opaquely with the later rule of general shortening. Kiparsky's (2001) Stratal OT analysis is similar to (3-58): pre-[ʔ]# closed syllable shortening occurs in the word-level stratum, at the same time as vowel lowering, so the interaction is transparent, while shortening of vowels before other consonants does not happen until the postlexical stratum, after long vowels have been lowered.

This example is a challenge to OT-CC because PREC(ID(high), ID(long)) has its opacity-promoting effect on all vowels that have been shortened, regardless of whether they are shortened in the pre-[ʔ]# context or elsewhere. Presumably, shortening in the pre-[ʔ]# context and shortening before other coda consonants violate exactly the same faithfulness constraints, so there is no way of constructing a PREC constraint that distinguishes between them. OT-CC uses faithfulness violations to detect opacity via PREC constraints, and situations that produce identical faithfulness violations are equivalent in the eyes of the PREC constraints.

Rule sandwiching effects are not very common, as Bye (2001: 65) notes, and even this particular example is dubious. The problem with (3-45) and its OT analogues involves the process of pre-[ʔ]# closed syllable shortening. Kiparsky's (2001: 15) Stratal OT analysis requires a markedness constraint or constraints against trimoraic syllables closed by [ʔ]. This constraint is ranked above IDENT(long) in the word stratum, whereas the general *[μμμ]$_\sigma$ constraint does not dominate IDENT(long) until the postlexical stratum. Kiparsky argues that CON must treat trimoraic syllables closed by [ʔ] as more marked than other trimoraic syllables, but this argument is not really relevant to the problem. Newman's (1944) original description is explicit that the transparent interaction of lowering with shortening is limited to vowels that precede [ʔ] *in word-final position in the future and absolutive suffixes*, and nowhere else. Closed syllable shortening before other [ʔ]s interacts with lowering in the usual opaque way: /wuːʔuj-iːn/ → [woʔjon] 'go to sleep (future)' (Newman 1944: 128) or /ʔiliːʔl-/ → [ʔileʔl-] 'fan repeatedly' (Newman 1944: 63). One might try to salvage the Stratal OT analysis by hypothesizing a markedness constraint in CON that is violated only by word-final trimoraic syllables that are closed by [ʔ] (cf. Bye 2001: 55). Positing a markedness constraint of such great specificity seems like a dubious move, and even then it does not explain the limitation to the future and absolutive suffixes. That pre-[ʔ]# closed syllable shortening is so severely limited in its applicability suggests that we are dealing here with a morphologized process that is outside the scope of any phonological analysis. It is certainly far too questionable to be used as evidence for or against some theory of opacity.

   Although Yawelmani is unimpressive as a potential counterexample to CC-OT, it adequately illustrates the claim: opaque interaction is tied to faithfulness violation. The empirical consequences of this claim are closely linked to the substantive properties of the theory of faithfulness, and a very rich faithfulness theory will weaken the predictions. To understand this connection, assume (absurdly) that Con includes a faithfulness constraint F that is violated only when a vowel is shortened before a word-final [ʔ]. Then by ranking Prec(F, Id(high)) above Prec(Id(high), Id(long)), it would be possible to rule out the chain *<ʔili:ʔ, ʔile:ʔ, ʔileʔ> with its LUMSeq <Id(high), F>. (For an actual case where a Prec constraint forces transparency by dominating another Prec constraint, see §4.3.4.) That there is no such constraint F is a substantive claim about Con rather than a formal property of OT-CC.

   Bye (2001) focuses on rule sandwiching in support of a revision of sympathy theory, and it is worth taking a look at some of his other examples to see whether they imperil OT-CC's prediction that processes producing identical faithfulness violations cannot differ in opacity. One of the examples comes from the Mizrahi variety of Modern Hebrew, based on a problem set in Kenstowicz and Kisseberth (1979: 134–135) and an OT analysis in Levi (2000).[38] The rule-sandwiching effect involves two consonant deletion processes and lowering in closed syllables, as shown in (3-59). If Con does not include a faithfulness constraint that deletion of [ʔ] violates and deletion of [ʕ] does not, then this opaque interaction cannot be obtained in OT-CC for the reasons already given in the discussion of Yawelmani.

(3-59)   Rule sandwiching in Modern Hebrew

	Underlying	/it-maleʔ-ti/	/it-pareʕ-ti/
Coda [ʔ] deletion		itmaleti	—
e → a/ __CC		—	itparaʕti
Coda [ʕ] deletion		—	itparati
Surface		[itmaleti]	[itparati]
		'I got full'	'I caused disorder'

The analysis in (3-59) is certainly incorrect, however.[39] The verbs in (3-59) are in the *hitpaʾel* pattern or *binyan*, a pattern that has underlying /e/ in the stem-final syllable. This /e/ shows up unchanged when no suffix follows ([itlabeʃ] 'he got dressed') and it lowers to [a] before consonant-initial suffixes ([itlaba**ʃ**ti] 'I got dressed'). By ordering /ʔ/-deletion early, (3-59) explains why /ʔ/-final *hitpaʾel* verbs have [e] in both contexts: [itmal**e**] 'he got full', [itmaleti]. But this completely misconstrues the problem that /ʔ/-final verbs present: they have

[e] presuffixally in other patterns, even those where the underlying vowel is not /e/. These include the *pa'al* pattern [saneti] 'I hated' from /sana?-ti/ (cf. [sana] 'he hated'), the *nif'al* pattern [niseti] 'I got married' from /nisa?-ti/ (cf. [nisa] 'he got married'), and the *hif'il* pattern [hisneti] 'I caused someone to be hated' from /hisni?-ti/ (cf. [hisni] 'he caused someone to be hated'). These facts show that the presence of [e] before suffixes in /?/-final verbs is a relatively systematic but idiosyncratic property of these verbs that has nothing whatsoever to do with the process that lowers /e/ to [a] before a cluster. There is simply no evidence for rule sandwiching here.

Another of Bye's examples is based on the interaction of stress and epenthesis in Mohawk (Iroquoian, Quebec and Ontario). Stress is assigned to the penult, including some but not all epenthetic vowels (Michelson 1988: 132ff.). Among the epenthetic vowels that are visible to stress are those that break up triconsonantal clusters, whereas vowels that split up biconsonantal C + resonant clusters are invisible to stress. A sandwiching derivation is given in (3-60).

(3-60) Rule sandwiching in Mohawk

Underlying	/wak-njak-s/	/ʌ-k-r-ʌʔ/
Ø → e/C__CC	wakenjaks	—
Penult stress	waˈkenjaks	ˈʌkrʌʔ
Ø → e/C__resonant	—	ˈʌkerʌʔ
Surface	[waˈkenjaks]	[ˈʌkerʌʔ]
	'I get married'	'I'll put it into a container'

In §4.2 we will see an OT-CC analysis of a similar example in Arabic. As for Mohawk, there is good reason to doubt that the two kinds of epenthetic vowels in (3-60) have the same representation. Hall (2003) argues persuasively that the intrusive vocoids that appear in C + resonant clusters of other languages are not actual segments at all. Rather, they are the result of incomplete overlap in the articulatory gestures of the abutting consonants. Such transitional vocoids are systematically invisible to the phonology: they do not make syllables of their own, and they are not independently stressable. Hagstrom's (1997) of Mohawk also treats the metrically invisible vowels as unsyllabified. This explains not only their invisibility to stress and other aspects of metrical structure assignment, but also the fact that they do not open the preceding syllable for the purposes of stressed-syllable lengthening (*[ˈʌːkerʌʔ]). If something like Hall's or Hagstrom's proposals is right, then Mohawk stress/epenthesis interaction is actually transparent, given the right representations for the two kinds of epenthetic vowels (cf. §2.3.4.1).

Bye (2001: chapter 7) finds four distinct rule-sandwiching effects in his analysis of West Finnmark Saami (Finno-Ugric, Norway and Finland). It would take another book to summarize this material fully and fairly, so a single remark will have to suffice: the cases of sandwiching depend on Bye's assumption that consonant gradation remains a live phonological process in this language and has not been morphologized. Saami gradation is usually regarded as morphologized, however, because the conditioning environment for the alternation has been obliterated by subsequent sound changes (Gordon 1996, McRobbie 1999). A purely phonological treatment of gradation therefore requires an extensive apparatus of 'ghost consonants' whose sole function is to trigger grade alternations. Indeed, Bye goes so far as to propose that '[a]ll "morphological conditioning" is reducible to the triggering and blocking effects of covert ("ghost") phonological elements' (Bye 2001: 21) and that 'learners must posit a covert functional phonological basis for any phonological alternation with only an overt morphological or syntactic trigger'.

As I noted in §2.2.3, the Natural Generative Phonologists and others have proposed that all opaque alternations are morphologized (Green 2004, Hooper [Bybee] 1976, 1979, Mielke, Hume, and Armstrong 2003, Sanders 2002, 2003, Vennemann 1974). Bye adopts a diametrically opposed position: no alternations, no matter how opaque, are ever morphologized. In my view, the right way to proceed is to focus on alternations that are clearly not morphologized and ask whether they can be opaque. That is the approach taken in §2.2.3, and it is the consistent strategy throughout the case studies in §4. When we look at evidence meeting these criteria, we find that phonological opacity really exists but that sandwiching effects probably do not.

3.5.2   Opacity as a result of allophonic alternations

One of OT's basic premises is *richness of the base* (ROTB), the thesis that there are no language-particular restrictions on inputs (see McCarthy 2002b: 70, 178 and references cited there, Prince and Smolensky 2004: 225). ROTB follows from the thesis that all systematic differences between languages are to be accounted for with differences in constraint ranking. Markedness constraints restrict outputs, but they say nothing about inputs. Hence, restrictions on inputs have no natural place in an OT system.

ROTB has obvious implications for the analysis of contrast: contrast and its absence must be accounted for in the grammar, without any assistance from restrictions on the lexicon (Kirchner 1997). For example, suppose that a language has predictable nasalization in vowels: vowels are nasal after nasal consonants and oral otherwise. Since nasalization is predictable in vowels, it is noncontrastive — there are no minimal pairs differing only in vowel nasality. A standard generative phonological analysis deals with this lack of contrast by restrictions on the lexicon, such as morpheme structure constraints, lexical redundancy rules, or underspecification. In OT, however, ROTB requires that the grammar alone do the job. This means that the grammar must enforce two types of unfaithful mappings, one that eliminates underlying oral vowels after nasal consonants and one that eliminates underlying nasal vowels in all other contexts. Suppose that nonconforming vowels are brought into line by changing their value for the feature [nasal]. Then the ranking $[{}^*NV_{[oral]} \gg {}^*V_{[nasal]} \gg \text{ID(nasal)}]$ has the desired effect (McCarthy and Prince 1995, 1999): /ba/ and /bã/ both map most harmonically to [ba], thereby satisfying ${}^*V_{[nasal]}$; and /ma/ and /mã/ map most harmonically to [mã], thereby satisfying top-ranked ${}^*NV_{[oral]}$.

As this example suggests, allophony can lead to indeterminacy in the underlying representation of noncontrastive features. Ito and Mester (2001: 280–281, 2003b) show that this indeterminacy has potentially problematic implications for faithfulness-based theories of opacity, such as sympathy. One of their examples, the interaction between nasalization of voiced velar stops and rendaku voicing in Japanese, nicely illustrates the point.

First, some background. In Tokyo Japanese, the voiced velar stop and its nasal counterpart are in complementary distribution, leading to alternations between an oral stop initially ([go] 'the game of go') and a nasal medially ([oki-ŋo] 'handicap go'). A morphophonological process known as *rendaku* voices an obstruent when it is initial in the second member of a compound: /maki-susi/ → [maki-zuʃi] 'rolled sushi'. There is a dissimilatory restriction on rendaku: it is blocked when the second member of the compound already contains a voiced obstruent, as in /mori-soba/ → [mori-soba] 'soba serving', *[mori-zoba].

Nasalization of /g/ and rendaku interact opaquely. In a rule-based derivation like (3-61), rendaku must apply before /g/-nasalization, since underlying /g/s that surface as [ŋ]s behave like other voiced obstruents in blocking rendaku. This is a case of counterfeeding order. If these rules were applied in the opposite order, then /g/-nasalization would feed rendaku: *[saka-doŋe]. The reason why /g/-nasalization would otherwise feed rendaku is that only voiced *obstruents* are involved in dissimilatory blocking of rendaku; a sonorant consonant in the second member of the compound does not block rendaku: /inu-sini/ → [inu-ʒini] 'useless death'.

(3-61) Interaction of rendaku with /g/-nasalization

Underlying	/saka-toge/
Rendaku	*blocked*
/g/-nasalization	saka-toŋe
Surface	[saka-toŋe] 'reverse thorn'

A rule-based analysis like (3-61) requires another, often tacit assumption: the language has a constraint that excludes /ŋ/ from underlying representations, thereby ensuring that all surface [ŋ]s are derived from underlying /g/s. This lexical constraint is necessary because rendaku never affects stems that contain a medial [ŋ], so all medial [ŋ]s must be derived from /g/s. Without such a restriction, there could be a stem /toŋe/ that does undergo rendaku: /saka-toŋe/ → *[saka-**d**oŋe]. Such behavior is not observed.

ROTB forbids restrictions on underlying representations, leading Ito and Mester to propose a Stratal OT analysis that uses an early stratum to approximate the effect of such a restriction. The unrestricted inputs to the first stratum include both /g/ and /ŋ/ in both initial and medial positions, but the phonology of the first stratum wipes out this potential distinction, mapping /ŋ/ to [g] in all contexts: /saka-to**g**e/, /saka-to**ŋ**e/ → [saka-to**g**e]. The output of the first stratum is the input to the second stratum, which nasalizes medial [g]s: [saka-to**ŋ**e]. In forms with input medial /ŋ/s, the result is a Duke-of-York derivation (§2.2.3, §2.3.2, §3.2.3): /saka-toŋe/ →$_{\text{stratum-1}}$ [saka-to**g**e] →$_{\text{stratum-2}}$ [saka-to**ŋ**e]. Rendaku is part of the grammar of the first stratum, where it interacts transparently with denasalization of /ŋ/ to [g]. In other words, there is no rendaku in /saka-toŋe/ →$_{\text{stratum-1}}$ [saka-**t**oge] because [toge] contains a voiced obstruent.

OT-CC has no difficulty with this example when the input is /saka-toge/. Suppose, following Ito and Mester (1986), that rendaku is the realization of a floating feature morpheme [+voice]. Rendaku is therefore compelled by a constraint like Max-Subseg (Zoll 1998), which requires floating features to dock onto segments, and rendaku is blocked by a higher-ranking constraint that prohibits the cooccurrence of two voiced obstruents in a stem. The only harmonically improving chains from /saka-toge/ are opaque <sa.ka.to.ge, sa.ka.to.ŋe> and transparent *<sa.ka.to.ge, sa.ka.to.ŋe, sa.ka.do.ŋe>. The opaque chain is favored over the transparent one if Prec(Id(voice), Id(nasal)) dominates Max-Subseg, as shown in (3-62). (To avoid cluttering this tableau, I have not shown the underlying floating [+voice] feature.)

(3-62) PREC(ID(voice), ID(nasal)) >> MAX-SUBSEG

/saka-toge/	PREC(ID(voice), ID(nasal))	MAX-SUBSEG
→ <sa.ka.to.ge, sa.ka.to.ŋe>	1	1
<sa.ka.to.ge, sa.ka.to.ŋe, sa.ka.do.ŋe>	W 2	L

If the input is /saka-toŋe/, however, there would appear to be no way of ruling out the chain <sakatoŋe, sakadoŋe>, which satisfies all of the high-ranking constraints and is completely transparent. The OT-CC analysis would seem to predict a nonexistent contrast between surface [ŋ]s that are incompatible with rendaku, because they are derived from /g/, and surface [ŋ]s that are compatible with rendaku, because they are derived from /ŋ/. As I noted previously, Japanese has no such contrast. Ito and Mester refer to this situation as 'allophonic masking': an allophonic process (here, /g/-nasalization) renders another process (here, rendaku) opaque. The input indeterminacy that goes with allophony under ROTB is likewise problematic for earlier faithfulness-based approaches to opacity like sympathy (§2.3.4.3) or turbidity (§2.3.4.1).

This problem would be solved if learners of Japanese were somehow forced to the conclusion that all surface [ŋ]s are derived from underlying /g/s. A learning algorithm with just that effect is proposed in McCarthy (2005b). Briefly and informally, the algorithm requires learners to attempt to generalize from alternations to nonalternating forms. A learner who has concluded from alternations like [go] ~ [oki-ŋo] that *some* [ŋ]s are derived from /g/s is obliged to test the hypothesis that *all* [ŋ]s are derived from /g/s. (This is referred to as 'taking a free ride' — the [ŋ]s that happen never to alternate with [g]s take a free ride on the independently motivated /g/ → [ŋ] mapping.) If a grammar can be found under this assumption, then the learner restructures underlying representations accordingly. Hence, a learner equipped with this algorithm concludes that no morphemes contain underlying /ŋ/ — not because there is a restriction on inputs, but because of how the learning algorithm works. This suggests a general solution to the problem of allophonic masking, coming from the theory of learning rather than from phonological theory proper. [40]

Before leaving this topic, it is worth noting that the learning problem addressed here is not some peculiar artifact of OT-CC and kindred theories of opacity. In a Stratal OT analysis like Ito and Mester's, it is equally necessary to explain how learners discover the constraint hierarchy of the earlier stratum, where all /ŋ/s become [g]s. *Pace* Bermúdez-Otero (2004), there are no known effective, worked-out learning algorithms for constraint ranking in nonsurface strata.

3.5.3 Faithfulness and PREC constraints in chain shifts

Chain shifts are a particular kind of counterfeeding opacity. In a chain shift, input segment /A/ becomes output [B] and input /B/ becomes output [C] in identical or overlapping environments. As we saw in §2.3.3, it is possible to analyze chain shifts within the limitations of classic OT, if the theory of faithfulness is rich enough. The example cited there comes from Bedouin Arabic. The vowel /a/ reduces to [i] but does not delete in /dafaʕ/ → [di.faʕ] 'he pushed', whereas the vowel /i/ deletes in /difiʔ/ → [dfiʔ] 'he was pushed'. Tableau (2-18) showed how a constraint MAX-A, which forbids deleting underlying low vowels, can be used to rule out the unwanted /dafaʕ/ → *[dfaʕ] mapping.

PREC constraints and constraints like MAX-A offer competing explanations for counterfeeding opacity. Are both necessary? This section develops an answer to that question.

PREC constraints are needed to analyze all of the cases of counterfeeding opacity that are not chain shifts. In §2.3.3 and §2.3.4.1, I argued that trying to analyze all types of counterfeeding opacity with faithfulness constraints leads to an overly rich theory of faithfulness and an insufficiently restrictive theory of opacity. For instance, to get the counterfeeding interaction in /gabr/ → [ga.bur] would require a faithfulness constraint that specifically prohibits raising a vowel if there is epenthesis after the immediately following consonant. On this rather bizarre view, the fact that the epenthetic vowel opens the syllable and thereby creates the context for raising is entirely accidental; indeed, there could just as well be a faithfulness constraint that forbids raising a vowel in an open syllable when another vowel is epenthesized to its left rather its right. Real cases of counterfeeding opacity never work like that. Rather, processes interact in a nonarbitrary way, and that is why PREC constraints are needed.

There is one type of chain shift, however, that cannot be handled with PREC constraints under the assumptions about faithfulness adopted here. This is the zero-terminating chain shift /A/ → [B], /B/ → Ø. The short explanation for why this is problematic is that the /A/ → [B] mapping violates an IDENT constraint while the /B/ → Ø mapping and the forbidden /A/ → Ø mappings both violate MAX but not IDENT. The long explanation follows.

Recall how PREC constraints usually work in counterfeeding opacity. In the analysis of /gabr/ → [ga.bur], for example, the constraint PREC(ID(low), DEP) rules out the sequence of LUMs in the transparent chain *<gab.r, ga.bur, gi.bur>, and the gradualness criterion invalidates the fell swoop **<gab.r, gi.bur>. The analysis of /dafaʕ/ → [di.faʕ] is crucially different, however. The chain *<dafaʕ, dfaʕ> is perfectly valid under gradualness, since only a single MAX-violating LUM is involved. The problem is that no workable PREC constraint will favor the intended winner <dafaʕ, difaʕ> over its transparent competitor *<dafaʕ, dfaʕ> without also disfavoring legitimate cases of syncope.

This problem arises consistently and exclusively with zero-terminating chain shifts. Its source is the vacuous-satisfaction property of IDENT constraints (McCarthy and Prince 1995, 1999): IDENT(F) forbids corresponding segments in input and output to differ in their value of F. IDENT(F) is not violated by input segments that have no output correspondent. That is why the chain <dafaʕ, dfaʕ> is valid while **<dafaʕ, difaʕ, dfaʕ> is not.

Another zero-terminating chain shift can be found in Cairene Arabic. In Cairene, high vowels in certain contexts are elided, but long high vowels resist elision in the same contexts. This resistance extends even to surface short high vowels that are derived from underlying long vowels by a process of unstressed syllable shortening: /ji-ʃiːl-uː-naː/ → [jiʃiˈluːna], *[jiʃˈluːna] 'they take us'. The chain shift is therefore /Vː/ → [V] and [V] → Ø in certain overlapping contexts.

Zero-terminating chain shifts like the ones in Bedouin and Cairene Arabic cannot be analyzed with PREC constraints, but they can be analyzed with positional faithfulness to prominent elements. (See Jesney (2005) for a similar, independently-developed proposal about chain shifts in language acquisition.) The Bedouin Arabic and Cairene Arabic chain shifts respectively preserve underlying low vowels and long vowels from deletion. Low vowels and long vowels are associated with greater prominence than their nonlow or short counterparts — for example, both low vowels and long vowels have greater duration and amplitude, and both are known to attract stress (de Lacy 2002, Gordon 1999, Kenstowicz 1996b, Lehiste 1970). This is consistent with the central tenet of the theory of positional faithfulness: there are constraints requiring greater faithfulness to more prominent elements (Beckman 1998, Casali 1997, Smith 2002 and others). One such constraint is MAX-Vː, which guards underlying long vowels from deletion (Gouskova 2003, McCarthy 2005a: 18). Another is MAX-A, which offers the same protection to underlying low vowels. Ranked above the markedness constraint that encourages deletion of high vowels, MAX-A correctly favors [difaʕ] over [dfaʕ] from /dafaʕ/.

The theory of positional faithfulness provides the conceptual framework for MAX-A, but it should be noted that this constraint is also well motivated on typological grounds. There is a body of typological work showing the need for MAX constraints that are differentiated by vowel height (Davis and Zawaydeh 1997, Howe and Pulleyblank 2004, Kaneko and Kawahara 2002, Pulleyblank

1998, Tranel 1999), though there is also a typological argument against this move (Gouskova 2003: 240–245). The independent typological support for MAX-A and the connection with positional faithfulness sharply distinguish it from the typologically dubious constraints required in a full faithfulness-based theory of counterfeeding opacity (see §2.3.4.1). For this reason, MAX-A, MAX-V:, and their kin plausibly supplement but do not supplant PREC. They are not helpful with the range of opaque interactions subsumed by PREC, but they do account for zero-terminating chain shifts, which stymie PREC. [41]

This approach to zero-terminating chain shifts makes a general typological prediction. In any chain shift of the form /A/ → [B] and /B/ → Ø, /A/ must be prominent in a way that is consistent with the general theory of positional faithfulness and /B/ must be less prominent than /A/ on the same dimension of prominence. This prediction follows because the constraint like MAX-A or MAX-V: that protects /A/ from deletion must not protect /B/. Therefore, /B/ must have less or none of whatever it is that causes /A/ to count as prominent for the theory of positional faithfulness. Many imaginable zero-terminating chain shifts fail to meet this standard, and so the range of possible zero-terminating chain shifts is limited. I know of no counterexamples to this typological prediction. [42]

A possible conceptual objection to prominence-based faithfulness in the context of OT-CC is that it seems to introduce an additional mechanism for dealing with opacity, in addition to PREC constraints.. There are two responses to this. First, it does not 'introduce' anything, since the evidence for greater faithfulness to prominent elements in Beckman's work and elsewhere is independent of opacity. In other words, MAX-A, MAX-V:, and the like are expected to exist under the independently motivated tenets of the theory of positional faithfulness. Second, Ito and Mester (2003c) rightly emphasize that OT need not contain some single mechanism that is an exact match with the opacity phenomenon; the constructs of linguistic theory are typically not in a one-to-one relationship with a pretheoretic classification of phenomena. Indeed, Kiparsky's (1973) original definition of opacity includes a clause ((c) in (2-6)) that classifies all neutralization processes as opaque, but the recent literature on opacity universally disregards neutralization since it offers no challenge to classic OT.

One last comment about MAX-A and MAX-V:. These constraints protect *underlying* low and long vowels from deletion, even when they are raised or shortened in surface forms. This behavior is consistent with and indeed expected under the proposal I made in §3.2.4.1: positional faithfulness constraints refer to the structural conditions obtaining in the fully faithful chain-initial form, even when these conditions differ in the ultimate output.

3.6   Comparison with other theories

Although OT-CC combines properties of several previous approaches to opacity, including rule ordering, it also differs significantly from each of them. This section structures the comparison around the main features of OT-CC: harmonic improvement (§3.6.1), gradualness (§3.6.2), and PREC constraints (§3.6.3). It complements the discussion in §2.2.3 (rule ordering) and §2.3.4 (previous theories of opacity in OT), and it expands on some of the remarks in §3.2.3 (precursors to candidate chains).

3.6.1   Harmonic improvement

In a valid candidate chain, successive forms must improve harmonically relative to the language's constraint hierarchy. When combined with the gradualness requirement on chains, the harmonic improvement requirement has many worthwhile consequences: it supports an analysis of opacity based on PREC constraints (the main goal, of course); it limits the size of the candidate set (§3.2.2); and it restricts classic OT's capacity for global optimization (§3.2.4.3).

Any classic OT grammar has an intrinsic harmonic improvement property (§2.3.1): the most harmonic candidate must be either (i) identical to the fully faithful candidate or (ii) less marked than the fully faithful candidate. Taking this a step further, one can say that *any* candidate that is more harmonic than the fully faithful candidate must be less marked than it. In OT-CC, the first form in any chain is fully faithful, and the second link in the chain is any form that is more harmonic than the first form and also satisfies the gradualness requirement. In general, for $[f_{i+1}]$ to be a valid successor to $[f_i]$ in the chain <... f_i, f_{i+1} ...>, it is necessary (but not sufficient) that the winner of a classic OT evaluation of the two-member candidate set $\{f_i, f_{i+1}\}$ be $[f_{i+1}]$.

Harmonic improvement distinguishes OT-CC from traditional rule ordering and its Stratal OT counterpart. Each rule in a grammar is entirely *sui generis*; the presence of a rule A→B/C__D says nothing whatsoever about what other rules the same grammar may contain, including even B→A/C__D (see §2.2.3, §2.3.2, and §3.2.3 on Duke-of-York derivations). Phonological rules state highly temporary generalizations, generalizations that can evaporate at the next step in the derivation. Grammars in rule-based phonology therefore lack *coherence*, in the sense that there are no connections among the various processes that coexist in a language. In theory, at least, a random sampling of rules from half a dozen different languages should also be a possible language. This is surely untrue, as was recognized quite early, particularly in the literature on conspiracies (Kisseberth 1970, also see the discussion in McCarthy 2002b: 53–55, 95–101).

It is the basis of one of OT's main critiques of rule-based phonology: a grammar in rule-based phonology is viewed as 'a more-or-less arbitrary assortment of formal rules', perhaps subject to naturalness requirements that are outside the theory of grammar (Prince and Smolensky 2004: 234).

Stratal OT shares this property of rule-based phonology, albeit in a milder form. There are no known constraints on how much the rankings of strata can differ within a single language (see §2.3.4.2), so each stratum can be literally any permutation of CON. Although the grammars of the individual strata are internally coherent in the same way that any classic OT grammar is, the phonological system of the language as a whole is noncoherent. This problem of system-level noncoherence is somewhat less severe than in rule-based phonology for two reasons. First, all strata contain the same constraints. Thus, the strata can only differ by as much as two OT grammars can differ, and this is not quite as unconstrained as 'a more-or-less arbitrary assortment of formal rules'. Second, any morphemes present at stratum n are subject to the phonology of that stratum and all subsequent strata. This means that roots undergo the phonology of all strata, and all morphemes eventually pass through the postlexical stratum. It should be noted, however, that some versions of Stratal OT do not impose even this very mild requirement, asserting a principle of stratal 'economy' according to which only forms with morphemes added at stratum n pass through stratum n's phonology (Inkelas and Orgun 1995, Yu 2000: 122).

Analyses of opacity in Stratal OT rely crucially on the noncoherence of a language's phonological system. For example, Kiparsky's (2001) Stratal OT analysis of Yawelmani deploys pre-[?]# closed syllable shortening (see (3-58)) in the word-level stratum, leaving general closed syllable shortening until the postlexical stratum. The similarity between these two strata is entirely accidental, however; nothing in the theory guarantees that the postlexical stratum should continue and expand the process of closed syllable shortening that began in an earlier stratum. Postlexically, closed syllables with long vowels could just as well have been left as-is or dealt with by epenthesis or consonant deletion rather than shortening.

In §3.5.3, I discussed the relevance of richness of the base to the analysis of opacity. It is also relevant to evaluating Stratal OT. Stratal OT has inherited from rule-based Lexical Phonology the premise that morphology and phonology occur in parallel. This means that some morphemes are not present until later strata. When combined with ROTB, this premise makes an unlikely prediction. Suppose that stratum 1 has the grammar $[*x \gg \text{FAITH}(x)]$. Any xs present in the input to stratum 1 will be treated unfaithfully, so the output of stratum 1 will be devoid of xs. ROTB entails that morphemes added at stratum

2 may also contain xs. If the grammar of stratum 2 is [FAITH(x) >> *x], it follows that the output of stratum 2 may contain xs in the stratum 2 morphemes. In general, Stratal OT with richness of the base predicts that the phonemic inventory of morphemes added in later strata is a (possibly improper) superset of the phonemic inventory of morphemes added earlier.[43] To my knowledge, the extant literature on Stratal OT has not examined whether this proposition is correct. Informal observation suggests that it is not.

3.6.2   Gradualness

In OT-CC, the successive forms in a chain cannot be too different from one another. There is gradual divergence from the faithful form that initiates the chain. The notion of a localized unfaithful mapping (LUM) was introduced as a measure of maximum distance between a form and its successor.

The gradualness requirement on chains is a very rough approximation to the steps in a traditional phonological derivation. Because the *SPE* formalism for stating rules is so rich, there are few if any limitations on the differences between successive forms in a derivation. More restrictive theories of rules, such as Archangeli and Pulleyblank's (1994) parametric system or Prince's (1983) Move-x, put much stricter limits on how much of a difference between forms a single rule can make. The LUM is closer to Archangeli and Pulleyblank's conception than to *SPE*, though the LUM is defined in terms of GEN's operations and CON's faithfulness constraints rather than rule parameters.

We saw in §3.3.4 that gradualness is necessary for the analysis of counterfeeding opacity in OT-CC. Gradualness also impacts the analysis of mappings that involve multiple processes. If the underlying and surface representations differ by n LUMs, then there must be $n-1$ intermediate forms in the chain, since gradualness forbids conflating two LUMs into a single link of a chain. When the multiple processes interact opaquely, such as Yawelmani /cʔuːm-hin/ → [cʔomhun], then PREC constraints will enforce a particular ordering of the LUMs, as is the case with the winning candidate <cʔuːmhin, cʔuːmhun, cʔoːmhun, cʔomhun> in (3-55).

Several theories of opacity described in §2.3.4.3 have problems dealing with multiple opaque processes. Sympathy theory is the obvious example. The sympathetic candidate is the most harmonic candidate that obeys a designated faithfulness constraint. In simple cases of counterbleeding opacity, the sympathetic candidate is identical to the intermediate form of a derivation or chain. For example, in the analysis of Bedouin Arabic /ħaːkim-iːn/ → [ħaːkʲmiːn], the sympathetic candidate must obey MAX and otherwise be maximally harmonic, therefore *[ħaːkʲimiːn] (see (2-29)). This is, of course, the same as the intermediate stage of the serial derivation (2-5) or the intermediate form of the winning candidate chain (d) in (3-27). Since a language may have several opaque processes — Yawelmani and Bedouin Arabic are nearby exemplars — sympathy theory has to allow for more than one designated faithfulness constraint and more than one sympathetic candidate at a time. But this move allows for impossible opaque interactions, as Kiparsky (2001) has shown and as we saw in (2-31), repeated here as (3-63).

(3-63) An unwelcome result of sympathy (= (2-31))

/pam/	Dep-C$_{\text{Dep-V}}$ (sympathy)	Max-V$_{\text{Max-C}}$ (sympathy)	No-Coda	Dep-V (selector)	Max-C (selector)
→ paə				1	1
a. pam	W$_1$	W$_1$	W$_1$	L	L
b. pamə (sympathetic via Max-C)	W$_1$			1	L
c. pa (sympathetic via Dep-V)		W$_1$		L	1

The problem with (3-63) is that a single markedness constraint, No-Coda, induces two unfaithful mappings, deletion and epenthesis, when either one alone would be enough. No-Coda does this by way of the sympathy system, which favors an output that simultaneously resembles both of the ways of satisfying No-Coda. The unwanted winner [pa.ə] could be avoided in a particular language by ranking Onset above either of the sympathy constraints, but that misses the point: sympathy theory with multiple selector constraints predicts an unattested and even bizarre type of opacity.

OT-CC does not make this prediction. By the gradualness criterion, the mapping /pam/ → [pa.ə] must proceed by way of one of the following putative candidate chains: <pam, pa.mə, pa.ə> or <pam, pa, pa.ə>. Both are harmonically improving in their initial subchains if No-Coda dominates Dep-V and Max-C, as in (3-63). But the next step in each chain is not harmonically improving under this ranking. No-Coda cannot compel the gratuitous additional unfaithful mapping in OT-CC for the same reason that it cannot do so in classic OT: there is no way to improve in markedness performance on a markedness constraint that is already fully satisfied. In sum, there are no valid chains ending in [pa.ə], starting from /pam/ under the given ranking. The existence of Prec constraints does not affect this result, since Prec constraints cannot favor a candidate that does not exist.

There are broader lessons to be drawn from this example. Sympathy theory analyzes opacity as the *intersecting* effects of two or more grammars with slightly different constraint rankings. One of these grammars has the basic ranking motivated by the language's transparent phonology, and the other grammars have each promoted one of the selector faithfulness constraints to the top of the hierarchy. The sympathy constraints determine how the special selector grammars affect the output. Stratal OT analyzes opacity as the serially *cumulative* effects of several grammars with different constraint rankings. The between-stratum ranking differences are relatively slight in practice, though unlimited in theory. Faithfulness constraints determine which effects of earlier strata are accumulated and which are not. The problem with sympathy theory that (3-63) illustrates is not shared with Stratal OT, suggesting that cumulativity rather than intersection is the right way to view opacity. But Stratal OT's failure to restrict divergence among the constituent grammars of a language is a significant liability.

OT-CC analyzes opacity as an effect of a single grammar that is used in a special way. The grammar — that is, EVAL and a single ranking of CON — not only evaluates candidates but also affects their construction via the harmonic improvement requirement. Opacity occurs when PREC constraints require that the effects of certain unfaithful mappings be cumulative in the case of counterbleeding opacity or anticumulative in the case of counterfeeding opacity. Because OT-CC shares with Stratal OT a cumulativity requirement, like Stratal OT it cannot produce the strange hypertrophy of counterbleeding opacity in (3-63). But because OT-CC derives opacity from a single grammar, it does not share Stratal OT's fundamental typological problem of unrestricted divergence among the component grammars of a single phonological system.

3.6.3   PREC constraints

The constraint PREC(A, B) favors those candidate chains in which any LUM that violates B is preceded by a LUM that violates A, or at least not followed by one. In a case of counterbleeding opacity like Bedouin Arabic <haː.ki.miːn, haː.kʲi.miːn, haːkʲ.miːn> (3-29), a PREC constraint favors palatalization before deletion over deletion alone. In a case of counterfeeding opacity like Bedouin Arabic <gabr, ga.bur> (3-37), a PREC constraint disfavors raising after epenthesis.

Although PREC constraints can induce or prevent unfaithful mappings under the right conditions, their power is held in check by the harmonic improvement requirement on chains and by the ranking metaconstraint (3-24). Because valid chains must improve harmonically, the potential effects of PREC constraints are also limited by the grammar as a whole. No PREC constraint can induce the mapping /x/ → [y] if [y] is more marked than [x] in the language in question.

And because the metaconstraint requires B to be ranked higher than PREC(A, B), PREC(A, B) can never affect satisfaction of B, though it certainly can and does affect satisfaction of A.

This view of opacity harks back to the 1970's idea that transparent rule orderings are natural and need not be stated in the grammar, whereas opaque orderings are the effect of special conditions on rule application (see §2.2.4, §2.2.5, and §2.3.4.4 for discussion and references). For example, Donegan and Stampe (1979: 147, 156–158) attribute counterfeeding order to a learned 'constraint' that has the effect of '[s]uppressing the application of a process to the output of another'. On this view or that of Anderson (1974), among others, most orderings are automatic consequences of basic principles of rule interaction, and only certain orderings, typically the opaque ones, need special treatment. The resemblance to OT-CC is clear.

Stratal OT is another theory of opacity based on ordering, but its character is somewhat different from the theories of the 1970's or OT-CC. Stratal OT derives the ordering of unfaithful mappings from the ordering of the strata in which they occur. Thus, /ħaːkim-iːn/ → [ħaːkʲmiːn] requires that palatalization occur in an earlier stratum than deletion, and /gabr/ → [gabur] requires that raising not occur in the same stratum as epenthesis, or any later stratum. The implicit claim, then, is that any independent evidence for the stratum at which an unfaithful mapping occurs should correlate with the evidence from opacity. As we saw in §2.3.4.2, however, this claim is counterexemplified in the literature on rule-based Lexical Phonology generally and in Bedouin Arabic specifically. OT-CC has no strata and therefore makes no such claim. PREC constraints do no more than stipulate opaque interactions, as stratal membership sometimes does, but perhaps this stipulation is the best that can be done.

OT-CC, Stratal OT, and sympathy theory analyze opacity as the required or prohibited interaction of certain processes. Two other theories of opacity in OT, local constraint conjunction and contrast preservation, look at opacity in very different ways. Constraint conjunction forbids violating two faithfulness constraints in proximity to one another. Proximity is defined by the specified domain of conjunction, and any two faithfulness constraints can be so combined. For example, [ID(low)&DEP]$_{Adj-\sigma}$ accounts for the counterfeeding result in /gabr/ → [gabur] (see (2-20)), blocking *[gɨbur] because the adjacent syllables contain violations of each of these constraints. Contrast preservation holds that opacity is a side effect of a neutralization process, avoiding merger by transposing the contrast to elsewhere in the form. For example, the presence of a low vowel in an open syllable in [ga.bur] is an indication of the following vowel's epenthetic status, avoiding merger with (hypothetical) underlying /gabur/. Likewise, the presence of a palatalized velar in [ħaːkʲmiːn] marks the omission of an underlying front vowel, avoiding merger of underlying /haːkimiːn/ with (also hypothetical) underlying /haːkmiːn/.

In §2.3.4.1 and §2.3.4.4, I argued that constraint conjunction and contrast preservation are not based on process interaction, to their detriment. By conjoining the wrong constraints or using the wrong domain, it is possible to produce blocking effects that are nothing like real counterfeeding opacity and are probably impossible. Attested cases of counterfeeding opacity can be described as 'process A cannot feed process B'. This is a very different proposition from the unattested pattern 'process A cannot apply in close proximity to process B', which constraint conjunction predicts. Contrast preservation also predicts impossible opaque interactions since it currently offers an insufficiently restrictive theory of where and how contrasts can be preserved. For example, in the case of /haːkim-iːn/ → [haːkʲmiːn], contrast preservation cannot relate the contrast-preserving palatalized velar to the nearness of the deleted vowel, to its frontness, or to the independent existence of a palatalization process in the language (though see Łubowicz (2003) for some related proposals that address these problems). Indeed, contrasts could in principle be preserved by outright markedness reversals similar to those that are produced by antifaithfulness constraints (cf. Alderete 2001a, 2001b).

OT-CC is an *interactional* theory of opacity, and the treatment of convergent chains is one of the principal reasons why it is interactional. (Convergence was defined in §3.3.1 and illustrated in §3.3.3.) Chains are convergent if they have the same output and their LUMSeqs are permutations of one another. Differences in LUM ordering between convergent chains are irrelevant and cannot affect the output. When all of the chains convergent on a particular output have been identified and intersected, the resulting LUMSeq (called the rLUMSeq) contains all and only those orderings that are crucial. Prec constraints attend only to these crucial orderings, ignoring the rest.

By discarding all but the crucial orders, chain convergence zeroes in on the situations of process interaction, since only interacting processes are relevant to opacity. To analyze the opaque interaction of palatalization and deletion in /kætaki/ → [kʲætakʲ], it is necessary to ignore the noninteracting palatalization of the first /k/. Chain convergence has that effect, as we saw in (3-34): the result is the same regardless of whether the LUM associated with palatalization of the first /k/ is ordered before or after the LUM associated with deletion of the final /i/, so this ordering information must be and is hidden from the Prec constraint. Without convergence, the opaque output [kʲætakʲ] would be harmonically bounded by *[kʲætak], which has only transparent palatalization. The convergent chains in (3-32) reveal what is wrong with *[kʲætak]: it substitutes pseudo-interaction, in the form of noncrucial LUM orderings, for authentic interaction, which is the only kind of interaction that survives chain convergence.

It is important to realize that OT-CC says nothing whatsoever about locality in the analysis of /kætaki/ → [kʲætakʲ] or similar cases. The LUM ordering of palatalization of the first /k/ and deletion of the final /i/ is filtered out by chain convergence because this order does not affect the output, *tout court*. There is no mention of another /k/ being closer to the deleted /i/ or of palatalization being limited to adjacent segments. Although both of these statements are certainly true, they are not and should not be part of the theory of opacity. This aspect of OT-CC stands in sharp contrast with, and is arguably superior to, the treatment of locality and of interaction in approaches like constraint conjunction and contrast preservation.

Notes

1   See Moreton (2003) on the existence of a fully faithful parse for every input and McCarthy (2002a, 2003a) on the role of this parse in comparative markedness theory.
2   'Basic faithfulness constraint' is a term of art. See §3.2.4.2 for the definition.
3   See Wilson (2003, 2004), which also uses harmonic evaluation in candidate construction.
4   I am indebted to Michael Becker for discussion of this topic.
5   This result does not change even if CON includes antifaithfulness constraints in the sense of Alderete (2001a, 2001b). The antifaithfulness constraint ¬DEP is satisfied if there is just one DEP violation in the input-output mapping. Therefore, it can justify only the very first step in the chain <pa, pa.ə, pa.ə.ə, pa.ə.ə.ə, …>.
6   I am grateful to Bruce Tesar for discussion of this issue.
7   I am grateful to Marc van Oostendorp for bringing this reference to my attention.
8   For a very different approach to the Beckman-Noyer problem that relies on revising OT-CC's gradualness requirement, see McCarthy (2006).
9   I am grateful to Joe Pater for pointing out this consequence of assuming that positional faithfulness refers to the chain-initial faithful syllabification.
10   On syllabicity contrasts and faithfulness, see Rosenthall (1994: 203ff.).
11   Constraints A and B are in a stringency relationship if every violation of A is also a violation of B, and not vice-versa. B is said to be more stringent because it is more severe in its assessments than A is.
12   I am grateful to Nicole Nelson for clarifying the role of I-CONTIG in cases like this.
13   I am indebted to Nicole Nelson for pointing this out.
14   The putative chain **<tʰo, tʰot, tʰo.ta> is invalid because its first step is not harmonically improving. Codas are nonmoraic in Axininca Campa and are limited to nasals in homorganic clusters, so [tʰot] does not satisfy FTBIN.

15   Parentheses delimit metrical feet. Where a parenthesis or stress mark coincides with a syllable boundary, I omit the period/full stop syllable boundary annotation, since it is superfluous in that situation. When syllabification is obvious or irrelevant or space is tight, I may also omit these annotations to save space or avoid visual distractions.

16   Hume (2001: 7): 'all regular cases of synchronic metathesis involve adjacent segments'.

17   These observations about metathesis in OT-CC are relevant to Horwood's (2002, 2004) proposal that infixation is reducible to metathesis. In his view, infixation in Tagalog /um-sulat/ → [sumulat] 'to write (actor focus)' is the result of a LINEARITY-violating transposition. If each transposition of a pair of adjacent segments is a LUM, as I have assumed, then this mapping would have to be obtained with a chain like <um.su.lat, us.mu.lat, su.mu.lat>. There is nothing in Tagalog phonology to support the requirement that this putative chain be harmonically improving in its initial subchain. Horwood's proposal would be a better fit to OT-CC if the entire morpheme /-um-/ could be shifted in a single LUM. Something like this may be necessary anyway to explain why infix morphemes normally remain contiguous even when the roots that they are infixed into do not.

18   For example, vowel coalescence in Attic Greek affects sequences of nonhigh vowels, preserving [+round] and [–ATR] from one of them (de Haas 1988, de Lacy 2002: 410ff., Sommerstein 1973): /tiːma-o-men/ → [tiːmoːmen] 'we honor'; /mistʰ-o-ɛː-te/ → [mistʰoːte] 'you (pl.) would hire out'. The assimilation + deletion approach therefore requires opaque assimilation of [+round] and [–ATR], both of which are observed to assimilate transparently in other languages. De Lacy (2002: 424) doubts the assimilation + deletion analysis because neither feature assimilates when one of the vowels is high (e.g., [poi.ɔː] 'I make', *[pou.ɔː]) — exactly the situation where deletion does not happen either. This argument does not go through, however, because the failure of assimilation when one vowel is high can be explained with independently motivated constraints. The feature value [+round] does not assimilate between high and nonhigh vowels because assimilation of this feature is often limited to vowels of the same height class. (Yawelmani is an example — see §2.3.4.3.) Therefore, the necessary restriction of [+round] assimilation to nonhigh vowels makes sense typologically. And assimilation of [–ATR] is limited to nonhigh vowels for the best of reasons: the language has no [–ATR] high vowels, which means there is an undominated markedness constraint against them.

19   Although the discussion in the text retains Walker's autosegmental perspective on Esimbi, the assimilatory approach to flop does not need to be couched in autosegmental terms.

20   Michael Becker and Fetiye Karabay raise an interesting question: how can the gradualness and harmonic improvement requirements accommodate reduplication? Must segments be copied one at a time, and if so how do we ensure monotonic harmonic improvement? The answer, somewhat surprisingly, is that reduplicative copying is not an unfaithful mapping, so it is not affected by the gradualness requirement. In the McCarthy and Prince (1995, 1999) theory of

reduplication, the exponence of the reduplicative morpheme RED is outside the scope of the input-output correspondence relation and therefore does not violate DEP_{IO} or any other input-output faithfulness constraint. If, on the contrary, DEP_{IO} were violated by reduplication, then in general any markedness constraint that dominates MAX_{BR} must also dominate DEP_{IO}, with unwelcome consequences for emergence of the unmarked (McCarthy and Prince 1994).

21 The phrase 'EVAL proper' refers to the pass through EVAL that is initiated by the single-headed arrow from GEN in the flowchart (3-5). EVAL proper is the point where completed candidate chains are compared and the optimal one is determined.

22 A and B are not limited to *basic* faithfulness constraints (cf. §3.2.4.2). That is, PREC can mention any faithfulness constraint in CON.

23 I am grateful to Michael Becker, Rachel Walker, and Matt Wolf for discussion of this point.

24 Abbreviations: *m.* masculine; *f.* feminine; *sg.* singular; *pl.* plural.

25 When the LUMSeq is empty < > or contains only a single LUM <A>, then the rLUMSeq is the empty set Ø, because there are no non-reflexive orderings in the LUMSeq.

26 In this tableau and others that evaluate chains, I label rows with the same letters (a), (b), etc. that are used to label the chains and their (r)LUMSeqs in a list like (3-27) or (3-28).

27 I am grateful to Colin Wilson for raising these issues and to him and Jason Riggle for related discussion.

28 In the notation used for LUMs, the locus of epenthesis can be relativized to the index of the preceding input segment or juncture.

29 I assume that a chain beginning <ga.br̩, ...>, with syllabic [r], is invalid because making a consonant syllabic is an unfaithful mapping (see §3.2.4.2).

30 Yawelmani was previously mentioned in §2.3.4.3, and references to the extensive literature on this language can be found there.

31 According to Blevins (2004), Yokuts does not have a general process of long-vowel lowering. In my view, the evidence against lowering is unconvincing, at least for the Yawelmani dialect. Lowering does not affect long high vowels derived by deletion and compensatory lengthing from /iʔCV/ and /uʔCV/, but this is simply an indication that lowering is itself opaque. There are also two registers where long high vowels are permitted: the *-wiyi* verbs, which are described as 'highly idiomatic and informal. They are primarily the property of children in everyday speech.' (Newman 1944: 56); and vowels that are 'rhetorically lengthened to express a retarded activity' (ibid., p. 57).

32 Color is a feature class in the sense of Padgett (1995). The Color class node in feature geometry was proposed by Odden (1991).

33 Tableaux (3-51), (3-52), and (3-53) omit the PREC constraints because, as was noted at the end of §3.3.2, PREC constraints are inherently irrelevant to determining chain validity.

34 The 'loser' chains in (3-51), (3-52), and (3-53) are not necessarily invalid; in fact, they are typically left-aligned subchains of the 'winner' chains, and so by downward entailment (§3.2.2) they must be valid.

35   I am grateful to Joe Pater and Anne-Michelle Tessier for discussion of learning-related matters.

36   There are there are $n*(n-1)$ logically possible PREC constraints because, for every constraint X, there is a logically possible constraint PREC(X, Y), where Y is any constraint other than X.

37   On learning by constraint demotion, see Tesar and Smolensky (1998, 2000).

38   The Mizrahi dialect is derived from the liturgical Hebrew of Jews in Arabic-speaking countries.

39   I am grateful to Michael Becker for pointing out the problems with (3-59).

40   An issue arises in examples like [ori-ŋami] 'paper folding' from /ori-kami/, where /k/ becomes [ŋ] via transparent interaction of rendaku and nasalization. By (3-24), ID(nasal) dominates PREC(ID(voice), ID(nasal)), and by (3-62), PREC(ID(voice), ID(nasal)) dominates MAX-SUBSEG. By transitivity of domination, then, IDENT(nasal) dominates MAX-SUBSEG. This ranking wrongly favors *[orikami], which violates only lower-ranking MAX-SUBSEG, over [oriŋami], which (supposedly) violates higher-ranking IDENT(nasal).

 In reality, there is no problem here because the /k/ → [ŋ] mapping does not actually violate IDENT(nasal). Because voiceless stops are universally incompatible with nasalization (cf. voiced stops in Piggott's (1992) Type B languages), they do not bear the feature [nasal]. The situation is analogous to the relationship between the feature [distributed] and coronality: noncoronals literally have no value for this feature (McCarthy 1988). If we assume, with Orgun (1996a), that IDENT(F) is violated only by corresponding segments that have *distinct* values for [F], then the mapping /k/ → [ŋ] indeed does not violate IDENT(nasal). (That this mapping is accomplished in a candidate chain with [g] as an intermediate stage is irrelevant, since faithfulness in chains is always determined relative to the input, not to any intermediate step (§3.2.1).)

41   There is a way of analyzing zero-terminating chain shifts with PREC constraints, but it requires a somewhat different theory of faithfulness than the one I have been assuming. It has been proposed that faithfulness to the properties of segments is the responsibility of MAX-*feature* constraints rather than IDENT constraints (Causley 1997, Lamontagne and Rice 1995, Lombardi 1998, 2001, McCarthy and Prince 1995, Walker 1997, 2001, Zoll 1998). The idea is that /a/ has more featural content than /i/, so deleting /a/ violates more MAX-*feature* constraints than deleting /i/ does. (This is reminiscent of some particle-based theories of segmental representation (e.g., Humbert 1995: 55, van der Hulst 1989: 281).) On this view, **<da.faʕ, d.faʕ> would not be a valid chain because it has violated more than one MAX-*feature* constraint in the space of a single LUM. A PREC constraint can then be invoked to favor counterfeeding <da.faʕ, di.faʕ> over the feeding chain *<da.faʕ, di.faʕ, d.faʕ>. See McCarthy (2007b) for related discussion.

42   The absence of such counterexamples would be more impressive if zero-terminating chain-shifts were more common. The Bedouin Arabic case is the only solid example of a zero-terminating chain shift that can be found in an unpublished collection of chain shifts compiled by Elliott Moreton (see Moreton and Smolensky 2002 for a less complete listing). The list includes two other

examples, but neither is very convincing. One of them is part of the Irish consonant mutation system, so it is undoubtedly morphological. The other, which is reported for Mwera (Bantu, Tanzania), involves voicing of voiceless obstruents after a nasal and deletion of a voiced obstruent in the same position (Kenstowicz and Kisseberth 1977: 157): /mp/ → [mb], /mb/ → [m]. From the description and examples in the original source, Harries (1950: 11–13, 20ff., 89–91), it appears that only certain nasal prefixes trigger these alternations, and even with these prefixes the result is sometimes inconsistent, so this chain shift may also be morphologized. Harries's grammar is little more than a sketch, so it is impossible to be more precise about what is going on, but on the whole this example is not compelling.

43 See Fitzgerald (2002: 267–268) on the similar prediction made by the version of Stratal OT that incorporates stratal economy.

4 Two Case Studies

4.1 Goals of this chapter

OT-CC offers some results that have little or nothing to do with phonological opacity (see especially §3.2.2, §3.2.4.3, and McCarthy (2007a, 2007b)), but it ultimately stands or falls on whether it provides a sufficient and a sufficiently restrictive theory of opacity. The previous chapter addressed questions of restrictiveness; this chapter contributes to demonstrating the sufficiency of OT-CC.

Obviously, it is not practical to attempt to reanalyze in OT-CC terms the vast range of opaque interactions in the phonological literature. In fact, this would not even be a good idea, since many of those interactions are embedded in dubiously phonological analyses of morphologized or lexicalized phenomena. Rather, the goal of this chapter is to present two extended case studies of phenomena in languages that have abundant opaque interactions. These case studies involve opaque interactions of processes whose phonological status is not in doubt — most are, as I note below, exceptionless, productive, and applicable in borrowed words, external sandhi, or language games.

Since the two case studies involve varieties of Arabic, a skeptic might ask whether we are looking here at two examples of the same thing and not two independent demonstrations of OT-CC at work. The answer is that these two Arabic 'dialects', Levantine and Arabian Bedouin, are actually distinct languages, at least as different as French and Spanish. The so-called sedentary dialects (*Ansässigendialekte*), including Levantine, separated from the Bedouin dialects at a very early period, perhaps not long after the spread of Islam to the Levant in 650CE. More to the point, the phenomena involved in opaque interactions are very different in these two speech varieties. The Bedouin dialect in particular has many situations of opacity with no parallel in Levantine.

The primary goal of this chapter is not polemical. Except for occasional digressions, I have not made a systematic effort to show that the analysis proposed here is somehow better than what can be achieved in rule-based phonology, Stratal OT, sympathy, or other approaches. For theory comparison, look to §2.3.4 and §3.6.

4.2   Levantine Arabic

4.2.1   Overview of the issues

The Arabic varieties spoken in the Levant — Lebanon, Syria, and Palestine — typically have complex opaque interactions among vowel epenthesis, stress assignment, and syncope. The data in (4-1) – (4-3) illustrate the range of these interactions as they are described by Abu-Salim (1982a: 196ff.) and Farwaneh (1995: 132ff.).

The data in (a) of (4-1) show that heavy penults normally attract stress. But the form in (b) has an epenthetic vowel in its penult, and as a result stress falls on the antepenult. Form (b), then, is a result of opaque interaction between stress and epenthesis: stress is assigned as if the epenthetic vowel were not present. Interestingly, when an epenthetic vowel in the penult breaks up cluster of four consonants (c), stress and epenthesis interact transparently, and stress is not retracted to the antepenult. (Throughout, epenthetic vowels will be italicized as an aid to understanding.)

(4-1)   Stress-epenthesis interaction I
    a. Stress falls on heavy penult
        /katab-na/   ka'tab.na   'we wrote'
        /katab-l-ak/   ka'tab.lak   'he wrote to you (m. sg.)'
    b. But not if the penult's vowel is epenthetic
        /katab-l-ha/   ka'ta.b*i*l.ha 'he wrote to her'
    c. Unless the epenthetic vowel breaks up a CCCC cluster
        /katab-t-l-ha/ ka.tab'*ti*l.ha 'I wrote to her'

The data in (4-2) illustrate a different opaque interaction of stress and epenthesis. Words with a light penult normally have stress on the antepenult (a), but if the final syllable has an epenthetic vowel then stress is assigned to the penult (b). In this case, stress is also being assigned as if the epenthetic vowel were not present, since *[ka'tabt] would be expected to have final stress.

(4-2)   Stress-epenthesis interaction II
    a. Stress skips a light penult
        /katab-u/   'ka.ta.bu 'they wrote'
    b. Unless the final syllable has an epenthetic vowel
        /katab-t/   ka'ta.b*i*t 'I wrote'

The situation in (4-3) involves the same stress opacity as (4-1), but with a further complication: epenthesis feeds syncope.

(4-3)   Interaction with syncope
    a. Short high vowels delete in nonfinal open syllables
      /fihim-it/   ˈfih.mit ‘she understood’
    b. Even when the resulting cluster requires epenthesis and opaque stress
      /ji-ktib-u/   ˈji.k*i*t.bu ‘they write’

It is clear from these data that Levantine Arabic phonology is rich in opacity. Furthermore, the processes involved are of undoubted generality, regularity, and productivity, so they cannot be dismissed as morphologized remnants of earlier phonology (cf. §2.2.3). Indeed, except for being opaque in the ways described, stress is virtually exceptionless in this and other varieties of Arabic.

The crux of the OT-CC analysis is the constraint PREC(ID(stress), DEP-V). It favors candidate chains in which all epenthetic LUMs are preceded by stress-assigning LUMs. The interaction of PREC(ID(stress), DEP-V) with other constraints accounts for the full range of opaque and transparent interactions seen in (4-1) (see §4.2.3), (4-2) (see §4.2.4), and (4-3) (see §4.2.5). In §4.2.6, there will also be discussion of a second PREC constraint that accounts for an opaque interaction between closed syllable shortening and vowel epenthesis.

These or similar data have been the subject of insightful analysis and theorizing in the previous phonological literature, particularly Abdul-Karim (1980), Abu-Mansour (1991), Abu-Salim (1980, 1982a, 1982b), Broselow (1980, 1982, 1992), Broselow, Chen, and Huffman (1997), Farwaneh (1995), Gouskova (2003: 218ff.), Hayes (1995: 125-130), Ito (1989), Johnson (1979), Kager (1999b), Kenstowicz (1983, 1986), Kiparsky (2003), Łubowicz (2003), and Selkirk (1981a). (Alderete (1999) is also relevant.) At appropriate junctures below, I will describe how the new analysis incorporates elements of this earlier work.

4.2.2   Stress and faithful syllabification

In Levantine Arabic, CV syllables are light (monomoraic), while CV: and CVC are normally heavy (bimoraic). Final consonants in this language are often described as extrametrical (e.g., by Hayes 1995: 125) to account for the fact that final CVC syllables are treated as light for stress purposes.[1] Rather than parse the final C as extrametrical, it makes more sense, in light of Broselow, Chen, and Huffman’s (1997) results, to adopt a shared-mora representation in which a single mora is linked to two segments. They present phonetic evidence for a shared-mora representation of CV:C syllables: these syllables are bimoraic, with a single mora assigned to both the second half of the long vowel and the coda, as shown in (a) of (4-4). Here, I will also assume a shared-mora representation for CVCC syllables and word-final CVC syllables ((b) and (c) in (4-4)).[2]

(4-4)   Shared-mora representation (after Broselow, Chen, and Huffman 1997: 57)
   a. CVːC syllables   b. CVCC syllables   c. Final CVC syllables

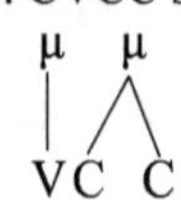

The Levantine Arabic stress pattern is of the Latin type: stress falls on the penult if it is heavy or if the word is disyllabic, and otherwise stress goes on the antepenult. The data are given in (4-5).

(4-5)   Stress in Levantine Arabic (Abu-Salim 1982a: 59ff.)
   a. Stress on heavy penult
      daˈras.na   'we studied'
      saˈmaː.na   'our sky'
      kaˈtab.lak   'he wrote to/for you (m. sg.)'
      maˈkaː.tib   'offices'
      makˈtab.na   'our office'
      ka.taˈbuː.ha   'they wrote it (f.)'

   b. Initial stress in disyllables
      ˈʔa.na   'I'
      ˈka.tab   'he wrote'

   c. Antepenult stress elsewhere
      ˈka.ta.bu   'they wrote'
      ˈmad.ra.sa   'school'
      ˈʕal.la.mat   'she taught'
      ʕalˈla.ma.to   'she taught him'

I assume that the parsing of words into feet follows the pattern illustrated in (4-6). (These parses are very similar, but not identical, to those in Hayes (1995: 125ff.).) Every heavy syllable is a foot on its own, and pairs of light syllables are grouped into trochaic feet, except that the word-final syllable must be left unfooted. As noted, final consonants do not project moras, so word-final CVC syllables are light, represented like (c) in (4-4). Words may contain several feet, with main stress assigned to the last of them.

(4-6)   Examples in (4-5) parsed metrically
   a. daˈras.na   L(ˈH)L
      saˈmaː.na   L(ˈH)L
      kaˈtab.lak   L(ˈH)L
      maˈkaː.tib   L(ˈH)L
      makˈtab.na   (ˌH)(ˈH)L
      ka.taˈbuː.ha   (ˌLL)(ˈH)L

b. ˈʔa.na   (ˈLL)
  ˈka.tab   (ˈLL)

c. ˈka.ta.bu   (ˈLL)L
  ˈmad.ra.sa   (ˈH)LL
  ˈʕal.la.mat   (ˈH)LL
  ʕalˈla.ma.to   (ˌH)(ˈLL)L

Although secondary stress is not usually reported for this language, there is a good reason to think that the nonprimary stressed feet in (4-6) are really there. Abu-Salim (1982a: 112ff.) presents data showing that a vowel is shortened in the syllable immediately before the main stress: /baːb-eːn/ → [baˈbeːn] 'two doors' (cf. [ˈbaːb] 'door'). There is no shortening when the long vowel and the stressed syllable are nonadjacent: [ʕaː.laˈmeːn] 'two worlds'. Vowel shortening limited to pretonic position can be rationalized as a way of avoiding stress clash. The stress clash in faithful *[(ˌbaː)(ˈbeːn)] is eliminated by shortening in *[ba(ˈbeːn)]. Changing the pretonic syllable from heavy to light by shorten- ing its vowel eliminates the necessity for stressing it under the constraints *Lapse (4-7) and Weight-to-Stress (4-17). This analysis predicts, somewhat surprisingly, that when the prestress long vowel is in a closed syllable, it will not shorten: vowel shortening in a closed syllable leaves a syllable that is still heavy, so the clash remains unresolved. This prediction is correct: [ma ʃaːfˈniːʃ] 'he didn't see me'.

Examples like (4-6) do not reveal whether foot parsing proceeds from left to right or from right to left; only words with a nonfinal sequence of three light syllables would help decide this question, but the native vocabulary supplies no examples. Hayes infers left-to-right parsing from the stress of Classical Arabic words like [ˈʃa.ʒa.ra.tun] 'a tree' as rendered by a Palestinian speaker (Kenstowicz 1981a), but this evidence is not unproblematic[3] and is in any case not the sort of evidence that is available to language learners.

To analyze the stress pattern in (4-6), I assume the rhythmically-based theory of metrical analysis proposed by Kager (2001) and discussed in McCarthy (2003b). The relevant constraints (see (4-7), (4-8), and (4-9)) regulate the pres- ence and distribution of stress lapses, which are defined as sequences of weak metrical elements. For a quantity-sensitive language like Levantine Arabic, the metrical elements are moras rather than syllables, so we are speaking here of moraic lapses (cf. Elenbaas and Kager 1999: 295, Prince 1983: 57ff.).

(4-7)   *Lapse (*Lps) (moraic version)
       Assign one violation mark for every sequence of unstressed moras.

(4-8)   Lapse-at-Peak (LpsPk) (moraic version)
       Assign one violation mark for every sequence of unstressed moras that is not
       adjacent to the stress peak.

(4-9)   LAPSE-AT-END (LPSEND) (moraic version)
Assign one violation mark for every nonfinal sequence of unstressed moras.

Since heavy syllables contain two moras and light syllables contain one, an unstressed heavy syllable constitutes a lapse, as does any sequence of unstressed light syllables. When a heavy syllable is stressed, the locus of stress prominence is the first mora (Kager 1993: 389, Prince 1983: 59-60). For example, in a 'HL sequence — that is, a stressed heavy syllable followed by an unstressed light syllable — the prominence is on the first of the three moras, so there is technically a lapse consisting of the second mora of the heavy syllable plus the mora of the light syllable.

The lapse constraints, which regulate rhythm, are sometimes in conflict with constraints that regulate foot form or location. The most important foot constraints in the current analysis are FOOT-BINARITY (4-10) and NONFINALITY (4-11). Both can compel violation of *LAPSE, as the ranking argument (4-12) shows. In this tableau and subsequently, I use a grid notation modeled on the one in Hayes (1995): 'x' stands for a prominent mora, '.' for a weak mora, and parentheses delimit metrical feet. I will also assume throughout that other constraints ensure that the locus of main stress is the rightmost foot (see McCarthy 2003b for a proposal).

(4-10)   FOOT-BINARITY (FTBIN) (moraic version) (Prince 1980)
Assign one violation mark for every foot that contains fewer than two moras.

(4-11)   NONFINALITY (NF)
Assign one violation mark for every foot that is final in some phonological word.

(4-12)   FOOT-BINARITY, NONFINALITY >> *LAPSE, LAPSE-AT-PEAK, LAPSE-AT-END

		FTBIN	NF	*LPS	LPSPK	LPSEND
	/katabu/					
→	'katabu (x .) .			1		
a.	ka'tabu . (x .)		W₁	L		
	/madrasa/					
→	'madrasa (x.) . .			2	1	1
b.	mad'rasa (x.)(x) .	W₁		L	L	L
c.	mad'rasa (x.)(x .)		W₁	L	L	L

In (4-12), the winner [('ka.ta)bu] violates only *LAPSE, a violation that it incurs because of the unstressed two-mora sequence [tabu]. It beats lapseless [ka('ta.bu)] with a final foot, since NONFINALITY dominates *LAPSE. The winner [('mad)ra.sa] has two overlapping lapses according to my assumptions about the locus of stress in heavy syllables and the moraic reckoning of lapses. These lapses are [d.ra] and [ra.sa], and the first is not word-final, so it violates LAPSE-AT-END, while the second is not adjacent to the peak, so it violates LAPSE-AT-PEAK. The losing candidates in (b) and (c) eliminate the lapses by fuller metrical parsing, but they do so by positing monomoraic or word-final feet, and such feet violate FOOT-BINARITY and NONFINALITY, respectively.

In longer words, nonprimary feet are required by *LAPSE. Because any sequence of nonprominent moras is a lapse, all nonfinal sequences of light syllables must carry a stress (see (4-13)).

(4-13) Minimal violation of *LAPSE

/katabuːha/	*Lᴘꜱ	LᴘꜱPᴋ	LᴘꜱEɴᴅ
→ kataˈbuːha (x .) (x.) .	1		
kataˈbuːha . . (x.) .	W₂		W₁

Disyllables like [ˈʔa.na] or [ˈka.tab] ((b) in (4-6)) and monosyllables like [ˈbaːb] 'door' require further attention. There are two logically possible ways of parsing the disyllables: by violating FOOT-BINARITY, as in [(ˈʔa)na], or by violating NONFINALITY, as in [(ˈʔa.na)]. The latter is correct. The argument depends on word-minimality effects. The basic logic of word minimality goes like this (Broselow 1982, McCarthy and Prince 1986/1996, Prince 1980): because the main-stressed foot is the head of the phonological word, every word must contain at least one foot to satisfy the constraint HEAD(Word) (see (4-14)). Because final consonants do not projects moras of their own, CVC monosyllables are monomoraic, which means they are too small to support a binary foot. Accordingly, the language has no CVC content words, and English borrowings like *bus* have to be augmented by epenthesis ([ˈba.sˤi]) or lengthening ([ˈbaːsˤ], [ˈbasˤsˤ]). Surface forms never violate FOOT-BINARITY, so it must be ranked higher than some appropriate faithfulness constraint, such as DEP-V (see (4-15)). On the other hand, since disyllables like [ˈʔa.na] and [ˈka.tab] and monosyllables like [ˈbaːsˤ] are possible words, NONFINALITY must be ranked below DEP-V (see (4-16)).

(4-14) HEAD(Word) (Hᴅ(Wᴅ)) (McCarthy and Prince 1986/1996, Selkirk 1980b)
Every phonological word contains a head foot.

(4-15) HEAD(Word), FOOT-BINARITY >> DEP-V

/ˈbasˤ/	Hᴅ(Wᴅ)	FᴛBɪɴ	Dᴇᴘ-V	NF
→ ˈbasˤi (x .)			ı	ı
a. ˈbasˤ (x)		W₁	L	ı
b. basˤ	W₁		L	L

(4-16) DEP-V >> NONFINALITY

/katab/	Hᴅ(Wᴅ)	FᴛBɪɴ	Dᴇᴘ-V	NF
→ ˈkatab (x .)				ı
a. ˈkatab (x) .		W₁		L
b. katab	W₁			L
c. ˈkatabi (x .) .			W₁	L

NONFINALITY is also violated by words ending in CVːC or CVCC, such as [baˈnaːt] 'girls', [dukˈkaːn] 'store', [ʔa.laˈmeːn] 'two pens', and [maˈħall] 'place'. Word-final CVːC and CVCC syllables have the shared mora representation depicted in (4-4) (a) and (b); they consist of a heavy, bimoraic syllable with an extra consonant adjoined to the second mora. These examples show that the imperative to stress heavy syllables overrides the imperative to keep final syllables unfooted. Formally, WEIGHT-TO-STRESS (4-17) is ranked above NONFINALITY, as shown in (4-18).

(4-17) WEIGHT-TO-STRESS (WᴛSᴛʀ) (cf. Prince 1990)

Assign one violation mark for every unstressed heavy syllable.

(4-18) WEIGHT-TO-STRESS >> NONFINALITY

/dukkaːn/	WᴛSᴛʀ	NF
→ dukˈkaːn (x .)(x .)		ı
ˈdukkaːn (x .) ..	W₁	L

This very nearly completes our survey of Levantine Arabic's basic system of stress and quantity. The rankings are summarized in (4-19). The three undominated constraints establish some unviolated restrictions on prosodic structure: feet contain at least two moras, every word contains at least one foot, and every heavy syllable is stressed. Word-final feet are avoided, but not categorically prohibited. Lapses are avoided insofar as possible, given the dominance of FOOT-BINARITY and NONFINALITY. Although there are differences of detail, this analysis has much in common with previous accounts of this and other Arabic dialects.

(4-19) Levantine ranking summary I

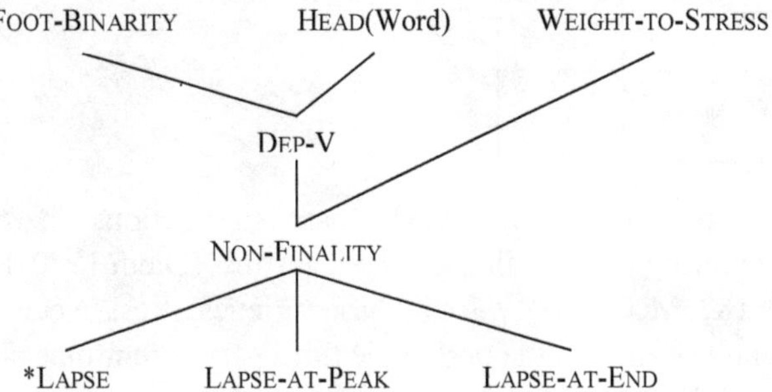

When stress is discussed in OT, there is usually no mention of faithfulness constraints. This is an unwarranted omission. The metrical literature contains many proposals for dealing with exceptional, unpredictable, or contrastive stress and accent by positing lexical markings of some sort. (See Hayes (1995: 112, 133, 144 et passim) for some examples.) Reconstructing this idea in OT requires that there be faithfulness to these lexical markings, whatever they are. Otherwise, in the absence of faithfulness, markedness would compel neutralization and contrastive stress would be universally impossible (see §3.2.4.1).

Alderete (2001b) argues for a particular conception of stress faithfulness that I will adopt here. He distinguishes between two constraints, MAX-PROM (MAX-PR) and DEP-PROM (DEP-PR) that respectively militate against removing prominence from and assigning prominence to a syllable-head. MAX-PROM is needed to preserve lexical stress markings in languages with free stress, like Russian, or in languages with lexically marked exceptions to a regular stress pattern. DEP-PROM preserves lexically marked unaccentedness, as in Japanese, or lexically marked unstressability, as in Lakota (Shaw 1980: 53ff.). There is much less evidence for faithfulness to degrees of stress, so I will assume that the difference between /patakama/ → [ˌpataˈkama] and /patakama/ → [ˈpataˌkama] does not involve faithfulness. None of these detailed assumptions is crucial; the only essential point is that the addition or removal of stress is an unfaithful act, a LUM.

Since no morphemes idiosyncratically resist receiving stress in Levantine Arabic, DEP-PROM is never visibly active. This means that it is dominated by constraints that require the presence of stress, such as *LAPSE (see (4-20)).

(4-20)   *LAPSE >> DEP-PROM

	/ʕallamato/	*LPS	DEP-PR
→	ʕalˈlamato (x.)(x .) .	1	2
a.	ʕalˈlamato . . (x .) .	W$_2$	L$_1$
b.	ˈʕallamato (x.) . . .	W$_3$	L$_1$

In some Levantine Arabic varieties, however, there are situations where MAX-PROM is active in favoring preservation of a lexical stress (Diem 1970, Fischer and Jastrow 1980: 182, McCarthy 1980). In these varieties, stress exceptionally falls on a light penult when it is the perfective third person feminine singular subject agreement suffix [-ət] and a heavy-light syllable sequence precedes it (4-21). Stress also exceptionally falls on a light penult in certain verb forms of the derivational classes known as Measures VII and VIII (4-22). (The data in (4-21) and (4-22) come from the Damascus dialect (Cowell 1965: 20).)

(4-21)   Exceptional stress I
ʕal.laˈmə.to   'she taught him'
kaː.taˈbə.to   'she wrote to him'
ʔak.raˈmə.to   'she honored him'

(4-22)   Exceptional stress II
bjəʃˈtə.ɣəl   'he works'
bəfˈtə.kər   'I think'
bjənˈħa.ka   'it is told'
mutˈta.həd   'united'

The data in (4-21) are particularly relevant to our current concerns. Suppose that the suffix [-ət] is marked with a lexical stress: /-ˈət/. Since that stress is preserved even when it falls on a light penult, MAX-PROM must dominate NONFINALITY. But because the same suffix is unstressed when word-final (e.g., [ˈʕal.la.met] 'she taught'), MAX-PROM must itself be dominated by FOOT-BINARITY. The ranking argument is given in (4-23). (On why this exceptional stress requires a preceding HL sequence, see McCarthy (1980).)

(4-23) Foot-Binarity >> Max-Prom >> Nonfinality (Damascus dialect)[4]

		FtBin	Max-Pr	NF
	/ʕallam-ˈət-o/			
→	ʕallaˈməto (x.) . (x .)			1
a.	ʕalˈlaməto (x.)(x .) .		W₁	L
	/ʕallam-ˈət/			
→	ˈʕallamət (x.) . .		1	
b.	ʕallaˈmət (x.) . (x)	W₁	L	W₁

4.2.3   Stress-epenthesis interaction I: Final clusters

As we saw in (4-2), when a word-final consonant cluster is broken up by epenthesis, stress is opaque, as if the epenthetic vowel were not actually present: /katab-t/ → [kaˈta.bit], *[ˈkata.bit] 'I wrote'. This pattern is extremely regular (Abu-Salim 1982b: 196ff.).

Before examining the candidate chains, we need to get a solid grip on the epenthesis process. The epenthetic vowel goes in the middle of a final cluster — that is, [kaˈta.bit] and not *[kaˈtab.ti] — because word-final epenthesis is prohibited in this language by undominated Align-R(Stem, Word) (Farwaneh 1995: 61-66, McCarthy and Prince 1993a: 126-127). The various Levantine varieties differ in which final clusters they split up and which they tolerate (Abu-Salim 1982a: 198ff., Farwaneh 1995: 72ff., Haddad 1984: 34ff.). For example, Haddad describes a Beirut dialect where relative sonority is a determinant of whether epenthesis is required, but there are also many complications: [mr] is permitted but [ml] is not; [lm] is permitted but [rm] is not; [rn] is questionable; clusters of coronal fricatives are worse than nonhomorganic fricative clusters; and almost all CG clusters, where G is a guttural consonant, require epenthesis regardless of the sonority of C or G. The ad hoc cover term Cluster-Condition (Cl-Cnd) will stand for the congeries of constraints on sonority and other factors that disfavor a tautosyllabic parse of the cluster in, say, /ʔibn/ 'son' but not /kalb/ 'dog'. Cluster-Condition dominates Dep-V (see (4-24)).

(4-24) CLUSTER-CONDITION >> DEP-V

	CL-CND	DEP-V
/ʔibn/		
→ (ˈʔi.b*i*n)		1
(ˈʔibn)	W$_1$	L
/kalb/		
→ (ˈkalb)		
(ˈka.l*i*b)		W$_1$

Valid candidate chains must have monotonically increasing harmony and monotonically decreasing faithfulness, so each chain member improves harmonically over its predecessors and accumulates all of its predecessors' LUMs. Furthermore, when there are several distinct ways of adding a violation of a particular faithfulness constraint, the most harmonic one is chosen. These basic principles are all important in the analysis of the /katab-t/ → [kaˈta.b*i*t] opaque mapping.

According to the local optimality requirement ((c) in (3-1)), candidate chains are initiated by the faithful parse of the input that is most harmonic according to the grammar of the language in question. Since stress assignment and epenthesis are unfaithful mappings, the faithful parses are limited to assigning segments to syllables. Given what was just said about CLUSTER-CONDITION, /katab-t/'s most harmonic faithful parse is presumably disyllabic [ka.tabt], with the shared-mora representation in (4-4) (b) for the syllable [tabt]. The minimal chain from input /katab-t/ is therefore <ka.tabt>.

The next member of any valid chain must be harmonically improving over [ka.tabt] and unfaithful by virtue of the addition of a single LUM. One way to improve harmony by adding a single LUM is to assign stress to some syllable. Stress assignment is a DEP-PROM-violating LUM. It represents harmonic improvement over a stressless form because it promotes better satisfaction of HEAD(Word) and *LAPSE, both of which dominate DEP-PROM (see (4-20)). Assigning stress to either syllable of [ka.tabt] would improve performance on HEAD(Word) and *LAPSE, so both [kaˈtabt] and [ˈka.tabt] meet the harmonic improvement requirement. But another aspect of the local optimality requirement on chains is also relevant here: when several distinct LUMs are possible in a form, and each violates the same basic faithfulness constraint, then the one that yields the most harmonic result is chosen over the rest. The forms [kaˈtabt] and [ˈka.tabt] have distinct LUMs that violate the same faithfulness constraint, DEP-PROM. The more harmonic of the two is [kaˈtabt] because it better satisfies FOOT-BINARITY and WEIGHT-TO-STRESS, as shown in (4-25). No known active constraint favors loser (a) in (4-25), and loser (b) is favored only by Nonfinality, which is ranked below Foot-Binarity (see (4-15)). Therefore, [ka('tabt)] is the proper continuation for the chain: <ka.tabt, ka('tabt)>.

(4-25) Relative harmony of Dep-Prom-violating LUMs

/katab-t/	FtBin	WtStr
→ ka'tabt .(x .)		
a. 'katabt (x .).		W_1
b. 'katabt (x)..	W_1	W_1

Vowel epenthesis offers another way of adding a single LUM to a chain. The chain <ka.tabt> can be extended by adding a Dep-V-violating LUM if the result is harmonically improving and it is more harmonic than any other way of adding a Dep-V-violating LUM. Most logically possible loci of vowel epenthesis are not even harmonically improving (e.g., *[*i*.ka.tabt]), so they are out of the picture. Two loci do offer improved performance on Cluster-Condition, however: [ka.ta.b*i*t] and [ka.tab.t*i*]. The form *[ka.tab.t*i*] is less harmonic than [ka.ta.b*i*t] because, as I noted previously, word-final epenthesis violates an undominated alignment constraint. Therefore, the chain continues by adding [ka.ta.b*i*t]: <ka.tabt, ka.ta.b*i*t>. The change in [b]'s status from weight-bearing coda to weightless onset happens as an automatic result of selecting the most harmonic form at each step. This is possible because decisions about prosodic parsing have no durability unless they involve faithfulness, and the alternation between a moraic coda and an onset is not a matter of faithfulness under the assumptions about moras in §3.2.4.2. A chain must accumulate LUMs monotonically, but it may be highly nonmonotonic with respect to those aspects of phonological representation, particularly syllabification, that are not guarded by faithfulness constraints.

We now need to check whether the two-form chains <ka.tabt, ka('tabt)> and <ka.tabt, ka.ta.b*i*t> can be further extended by adding other harmony-improving LUMs. Adding a Dep-V-violating LUM to the first of these chains is one possibility. The form [ka('ta.b*i*t)] improves harmonically over [ka('tabt)] because Cluster-Condition dominates Dep-V. Therefore, <ka.tabt, ka('tabt), ka('ta.b*i*t)> can be added to the set of candidate chains.

Adding a Dep-Prom-violating LUM to <ka.tabt, ka.ta.b*i*t> offers another obvious gain in harmony, since undominated Head(Word) says that it is always better to stress a stressless word. The most harmonic way of adding this LUM is [('ka.ta)b*i*t], with the usual antepenultimate stress of words consisting of three light syllables. Therefore, <ka.tabt, ka.ta.b*it* ('ka.ta)b*it*> can also be added to the set of candidate chains.

Further harmonic improvements are not possible, so there are no other chains. For example, adding another DEP-PROM-violating LUM to <ka.tabt, ka('tabt)> does not yield any further harmonic improvement, since the initial foot in *[(ˌka)('tabt)] pointlessly violates undominated FOOT-BINARITY. Likewise, adding another DEP-V-violating LUM to <ka.tabt, ka.ta.b*it*> will not gain any improvement in harmony. Something like **<ka.tabt, ka('tabt), ka('tab*it*), ('kata)b*it*>, with shift of a previously assigned stress, is not a valid chain. It is invalid because it is inconsistent with the requirement that chains monotonically increase in unfaithfulness, accumulating all of the LUMs that they have acquired along the way.

The five chains listed in (4-26) constitute the entire candidate set. To save space and increase clarity, I have omitted the indices from the LUMs whenever there is no danger of ambiguity.

(4-26) Valid chains for input /katabt/ and their LUMSeqs

Chain	LUMSeq	Description
a. <ka.tabt>	<>	Faithful.
b. <ka.tabt, ka('tabt)>	<DEP-PR@4>	Stress, no epenthesis.
c. <ka.tabt, ka.ta.b*it*>	<DEP-V>	Epenthesis, no stress.
d. <ka.tabt, ka('tabt), ka('tab*it*)>✓	<DEP-PR@4, DEP-V>	Opaque winner.
e. <ka.tabt, ka.ta.b*it* ('ka.ta)b*it*>	<DEP-V, DEP-PR@2>	Transparent loser.

There are no convergent chains in (4-26), so the LUMSeqs and rLUMSeqs are identical. Transparent (e) is less marked than opaque (d), since (d)'s output violates NONFINALITY and (e)'s does not. Nonetheless, (d) is optimal because a PREC constraint overrides its NONFINALITY violation. Specifically, PREC(DEP-PR, DEP-V) requires all DEP-V-violating LUMs to be preceded and not followed in their rLUMSeqs by DEP-PROM-violating LUMs. (In effect, stress assignment must precede and not follow epenthesis.) The triumph of the opaque winner (d) is ensured, as in (4-27), by ranking PREC(DEP-PR, DEP-V) above (d)'s worst mark that is not shared with (e), and that is (d)'s violation of NONFINALITY. In addition to this ranking, tableau (4-27) shows DEP-V dominating PREC(DEP-PR, DEP-V) as required by the ranking metaconstraint (3-24).

(4-27) PREC(DEP-PR, DEP-V) >> NONFINALITY

	/katabt/	CL-CND	HD(WD)	DEP-V	PREC(DEP-PR, DEP-V)	NF	*LPS	DEP-PR
d. →	ka('tab*i*t) <DEP-PR@4, DEP-V>			1		1		1
a.	ka.tabt <>	W₁	W₁	L		L	W₂	L
b.	ka('tabt) <DEP-PR@4>	W₁		L		1		1
c.	ka.ta.b*i*t <DEP-V>		W₁	1	W₁	L	W₂	L
e.	('ka.ta)b*i*t <DEP-V, DEP-PR@2>			1	W₂	L	W₁	1

Tableau (4-27) merits close inspection, since it is the crux of the analysis. The winning candidate (d) is opaque by virtue of violating NONFINALITY, which the transparent candidate in row (e) obeys. PREC(DEP-PR, DEP-V), by dominating NONFINALITY, allows the opaque candidate to win. PREC(DEP-PR, DEP-V) assigns violations to chains in which a DEP-V-violating LUM is not preceded and/or is followed by a DEP-PROM-violating LUM. The transparent chain (e) has both of these flaws, so it is nonoptimal. The other candidates (a), (b), and (c) violate the undominated markedness constraints CLUSTER-CONDITION or HEAD(Word), so they are nonstarters in this competition.

This case of opacity is a good example of OT-CC at work. Starting from a well-motivated analysis of the transparent phonology in §4.2.2, I have introduced one novel ranking stipulation — PREC(DEP-PR, DEP-V) dominates NONFINALITY — to favor [ka('ta.b*i*t)] over *[('ka.ta)b*i*t]. Interestingly, this is not the only situation in the language where NONFINALITY is violated, as disyllables like [('ka.tab)] show. This sort of structural similarity between opaque and transparent derivation is not unexpected in OT-CC, because PREC is just another rankable constraint that can, like FOOT-BINARITY in the case of [('ka.tab)], compel violation of NONFINALITY. This result therefore accords with one of OT-CC's central premises: PREC constraints are ranked within a single grammar that is responsible for opaque and transparent phonology together.

4.2.4   Stress-epenthesis interaction II: Medial clusters

When medial clusters are resolved by epenthesis, the interaction with stress is opaque in one situation and transparent in another. A medial cluster of three consonants $C_1C_2C_3$ is normally resolved by epenthesizing a vowel between

C_1 and C_2. Stress is opaque because it skips over the heavy penult created by epenthesis: /katab-l-ha/ 'he wrote to her' becomes [ka'ta.b*i*l.ha] and not *[ka.ta'b*i*l.ha]. When the penult syllable is heavy and has a *non*-epenthetic vowel, penult stress is the norm: [da'ras.na]. Medial clusters of four consonants $C_1C_2C_3C_4$ are resolved by epenthesis between C_2 and C_3. In this case, however, stress is assigned transparently to the heavy penult: /katab-t-l-ha/ → [ka.tab't*i*l.ha].

This difference between three- and four-consonant clusters, I will argue, is the result of Prec(Dep-Pr, Dep-V)'s place in the constraint hierarchy. Prec is ranked high enough to force a violation of Weight-to-Stress in [ka('ta.b*i*l)ha]. But more than just Weight-to-Stress is violated by *[ka('tab)t*i*l.ha]: this form contains a type of highly marked lapse that the language never permits. (Essentially, stress has been retracted too far, moraically, from the end of the word.) Therefore, Prec(Dep-Pr, Dep-V) is ranked below the relevant antilapse constraint. We will now examine the details of this analysis.

All chains from the input /katab-l-ha/ are initiated by its most harmonic faithful parse. This is presumably [ka.tabl.ha], with the [l] parsed as part of a complex coda with mora sharing, like (b) in (4-4). Faithful [ka.tabl.ha] constitutes the shortest chain, <ka.tabl.ha>.

Because Head(Word) and other constraints dominate Dep-Prom, a form with stress somewhere is more harmonic than an otherwise identical form with stress nowhere. The most harmonic way of adding a Dep-Prom-violating LUM to the minimal chain is [ka('tabl)ha]. Local optimality requires placing stress in the most harmonic spot, and stressing either [ka] or [ha] would clearly be less harmonic because it would needlessly violate one or more of the constraints Foot-Binarity, Weight-to-Stress, and Nonfinality: *[('ka.tabl)ha], *[('ka)tabl.ha], *[ka.tabl('ha)]. The resulting two-link, Dep-Prom-violating chain is therefore <ka.tabl.ha, ka('tabl)ha>.

The previous section showed that epenthesis in final $C_1C_2\#$ is a response to sonority and other factors embodied in the cover constraint Cluster-Condition. These same factors also condition epenthesis in medial $C_1C_2C_3$ (Abu-Salim 1982a: 199, Haddad 1984: 36), so epenthesis in /ʔibn/ → ['ʔi.b*i*n] is paralleled by epenthesis in /ʔibn-ha/ → ['ʔi.b*i*n.ha] 'her son', and lack of epenthesis in ['kalb] is paralleled by lack of epenthesis in ['kalb.na] 'our dog'. Therefore, the same ranking that determines whether or not epenthesis affects final $C_1C_2\#$, [Custer-Condition >> Dep-V] in (4-24), also determines whether it affects medial $C_1C_2C_3$.

Because Cluster-Condition dominates Dep-V, adding a Dep-V-violating LUM to <ka.tabl.ha> is harmonically improving. Local optimality requires choosing the most harmonic locus for the Dep-V violation, and there are two possibilities, either of which would satisfy CLUSTER-CONDITION: [ka.ta.b*i*l.ha], with epenthesis between C_1 and C_2, and [ka.tab.l*i*.ha], with epenthesis between C_2 and C_3. Arabic dialects are divided between those that favor the first locus of epenthesis, such as Levantine, Maltese, and Iraqi, and those that favor the second, such as Egyptian and Saudi (Broselow 1992, Farwaneh 1995, Kiparsky 2003).

The constraint that decides the locus of epenthesis is WEAK<*i* (4-38). The scholarship and the typology that justify this constraint will be discussed in detail in §4.2.5. Essentially, WEAK<*i* requires low-sonority [ə] nuclei in low-prominence syllables. To continue the chain <ka.tabl.ha, ka('tabl)ha>, we have to select the most harmonic locus of DEP-V violation. According to WEAK<*i*, [ka('ta.b*i*l)ha] is a more harmonic way of adding a DEP-V violating LUM to [ka('tabl)ha] than *[ka('tab)l*i*ha] is, since *[ka('tab)l*i*ha] introduces a violation of WEAK<*i* because of the syllable [l*i*], while [ka('ta.b*i*l)ha] does not.

To continue the chain <ka.tabl.ha, ka('tabl)ha> with the form [ka('ta.b*i*l)ha], harmonic improvement must also be assured. Therefore, [ka('ta.b*i*l)ha] must be more harmonic than [ka('tabl)ha]. That requires ranking CLUSTER-CONDITION above WEIGHT-TO-STRESS, as shown in tableau (4-28). Since a previously assigned stress cannot be shifted or removed in a valid chain, **<ka.tabl.ha, ka('tabl)ha, ka.ta('b*i*l)ha> is simply not in the space of legitimate candidates.

(4-28) CLUSTER-CONDITION >> WEIGHT-TO-STRESS from chain validity

	/katab-l-ha/	ClCnd	WtStr
→	ka'tab*i*lha . (x ..) .		1
	ka'tablha . (x .) .	W₁	L

This exhausts the valid chains where the first LUM involves stress assignment. We must also consider the possibility of chains where the first LUM involves epenthesis. The two logically possible epenthesizing continuations of the singleton chain <ka.tabl.ha> are [ka.ta.b*i*l.ha] and [ka.tab.l*i*.ha]. They equally violate WEAK<*i*. Which of these is more harmonic depends on other, lower-ranking markedness constraints whose identity may be unknown. Rather than base the argument on speculation about those constraints, I will show that we get the right result even if *both* <ka.tabl.ha, ka.ta.b*i*l.ha> and <ka.tabl.ha, ka.tab.l*i*.ha> are among the valid candidate chains, as are their DEP-PROM-violating continuations <ka.tabl.ha, ka.ta.b*i*l.ha, ka.ta('b*i*l)ha>, <ka.tabl.ha, ka.tab.l*i*.ha,

ka('tab)l*i*.ha>, and <ka.tabl.ha, ka.ta.b*i*l.ha, ka.ta('b*i*l)ha, (ˌkata)('b*i*l)ha>. (The last of these chains is the result of adding a second DEP-PROM-violating LUM at a different locus. This additional step is harmonically improving because *LAPSE dominates DEP-PROM.)

This exhausts the full range of valid chains, and the results are collected in (4-29). The intended winner is (d), and its most harmonic transparent competitors are (e) or (e′) and (f). The difference between the opaque winner and the transparent losers is that the winner satisfies PREC(DEP-PR, DEP-V), while the transparent losers do not. Since WEIGHT-TO-STRESS favors the losers, PREC(DEP-PR, DEP-V) must dominate WEIGHT-TO-STRESS.

(4-29)   Valid chains for input /katab-l-ha/ and their LUMSeqs

    a. <ka.tabl.ha>   Faithful.
      < >

    b. <ka.tabl.ha, ka('tabl)ha>   No epenthesis.
      <DEP-PR@4>

    c. <ka.tabl.ha, ka.ta.b*i*l.ha>   No stress.
      <DEP-V@5>

    c′. <ka.tabl.ha, ka.tab.l*i*.ha>   No stress.
      <DEP-V@6>

    d. <ka.tabl.ha, ka('tabl)ha, ka('ta.b*i*l)ha>✓   Opaque winner.
      <DEP-PR@4, DEP-V@5>

    e. <ka.tabl.ha, ka.ta.b*i*l.ha, kata('b*i*l)ha>   Transparent loser.
      <DEP-V@5, DEP-PR@6>

    e′. <ka.tabl.ha, ka.tab.l*i*.ha, ka('tab)l*i*.ha>   Transparent loser.
      <DEP-V@6, DEP-PR@4>

    f. <ka.tabl.ha, ka.ta.b*i*l.ha, ka.ta('b*i*l)ha, (ˌka.ta)('b*i*l)ha>   Transparent loser.
      <DEP-V@5, DEP-PR@6, DEP-PR@2>

Tableau (4-30) presents the argument for ranking PREC(DEP-PR, DEP-V) above WEIGHT-TO-STRESS. Only the most important candidate comparisons are included, so the tableau omits candidates (a), (b), (c), and (c′) because their outputs violate undominated markedness constraints, HEAD(Word) in the case of stressless (a), (c), and (c′), and CLUSTER-CONDITION in the case of unepenthesized (b). (The effects of those constraints can be seen in tableau (4-27), however.)

(4-30) PREC(DEP-PR, DEP-V) >> WEIGHT-TO-STRESS[5]

	/katab-l-ha/	WK<i	DEP-V	PREC	WTSTR	*LPS	DEP-PR
d. →	ka('ta.bil)ha <DEP-PR@4, DEP-V@5>	1	1		1	2	1
e.	ka.ta('bil)ha <DEP-V@5, DEP-PR@6>	W$_2$	1	W$_2$	L	2	1
e′	ka('tab)li.ha <DEP-V@6, DEP-PR@4>	W$_2$	1	W$_2$	L	2	1
f.	(ˌka.ta)('bil)ha <DEP-V@5, DEP-PR@6, DEP-PR@2>	1	1	W$_2$	L	L$_1$	W$_2$

The argument for this PREC constraint and its ranking comes from comparing
the winner with loser (f) in tableau (4-30). (Candidates (e) and (e′) are not as
useful because they are also disfavored by WEAK<i, whose ranking with respect
to PREC(DEP-PR, DEP-V) is not known.) The winner violates WEIGHT-TO-STRESS,
but loser (f) does not. The winner triumphs because PREC(DEP-PR, DEP-V) is
ranked higher than WEIGHT-TO-STRESS, favoring the winner's LUMSeq where
the DEP-PROM-violating LUM precedes the DEP-V-violating LUM.

This analysis is noteworthy because it illustrates convergence of different
sources of ranking evidence. Tableau (4-30) shows that PREC(DEP-PR, DEP-V)
dominates WEIGHT-TO-STRESS. By the ranking metaconstraint (3-24), DEP-V
must dominate PREC(DEP-PR, DEP-V), giving the partial hierarchy ⟦DEP-V >>
PREC(DEP-PR, DEP-V) >> WEIGHT-TO-STRESS⟧. The epenthesis process shows
that CLUSTER-CONDITION dominates DEP-V (4-24). Putting these ranking results
together, we get the fuller hierarchy ⟦CLUSTER-CONDITION >> DEP-V >> PREC(DEP-
PR, DEP-V) >> WEIGHT-TO-STRESS⟧ (see (4-35) for a diagram). From transitivity
of the constraint domination relation, it follows that CLUSTER-CONDITION must
dominate WEIGHT-TO-STRESS. This ranking inferred from transitivity is identical
to the ranking required for chain validity in (4-28). Because OT-CC requires
that transparent and opaque interactions coexist in a single grammar, convergent
rankings like this are expected and inconsistent rankings are predicted to be
impossible.

Another situation of ranking convergence arises when we compare the two
situations of opacity, final C_1C_2# and medial $C_1C_2C_3$. Tableau (4-30) shows that
opaque stress with $C_1C_2C_3$ inputs is a result of ranking PREC(DEP-PR, DEP-V)
above WEIGHT-TO-STRESS, since winning [ka('tab$i$l)ha]'s worst markedness
problem is its stressless heavy penult. We can show independently (see (4-18))
that WEIGHT-TO-STRESS dominates NONFINALITY. The hierarchy is therefore

⟦PREC(DEP-PR, DEP-V) >> WEIGHT-TO-STRESS >> NONFINALITY⟧ (see (4-35) for a diagram). From transitivity, then, PREC(DEP-PR, DEP-V) dominates NONFINALITY. Tableau (4-27) shows that opaque stress with C_1C_2# inputs requires ranking PREC(DEP-PR, DEP-V) above NONFINALITY, since winning [ka('tab*i*t)]'s worst markedness problem is its word-final foot. The ranking relation between PREC(DEP-PR, DEP-V) and NONFINALITY is therefore proven by convergent evidence from transitivity of domination and from direct argument.

Some interesting typological predictions can be derived from permuting the hierarchy ⟦PREC(DEP-PR, DEP-V) >> WEIGHT-TO-STRESS >> NONFINALITY⟧. Because PREC(DEP-PR, DEP-V) dominates both WEIGHT-TO-STRESS and NONFINALITY in Levantine Arabic, both $C_1C_2C_3$ and final C_1C_2# inputs have opaque interaction of stress and epenthesis. If PREC(DEP-PR, DEP-V) is ranked immediately below WEIGHT-TO-STRESS, however, stress will be transparent with medial $C_1C_2C_3$ inputs, though C_1C_2# inputs will have opaque stress. Exactly this situation is found in the Iraqi, Abu Dabi, and Omani varieties, which have forms like [kata'b*i*lha] (Farwaneh 1995: 136-142). Interdialectal variation between opaque and transparent stress is therefore a result of differences in constraint ranking rather than differences in rule ordering or assignment of processes to strata. In fact, Iraqi Arabic is described as having *intra*dialectal variation between opaque and transparent stress (Erwin 1963: 41), indicating that Iraqi has variable ranking of PREC(DEP-PR, DEP-V) and WEIGHT-TO-STRESS.[6]

The hierarchy ⟦PREC(DEP-PR, DEP-V) >> WEIGHT-TO-STRESS >> NONFINALITY⟧ leads to a related prediction: in any Arabic dialect where WEIGHT-TO-STRESS dominates NONFINALITY, opaque stress with $C_1C_2C_3$ inputs entails opaque stress with C_1C_2# inputs, but not vice-versa. In other words, there should be no dialect that has opaque stress in [ka'tab*i*lha] and transparent stress in ['katab*i*t]. The logic of this prediction goes like this. Given ⟦WEIGHT-TO-STRESS >> NONFINALITY⟧, there are only three places to rank PREC(DEP-PR, DEP-V):

i) If PREC(DEP-PR, DEP-V) is ranked *above* WEIGHT-TO-STRESS, the result is the Levantine pattern with opaque stress in both C_1C_2# and $C_1C_2C_3$: [ka'tab*i*t], [ka'tab*i*lha].

ii) If PREC(DEP-PR, DEP-V) is ranked *between* WEIGHT-TO-STRESS and NONFINALITY, the result is the Iraqi and Gulf pattern with opaque stress in C_1C_2# but not $C_1C_2C_3$: [ka'tab*i*t], [kata'b*i*lha].

iii) If PREC(DEP-PR, DEP-V) is ranked *below* NONFINALITY, then stress is transparent across the board: ['katab*i*t], [kata'b*i*lha]. This pattern is not attested in the Arabic dialects, though obviously there are other languages where stress and epenthesis interact transparently.

As long as WEIGHT-TO-STRESS dominates NONFINALITY, there is no way of getting opaque stress in $C_1C_2C_3$ but not $C_1C_2\#$ because there is no way of ranking PREC(DEP-PR, DEP-V) above WEIGHT-TO-STRESS without having it also dominate NONFINALITY. As it happens, the ranking [WEIGHT-TO-STRESS >> NONFINALITY] is ubiquitous in those varieties of Arabic that have well-understood stress systems, and concomitantly no Arabic variety has opaque stress in $C_1C_2C_3$ but not $C_1C_2\#$.

Epenthesis into quadriconsonantal clusters interacts transparently with stress in Levantine Arabic and other varieties (Broselow 1992: 41, Farwaneh 1995: 151, Kenstowicz 1983, Kiparsky 2003: 163): /katab-t-l-ha/ → [ka.tab'til.ha]. The explanation: there is no way to satisfy PREC(DEP-PR, DEP-V) without violating an undominated markedness constraint, so PREC(DEP-PR, DEP-V) is unable to favor an opaque chain, leaving transparent stress as the only viable option. The problem with opaque *[ka('tab)til.ha] is the long stress lapse between the main-stressed mora and the end of the word. Schematically, this form is *[. (x .) . . .], and it competes unsuccessfully with transparent [. (x .)(x .) .] (i.e., [ka(₁tab)('til)ha]).

Elenbaas and Kager (1999), Gordon (2003), and Steriade (1997: 35) have proposed constraints against *long* lapses, defined as sequences of three unstressed metrical elements. As I noted previously, Kager (2001) argues that (short) lapses may be licensed in certain positions — finally or near a stress peak — even in languages that generally avoid lapses (see (4-7)-(4-9)). Aden (2006) shows that long lapses can also be positionally licensed. In Tripura Bangla (Das 2002), long lapses are forbidden everywhere except word-finally: ['a.ra.sa.li] 'trouble-making', ['ɔ.no.nu₁kɔ.ro.ni.jɔ] 'inimitable'. She concludes that CON must include the constraint (4-32) (and presumably (4-33)) in addition to the basic constraint (4-31).

(4-31) *LONG-LAPSE (*LNGLPS) (cf. (4-7)) (moraic version)
Assign one violation mark for every sequence of three unstressed moras.

(4-32) LONG-LAPSE-AT-END (LNGLPSEND) (cf. (4-8)) (moraic version)
Assign one violation mark for every nonfinal sequence of three unstressed moras.

(4-33) LONG-LAPSE-AT-PEAK (LNGLPSPK) (cf. (4-9)) (moraic version)
Assign one violation mark for every sequence of three unstressed moras that is not adjacent to the stress peak.

Levantine Arabic permits long moraic lapses in forms without and with epenthesis: ['mad.ra.sa]/[(x .) . .], [ka('ta.bil)ha]/[. (x ..) .]. But all permissible long lapses adjoin the peak and the end of the word, so both Long-Lapse-at-End and Long-Lapse-at-Peak are satisfied. The form *[ka('tab)t*i*l.ha]/*[. (x .) . . .] contains two (overlapping) long lapses, one of which adjoins the peak and the other of which adjoins the end: [b$_\mu$.ti$_\mu$l$_\mu$] and [ti$_\mu$l$_\mu$.ha$_\mu$]. Therefore, this form violates both Long-Lapse-at-End and Long-Lapse-at-Peak. It follows, then, that ranking either one of these constraints above Prec(Dep-Pr, Dep-V) will crucially disfavor opaque *[ka('tab)t*i*l.ha] relative to transparent [ka(‚tab)('t*i*l)ha]. I have arbitrarily selected Long-Lapse-at-End as the high-ranking constraint for the ranking argument in (4-34).

(4-34)   Long-Lapse-at-End >> Prec(Dep-Pr, Dep-V)

/katab-t-l-ha/	LngLpsEnd	Prec(Dep-Pr, Dep-V)
→ katab't*i*lha . (x.)(x.) .		2
ka'tabt*i*lha . (x .) . . .	W$_1$	L

This explanation for transparent stress with $C_1C_2C_3C_4$ inputs can be compared with proposals by Farwaneh (1995: 46ff.) and Kiparsky (2003: 163). They also attribute transparent stress to something special about the result of parsing a four-consonant sequence, with two 'extra' consonants to deal with instead of just one. In Farwaneh's analysis, for example, C_2 and C_3 are syllabified as the onset and coda of a degenerate heavy syllable, which then attracts stress in the usual way. In Kiparsky's Stratal OT account, stray consonants in the lexical stratum are normally parsed as 'semisyllables', which are unsyllabified consonants that are individually licensed by moras. Epenthesis is delayed until the postlexical stratum; since stress is assigned in the lexical stratum, it ignores the unsyllabified semisyllables. The special status of $C_1C_2C_3C_4$ inputs is ascribed to a prohibition on *adjacent* semisyllables that is active in the lexical stratum (Kiparsky 2003: 163), dominating Dep-V and forcing lexical epenthesis in [ka.tab't*i*l.ha]. Because the epenthetic vowel in [ka.tab't*i*l.ha] is present in the output of the lexical stratum, it is visible to stress assignment.

Farwaneh's and Kiparsky's analyses both locate the explanation for transparent stress in restrictions on syllabification that apply early in the derivation. In contrast, the analysis proposed here locates the explanation in a restriction on stress in surface forms, the unviolated constraint Long-Lapse-at-End. Stress is transparent because opaque stress is rhythmically unsupportable according to a typologically justified universal constraint.

Diagram (4-35) updates the constraint hierarchy in (4-19) to reflect the additional information about ranking that has been developed. (Some less relevant constraints have been omitted.) The nexus of interest surrounds the PREC constraint. DEP-V and consequently CLUSTER-CONDITION dominate PREC because of the metaconstraint (3-24). This ranking ensures that transparent interaction of stress and epenthesis cannot be obtained by suppressing epenthesis (see §3.3.3). LONG-LAPSE-AT-END also dominates PREC, with the effect of forcing transparent interaction when opaque interaction would produce an impermissible type of lapse. Ranked below PREC are WEIGHT-TO-STRESS and NONFINALITY, constraints that characterize the two ways in which opaque forms are anomalous.

(4-35)   Levantine ranking summary II

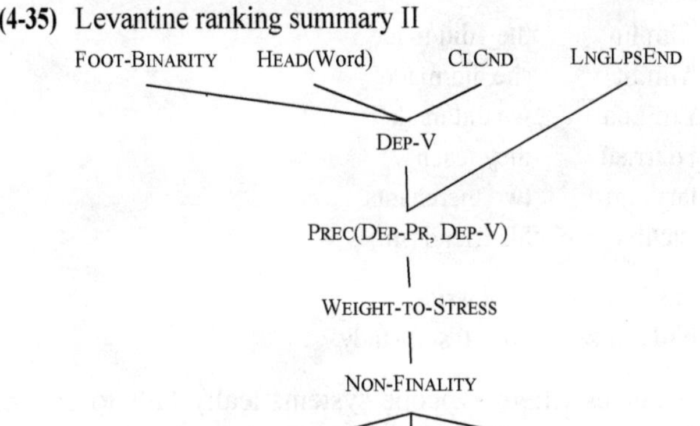

We have now seen the range of stress/epenthesis interactions in Levantine Arabic. By dominating both WEIGHT-TO-STRESS and NONFINALITY, PREC(DEP-PR, DEP-V) accounts for the opaquely unstressed heavy penult of [ka'ta.b*i*l.ha] and the opaquely stressed light penult of [ka'ta.b*i*t]. Transparent stress in [ka.tab't*i*l.ha] is a result of crucial domination of PREC(DEP-PR, DEP-V) by LONG-LAPSE-AT-END. Under the OT-CC thesis that candidates consist of chains of unfaithful mappings, constraint ranking — OT's most fundamental property — is sufficient to account for this rather complex system of opacity and transparency.

4.2.5   Syncope-epenthesis interaction

Syncope is relevant to understanding the locus of vowel epenthesis in medial clusters ([ka.ta.b*i*l.ha] vs. *[ka.tab.l*i*.ha]), and shortening interacts opaquely with epenthesis. The well-known cyclicity effects of Levantine Arabic will also be addressed.

Syncope is pervasive in colloquial Arabic, although there are important differences among the dialects. The Levantine version of syncope is illustrated in (4-36): short high vowels are deleted in nonfinal open syllables, even if a geminate or long vowel precedes. When a nongeminate cluster precedes, as in (b), syncope has the potential to introduce violations of CLUSTER-CONDITION, so epenthesis also occurs, though in a different place from the deletion site. Syncope and epenthesis together look like metathesis, but the basic mapping does not seem to be metathetic since syncope and epenthesis both occur independently as well. (On why the epenthetic vowel is high, see Gouskova (2003).)

(4-36) Syncope (Abu-Salim 1982a: 136, 162ff., Farwaneh 1995: 97ff.)

a. /ʕimil-uː/	ˈʕim.lu	'they did/made'
/ʕimil-it/	ˈʕim.lit	'she did/made'
/ʕimil-naː/	ʕˈmil.na	'we did/made'
/j-darris-uː/	jˈdarr.su	'they teach'
/taːʒir-eːn/	taːʒˈreːn	'two merchants'
/saːħib-uː/	ˈsaːħbu	'his friend (m.)'
b. /ji-ktib-uː/	ˈji.kɨt.bu	'they write'
/bi-ti-drus-iː/	bˈtu.dɯr.si	'you (f. sg.) study'

There are a few circumstances where syncope systematically fails to occur. Underlying long vowels are immune to deletion, even when shortened. Any short high vowels that look like they should have syncopated but did not may be the result of shortening processes. Levantine Arabic's well-known 'cyclic' stress, discussed below, is another source of immunity from syncope. Finally, vowels in a $C_iC_i\_\_C_i$ context do not syncopate for reasons discussed in McCarthy (1986).

When these cases have been set aside, the net effect of syncope is to ensure the validity of the following surface generalization: short high vowels in unstressed nonfinal open syllables are prohibited. The syllables that syncope eliminates are therefore the weakest of the weak (cf. Angoujard 1986). A syllable's weakness, in this sense, is primarily or entirely a function of its duration: short vowels are obviously shorter than long vowels; *ceteris paribus*, open syllables are shorter than closed syllables; unstressed syllables are shorter than stressed syllables (Lehiste 1970: 36); and medial syllables are shorter than final syllables (because of final lengthening (Lindblom 1978)).[7] In Levantine Arabic, the syllables subject to syncope are short in every one of these senses.

Cross-linguistically, vowel reduction processes are also sensitive to syllable duration and other aspects of prominence. Crosswhite (2000a) identifies a type of reduction that affects vowels in 'ultra-short syllables', changing them into vowels of lower sonority, typically schwa or the high vowels. In Bedouin Arabic (§4.3), syncope of high vowels and reduction of low vowels to high occur in exactly the same range of prosodic contexts, all of which are associated with shorter duration than prosodic contexts where syncope or reduction do not occur.

A complete cross-linguistic typology of durational effects on syncope and reduction would be a distraction from the main goal here. I will therefore propose some constraints that are sufficient for the examples discussed in this chapter but not for the full range of phenomena found in other languages. These constraints are not so much ad hoc as incomplete: they are merely representative of the broader constraint family required for the analysis of syncope (Gouskova 2003), reduction (Crosswhite 1999, 2000a, 2000b), and sonority-driven stress (de Lacy 2002: 55ff., Kenstowicz 1996b). See these works for detailed proposals along the same general lines.

In defining the constraints, I will refer to a syllable as *weak* if it has all of the following characteristics that, as was just noted, lead to shorter overall duration: it is an open syllable, its vowel is short, it is unstressed, and it is nonfinal. Weak syllables favor vowels of lower sonority, according to the constraints WEAK<*a* (4-37) and WEAK<*i* (4-38). Since high vowels are less sonorous than low vowels, these constraints are in a stringency relationship: every violation of WEAK<*a* is also a violation of WEAK<*i*, but not vice-versa.

(4-37)   WEAK<*a* (WK<*a*)
    Assign a violation mark for every weak syllable with a nucleus whose sonority
      is equal to or greater than that of a [+low] vowel.

(4-38)   WEAK<*i* (WK<*i*)
    Assign a violation mark for every weak syllable with a nucleus whose sonority
      is equal to or greater than that of a [+high] vowel.

In Levantine Arabic, WEAK<*i* compels deletion of /i/ but not /a/. Since [i] and [a] in weak syllables equally violate WEAK<*i*, deletion of /a/ must be prevented by a faithfulness constraint that is sensitive to the greater intrinsic prominence of low vowels, MAX-A (4-39). (On MAX-A, see §2.3.3 and §3.5.3. For MAX-A in Cairene Arabic, see Davis and Zawaydeh (1997).) As shown in (4-41), MAX-A dominates WEAK<*i*, so underlying low vowels are preserved. WEAK<*i* itself dominates MAX-I (4-40), so high vowels in weak syllables are deleted. By transitivity, MAX-A dominates MAX-I, a ranking that is presumably required universally under the positional-faithfulness interpretation of MAX-A proposed in §3.5.3.[8]

(4-39) Max-A

Assign a violation mark for every input low vowel that has no output correspondent.

(4-40) Max-I

Assign a violation mark for every input nonlow vowel that has no output correspondent.

(4-41) Max-A >> Weak<i >> Max-I

/ʕimil-it/	Max-A	Wk<i	Max-I
/ʕimil-it/			
→ ˈʕim.lit			1
a. ˈʕi.mi.lit		W₁	L
/katab-it/			
→ ˈka.ta.bit		1	
b. ˈkat.bit	W₁	L	W₁

The constraint Weak<i could in principle be satisfied by changing /i/ to some less sonorous vowel, such as [ə]. The Levantine vowel system does not include [ə], however, so candidates like *[ˈʕiməlit] are ruled out by an undominated markedness constraint. Likewise, Weak<a could in principle be satisfied by changing /a/ into the less sonorous vowel [i]. Since this reduction process does not occur in Levantine Arabic (/katab-it/ → *[ˈka.ti.bit]), Ident(+low) must dominate Weak<a. For the opposite ranking in Bedouin Arabic, see (4-75).

Syncope can create word-initial clusters, as in [ʕˈmil.na] from /ʕimil-na/, and shared-mora representations like (4-4), as in [taːʒˈreːn] from /taːʒireːn/. Therefore, Weak<i must dominate the markedness constraints that are violated by these configurations.

The constraint Weak<i is also responsible for determining the locus of epenthesis. As I noted in §4.2.4, medial triconsonantal clusters could in principle be resolved with epenthesis before or after the second consonant: [kaˈta.bil.ha] vs. *[kaˈtab.li.ha]. Since *[kaˈtab.li.ha] has the decided advantage of transparent stress, some constraint that disfavors it must be ranked above [kaˈta.bil.ha]'s worst comparative violation, Weight-to-Stress. The identity of that higher-ranked constraint is now clear: it is Weak<i. By dominating Weight-to-Stress, as shown in (4-42), it correctly favors [kaˈta.bil.ha].

(4-42) WEAK<*i* >> WEIGHT-TO-STRESS

/katab-l-ha/	WK<*i*	WTSTR
→ ka'ta.b*i*l.ha	1	1
ka'tab.l*i*.ha	W 2	L

As we first saw in (4-3), there is an interesting interaction between syncope on the one hand and stress and epenthesis on the other. Syncope can create medial triconsonantal clusters, and if the result would violate CLUSTER-CONDITION, epenthesis with opaque stress occurs as well: /ji-ktib-uː/ → ['ji.k*i*t.bu]; /bi-ti-dr*u*s-iː/ → [b'tu.d*u*r.si]. Because the epenthesized vowel matches the deleted vowel in color, this looks like metathesis, but the basic process is not really metathetic. The language has a weak or nonexistent contrast between short [i] and [u] (Haddad 1984: 256ff., Herzallah 1990: 146ff., Kenstowicz 1981b), and the factors that condition the [u] allophone of the second high vowel in [b'tu.dur.si] are the same as the factors that condition it in [b'tud.rus] 'she studies'.

Apart from metathesis, there are two logically possible paths from /ji-ktib-uː/ to ['ji.k*i*t.bu]. One route involves epenthesis followed by syncope, going by way of ['ji.k*i*.ti.bu]. The problem with this chain is that the change from ['jik.ti.bu] to ['ji.k*i*.ti.bu] is not harmonically improving, given the rest of the grammar of Levantine Arabic. (That is, no constraint ranked higher than DEP-V favors epenthetic ['ji.k*i*.ti.bu] over more faithful ['jik.ti.bu].) The other path puts syncope before epenthesis, proceeding by way of ['jikt.bu]. The change from ['jik.ti.bu] to ['jikt.bu] is harmonically improving if WEAK<*i* dominates CLUSTER-CONDITION, as shown in (4-43). With this ranking, there can be a valid chain from /ji-ktib-uː/ via ['jikt.bu] to ['ji.k*i*t.bu]. (This ranking, it may be noted, is consistent with the ranking result in (4-42), since CLUSTER-CONDITION dominates WEIGHT-TO-STRESS by transitivity (see (4-35).)

(4-43) WEAK<*i* >> CLUSTER-CONDITION from chain validity

/ji-ktib-uː/	WK<*i*	CLCND
→ 'jikt.bu		1
'jik.ti.bu	W 1	L

The analysis of /ji-ktib-uː/ → ['ji.k*i*t.bu] is now in place. To keep the number and length of the chains more easily manageable, I will disregard final vowel shortening, pretending that the input is /ji-ktib-u/. The shortest chain from this input is faithful <jik.ti.bu> (= (a) in (4-44)). This chain can be improved on harmonically by adding stress to give <jik.ti.bu, ('jik)ti.bu> (= (b) in (4-44)). Because Weak<*i* dominates Cluster-Condition, the other way of improving harmonically is to delete [i] from the second syllable, forming <jik.ti.bu, jikt.bu> (= (c) in (4-44)). Two converging chains (= (d) in (4-44)) add syncope after stress, yielding <jik.ti.bu, ('jik)ti.bu, ('jikt)bu>, or stress after syncope, yielding <jik.ti.bu, jikt.bu, ('jikt)bu>. Two other converging chains (= (e) in (4-44)) follow syncope with epenthesis, a harmonic improvement because Cluster-Condition dominates Dep-V. The sequence **<jik.ti.bu, jikt.bu, ji.k*i*t.bu, ji('k*i*t)bu> is not harmonically improving, and hence invalid as a chain, because the <…, jikt.bu, ji.k*i*t.bu, …> step introduces a violation of Weak<*i* solely to improve performance on lower-ranking Cluster-Condition. The winning chains in (e) do not have this problem because the initial syllable is stressed before it is opened by epenthesis.

(4-44) Valid chains for input /ji-ktib-u/ and their (r)LUMSeqs

    a. <jik.ti.bu>   Faithful.
       < >

    b. <jik.ti.bu, ('jik)ti.bu>   No syncope.
       <Dep-Pr@2>

    c. <jik.ti.bu, jikt.bu>   No stress.
       <Max-I>

    d. <jik.ti.bu, ('jik)ti.bu,('jikt)bu>   No epenthesis.
       <jik.ti.bu, jikt.bu, ('jikt)bu>
        ℒ = {Dep-Pr@2, Max-I}
        rL = < >

    e. <jik.ti.bu, ('jik)ti.bu,('jikt)bu,('ji.k*i*t)bu>✓   Opaque.
       <jik.ti.bu, jikt.bu, ('jikt)bu,('ji.k*i*t)bu>✓
        ℒ = {Dep-Pr@2, Dep-V, Max-I}
        rL= {<Dep-Pr@2, Dep-V>, <Max-I, Dep-V>}

The opaque winner (e) in (4-44) obeys Prec(Dep-Pr, Dep-V), but its status as winner is assured by constraints that are ranked even higher. Candidates (a) and (c) are out because they lack stress entirely and so violate undominated Head(Word). Candidate (b) violates Weak<*i*, and (d) violates Cluster-Condition. That leaves opaque (e) as the only viable candidate, so the correct mapping /ji-ktib-uː/ → [ˈji.kɪt.bu] is assured. In short, nothing new needs to be said to accommodate this case of opacity.

Perhaps the best known phenomenon in Levantine Arabic is the effect of 'cyclic' stress on syncope (Brame 1973, 1974). As the data in (4-45) show, suffixation of object agreement or negation causes rightward displacement of main stress. Even when the main stress shifts, however, the short high vowel in the initial syllable does not delete: [siˈmiʕkum], not *[sˈmiʕ.kum]. There is no cyclic effect when subject agreement suffixes are added, leading to minimal pairs like [fˈhim-na$_{Subj}$] 'we understood' versus [fiˈhim-na$_{Obj}$] 'he understood us'.

(4-45) Syncope and cyclicity

ˈsimiʕ	siˈmiʕkum	'he heard'/'he heard you (pl.)'
ˈfihim	fiˈhimna	'he understood'/'he understood us'
ˈʃirib	ʃiˈribha	'he drank'/'he drank it (f.)'
	ma ʃiˈribiʃ	'he didn't drink'

The standard analysis of these facts is that [siˈmiʕ.kum] 'he heard you (pl.)' is derived cyclically. Stress is first assigned on the inner cycle to the initial syllable of [ˈsi.miʕ] 'he heard', protecting the first [i] from syncope. On the outer cycle, main stress is reassigned to the penult, but the stress inherited from the previous cycle is retained and subordinated to the new main stress: [ˌsiˈmiʕ.kum]. This inherited, now secondary stress is sufficient to block syncope on the outer cycle.[9]

Only object agreement suffixes produce cyclic effects because only these suffixes attach to free stems. Because subject agreement is obligatory, subject agreement suffixes attach to bound stems, and bound stems are not cyclic domains (Benua 1997, Brame 1973: 54-55, Inkelas 1989, Kager 1999a: 282, Kiparsky 1982, 1985). In other words, for A to be a cyclic domain in [[A]+B], [A] must be a free-standing word from which [[A]+B] is derived compositionally, since otherwise [A] is a bound stem. The stem [ˈsi.miʕ] inside of [siˈmiʕ.kum] is a free-standing word and the semantic relationship of stem + suffix is compositional: [['he heard']+'you (pl.)']. But the stem inside of [sˈmiʕ.na] 'we heard' is bound, since it is not a free-standing word in a compositional relationship. (The form [ˈsi.miʕ] is a free-standing word, but its meaning 'he heard' cannot be composed with the meaning of the suffix 'we' to make 'we heard'.)

OT-CC does not require a commitment to any particular theory of cyclic effects in OT, but since it is a single-grammar theory of opacity, its natural affinity is with a single-grammar theory of cyclicity like the one in Benua (1997) and Kager (1999a), rather than multi-grammar Stratal OT. (For a more literally cyclic approach under a somewhat different version of OT-CC, see the end of §3.2.4.2.) Benua draws a distinction between input-output (IO) and output-output (OO) faithfulness constraints. All of the faithfulness constraints discussed so far have been of the IO type; they require identity between the lexical forms of morphemes and their surface exponents. OO faithfulness constraints require identity between the surface form of a derived word and the surface form of the simpler word from which it is compositionally derived, if any. Thus, OO faithfulness constraints require surface [[A]+B] to resemble surface [A], if /A+B/ is derived compositionally from /A/ and if [A] exists. Only free-standing words and not bound stems can be cyclic domains precisely because OO faithfulness refers to free-standing output forms. Bound stems, by definition, do not have free-standing output forms. (See Benua 1997: 199-205 for the original statement of this argument.)

In Levantine Arabic, the active OO constraint is a type of positional faithfulness requiring preservation of main-stressed vowels: OO-Max-$'$V. (Kiparsky (2003: 162-163) proposes a similar constraint in the context of his Stratal OT analysis of these facts.) By dominating Weak$<i$, as shown in (4-46), OO-Max-$'$V overrides the imperative for syncope and requires preservation of a short high vowel in a situation where it would otherwise be expected to delete. OO-Max-$'$V is vacuously satisfied by forms with subject agreement like [s$'$miʕ.na], since [s$'$miʕ.na] is not a derived form in the relevant sense. Furthermore, OO-Max-$'$V has no protective effect on vowels that are not stressed in the underived form, so syncope is not impeded in [$'$sim.ʕo] 'he heard him'.

(4-46) OO-Max-$'$V >> Weak$<i$

/simiʕ-kum/	OO-Max-$'$V (cf. [$'$simiʕ])	Wk$<i$
→ si$'$miʕ.kum		1
s$'$miʕ.kum	W 1	L

In Stratal OT, cyclicity and opacity are deeply connected with one another: both are consequences of serial application of multiple OT grammars. OT-CC makes no such connection: opacity is attributed to constraints on chains whereas cyclicity has other sources, such as output-output faithfulness. We previously saw reasons to doubt the connection that Stratal OT makes (see §2.3.4.2), and the facts of Levantine Arabic, while probably compatible with Stratal OT (as the analysis briefly sketched in Kiparsky (2003) suggests), offer no support for the opacity/cyclicity connection. The 'cyclic' effect is actually failure of syncope through crucial domination of Weak$<i$. Syncope is never opaque in Levantine Arabic, however; in terms of the present analysis, no relevant Prec constraint dominates Weak$<i$.

4.2.6   Vowel shortening-epenthesis interaction

Like stress, vowel shortening interacts opaquely with epenthesis (Abu-Salim 1982a: 112ff., Farwaneh 1995: 151ff.). The examples in (4-47) show that there is no general process of closed syllable shortening. Vowels are shortened, however, before medial triconsonantal and final biconsonantal clusters, even when those clusters end up being split by epenthesis (4-48). This is a type of counterbleeding opacity: because of epenthesis, the long vowels in (4-48) should not need to shorten, but they do so anyway.

(4-47)   No closed syllable shortening
    /ʒaːb-ha/   ˈʒaːb.ha   'he brought her'
    /ʒaːb-l-u/   ˈʒaːb.lu   'he brought for him'[10]

(4-48)   Pre-/CCC/ and /CC#/ shortening
    /ʃaːf-l-ha/   ˈʃa.fil.ha   'he saw for her'
    /ʒaːb-l-ha/   ˈʒa.bil.ha   'he brought for her'
    /ma ʒaːb-ʃ/   ma ˈʒa.biʃ   'he didn't bring'

Inputs like /ʒaːb-ha/ do not require shortening or epenthesis because CV:C syllables are tolerated. Their shared-mora representation (4-4) presumably violates some markedness constraint that is ranked too low to matter, and they obey CLUSTER-CONDITION, since they have no tautosyllabic clusters. But an input like /ʃaːf-l-ha/ presents the further problem of parsing the /l/, either by adjoining it to make a CV:CC syllable or by attaching it as an immediate constituent of the phonological word.

Let *WORD-APPENDIX (*WDAPP) be the constraint that is violated when a segment is an immediate constituent of the phonological word node. The faithful parse [ʃaːf⟨l⟩ha] violates this constraint. (The angled brackets are used here to indicate that a segment is unsyllabified.) If *WORD-APPENDIX dominates IDENT(long) and CLUSTER-CONDITION as in (4-49), then the path from faithful [ʃaːf⟨l⟩ha] to output [ˈʃa.fil.ha] via [ʃafl.ha] is harmonically improving.

(4-49)   *WORD-APPENDIX >> IDENT(long), CLUSTER-CONDITION from chain validity

/ʃaːf-l-ha/	*WDAPP	ID(long)	CLCND
→ ʃafl.ha		1	1
ʃaːf⟨l⟩ha	W₁	L	L

The competing chains for opaque [ˈʃa.fil.ha] and its principal transparent competitors are given in (4-50). The first two chains are convergent: they produce the same output with different permutations of the same LUMs. Chains (b), (c), and (d) exhibit various combinations of opacity and transparency of stress and shortening. Penult stress and no shortening are the two transparent situations, since they accord with the properties that are visible in surface structure: the initial syllable is open and the second syllable is closed.

(4-50) Some chains from /ʃaːf-l-ha/ and their (r)LUMSeqs
    a. <ʃaːf⟨l⟩ha, ʃafl.ha, ˈʃafl.ha, ˈʃa.fɪl.ha>✓   Opaque stress and shortening.
       <ʃaːf⟨l⟩ha, ˈʃaːf⟨l⟩ha, ˈʃafl.ha, ˈʃa.fɪl.ha>✓
         ℒ = {Dep-Pr@2, Id(long), Dep-V}
         rL = {<Id(long), Dep-V>, <Dep-Pr@2, Dep-V>}

    b. <ʃaːf⟨l⟩ha, ʃaː.fɪl.ha, ʃaːˈfɪl.ha>   Transparent stress, no
       <Dep-V, Dep-Pr@4>   shortening.

    c. <ʃaːf⟨l⟩ha, ˈʃaːf⟨l⟩ha, ˈʃaː.fɪl.ha>   Opaque stress, no shortening.
       <Dep-Pr@2, Dep-V>

    d. <ʃaːf⟨l⟩ha, ʃafl.ha, ʃa.fɪl.ha, ʃaˈfɪl.ha>   Transparent stress, opaque
       <Id(long), Dep-V, Dep-Pr@4>   shortening.

Prec(Dep-Pr, Dep-V) rules out the chains with transparent stress on the epenthetic vowel, (b) and (d) in (4-50). The interesting loser is therefore (c), which has opaque stress but a transparent interaction of shortening and epenthesis. Since (a) is the winner, we require another Prec constraint to choose (a) over (c). Prec(Id(long), Dep-V) favors those chains where any epenthesizing LUM is preceded and not followed by a vowel shortening LUM. In the rLUMSeq derived from the chains in (a), this constraint is satisfied. But chain (c) violates it because its epenthesizing LUM is not preceded by a shortening LUM. To have the desired effect, Prec(Id(long), Dep-V) must be ranked above (a)'s worst violation relative to (c), and that is Ident(long). This ranking result is certified in (4-51).

(4-51) Prec(Id(long), Dep-V) >> Ident(long)

	/ʃaːf-l-ha/	Prec(Id(long), Dep-V)	Id(long)
a. →	ˈʃa.fɪl.ha {Dep-Pr@2, Id(long), Dep-V} {<Id(long), Dep-V>, <Dep-Pr@2, Dep-V>}		1
c.	ʃaːˈfɪl.ha <Dep-Pr@2, Dep-V>	W₁	L

4.2.7 Summary

When PREC constraints are visibly active, opaque outcomes are favored. In Levantine Arabic, the constraint PREC(DEP-PR, DEP-V) requires any epenthetic LUM to be preceded by a stress-assigning LUM. It thereby supports opaque interaction of stress and epenthesis, displacing stress to the right of its expected position in [ka'ta.b*i*t] and to the left in [ka'ta.b*i*l.ha]. Because PREC constraints are no different in kind from other OT constraints, they may be crucially dominated, yielding transparency in the midst of a basically opaque pattern. This too occurs in Levantine Arabic, when the epenthetic vowel is transparently stressed in [ka.tab'*ti*l.ha] because PREC(DEP-PR, DEP-V) is dominated by a constraint against the long lapse of opaque *[ka'tab.t*i*l.ha]. Another constraint, PREC(ID(long), DEP-V), is responsible for the opaque interaction of epenthesis and closed syllable shortening that yields ['ʃa.f*i*l.ha] from /ʃaːf-l-ha/. In concert with *WORD-APPENDIX, this constraint explains why there is shortening in the surface open syllable of ['ʃa.f*i*l.ha] and, paradoxically, why there is no shortening in the surface closed syllable of ['ʒaːb.lu] from /ʒaːb-l-u/.

This account of Levantine Arabic shows that it is possible to analyze a complex but well understood set of opaque interactions within a single OT grammar. Multigrammar approaches like Stratal OT or sympathy do not seem to be necessary, nor are ordered rules. The key to the present analysis is the recognition that candidates include more information than just the output form and the input-output relation; they also encode the sequence of operations that maps input to output. By regulating that sequence of operations, PREC constraints are able to favor opaque interactions in a way that is fundamentally integrated with classic OT's bias toward transparency.

4.3 Bedouin Arabic

4.3.1 Background

The phonology of the Bedouin dialects of Arabic is very different from the phonology of sedentary dialects like Levantine. Processes that are unusual or nonexistent in sedentary dialects, such as raising of low vowels in open syllables or deletion of low vowels in the context __CVCV, are pervasive in the Bedouin varieties, and Bedouin stress is typically iambic rather than trochaic. Bedouin Arabic has no shortage of opaque interactions, and they have been investigated with great insight and thoroughness by Al-Mozainy (1976, 1981). Several of these phenomena were recruited as examples in previous chapters, and further details were promised later. This section redeems that promissory note.

Al-Mozainy belongs to the Bani Sâlim branch of the Harb tribe. Although he is a native speaker of this dialect (in fact, a text dictated by him has been published in Ingham (1982: 112-115)), his primary source of material was the language of older, illiterate speakers, who were chosen to avoid unwanted influence from Standard Arabic or other dialects. All of the data here are drawn from Al-Mozainy's work, and parenthesized page numbers in the examples indicate where the forms can be found in Al-Mozainy (1981). Throughout, when I refer to unqualified 'Bedouin Arabic', I mean the variety that Al-Mozainy speaks and has described. In addition to the published data, I have checked various additional forms with Al-Mozainy via email, and a few come from Al-Mozainy, Bley-Vroman, and McCarthy (1985). Somewhat similar phenomena can be found in other Arabian Bedouin dialects, such as those described by Abboud (1979), Johnstone (1967a, 1967b), and Prochazka (1988). The Levantine and North African Bedouin dialects described by Blanc (1970), Irshied (1984), Irshied and Kenstowicz (1984), and Mitchell (1960) differ significantly.

I have made a few simplifications in Al-Mozainy's transcriptions. I do not indicate palatalization of [k] and [g] or pharyngealization of [r] and [l]. (Al-Mozainy is somewhat inconsistent in marking palatalization.) I will always transcribe the high vowel produced by the raising process as [i], although its actual color varies automatically among [i], [ɨ], and [u], depending on details of the segmental context (Al-Mozainy 1981: 64ff.). Since Al-Mozainy does not usually distinguish the front and back allophones of the low vowel in his transcriptions, neither do I.

The discussion of Bedouin Arabic is organized around the principal phonological phenomena and their interactions. The foundations of the analysis are laid in §4.3.2 with an argument for iambic stress and an account of vowel deletion in the __CVCV context. A minor opaque interaction is dealt with in passing, but more importantly this section shows how the harmonic improvement requirement on chains resolves a problem with a classic OT analysis of the same facts and with the general problem of segmental alternations that improve metrical structure. The opaque interaction of stress with two reduction processes, syncope of high vowels and raising of low vowels, is the topic of §4.3.3. Syncope, raising, and stress all interact opaquely with epenthesis for reasons that will be discussed in §4.3.4. The opaque interaction of raising, syncope, and a metathesis process is analyzed in §4.3.5. Finally, to these cases should be added the opaque interaction of syncope and palatalization, which was analyzed in §3.3.3. From this summary, it is clear that Bedouin Arabic phonology has many opaque interactions, so it is an excellent test-bed for OT-CC.

4.3.2   Stress and trisyllabic deletion

Although the sedentary Arabic dialects have trochaic stress, Bedouin Arabic stress is iambic. This important insight, due to Hayes (1995: 226ff.), is not at all obvious from the observed stress patterns, but it helps to make sense of some otherwise puzzling features of Bedouin Arabic phonology. The basic data are given in (4-52), organized by the surface syllable pattern.

(4-52) Bedouin Arabic stress

    a. Monosyllables
/kitib/	kˈtib	'it was written' (149)
/ʃirib/	ʃˈrib	'it was drunk' (151)

    b. Disyllables with light penult
/katab/	ˈki.tab	'he wrote' (133)
/ʁazaː/	ˈʁa.za	'he raided' (133)

    c. Heavy penult
/ʃarib-at/	ˈʃar.bat	'she drank' (147)
/maktuːf-ah/	makˈtuː.fah	'tied (f. sg.)' (132)

    d. Heavy antepenult and light penult
/maħkam-ah/	ˈmaħ.ku.mah	'court' (187)
/ðˤarabt-kum/	ðˤaˈrab.tu.kum	'I hit you (m. pl.)' (151)

    e. Light antepenult and penult
/ʔakal-at/	ʔaˈka.lat	'she ate' (164)
/ʔakað-at/	ʔaˈka.ðat	'she took' (146)

    f. Degenerate syllable before light penult
/saħab-at/	sˈħa.bat	'she pulled'[11] (61)
/katab-at/	kˈti.bat	'she wrote' (146)
/ʔinkasar-at/	ʔin.kˈsa.rat	'it (f.) got broken' (153)
/ʔiftakar-aw/	ʔif.tˈka.raw	'they (m.) remembered' (153)

    g. CVːC or CVCC ultima
/ðˤarab-t/	ðˤaˈrabt	'I hit' (132)
/ja-χdim-uːn/	jχadˈmuːn	'they (m.) serve' (175)

Which is the correct metrical analysis, iambic [(ðˤaˈrab)tu.kum] or trochaic [ðˤa(ˈrab)tu.kum]? Just looking at the distribution of stress is not very helpful, since most of the data seem to fit well with both iambic and trochaic stress (c, d, g) or with neither (a, f). Although there are some words with overtly iambic stress (e), the principal argument for iambic stress comes not from the distribution of stress but from the vowel deletion process exemplified in (f).

The [ʔ]-initial words like [ʔaˈka.lat] in (e) have a stress pattern that could only be analyzed as iambic: [(ʔaˈka)lat]. A trochaic parse *[ʔa(ˈka.lat)] is out of the question because Bedouin Arabic, like Levantine, consistently respects NONFINALITY unless the final syllable is heavy or the word is disyllabic. Iambic stress shows, of course, that IAMB (4-53) dominates TROCHEE. NONFINALITY, no matter where it is ranked, favors the parse [(ʔaˈka)lat] over end-stressed *[ʔa(kaˈlat)], as usual in iambic systems. The reason why these words are always [ʔ]-initial will be given shortly.

(4-53) IAMB

Assign one violation mark for every foot that is not left-headed.

Some words that look like [ʔaˈka.lat] but have a different stress pattern are listed in (4-54). These words have stems that begin with /ʔ/, which is deleted after the definite article /ʔal/ (cf. [ˈʔa.sad] 'a lion', etc.). The naïve expectation is that 'the lion' will be pronounced with peninitial stress, *[ʔaˈla.sad], just like [ʔaˈka.lat]. The actual stress pattern is opaque, however: [ˈʔa.la.sad] is stressed as if it were *[ˈʔal.ʔa.sad], like the other [(ˈH)LL] words in (d) of (4-52). This instance of opaque stress requires the constraint PREC(DEP-PR, MAX-C) to favor the opaque chain <ʔal.ʔa.sad, (ˈʔal)ʔa.sad, (ˈʔa.la)sad> over its transparent competitor *<ʔal.ʔa.sad, ʔa.la.sad, (ʔaˈla)sad>. Since [(ˈʔa.la)sad] has a trochaic foot to *[(ʔaˈla)sad]'s iamb foot, PREC(DEP-PR, MAX-C) must dominate IAMB, as shown in (4-55). By the ranking metaconstraint (3-24), PREC(DEP-PR, MAX-C) must be ranked below MAX-C, and MAX-C must itself be ranked below whatever markedness constraint militates against faithful analysis of VCʔV sequences. These additional ranking requirements need not detain us further, since they in no way affect the main points of the analysis.

(4-54) Nouns with initial /ʔal-ʔ/ (Al-Mozainy 1981: 138)

/ʔal-ʔasad/	ˈʔa.la.sad	'the lion'
/ʔal-ʔaxu/	ˈʔa.lu.xu	'the brother'
/ʔal-ʔabu/	ˈʔa.li.bu	'the father'

(4-55) PREC(DEP-PR, MAX-C) >> IAMB

/ʔal-ʔasad/	PREC(DEP-PR, MAX-C)	IAMB
→ <ʔal.ʔa.sad, (ˈʔal)ʔa.sad, (ˈʔa.la)sad> <DEP-PR@2, MAX-C@3>		1
<ʔal.ʔa.sad, ʔa.la.sad, (ʔaˈla)sad> <MAX-C@3, DEP-PR@4>	W₂	L

The main evidence for iambic prosody comes from the process of trisyllabic deletion. Descriptively, the vowel /a/ is deleted from a light syllable that is followed by a nonfinal light syllable: /saħab-at / → [sˈħa.bat]. This process is extremely general; in fact, I know of no lexical exceptions. It is also productive; for instance, Al-Mozainy (1981: 85) cites the borrowing [ʔal-ʕgi.bah] for the Jordanian Arabic original [ʔal-ʕaqabah] 'Aqaba', and further evidence can be garnered from the secret language exemplified in (4-73) (see note 16).

Trisyllabic deletion only affects light syllables, so neither long vowels nor vowels in closed syllables are vulnerable. Furthermore, the following syllable must also be light; there is no deletion from the initial syllable of [ðˤaˈrab.tu.kum] because the following syllable is heavy. This sequence of two light syllables must itself be nonfinal: /ʁa.zaː/ → [ˈʁa.za], *[ʁˈza(ː)]. The rule 'a → Ø/__CVCV' abbreviates all of these conditions, but obviously explains none of them. OT demands that we explain why trisyllabic deletion occurs by identifying the responsible markedness constraints. Those constraints, I propose in McCarthy (2003c), come from metrical theory.

The analysis begins with an analogous example from another language, trisyllabic shortening in English. Pairs like *serene/serenity*, *grateful/gratitude*, and *derive/derivative* show that, descriptively, a long vowel is shortened when followed by an unstressed syllable that is itself nonfinal. The standard analysis of trisyllabic shortening (Chomsky and Halle 1968) uses a purely descriptive rule with a complex, nonlocal environment, much like 'a → Ø/__CVCV'. The explanation for trisyllabic shortening comes from metrical theory. According to Myers (1987) and Prince (1990), trisyllabic shortening is conditioned by foot structure, in top-down fashion. The stress pattern of nouns with a light penult is a trochaic foot over penult and antepenult, with final syllable extrametricality: *se (réni)*$_\text{Ft}$ *⟨ty⟩*. Shortening improves the well-formedness of the trochaic foot, replacing a HL (heavy-light) trochee with a more harmonic LL trochee. This approach has answers to the *why*'s of trisyllabic shortening, as Prince (1996) emphasizes. Why shortening and not, say, lengthening? Because shortening improves the match with the preferred bimoraic foot. Why a following unstressed syllable? Because a following unstressed syllable is a descriptive artifact of the real foot-based condition — the second syllable of a trochee is by definition unstressed. And why, in nonlocal fashion, must there be another syllable after that? Because of English's regular noun extrametricality rule. The answers to these questions emerge clearly once the role of trochaic foot structure in English is properly understood.

Similarly, I propose that the key to understanding trisyllabic deletion in Bedouin Arabic is placing it in the context of an *iambic* stress system. Iambic feet are subject to strong quantitative requirements. According to the Iambic/

Trochaic Law (Hayes 1987, 1995: 80) or Grouping Harmony (Prince 1990) (see also Kager 1993, McCarthy and Prince 1986/1996), iambic feet tend to favor quantitative reinforcement of the prominential contrast, so a L'H iamb is better than a L'L iamb. For concreteness, I will assume that the GROUPING-HARMONY constraint is defined as in (4-56).[12]

(4-56) GROUPING-HARMONY (GRPHARM)
  In a foot (x y), |y| > |x|.   (|α| ≡ weight of α)

Because of GROUPING-HARMONY, many languages have iambic lengthening processes, which improve LL iambs by lengthening the second syllable: /pakata/ → [(pa'ka:)ta] *or* [(pa'kat)ta]. Another logically possible consequence of GROUPING-HARMONY is reduction of unstressed syllables in iambic feet, enhancing the quantitative contrast by weakening the weak rather than strengthening the strong. Hayes (1995: 213) reports that this occurs in Delaware, and it is an element of Kager's (1997) analysis of Macushi Carib. The Bedouin Arabic process is exactly this: reduction of the unstressed syllable in a (L'L) iambic foot to enhance the quantitative contrast.

  The most harmonic segmentally faithful iambic parse of /sahab-at/ is [(sa'ħa)bat]. (The alternative parses *[sa('ħa.bat)] and *[sa(ħa'bat)] are ruled out by NONFINALITY.) The iambic foot [(sa'ħa)] violates GROUPING-HARMONY, since its unstressed and stressed syllables are of equal weight, both light, and iambs prefer unequal quantity. As I just noted. many languages improve on this situation by lengthening the stressed syllable, but that option is ruled out in Bedouin Arabic by IDENT(-long) or some equivalent constraint. In Bedouin Arabic, I claim, a (L'L) iamb loses out to an iamb where the first syllable has lost its nucleus and therefore has no moras at all. A moraless or 'degenerate' syllable is obviously lighter than a monomoraic syllable, so this move improves performance on GROUPING-HARMONY. Diagram (4-57) shows how an iambic foot with an initial degenerate syllable is represented. From now on, I will use the more compact notation [s.ħa] or [(s'ħa)] to indicate the presence of a degenerate syllable. It should be noted that this structure can also occur word-internally, as in [ʔin(k'sa)rat] from /ʔinkasar-at/.

(4-57) Satisfying GROUPING-HARMONY with a degenerate syllable[13]

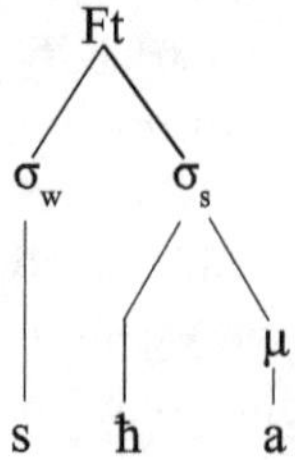

By ranking Grouping-Harmony and Ident(-long) above Max-A, as shown in tableau (4-58), we account for the full range of observed conditions on this deletion process, conditions that are only stipulated in the rule 'a → Ø/__CVCV'. Only vowels in light syllables are deleted because a disyllabic iamb can never begin with a heavy syllable, and Grouping-Harmony is only relevant to disyllabic feet. The syllable following the affected vowel must also be light because, if it were heavy, Grouping-Harmony would be satisfied without further ado: [(ðˤaˈrab)tu.kum]. The last CV in the rule is there to ensure that the affected light-light sequence is nonfinal. The real explanation: final light-light sequences are always stressed trochaically because of Nonfinality (e.g., [ˈʁa.za]), and trochees have different quantitative requirements than iambs (Hayes 1995, Prince 1990). The fact that only the vowel /a/ seems to be targeted for deletion by this process is an analytic artifact with a trivial explanation: high vowels are deleted by a notionally distinct process, discussed below.[14]

(4-58) Grouping-Harmony, Ident(-long) >> Max-A

/saħab-at/		GrpHarm	Id(-long)	Max-A
→	(sˈħa)bat			1
a.	(saˈħa)bat	W₁		L
b.	(saˈħaː)bat		W₁	L

The peculiarity of [ʔ]-initial words like [(ʔaˈka)lat] is not their iambic stress but rather their failure to show the effects of trisyllabic deletion. Expected *[(ʔˈka)lat] is presumably ruled out because of some difficulty associated with degenerate syllables consisting of only [ʔ]. The markedness constraint that *[(ʔˈka)lat] violates — I will give it the ad hoc designation *[ʔ]σ — must therefore dominate Grouping-Harmony, as shown in (4-59).

(4-59) *[ʔ]σ >> Grouping-Harmony

/ʔakal-at/		*[ʔ]σ	GrpHarm
→	(ʔaˈka)lat		1
	(ʔˈka)lat	W₁	

Although the ranking shown in (4-58) is a big part of the trisyllabic deletion story, it is not the whole thing. The form *[(ˈsaħ)bat] is at least as unmarked and no more unfaithful than the winner in (4-58). The monosyllabic foot [(ˈsaħ)] satisfies Grouping-Harmony just as well as [(sˈħa)] does; worse yet, [(sˈħa)] must be more marked than [(ˈsaħ)] because the language parses consonants as codas rather than degenerate syllables whenever possible. This means that *[('saħ)bat] is wrongly predicted to be more harmonic than the real winner [(s'ħa)bat].

The explanation for [(s'ħa)bat]'s greater harmony comes from OT-CC. Winning [(s'ħa)bat] is the endpoint of a valid, harmonically improving candidate chain: <sa.ħa.bat, (sa'ħa)bat, (s'ħa)bat>. This chain is harmonically improving because the presence of a stress is more harmonic than its absence, as in Levantine Arabic, and because of the ranking in (4-58), which allows deletion in support of GROUPING-HARMONY. Since chains must monotonically accumulate LUMs, there is no way to get to *[('saħ)bat] with a similar chain — a chain with stress shift like <sa.ħa.bat, (sa'ħa)bat, ('saħ)bat> is inherently invalid because it is noncumulative. There are two alternative routes to *[('saħ)bat] that need to be considered, however.

One possible way of getting to *[('saħ)bat] is via a sequence of forms that delete the vowel in the penult before it gets a chance to be stressed: <sa.ħa.bat, saħ.bat, ('saħ)bat>. This putative chain is invalid, however, because the initial /a/-deletion step is not harmonically improving. Neither GROUPING-HARMONY nor any other markedness constraint ranked higher than MAX-A will favor [saħ] over [saħa] when foot structure is not present. The other possible route to *[('saħ)bat] involves assigning trochaic stress and deleting the unstressed syllable: <sa.ħa.bat, ('saħa)bat, ('saħ)bat>. This chain is invalid because stress is iambic, except finally, so trochaic stress is not the most harmonic way of assigning a DEP-PROM-violating LUM. In short, *[('saħ)bat] is not even a member of the candidate set, so it offers no competition at all for the real winner [(s'ħa)bat].

This argument has significance that goes well beyond this particular example (also see §3.2.4.3 on other effects of requiring chains to improve harmonically). The pre-OT stress literature, such as Hayes (1995), is replete with insightful analyses that involve first assigning metrical feet and then invoking processes that have the effect of 'improving' the metrical analysis. Vowel reduction and deletion are among these processes, as we have seen. As in rule-based phonology generally, these analyses can have basic problems of formalization: there is a lurking danger that the notion of improvement is in the textual interpretation of the analysis and not the analysis itself. OT solves this problem by giving well-definition to improvement, but classic OT also introduces a problem of its own: how is it possible to reproduce the effect of ordering the stress rule first and then applying the improvement rules to the resulting metrical structure?

The competition between [(s'ħa)bat] and *[('saħ)bat] is an instance of this problem. Winning [(s'ħa)bat] has the same basic stress pattern as segmentally faithful [(sa'ħa)bat], but *[('saħ)bat] has a different stress pattern. In rule-based phonology, this is the result of ordering stress before vowel deletion (and not subsequently shifting stress). But in classic OT, where the effects of all processes are evaluated in parallel, there is no way of limiting the viable candidates to those that share segmentally faithful [(sa'ħa)bat]'s stress pattern. This problem for classic OT was first identified by Kager (1997), who develops some ideas about how it can be gotten around in two languages with stress-sensitive vowel deletion, Macushi Carib and Southeastern Tepehuan. A general solution has proven elusive, however, because no general solution can be reconciled with classic OT's basic premises.

The analysis of Bedouin Arabic suggests how OT-CC can provide a fully general account of processes that optimize metrical structure by altering segments. Because chains must show harmonic improvement at every step, processes like deletion or lengthening can respond to metrical well-formedness requirements, but they cannot anticipate those requirements by making changes that will later turn out to be providential. As I noted a few paragraphs ago, *[('saħ)bat] can only be derived by a putative chain like <sa.ħa.bat, saħ.bat, ('saħ)bat>, in which the vowel-deleting LUM precedes the stress-assigning LUM. But because no metrical structure is present yet, vowel deletion in the <sa.ħa.bat, saħ.bat> subchain offers no immediate harmonic improvement. On the one hand, because classic OT optimizes globally, a classic OT analysis ends up wrongly favoring *[('saħ)bat] because this form offers the best combination of metrical structure and vowel deletion. OT-CC, on the other hand, is locally optimizing and incapable of producing this sort of global effect: for deletion to occur first, it must offer immediate harmonic improvement all by itself, and if deletion is a response to metrical well-formedness, then metrical structure must already be present when deletion occurs.

To sum up, the trisyllabic deletion process makes sense in the context of an iambic analysis of the stress patterns in (4-52), but it would not make sense in a trochaic analysis. As we have seen, words like [(s'ħa)bat] show that the modal foot is iambic, albeit somewhat covertly. Feet are overtly iambic in the [(ʔa'ka)lat] case, where trisyllabic deletion is blocked.

Although Bedouin Arabic is modally iambic, trochaic feet do occur under conditions where IAMB is crucially dominated. The opaque stress in (4-55) is one example; another is the stress pattern of disyllables like [('sa.ħab)] ((b) in (4-52)). Reversal of iambic prominence word-finally is common; for another example, see the analysis of Axininca Campa in McCarthy and Prince (1993b). Final reversal shows that NONFINALITY('σ) (4-60) dominates IAMB (see tableau (4-61)). (As in Levantine Arabic (§4.2.2), I assume that final CVC syllables are parsed as light, and final CV: syllables are shortened.)

(4-60) NONFINALITY($'\sigma$) (NF($'\sigma$))

Assign one violation mark for every stressed syllable that is final in some phonological word.

(4-61) NONFINALITY($'\sigma$) >> IAMB[15]

	/sahab/	NF($'\sigma$)	IAMB
→	('sa.hab)		1
a.	(sa'ħab)	W 1	L
b.	(s'ħab)	W 1	L

The current state of the constraint hierarchy is summarized in (4-62). (The ad hoc constraint on [ʔ] has been included to clarify some of the interactions.) Feet are normally iambic, but they are trochaic under two circumstances: in opaque derivations like /ʔal-ʔasad/ → ['ʔa.la.sad], where trochaic stress is necessary to satisfy PREC(DEP-PR, MAX-C); and in disyllables, where stressed-syllable non-finality rules out the iambic parse. The other important element of this system is the interaction of GROUPING-HARMONY with MAX-A, which is responsible for the trisyllabic deletion process that we examined at length.

(4-62) Bedouin Arabic ranking summary I

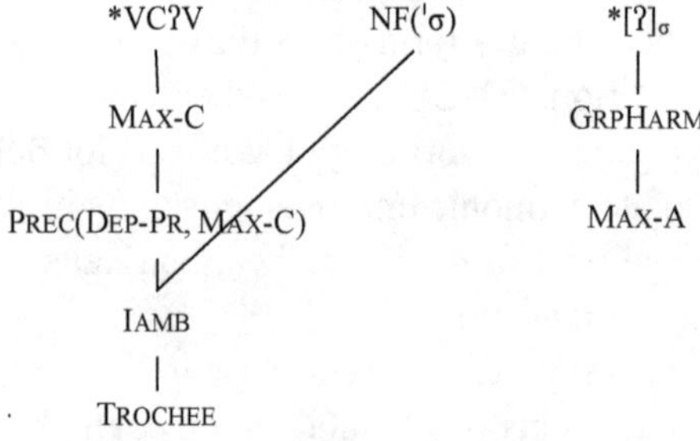

4.3.3   Syncope and raising

Like Levantine Arabic, Bedouin Arabic deletes short high vowels from nonfinal open syllables. Some examples are given in (4-63); evidence of productivity comes from borrowings like [slinder] for English *cylinder* (Al-Mozainy 1981: 84). As in Levantine, these data show that WEAK<*i* (4-38) dominates MAX-I (see (4-64)).

(4-63) Syncope of high vowels, part I

/kitib-t/	kˈtibt	‘you (m. sg.) were written’ (59)
/ti-rsil-uːn/	tirsˈluːn	‘you (m. sg.) send’ (46)
/ja-gʕud-uːn/	jagʕˈduːn	‘you (m. pl.) sit’ (46)
/ja-ktub-in/	ˈjaktbin	‘they (f.) write’ (142)

(4-64) Wᴇᴀᴋ<*i* >> Mᴀx-I

/kitib-t/	Wᴋ<*i*	Mᴀx-I
→ kˈtibt		1
kiˈtibt	W₁	L

Syncope works somewhat differently in Bedouin Arabic than Levantine, however, as the data in (4-65) reveal. Bedouin Arabic elides high vowels from positions where they would otherwise be stressed. Thus, /kitib/ becomes [kˈtib] and not *[ˈki.tib], or /ʃarib-at/ becomes [ˈʃar.bat] and not *[ʃˈri.bat] (cf. [kˈti.bat] ‘she wrote’ from /katab-at/).

(4-65) Syncope of high vowels, part II

/kitib/	kˈtib	‘it (m.) was written’ (149)
/kitib-at/	ˈkitbat	‘it (f.) was written’ (59)
/ʃarib-at/	ˈʃarbat	‘she drank’ (147)

Syncope of high vowels from positions where they would otherwise be stressed is evidence of an opaque, counterbleeding interaction between stress and syncope. Stress has no protective effect on the deleted high vowels in (4-65) because the Mᴀx-I-violating LUM is ordered before any Dᴇᴘ-Pʀᴏᴍ-violating LUM. This LUM ordering is required by Pʀᴇᴄ(Mᴀx-I, Dᴇᴘ-Pʀ), which must dominate both Nᴏɴғɪɴᴀʟɪᴛʏ(ˈσ) and Mᴀx-I to favor opaque [kˈtib] over transparent *[ˈkitib] (see (4-66)).

(4-66) Pʀᴇᴄ(Mᴀx-I, Dᴇᴘ-Pʀ) >> Nᴏɴғɪɴᴀʟɪᴛʏ(ˈσ), Mᴀx-I

/kitib/	Pʀᴇᴄ(Mᴀx-I, Dᴇᴘ-Pʀ)	NF(ˈσ)	Mᴀx-I
→ <ki.tib, k.tib, (kˈtib)> <Mᴀx-I@2, Dᴇᴘ-Pʀ@4>		1	1
<ki.tib, (ˈki.tib)> <Dᴇᴘ-Pʀ@2>	W₁	L	L

The new ranking results in (4-64) and (4-66) should be incorporated into the hierarchy before the analysis goes any further. To keep the diagram in (4-67) simple, I have omitted some of the less relevant constraints in the earlier diagram (4-62). The ranking of MAX-A over MAX-I is obtained from basic typological considerations (see §3.5.3, §4.2.5 above, and note 14).

(4-67) Bedouin Arabic ranking summary II

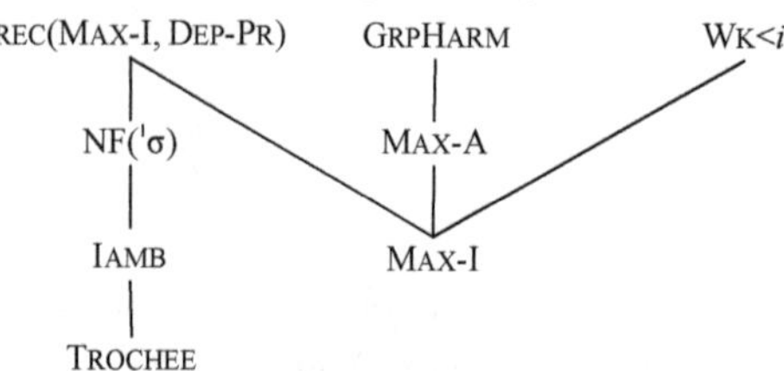

We have seen that low vowels delete to satisfy GROUPING-HARMONY, while high vowels delete because of WEAK<i. What happens when a stem contains both a low vowel and a high vowel, with each of them in positions that favor deletion? A relevant datum is /ʃarib-at/ 'she drank'. The interesting candidates are ['ʃar.bat], with deletion of /i/, and *[ʃ'ri.bat], with deletion of /a/. (Deletion of both vowels is ruled out by undominated constraints on syllable structure: *[ʃrbat].) The chains and their LUMSeqs appear in (4-68). No new ranking is necessary to explain why (a) is more harmonic than (b); indeed, there is already more than one explanation at hand. First, (b) violates MAX-A and (a) violates MAX-I. Because MAX-A universally dominates MAX-I, (b) is disfavored. Second, PREC(MAX-I, DEP-PR) favors chain (a) over chain (b), since the latter includes a DEP-PROM-violating LUM with no preceding MAX-I-violating LUM.

(4-68) Some chains from /ʃarib-at/ and their LUMSeqs
    a. <ʃa.ri.bat, ʃar.bat, ('ʃar)bat>✓   <MAX-I@4, DEP-PR@2>
    b. <ʃa.ri.bat, (ʃa'ri)bat, (ʃ'ri)bat>   <DEP-PR@4, MAX-A@2>

Although low vowels do not delete in the same contexts as high vowels, they do sometimes turn into high vowels by a process I will refer to as raising. The conditions under which raising does or does not occur are interesting in themselves, but raising is also important because of its opaque interactions with the rest of the phonology. Raising, like high-vowel syncope, is not bled by stress assignment, so the vowel in the first syllable of ['simiʕ] from /samiʕ/ 'he heard' is both raised and stressed. Furthermore, raising does not feed syncope of high vowels, so /samiʕ/ does not become *[s'miʕ]. Nor is raising fed by processes like epenthesis or glide vocalization that create open syllables: /badw/ → ['ba.du], *['bi.du] 'a Bedouin'.

As the examples in (4-69) show, short low vowels become high in nonfinal open syllables. These examples are representative of hundreds of noun, verb, and adjective forms cited by Al-Mozainy.

(4-69) Paradigm of /katab/ (58)
    'kitab   'he wrote'
    ki'tabt   'you (m. sg.) wrote'
    ki'tabtum 'you (m. pl.) wrote'
    ki'tabna 'we wrote'
    k'tibat   'she wrote'

The vowel of /katab/'s second syllable alternates between [a] and [i], so positing /a/ for the underlying representation of the second vowel is not unreasonable. Furthermore, underlying /a/ in this position is necessary to differentiate it from the behavior of underlying /i/, which deletes in ['ʃar.bat] from /ʃarib-at/ 'she drank' (Al-Mozainy 1981: 3-4). But the vowel of /katab/'s first syllable never shows up as [a]; it alternates between [i] — the result of raising — and zero — the result of trisyllabic deletion. What, then, is the rationale for positing underlying /a/ in /katab/'s first syllable? This question receives very careful attention from Al-Mozainy, and I summarize his arguments here. (Other treatments of raising in Bedouin Arabic include Kirchner (1996), McCarthy (1993b, 1994a, 1994b), and Parkinson (1992).)

For one thing, the first underlying /a/ of /katab/ is justified by the usual logic of underlying representations: different patterns of surface alternation require different underlying structures. Since the vowel of the first syllable in the passive verb [k'tib]~[k'tibt]~['kit.bat] 'he~you~she was written' alternates differently from its active counterpart ['ki.tab]~[ki'tabt]~[k'ti.bat] 'he~you~she wrote', the passive and active verbs must have different vowels in their initial syllables. Since the passive must have underlying /i/ in the first syllable to account for deletion in [k'tib], the active must have a different, less readily deleteable vowel — therefore /a/.

Another argument for underlying /a/ is that raising is sometimes blocked by the consonantal and/or vocalic context. The examples in (4-70) show that raising is blocked by an adjacent guttural consonant (McCarthy 1994b), unless a high vowel follows. Raising is also blocked if the vowel in the next syllable is low and the intervening consonant is a guttural or a coronal sonorant (4-71). Because raising is sometimes blocked, there are overt [a]~[i] alternations across different words with the same underlying vowel melody in the sense of McCarthy (1979, 1981). The vowels in the initial syllables of ['ki.tab] 'he wrote' and ['ʕa.bad] 'he worshiped' come from the same underlying source: the /a-a/ melodic morpheme of perfective active verbs. The same is true of [gɨ.waː.niːn] 'laws' (67) and [ga'raː.jib] 'relatives' (195), which share the /a-aː-i(ː)/ melodic morpheme of the broken plural template (McCarthy and Prince 1990a).

(4-70) a. Raising blocked by an adjacent guttural (56, 68, 164)
      ˈʕabad 'he worshiped'
      ˈħakam 'he ruled'
      ˈʁanam 'sheep'
      ˈχadaʕ 'he cheated'
      ˈsaħab 'he pulled'
      ˈnaʕas 'he dozed'
      ˈnaχal 'palm trees'
      ˈbaʁal 'mule'

      b. But not if a high vowel follows
      ˈħilim 'he dreamt'
      ˈʕitˤiʃ 'he became thirsty'
      ˈfihim 'he understood'

(4-71) a. Raising blocked by following [a] across coronal sonorant (56, 68)
      ˈsarag 'he stole'
      ˈbalah 'dates'
      ˈmanaʕ 'he prohibited'

      b. But not by a following high vowel
      ˈkirih 'he disliked'

Al-Mozainy develops another argument for underlying /a/ — and for the productivity of the raising process — on the basis of a secret language that involves permuting the root consonants. When the result of root permutation alters the conditions that permit and block raising, the process succeeds or fails exactly as predicted (see (4-72) and (2-8)). In addition to this naturally-occurring secret language, Al-Mozainy's evidence extends to a contrived secret language that involves infixing the syllable [ħar] after the first vowel. The prediction is that the presence of a guttural plus [a] sequence will block raising of a preceding /a/, and this prediction was borne out in the responses of his consultants (4-73).

(4-72) Raising and blocking in a natural secret language (86ff.)

Real language	Secret language forms
ðˤarab 'he hit'	ribaðˤ, biðˤar, riðˤab, ðˤibar
	baraðˤ
ðˤribat 'she hit'	rbiðˤat, rðˤibat, briðˤat
	bðˤarat, ðˤbarat
difaʕ 'he pushed'	fidaʕ, ʕadaf, daʕaf, ʕafad, faʕad
ʒibal 'mountain'	biʒal, liʒab
	ʒalab

(4-73) Raising and blocking in an artificial secret language (92ff.)[16]
    kitab 'he wrote'   kaḥartab
    ktibat 'she wrote'   kaḥartibat
    giba:jil 'tribes'   gaḥarba:jil

The data in (4-74) show that raising is also productive in borrowed words. This is scarcely unexpected, given all of the other evidence we have seen in support of this process.

(4-74) Raising in borrowed words (84ff.)

Source word	Source language	Borrowed word	Gloss
kabak	Turkish	kibak	'cufflink'
ʔalʕaqabah	Jordanian Arabic	ʔalʕgibah	'Aqaba'
madrasah	Standard Arabic	madrisah	'school'

Al-Mozainy's final piece of evidence for underlying /a/ and the productivity of raising comes from his observations of children's spelling errors — or rather the lack of them. Children learn to write Standard Arabic in school, and the vowels of Standard Arabic are a frequent source of difficulty for children and adults who speak other varieties of colloquial Arabic. Surprisingly, these Bedouin Arabic speaking children make few errors in spelling the Standard Arabic vowels. According to Al-Mozainy, spelling Standard Arabic vowels is easier for these children because the Standard Arabic form is similar to their internalized representation of their native language. For instance, underlying /katab/ is similar to Standard Arabic [kataba].

This is an impressive array of evidence for the regularity and productivity of the raising process and for the underlying representations that it presupposes. Since raising is also opaque, this evidence refutes claims that all cases of opacity can be explained away as the morphologized remnants of phonological processes that are no longer productive (see §2.2.3). Raising is clearly alive and kicking in Bedouin Arabic. We will now proceed to explore the details of this phenomenon and its interaction with the rest of the phonology.

Raising of /a/, like syncope of /i/, is a reduction process. The idea that raising is a type of vowel reduction is supported by similar phenomena in other languages, such as Russian (see Crosswhite (1999, 2000a) and the related discussion in §4.2.5). In fact, raising and syncope affect syllables of exactly the same type: those that are light and nonfinal. Raising is compelled by a markedness constraint from the same family as the constraint that produces syncope. WEAK<*a* (4-37) favors less sonorous vowels in weak (= nonfinal, light, and unstressed) syllables. By ranking WEAK<*a* above IDENT(+low), as in (4-75), low vowels are forced to reduce in sonority when they occur in weak syllables.

(4-75) WEAK<*a* >> IDENT(+low)

/katab-t/	WK<*a*	ID(+low)
→ ki'tabt		1
ka'tabt	W₁	L

Reduction is not the only point of resemblance between syncope and raising. Raising, like syncope, is in a counterbleeding interaction with stress. Just as syncope can affect vowels in syllables where they would otherwise have been stressed, so too can raising affect vowels in syllables that end up being stressed in surface forms: ['ki.tab], ['ʃi.rib], etc. The constraint PREC(ID(+low), DEP-PR) favors chains where the raising LUM precedes the stress-assigning LUM. It dominates IDENT(+low), thereby favoring reduction even in forms where stress would render reduction unnecessary. See (4-76) for the ranking argument and compare (4-66) for the parallel argument with syncope.

(4-76) PREC(ID(+low), DEP-PR) >> IDENT(+low)

/katab/	PREC(ID(+low), DEP-PR)	ID(+low)
→ <ka.tab, ki.tab, ('ki.tab)> <ID(+low)@2, DEP-PR@2>		1
<ka.tab, ('ka.tab)> <DEP-PR@2>	W₁	L

This opaque analysis rests on the assumption that raising is a reduction process that could be bled by stress, so PREC(ID(+low), DEP-PR) forces a counterbleeding interaction. The principal arguments for raising as reduction are two: the existence of similar reduction processes in other languages, as I have already noted; and the lack of reasonable alternatives. For Kirchner (1996: 347), raising and syncope are responses to an imperative to '[m]inimize the duration of a short vowel in an open syllable' — in other words, they are a kind of reduction. For Parkinson (1992: (19)), raising is a process of height dissimilation that affects the first of two /a/s in adjacent syllables: /katab/ → ['ki.tab]. (Height assimilation is then responsible for raising in /ʃarib/ → ['ʃi.rib].) The problem with this approach is that it cannot explain why dissimilation consistently targets the first of the two /a/s, and then only when it is in a light syllable. Why only a light syllable? Because raising is reduction.

Although raising interacts opaquely with stress, it usually interacts transparently with the conditions that are responsible for the preservation of unraised low vowels in examples like ['ʕa.bad] or ['sa.ħab] (see (4-70) and (4-71)). These conditions are all assimilatory. Guttural consonants and low vowels are acoustically and articulatorily similar, indicating that they have some feature value in common. For simplicity, we can refer to that feature value as [+low], but see McCarthy (1991, 1994b) for a more nuanced view. The reason why /ʕabad/ does not raise to *[ˈʕi.bad] and /saħab/ does not raise to *[ˈsi.ħab] is that [+low] vowels are favored when they are adjacent to [+low] consonants. This requirement is not able to force high vowels to lower — compare /samiʕ/ → [ˈsi.miʕ], *[ˈsimaʕ] — but it is able to block raising in [ˈʕa.bad] and [ˈsa.ħab].

The preference for low vowels next to guttural consonants is subsumed by the general theory of interactions between consonant place and vowel quality (see Clements and Hume 1995: 277ff. for a review). This theory, no matter how it is constructed, will have to contain constraints with the force (though perhaps not the formulation) of ATTRACT-LOW in (4-77). In Bedouin Arabic, ATTRACT-LOW is ranked beneath IDENT(-low), since it does not cause vowel lowering, but above WEAK<a, since it blocks raising. Both of these ranking arguments are supplied in (4-78).

(4-77) ATTRACT-LOW (ATTRLO)
      Assign one violation mark for every nonlow vowel that is adjacent to a guttural consonant.

(4-78) IDENT(-low) >> ATTRACT-LOW >> WEAK<a >> IDENT(+low)

		ID(-low)	ATTRLO	WK<a	ID(+low)
	/ʕabad-na/				
→	ʕaˈbad.na			1	
a.	ʕiˈbad.na		W₁	L	W₁
	/samiʕ-na/				
→	siˈmiʕ.na		1		1
b.	siˈmaʕ.na	W₁	L		1
c.	saˈmiʕ.na		1	W₁	L
d.	saˈmaʕ.na	W₁	L	W₁	L

The lowering effect of an adjacent guttural is overridden when a high vowel follows in the next syllable. Forms like [ˈħi.lim] and [ˈfi.him] in (4-70) would be expected to surface as *[ˈħa.lim] and *[ˈfa.him] if ATTRACT-LOW were satisfied. This resistance to lowering is a type of vowel height harmony. For present purposes, it is enough to recruit the ad hoc constraint *aCi to account for this phenomenon. As shown in tableau (4-79), *aCi is ranked above ATTRACT-LOW, so it can block the lowering effect of an adjacent guttural.

(4-79) IDENT(-low), *aCi >> ATTRACT-LOW >> WEAK<a >> IDENT(+low)

		ID(-low)	*aCi	ATTRLO	WK<a	ID(+low)
	/ħalim-na/					
→	hi'lim.na			1		1
a.	ħa'lim.na		W₁	L	W₁	L
b.	ħa'lam.na	W₁		L		L

Examples like ['**sa.ra**g] in (4-71) illustrate one last condition under which there is no raising: when the target vowel is followed by a coronal sonorant and another low vowel. This phenomenon is also a type of vowel harmony, but it is harmony to which only coronal sonorants are transparent. This harmony process is quite interesting in itself, but it is not very relevant to our concerns here. Since it has been discussed elsewhere (Gafos and Lombardi 1999, McCarthy 1994a, Parkinson 1992), it will not detain us further.

Now that we have the basics of raising and syncope in hand, we can return to two issues that were raised in previous chapters. One involves the interaction of raising and syncope, with relevance to the analysis of zero-terminating chain shifts, and the other has to do with phrase-level syncope and Stratal OT. This section concludes with a summary of the constraint hierarchy (4-84) and presentation of some fully worked-out examples ((4-86)-(4-93)).

The interaction of raising and syncope. As I observed in §3.5.3, raising of low vowels and syncope of high vowels are in a counterfeeding or chain-shift relationship. In rule-based phonology, this means that the syncope rule is ordered before the raising rule, so a high vowel that is the output of raising cannot serve as the input to syncope. This counterfeeding relationship leads to a transformation of some underlying /a/~/i/ contrasts into surface [i]~Ø contrasts, such as /samiʕ-t/ → [si'miʕt], *[s'miʕt] 'I heard' versus /simiʕ-t/ → [s'miʕt] 'I was heard'.

In OT terms, the nonoptimal mapping /samiʕ-t/ → *[s'miʕt] provides a way of satisfying both WEAK<i and WEAK<a, while the optimal mapping /samiʕ-t/ → [si'miʕt] satisfies only WEAK<a. For that reason, we require the constraint MAX-A (4-39), which forbids deletion of underlying low vowels. If MAX-A is ranked above WEAK<i and IDENT(+low), as in (4-80), then the problematic mapping /samiʕ-t/ → *[s'miʕt] is ruled out. In OT-CC terms, this means that the putative candidate chain **<sa.miʕt, s.miʕt, s'miʕt> is invalid because it is not harmonically improving: although the initial subchain <sa.miʕt, s.miʕt> offers better performance on WEAK<i, it introduces a violation of the higher-ranking constraint MAX-A.

(4-80) Max-A >> Weak<*i*, Ident(+low)

/samiʕ-t/	Max-A	Weak<*i*	Id(+low)
→ siˈmiʕt		₁	₁
sˈmiʕt	W₁	L	L

The interaction of raising and syncope in Bedouin Arabic was discussed earlier (see §3.5.3). I explained why this type of opaque interaction — a zero-terminating chain shift — must be analyzed with a prominence-sensitive faithfulness constraint rather than a Prec constraint. It is appropriate to revisit that argument here, filling in the technical details.

Raising and syncope are in a counterfeeding relationship, so mappings like /samiʕ-t/ → *[sˈmiʕt] or /katab-t/ → *[kˈtabt] have to be prevented. As we just saw, Max-A rules out these mappings by ensuring that the chains that would produce them are not harmonically improving. To show that Max-A is necessary, then, we should ask what would happen if it did not exist.

Without Max-A, there would be a harmonically improving path from /katab-t/ to *[kˈtabt]. In fact, there would be two such paths, the convergent chains listed in (4-81). These chains are valid because, without Max-A, deletion of /a/ is a harmonically improving way of satisfying Weak<*i* (cf. (4-80)). The correct mapping is /katab-t/ → [kiˈtabt], and it too is obtained from a pair of convergent chains, which are supplied in (4-82).

(4-81) /katab-t/ → *[kˈtabt] chains valid without Max-A

  <ka.tabt, k.tabt, k(ˈtabt)>   <Max-A@2, Dep-Pr@4>
  <ka.tabt, ka(ˈtabt), k(ˈtabt)>   <Dep-Pr@4, Id(+low)@2>
   $\mathcal{L}$ = {Max-A@2, Dep-Pr@4}
   rL = Ø

(4-82) /katab-t/ → [kiˈtabt] chains

  <ka.tab.t, ki.tab.t, ki(ˈtab)t>   <Id(+low)@2, Dep-Pr@4>
  <ka.tab.t, ka(ˈtab)t, ki(ˈtab)t>   <Dep-Pr@4, Id(+low)@2>
   $\mathcal{L}$ = {Id(+low)@2, Dep-Pr@4}
   rL = Ø

If the chains in (4-81) were valid, then they would threaten the optimality of the chains in (4-82), which lead to the desired outcome. We cannot appeal to constraints of the form Prec(X, Dep-Pr); they are useless in making this determination, since the empty rLUMSeqs of these chains violate all Prec(X, Dep-Pr) constraints equally. Worse yet, the markedness constraint Weak<*i* favors the

/katab-t/ → *[kˈtabt] mapping. This means that (4-81) can only be eliminated with a faithfulness constraint. As we have seen, that constraint is MAX-A.

This result is a consequence of the theory of faithfulness as well as OT-CC. In counterfeeding opacity, a PREC constraint favors the <A, B> chain over the <A, B, C> chain by penalizing chains in which the LUM incurred by the B → C mapping crucially follows the LUM incurred by the A→ B mapping. The gradualness requirement on chains rules out <A, C>, which would otherwise triumph (see §3.3.4). But because deletion vacuously satisfies all IDENT constraints (McCarthy and Prince 1995, 1999), in a zero-terminating chain shift the <A, Ø> chain is not prohibited by gradualness while the <A, B, Ø > chain is. That is why Bedouin Arabic requires MAX-A.

The principles of OT-CC that have led us to this result about zero-terminating chain shifts — the definition of PREC and the ranking metaconstraint — are important and desirable elements of the theory's typological predictions. (The vacuous satisfaction property of IDENT is less central and could be modified without affecting OT-CC's fundamentals.) I suggested in §3.5.3 that the result itself is also desirable. The inability of PREC constraints to account for zero-terminating chain shifts forces an alternative approach based on positional faithfulness constraints like MAX-A. This alternative predicts that zero-terminating chain shifts will always be initiated by elements whose intrinsic prominence protects them from deletion via constraints like MAX-A. This prediction is in itself a result — a correct result, so far as I know.

Phrase-level syncope and Stratal OT. In §2.3.4.2, I offered a criticism of Lexical Phonology and Stratal OT based on the domains of syncope and raising. Syncope and raising have different domains in Bedouin Arabic. Syllables are subject to syncope if they are weak by virtue of phrasal syllabification across word juncture (see (4-83)). But syllables are not subject to raising under the same circumstances. As an example of raising in a syllable that is weak because of junctural syllabification, Al-Mozainy (1981: 54) cites only the lexicalized expression /baːrak alˤlˤah fiːk/ → [baː.ri.k alˤ.lˤah.fiːk] 'may Allah bless you', and he has confirmed to me via email that this example is unique. Thus, the usual behavior of raising is exemplified by [ʕa.ba.dalˤ.lˤah] 'he worshiped Allah', with the second vowel of /ʕabad/ remaining low in a juncturally open syllable.

(4-83) Phrase-level syncope (= (2-7))

/kaːtib al-ʒawaːb/	kaːt.bal.ʒu.waːb	'writing the letter'
	*kaː.ti.bal.ʒu.waːb	
/tiʕtˤuːnih al-museːʕiːdi/	tiʕ.tˤuːn.hal.m.seː.ʕiː.di	'you give it to the one
	*tiʕ.tˤuː.ni.hal.m.seː.ʕiː.di	from the clan of
		Musaiʕīd'

This difference between syncope and raising leads to problems for Lexical Phonology and Stratal OT. In Lexical Phonology, the domain of a process is determined by the stratum it is assigned to. For reasons of parsimony, then, Lexical Phonology should have no other mechanism for specifying the domains of processes, such as the parametric rule domains in the theory of prosodic phonology (Nespor and Vogel 1986, Selkirk 1980a). Since raising is word-bounded and syncope is not, raising must be assigned to the lexical stratum and syncope must be assigned to the postlexical stratum. Although syncope could also be applicable at the lexical stratum, raising emphatically must not persist until the postlexical stratum, or else postlexical resyllabification would produce results like *[ʕa.bi.dalˤ.lˤah] from /ʕabad/. This reasoning applies with equal force to Stratal OT: the lexical ranking that is responsible for raising, [Weak<a >> Id(+low)], has to be reversed postlexically.

The problem is that this assignment of processes to strata wreaks havoc with the raising/syncope chain shift. Any low vowel that is raised to high in the lexical phonology is subject to deletion in the postlexical phonology, and nothing can be done to prevent this from happening. For example, /katabt/ will map to [kiˈtabt] in the lexical phonology; then the postlexical phonology, where syncope is still active, will change its input [kiˈtabt] into the final output *[kˈtabt].

Rule-based Lexical Phonology could perhaps call on the strict cycle or one of its descendants to explain why postlexical syncope cannot dip inside the lexical output/postlexical input /kiˈtabt/ (cf. Kiparsky 1993: 284-285). To my knowledge, though, nothing akin to strict cyclicity has been proposed in relation to Stratal OT, and the only extant proposal for introducing a replacement for strict cyclicity in classic OT, that of Łubowicz (2002), is not applicable in this case. The constraint Max-A is also of no use: it cannot rule out the postlexical mapping [kiˈtabt] → *[kˈtabt] because the deleted vowel is not /a/ in the input to this stratum. Allowing Max-A to look back to the original input is antithetical to Stratal OT's basic premises and to its critique of output-output faithfulness: Stratal OT has only one kind of faithfulness, which relates the input of a stratum to the output of that same stratum.

The essence of Stratal OT's predicament is the deep connection that it establishes between opacity and strata. The Bedouin Arabic examples reveal that this connection is too deep: contrary to Stratal OT's prediction, it is possible for an opaque process B to have a bigger domain than process A even if A is the process that makes B opaque.

OT-CC does not insist on a connection between opacity and cyclicity, since the latter is attributed to output-output faithfulness constraints (see §2.3.4.2 and §4.2.5 for references and further discussion). In the case at hand, the ill-formedness of *[ʕa.bi.dalˤ.lˤah] from /ʕabad/ is a consequence of faithfulness of a word in context to its output citation form, ['ʕa.bad]. (On extending output-output faithfulness to phrasal phonology, see McCarthy (2000b), Steriade (1999a, 1999b), and Truckenbrodt (2002).) The faithfulness constraint OO-IDENT(+low) that is proper to this dimension of output-output correspondence requires that all contextual forms of /ʕabad/ match the low vowels of its citation form ['ʕa.bad]. Ranked above WEAK<a, this faithfulness constraint rules out *[ʕa.bi.dalˤ.lˤah]. OO-MAX-I is ranked below WEAK<i, however, accounting for syncope in [kaːt.bal.ʒu.waːb] from /kaːtib/ despite the lack of identity with the citation form ['kaː.tib]. In this way, output-output faithfulness offers a general theory of processes that are and are not limited to a word domain.

Summary. The constraint rankings are once again summarized in (4-84). This diagram incorporates one ranking relation that has not yet been proven, [MAX-A >> WEAK<a]. This ranking is necessary in interactions where ATTRACT-LOW is active, such as /ʕabad-na/ → [ʕa'bad.na] in (4-78). Without this ranking, *[ʕ'bad.na] would offer a way of satisfying both WEAK<a and ATTRACT-LOW, whereas the actual winner violates WEAK<a. Tableau (4-84) certifies this ranking argument.

(4-84)   Bedouin Arabic ranking summary III

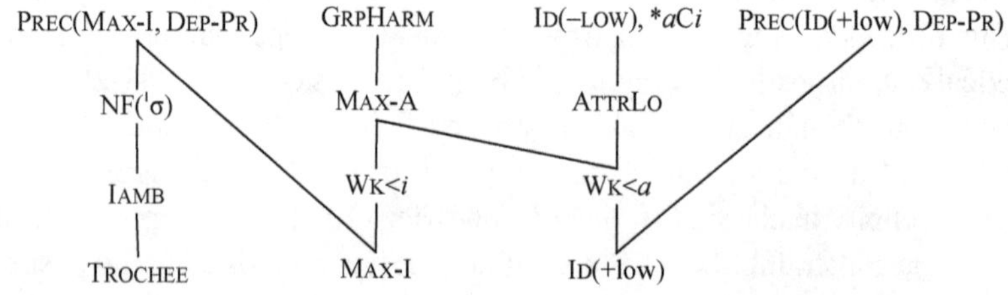

(4-85)   MAX-A >> WEAK<a

	/ʕabad-na/	MAX-A	ID(-low)	ATTRLO	WK<a
→	ʕa'bad.na				₁
a.	ʕ'bad.na	W₁			L
b.	ʕi'bad.na		W₁	W₁	L

There are two PREC constraints in (4-84). One of them, PREC(MAX-I, DEP-PR), is responsible for the counterbleeding interaction between stress and syncope, with high vowels deleting in positions where they would otherwise receive stress. The other, PREC(ID(+low), DEP-PR), is responsible for the counterbleeding interaction between stress and the other reductive process, raising. It accounts for the presence of raised vowels in surface stressed syllables.

It is also appropriate at this point to do a check on the overall success of the analysis by challenging it with some of the basic patterns of alternation. We will begin with the /katab/ → ['ki.tab] mapping. The valid candidate chains are listed in (4-86). (Here and subsequently, I omit those chains whose outputs fatally violate HEAD(Word) by failing to assign stress.) In chain (a), stress and raising interact transparently — stress bleeds raising — and in chain (b) they have an opaque, counterbleeding interaction. Although (a) is more faithful than (b) by virtue of obeying IDENT(+low), the constraint PREC(ID(+low), DEP-PR) favors (b) and dominates IDENT(+low), with fatal consequences for (a).

(4-86) Chains from /katab/ and their LUMSeqs

    a. <ka.tab, ('ka.tab)>   <DEP-PR@2>

    b. <ka.tab, ki.tab, ('ki.tab)>   <ID(+low)@2, DEP-PR@2>

A more complex example is /katab-at/ → [k'ti.bat]. The valid chains are given in (4-87). These chains are more diverse than in the previous case because the first two syllables present many more opportunities for reduction or deletion. But because convergent chains are conflated into a single candidate, the candidates that are evaluated are not as numerous as the chains. Tableau (4-88) compares the six distinct candidates in (4-87) over all the constraints on which they differ. (To save space, I have omitted the chains themselves from the tableau.) The losers are all ruled out by one or both of the top-ranked constraints, PREC(ID(+low), DEP-PR) and GROUPING-HARMONY. The violators of the PREC constraint are those that fail to lower the vowel in the second syllable of /katab-at/; they have failed to do so because their rLUMSeqs include a premature violation of DEP-PROM. The violators of GROUPING-HARMONY are those output forms with a (L'L) iambic foot. Only one chain satisfies both of these constraints, and it is the chain that produces the correct mapping, /katab-at/ → [k'ti.bat].

(4-87) Chains from /katab-at/ and their LUMSeqs

    a. <ka.ta.bat, (ka'ta)bat>   <DEP-PR@4>

    b. <ka.ta.bat, (ka'ta)bat, (k'ta)bat>   <DEP-PR@4, MAX-A@2>

    c. <ka.ta.bat, (ka'ta)bat, (ki'ta)bat>   <DEP-PR@4, ID(+low)@2>
       <ka.ta.bat, ki.ta.bat, (ki'ta)bat>   <ID(+low)@2, DEP-PR@4>

    d. <ka.ta.bat, ka.ti.bat, (ka'ti)bat>   <ID(+low)@4, DEP-PR@4>

    e. <ka.ta.bat, ka.ti.bat, (ka'ti)bat, (k'ti)bat> ✓ <ID(+low)@4, DEP-PR@4, MAX-A@2>

   f. <ka.ta.bat, ka.ti.bat, ki.ti.bat, (ki'ti)bat>   <ID(+low)@4, ID(+low)@2, DEP-PR@4>

   <ka.ta.bat, ki.ta.bat, ki.ti.bat, (ki'ti)bat>   <ID(+low)@2, ID(+low)@4, DEP-PR@4>

   <ka.ta.bat, ka.ti.bat, (ka'ti)bat, (ki'ti)bat>   <ID(+low)@4, DEP-PR@4, ID(+low)@4>

(4-88) /katab-at/ → [k'tibat]

	/katab-at/	GRPHARM	PREC(ID(+low), DEP-PR)	PREC(MAX-I, DEP-PR)	MAX-A	WK<*i*	WK<*a*	ID(+low)
e. →	(k'ti)bat <ID(+low)@4, DEP-PR@4, MAX-A@2>			1	1			1
a.	(ka'ta)bat <DEP-PR@4>	W_1	W_1	1	L	W_1	W_1	L
b.	(k'ta)bat <DEP-PR@4, MAX-A@2>		W_1	1	1			L
c.	(ki'ta)bat {DEP-PR, ID(+low)@2} Ø	W_1	W_2	1	L	W_1		1
d.	(ka'ti)bat <ID(+low)@4, DEP-PR@4>	W_1		1	L	W_1	W_1	1
f.	(ki'ti)bat {ID(+low)@4, ID(+low)@2, DEP-PR} {<ID(+low)@4, DEP-PR>}	W_1		1	L	W_1		W_2

Although it looks as if the winner in (4-88) is violating an undominated constraint, PREC(MAX-I, DEP-PR), in reality no PREC constraint can be undominated because of the ranking metaconstraint (3-24). PREC(MAX-I, DEP-PR) is dominated by DEP-PROM and therefore it is also dominated by HEAD(Word) and any other constraints that require the presence of stress. These higher-ranking constraints rule out candidate chains with no stress, such as <ka.ta.bat, ka.ti.bat, ki.ti.bat>, which would otherwise vacuously satisfy PREC(MAX-I, DEP-PR) (see §3.3.3 and §3.3.4).

There are fewer valid candidate chains for the mapping /sahab-at/ → [s'ha.bat] than for the /katab-at/ mapping because ATTRACT-LOW dominates WEAK<*a*, so raising is not harmonically improving in the vicinity of the guttural consonant [ħ]. The two candidates appear in (4-89), and tableau (4-90) compares them.

(4-89) Chains from /sahab-at/ and their LUMSeqs

   a. <sa.ħa.bat, (sa'ħa)bat>   <DEP-PR@4>

   b. <sa.ħa.bat, (sa'ħa)bat, (s'ħa)bat>✓ <DEP-PR@4, MAX-A@2>

(4-90) /saḥab-at/ → [sˈḥabat]

/saḥab-at/		GRPHARM	PREC(ID(+low), DEP-PR)	PREC(MAX-I, DEP-PR)	MAX-A	WK<*i*	WK<*a*
b. →	(sˈḥa)bat <DEP-PR@4, MAX-A@2>		1	1	1		
a.	(saˈḥa)bat <DEP-PR@4>	W₁	1	1	L	W₁	W₁

Another mapping of interest is /kitib-at/ → [ˈkit.bat]. The valid candidate chains are listed in (4-91). The two chains in (b) converge because deletion of the first /i/ does not interact with stress assignment, so the resulting rLUMSeq is empty. Tableau (4-92) shows how the treatment of convergent chains distinguishes between the winner's crucial LUM ordering and loser (b)'s noncrucial ordering. Because (b)'s rLUMSeq is empty but the ℒ-set includes a DEP-PROM violation, (b) cannot be in compliance with PREC(MAX-I, DEP-PR).

(4-91) Chains from /kitib-at/ and their (r)LUMSeqs

    a. <ki.ti.bat, (kiˈti)bat>   <DEP-PR@4>

    b. <ki.ti.bat, (kiˈti)bat, (kˈti)bat>   ℒ = {DEP-PR@4, MAX-I@2}
       <ki.ti.bat, ktibat, (kˈti)bat>   rL = Ø

    c. <ki.ti.bat, kitbat, (ˈkit)bat>✓   <MAX-I@4, DEP-PR@2>

(4-92) /kitib-at/ → [ˈkitbat]

/kitib-at/		GRPHARM	PREC(MAX-I, DEP-PR)	WK<*i*	MAX-I
c. →	(ˈkit)bat <MAX-I@4, DEP-PR@2>				1
a.	(kiˈti)bat <DEP-PR@4>	W₁	W₁	W₁	L
b.	(kˈti)bat {DEP-PR@4, MAX-I@2} Ø		W₁		1

The final mapping to be examined is /ʃarib-at/ → [ˈʃar.bat]. We earlier looked at the question of why [ˈʃar.bat] is more harmonic than *[ʃˈri.bat] (see (4-68)). An even more interesting issue is raised by the form *[ˈʃir.bat], where the vowel of the first syllable has raised. The candidate chains are listed in (4-93).

(4-93) Chains from /ʃarib-at/ and their (r)LUMSeqs[17]

    a. <ʃa.ri.bat, (ʃaˈri)bat>   < DEP-PR@4>

    b. <ʃa.ri.bat, ʃar.bat, (ˈʃar)bat>✓   <MAX-I@4, DEP-PR@2>

    c. <ʃa.ri.bat, (ʃaˈri)bat, (ʃˈri)bat>   <DEP-PR@4, MAX-A@2>

    d. <ʃa.ri.bat, (ʃaˈri)bat, (ʃiˈri)bat>   ℒ = {DEP-PR@4, ID(+low)@2}
       <ʃa.ri.bat, ʃi.ri.bat, (ʃiˈri)bat>   rL = Ø

    e. <ʃa.ri.bat, ʃi.ri.bat, ʃir.bat, (ˈʃir)bat>   <ID(+low)@2, MAX-I@4, DEP-PR@2>

The winning candidate chain in (4-93) is (b), with syncope only. Its main competitor is (e), with raising and then syncope. Chain (e) has the advantage of satisfying both of the PREC constraints, PREC(ID(+low), DEP-PR) and PREC(MAX-I, DEP-PR). In contrast, the winner satisfies only PREC(MAX-I, DEP-PR). This means that some constraint C that is satisfied by the winner (b) and violated by the loser (e) crucially dominates PREC(ID(+low), DEP-PR), thereby preventing raising in the first syllable of /ʃarib-at/. C cannot be a faithfulness constraint, since the faithfulness constraint that distinguishes between these two candidates is IDENT(+low), and it is of no use because it is ranked below PREC(ID(+low), DEP-PR) (see (4-76)). Nor can C be a PREC constraint. The only PREC constraint that would be useful in this situation is PREC(MAX-I, ID(+low)), and it must be ranked below IDENT(+low) because of the ranking metaconstraint (3-24). With all of the potentially useful faithfulness and PREC constraints ranked too low to matter, the constraint that favors [('ʃar)bat] over *[('ʃir)bat] must be some type of markedness. Specifically, C is a constraint prohibiting high vowels in closed syllables. Typological precedent for this constraint comes from Saipanese Chamorro, which has a process lowering high vowels to mid in closed stressed syllables (Chung 1983, Crosswhite 1998). Since C need only dominate PREC(MAX-I, ID(+low)) and IDENT(+low), there is no danger of it causing wholesale lowering of vowels in closed syllables or affecting results elsewhere in the analysis.

4.3.4   Epenthesis

The previous section showed how syncope and raising are rendered opaque by stress. This section describes how syncope and raising are also rendered opaque by epenthesis. As in Levantine Arabic, epenthesis is a result of ranking CLUSTER-CONDITION above DEP-V. Examples like (4-94) show that high vowels are not deleted in syllables that are open by virtue of epenthesis. In consequence, there is a surface contrast between epenthetic ['ħibir] from /ħibr/ and nonepenthetic [k'tib] from /kitib/. For the same reason, an underlying contrast between /a/ and /i/ is neutralized: nonepenthetic /gadir/ 'he became able' maps to ['gi.dir] by raising, and /gidr/ 'pot' also maps to ['gi.dir] by epenthesis (Al-Mozainy 1981: 71). Similarly, the data in (4-95) show that low vowels are not raised in syllables that are open by virtue of epenthesis. This resistance of pre-epenthetic vowels to raising is the source of the surface contrast between epenthetic ['ga.bil] from /gabl/ 'before' and nonepenthetic ['gi.bil] from /gabil/ 'he accepted'.

(4-94) Epenthesis and syncope (47, 71-72, 123, 209)

/libn/	ˈlib*i*n	'clay'
/gitˤn/	ˈgitˤ*i*n	'cotton'
/ħibr/	ˈħib*i*r	'ink'
/χibl/	ˈχib*i*l	'crazy'
/siʒn/	ˈsiʒ*i*n	'prison'

(4-95) Epenthesis and raising (56, 70, 123)

/gabr/	ˈgab*u*r	'grave'
/gabl/	ˈgab*i*l	'before'

To understand what is going on here and to integrate it with the rest of the analysis, we need to look closely at the candidate chains that compete to produce these mappings. We will focus on the /libn/ → [ˈli.b*i*n], *[lˈb*i*n] case as an example, but the discussion could equally well have concentrated on /gabl/ → [ˈga.b*i*l]. The valid candidate chains from input /libn/ are given in (4-96). (To keep things simple, I omit chains that are hopeless because they violate undominated markedness constraints by lacking required stress or epenthesis.) The two chains in (a) are convergent, with an empty rLUMSeq. That is because the order of stress and epenthesis does not matter in surface disyllables, where NONFINALITY(ˈσ) decides the locus of stress. The other chain, (b), is the expected result of transparent interaction of syncope and epenthesis.

(4-96) Chains from /libn/ and their (r)LUMSeqs

a. <libn, (ˈlibn), (ˈlib*i*n)>✓   ℒ = {DEP-PR@2, DEP-V@4}
   <libn, lib*i*n, (ˈlib*i*n)>✓   rL = ∅

b. <libn, li.b*i*n, l.b*i*n, (lˈb*i*n)>   <DEP-V@4, MAX-I@2, DEP-PR@4>

The winning candidate chains in (a) share a rLUMSeq that violates PREC(MAX-I, DEP-PR): their ℒ-set {DEP-PR@2, DEP-V@4} includes a DEP-PROM-violating LUM, and in the empty rLUMSeq there is no MAX-I-violating LUM ordered before the DEP-PROM violation. The loser (b) obeys PREC(MAX-I, DEP-PR). Therefore, PREC(MAX-I, DEP-PR) must be dominated by some constraint that (a) obeys and (b) violates. The only faithfulness or markedness constraints that favor (a) over (b) have to be ranked below PREC(MAX-I, DEP-PR) because of the nonepenthetic mapping /kitib/ → [kˈtib], *[ˈki.tib] (see (4-66)). This leaves only one possibility: the constraint that crucially favors (a) is from the PREC family. In fact, it is a constraint previously seen in the analysis of Levantine Arabic, PREC(DEP-PR, DEP-V).

In Levantine Arabic, PREC(DEP-PR, DEP-V) is a cause of opaque stress in the vicinity of epenthetic vowels, such as the unstressed epenthetic penult of [kaˈta.bil.ha] (see (4-30)). This constraint is active under identical circumstances in Bedouin Arabic, producing an opaque interaction of stress and epenthesis in (4-97) (cf. their Levantine counterparts in (4-44)).

(4-97) Effect of PREC(DEP-PR, DEP-V)[18]

/ja-bruk-in/	ˈjaburkin	'they (she-camels) kneel'
/ja-srug-in/	ˈjasurgin	'they (f.) steal'

If PREC(DEP-PR, DEP-V) is ranked above PREC(MAX-I, DEP-PR), then the right result is obtained for the epenthesis-syncope interaction /libn/ → [ˈli.bin] and the other examples in (4-94). The ranking argument is given in (4-98). The convergent chains that produce the output [ˈli.bin] fare worse than the *[lˈbin] chain on the lower ranking constraint, since the *[lˈbin] chain violates DEP-PR but not MAX-I. But the *[lˈbin] chain has a more serious problem: it has a DEP-V violation with a following and without a preceding DEP-PROM violation. That is deadly, given PREC(DEP-PR, DEP-V)'s higher rank. The [ˈli.bin] chains violate this constraint as well, but less seriously, since the rLUMSeq has no LUM orderings at all.

(4-98) PREC(DEP-PR, DEP-V) >> PREC(MAX-I, DEP-PR)

/libn/		PREC(DEP-PR, DEP-V)	PREC(MAX-I, DEP-PR)
a. →	(ˈlibin) {DEP-PR@2, DEP-V@4} < >	1	1
b.	(lˈbin) <DEP-V@4, MAX-I@2, DEP-PR@4>	W$_2$	L

This argument straightforwardly generalizes to the /gabl/ → [ˈga.bil] case. Because epenthesis and raising also interact opaquely, PREC(DEP-PR, DEP-V) must dominate PREC(ID(+low), DEP-PR) as well.

Tableau (4-98) explains why underlying /i/ survives before an epenthetic vowel and deletes before an underlying vowel: /libn/ → [ˈli.bin] versus /kitib/ → [kˈtib]. The reason: high-ranking PREC(DEP-PR, DEP-V) can only be active when candidate chains have epenthesis, and chains can have epenthesis only when epenthesis is harmonically improving. When the input ends in a cluster, like /libn/, then epenthesis is harmonically improving, PREC(DEP-PR, DEP-V) is active, and PREC(MAX-I, DEP-PR) is overridden. Succinctly, the form [ˈli.bin] is transparent with respect to the stress-syncope interaction in order to be opaque with respect to the stress-epenthesis interaction.

Tableau (4-98) shows a type of ranking that we have not seen previously: one PREC constraint crucially dominating another. That this should happen is hardly a surprise; PREC constraints can conflict with one another, and conflict is the basis of all direct ranking arguments. The possibility of rankings like this follows, then, from OT-CC's (and OT's) central assumptions.

4.3.5   Metathesis

Under some conditions, tautosyllabic sequences of a low vowel followed by a guttural consonant are metathesized, placing the guttural in onset position, as in (4-99). In contrast, examples like ['jiħ.mal] 'it is carried' show that only low vowels can be metathesized.

(4-99) [a]+guttural metathesis (168, 184ff.)

/ja-χdim/	j'χadim	'he serves'
/ja-χdim-uːn/	jχad'muːn	'they serve'
/dahma/	d'hama	'dark red'
/laħm-ah/	l'ħam-ah	'piece of meat'
/ma-ʕzuːm/	mʕa'zuːm	'invited (masculine singular)'
/ma-ħzuːm-ah/	mħa'zuːmah	'tied (feminine singular)'
/ʔista-ʕʒal/	ʔist'ʕaʒal	'got in a hurry'
/ʔista-ʕzam/	ʔist'ʕazam	'accepted an invitation'

I conjecture that metathesis is a response to the difficulty, familiar to any student of Arabic, of hearing the difference between tautosyllabic [aG] and [Ga], where G is a guttural (See Hall 2003: 31, 87 for a different view.) This perceptual problem is a result of the many acoustic similarities between the low vowel and the gutturals. When the vowel is nonlow or the consonant is not a guttural, the perceptual challenges of detecting the order of articulation are lessened, and there is no motive for metathesis. The ad hoc constraint in (4-100) is a stand-in for an authentic theory of perceptually-based markedness constraints in phonology, such as the one proposed by Boersma (1998). This constraint is ranked above the antimetathetic faithfulness constraint LINEARITY (LIN) (McCarthy and Prince 1995, 1999), as shown by tableau (4-101).

(4-100) *aG]$_\sigma$ (ad hoc constraint)

    Assign one violation mark for every tautosyllabic sequence of a low vowel and a guttural consonant, in that order.

(4-101) *aG]$_\sigma$ >> LINEARITY

/ja-χdim/	*aG]$_\sigma$	LIN
→ j'χa.dim		1
'jaχ.dim	W$_1$	L

Under various circumstances, metathesis is blocked by constraints that must be ranked higher than *aG]$_\sigma$. Stem-final gutturals do not metathesize (4-102) because the right edge of the stem must be aligned with the right edge of a syllable (McCarthy and Prince 1993a: 127). The constraint *[ʔ]$_\sigma$, which prohibits degenerate syllables consisting solely of glottal stop, blocks metathesis (4-103), just as it blocks deletion in situations where GROUPING-HARMONY is active (cf. (4-59)).[19] Metathesis into a geminate guttural is forbidden (4-104) as a breach of geminate integrity (Guerssel 1977, Hayes 1986). It should be noted, however, that there are also some as-yet unexplained metathetic alternations (e.g., [m'χa.raʒ] 'exit (190)' ~ ['maχ.ri.ʒi] 'my exit (187)') as well as some outright exceptions (e.g., ['gah.wa] 'he served coffee (188)' vs. [g'ha.wa] from /gahwa/ 'coffee'). Thus, the evidence for opacity and for OT-CC from this metathesis process is not quite as robust as the other evidence discussed in this chapter.

(4-102) No metathesis of stem-final guttural (88-89)

'difaʕ, *'difʕa	'he pushed'
di'faʕt	'you (masc. sg.) pushed'
di'faʕna	'we pushed'

(4-103) Effect of *[ʔ]$_\sigma$ on metathesis (187-188)

'ʔahda, *ʔ'hada	'he gave a present'
'ʔaχlaf, *ʔ'χalaf	'he changed something'
'ʔaʕtaːd, *ʔ'ʕataːd	'I became used to'

(4-104) No metathesis into geminate guttural (187)

'ʃaχχasˁ, *ʃ'χaχasˁ	'he dressed up'
'ʃaʁʁal	'he made something work (started a car)'
'laħħaf	'he covered up'

Metathesis has an opaque, counterfeeding relationship with raising. The [a] vowels in [j'χa.dim] and [m.ʕa'zuːm] are unexpected, since normally a low vowel in an open syllable is raised, despite a preceding guttural, if the vowel in the next syllable is high. This phenomenon is exemplified by /ħalim/ → ['ħi.lim] and other forms in (4-70), and in tableau (4-79) it is attributed to the ad hoc harmony constraint *aCi. If the interaction of metathesis with raising were transparent rather than opaque, /ja-χdim/ would be expected to surface as *[j'χi.dim].

This case of opacity shows that *aCi is crucially dominated by the constraint Prec(Id(+low), Lin). The choice, as seen in tableau (4-105), is between the opaque chain <jaχ.dim, j.**χa**.dim, j'**χa**.dim> and its transparent competitor *<jaχ.dim, j.**χa**.dim, j.**χi**.dim, j'**χi**.dim>. Both chains are valid if *aG]$_\sigma$ dominates *aCi. Both chains violate Prec(Id(+low), Lin) because neither presents an Ident(+low)-violating LUM ordered before a Linearity-violating LUM. But the transparent chain's breach of this Prec constraint is more serious, incurring two violations, since it has exactly the wrong order of these LUMs. This is a typical case of counterfeeding opacity in OT-CC.

(4-105) Prec(Id(+low), Lin) >> *aCi

/jaxdim/	Prec(Id(+low), Lin)	*aCi
→ <jaχ.dim, j.χa.dim, j'χa.dim> <Lin@2, Dep-Pr@2>	1	1
<jaχ.dim, j.χa.dim, j.χi.dim, j'χi.dim> <Lin@2, Id(+low)@2, Dep-Pr@2>	W$_2$	L

There is another opaque interaction involving metathesis: it is not fed by syncope. This counterfeeding interaction can be observed in the mapping /jiʃtaʁilin/ → [jiʃ'taʁ.lin], *[jiʃ.t'ʁa.lin] 'they (f.) work' (Al-Mozainy email, 11/25/05). The responsible constraint is Prec(Lin, Max-I), and it crucially dominates the markedness constraint that normally compels metathesis, *aG]$_\sigma$. In this way, the chain <jiʃ.ta.ʁi.lin, jiʃ.taʁ.lin, jiʃ'taʁ.lin> is favored over *<jiʃ.ta.ʁi.lin, jiʃ.taʁ.lin, jiʃ.t.ʁa.lin, jiʃ.t'ʁa.lin>.

These two opaque interactions involving metathesis lead to problems for theories of opacity based on rule ordering or its equivalent. From the evidence just discussed, a metathesis rule would have to be ordered after raising and before syncope: raising → metathesis → syncope. Since rule ordering is standardly regarded as a transitive relation (though see Anderson 1974), this arrangement entails that raising precede syncope. But, as we saw in §4.3.3, the counterfeeding relationship between raising and syncope requires the ordering syncope → raising — a contradiction. Similar issues will arise in Stratal OT, which is minimally different from standard generative phonology in the relevant respect.

The source of this ordering paradox is a collection of counterfeeding interactions: raising cannot feed syncope, so syncope must precede raising; metathesis cannot feed raising, so raising must precede metathesis; and syncope cannot feed metathesis, so metathesis must precede syncope. In the analysis presented here, there is no paradox. Counterfeeding interactions are the result of visible activity by faithfulness constraints (raising and syncope) or Prec constraints (metathesis and raising, metathesis and syncope). There is no need to find an order of processes — or an ordering of strata that effect those processes — that is consistent with all of the attested counterfeeding interactions.

4.3.6   Summary

This analysis of Bedouin Arabic more than confirms a point made at the end of the section on Levantine Arabic: OT-CC has the means to analyze complex opaque phonology in sensible, typologically justifiable ways. In fact, the richness and complexity of the opaque phonology of Bedouin Arabic even exceeds that of Levantine Arabic, yet at the same time the regularity and productivity of the opaque processes is well supported — thanks to the work of Al-Mozainy (1981).

Among the phenomena that have been accounted for is the ability of reductive processes — syncope and raising — to affect vowels in positions where they are or would be stressed. The explanation is that the unfaithful mappings associated with reduction and deletion are obliged by a Prec constraint to precede any stress-assigning mapping, and that is how they seem to affect (would-be) stressed syllables. These same processes fail to affect stressed syllables that are open by virtue of epenthesis because the ordering of the epenthesizing and stress-assigning mappings is fixed by a different, higher ranking Prec constraint. Finally, the examination of guttural metathesis showed that it is not fed by syncope and does not feed raising. These interactions, which can also be accounted for with Prec constraints, do not seem to be compatible with theories of opacity based on linearly ordered rules or the equivalent.

The analysis of Bedouin Arabic also provides support for a point made in §3.2.4.3: the harmonic improvement requirement on chains restricts the possible mappings that a grammar can perform, relative to classic OT. The specific problem addressed was the existence of segmental processes, such as deletion, that improve metrical structure. The analysis of Bedouin Arabic shows how OT-CC can recapture traditional insights like this one that have proven elusive in classic OT terms.

Notes

1   The lightness of final CVC syllables in this and other Arabic dialects is related to a general process that shortens final CV: (Abu-Salim 1982a: 134ff., McCarthy 2005a).

2   On appendices, weightless codas, extrasyllabic consonants, and kindred notions, see among many others Borowsky (1986), Clements (1990), Morén (1999), Selkirk (1982a), Sherer (1994), and, for a comprehensive review and bibliography, Vaux (to appear).

3   The problem with using Classical Arabic ['ʃaʒaratun] as evidence of Palestinian stress is that it may actually be Cairene stress. Al-Azhar University in Cairo, where Mitchell (1960) encountered the ['ʃaʒaratun] stress pattern, is a major center for Arabic and Islamic learning with far-ranging influence.

4   In tableau (4-23), I have suppressed the alternation between [ə] and [e].

5   Recall from §3 that I am using a typographic shortcut in tableaux: the $\mathcal{L}$-set and rLUMSeq are given only when they are the result of convergence of two or more chains. Otherwise, I give the LUMSeq, which is a little easier to deal with. Bear in mind, however, that the actual definition of Prec in (3-23) refers to $\mathcal{L}$-sets and rLUMSeqs, not LUMSeqs.

6   On variable constraint ranking as a source of within-language variation, see the references in McCarthy (2002b: 233) as well as Boersma (1997) and Boersma and Hayes (2001).

7   The special status of word-final syllables can be seen clearly in Syrian Arabic, where only final CVC maintains a contrast between short /i/ and /u/ (Ambros 1977: 17, Grotzfeld 1965: 12).

8   The ranking of Max-A and Weak<*i* is responsible for the distinction between 'differential' and 'nondifferential' Arabic dialects. These terms, which come from Cantineau (1939), refer to whether high vowels are differentiated from low vowels in syncope. Levantine is differential because only high vowels syncopate; in a nondifferential dialect, Max-A is ranked below Weak<*i* so vowels of both types syncopate.

9   Brame (1974: 44) concedes that the hypothesized secondary stress of [ˌsiˈmiʕkum] may not be audible.

10 The form [ʒaːb.lu] comes from Farwaneh's Southern Palestinian dialect (Farwaneh 1995: 162). Abu-Salim reports shortening before the monoconsonantal suffix [-l-] 'dative/benefactive': ['ʒab.lu]. This is perhaps a paradigm uniformity effect (cf. Downing, Hall, and Raffelsiefen (eds) 2005), extending the shortening that is required in (4-48) to all verbs in the dative/benefactive subparadigm.

11 This form is cited from Al-Mozainy, Bley-Vroman, and McCarthy (1985: 136).

12 The definition of Grouping-Harmony in (4-56) follows Prince (1990) in not mentioning prominence. It is therefore a constraint on feet in general rather than iambs in particular, favoring greater length constituent-finally. The reason: although iambic systems satisfy Grouping-Harmony by reducing the first syllable in a foot or expanding the second syllable, they never never seem to accomplish this end by relabeling the iamb as a trochee. An iamb-specific grouping harmony constraint would predict this last, unattested possibility.

13 There is much precedent in the literature for degenerate syllables or similar notions in Arabic (Aoun 1979, Broselow 1992, Farwaneh 1995, Kiparsky 2003, McCarthy and Prince 1990a, 1990b, Selkirk 1981a), in other languages (e.g., Cho and King 2003, Féry 2003), and in analyses of epenthesis (Hyman 1985, Piggott 1995, Selkirk 1981a).

14   High-ranking MAX-I cannot be invoked to explain why GROUPING-HARMONY does
     not compel deletion of high vowels since low vowels are more prominent than
     high vowels, so MAX-A universally dominates MAX-I. See §3.5.3 and §4.2.5.

15   As it is defined in (4-56), GROUPING-HARMONY favors neither [('saħab)] nor
     *[(sa'ħab)] since both have (LL) feet. Hence, although GROUPING-HARMONY later
     turns out to dominate NONFINALITY('σ) (see (4-67)), the ranking argument in (4-
     61) remains valid.

16   The secret-language form [kaħartibat] for [ktibat] from /katabat/ also shows
     that trisyllabic deletion is a productive process. The first vowel in [kaħartibat]
     is not deleted because the following syllable is heavy, so there is already an
     impeccable (L'H) foot. The first vowel in /katabat/ enjoys no such protection and
     therefore deletes in [ktibat].

17   Candidate (e) in (4-93) takes the typographic shortcut of substituting the
     LUMSeq for the informationally equivalent rLUMSeq.

18   These examples are from Al-Mozainy (1981: 228–229), with the stress position
     confirmed by him in e-mail on October 25, 2005.

19   With adjectives of color and bodily defect, such as /ʔa-ħmar/ 'red' or /ʔa-ħwal/
     'cross-eyed', there is variation between a form that accommodates metathesis by
     deleting [ʔ] and a form with vowel-copying epenthesis: ['ħamar] ~ [ʔa'ħamar],
     ['ħawal] ~ [ʔa'ħawal].

5 Postscript

One premise of this book is that Optimality Theory can benefit from a change in its modular organization. Candidate chains require a different relationship between GEN and EVAL, a relationship that is two-way rather than exclusively one-way. This change was first suggested by Prince and Smolensky in their 1993 manuscript. Now, more than a dozen years later, that suggestion is yielding results that could not have been anticipated in 1993.

Another premise of this book is that derivations (of a sort) are compared. The central assumptions of OT are two: candidates are compared for relative harmony, and comparison is done by ranked, violable constraints. Candidate chains, which are a type of derivation, are compared by the same basic EVAL mechanism that is used to compare candidate output forms in classic OT. The most harmonic derivation is an optimal candidate chain. It is optimal according to a hierarchy of constraints that evaluate the output of the derivation, the faithfulness violations accumulated along the way from input to output, and the order in which those faithfulness violations are acquired.

The connection between these two premises was made in §3.3 and elsewhere. Chain formation in GEN requires information that only EVAL can provide. Chains must be harmonically improving, and each chain member must be more harmonic than a small set of alternatives. These conditions on chain validity are essential to the success of the theory of chain comparison.

These two premises are supported by two main kinds of evidence. In §3.2 and in McCarthy (2007a), I argue that a two-way GEN-EVAL relationship establishes necessary limits on certain kinds of global optimization. Output candidates do not spring fully formed from the brow of GEN; rather, they are produced by a succession of operations, each of which yields a form that improves harmonically over its predecessor. The global optimizations that are eliminated in this theory are those where several operations are necessary before any harmonic improvement is obtained.

The other source of evidence — and the principal empirical focus of this book — is phonological opacity. I argued that opacity is an authentic property of human language, and I showed how a wide variety of opaque interactions can be analyzed in OT if the candidates include derivational information in the form of chains. I have no doubt that there are purported opaque interactions in the literature that cannot be analyzed in these terms. I also have no doubt that many purported opaque interactions in the literature are the imaginings of overly zealous analysts. That is why I placed particular emphasis on establishing the systematic character and robustness of the opaque interactions that are the object of study in §4.

What's next? There will always be more work to do on the topic of phonological opacity: winnowing the wheat from the chaff in that vast literature, and establishing whether certain opaque interactions are impossible or merely rare. A very promising line of inquiry — and one that has barely been started — concerns the matter of global optimization and its limits. I hope to see and do more work on this topic in the future.

References

Abboud, Peter (1979) The verb in Northern Najdi Arabic. *Bulletin of the School of Oriental and African Studies* 42: 467–499.

Abdul-Karim, Kamal (1980) *Aspects of the Phonology of Lebanese Arabic.* Doctoral dissertation. Urbana, IL: University of Illinois.

Abu-Mansour, Mahasen Hasan (1991) Epenthesis in Makkan Arabic: Unsyllabifiable consonants versus degenerate syllables. In Mushira Eid and John J. McCarthy (eds) *Perspectives on Arabic Linguistics III: Papers from the Third Annual Symposium on Arabic Linguistics* 137–159. Amsterdam: John Benjamins.

Abu-Salim, Issam M. (1980) Epenthesis and geminate consonants in Palestinian Arabic. *Studies in the Linguistic Sciences* 10: 1–11.

Abu-Salim, Issam M. (1982a) *A Reanalysis of Some Aspects of Arabic Phonology: A Metrical Approach.* Doctoral dissertation. Urbana, IL: University of Illinois.

Abu-Salim, Issam M. (1982b) Syllable structure in Palestinian Arabic. *Studies in the Linguistic Sciences* 12: 1–28.

Aden, Paula S. (2006) *Ternary Stress.* BA honors thesis. Amherst, MA: University of Massachusetts Amherst.

Al-Mozainy, Hamza Q. (1976) *Vowel deletion and the segmental cycle in the Arabic dialect of Hijaz (Saudi Arabia).* Master's thesis. Austin, TX: University of Texas, Austin.

Al-Mozainy, Hamza Q. (1981) *Vowel Alternations in a Bedouin Hijazi Arabic Dialect: Abstractness and Stress.* Doctoral dissertation. Austin, TX: University of Texas, Austin.

Al-Mozainy, Hamza Q., Bley-Vroman, Robert, and McCarthy, John J. (1985) Stress shift and metrical structure. *Linguistic Inquiry* 16: 135–144.

Albright, Adam (2002) *The Identification of Bases in Morphological Paradigms.* Doctoral dissertation. Los Angeles: UCLA. [Available at http://web.mit.edu/albright/www/AlbrightDiss.html.]

Alderete, John (1997) Dissimilation as local conjunction. In Kiyomi Kusumoto (ed.) *Proceedings of the North East Linguistic Society 27* 17–32. Amherst, MA: GLSA Publications.

Alderete, John (1999) Head dependence in stress-epenthesis interaction. In
Ben Hermans and Marc van Oostendorp (eds) *The Derivational Residue
in Phonological Optimality Theory* 29–50. Amsterdam: John Benjamins.
[Available on Rutgers Optimality Archive, ROA-453.]
Alderete, John (2001a) Dominance effects as transderivational anti-faithfulness.
Phonology 18: 201–253.
Alderete, John (2001b) *Morphologically Governed Accent in Optimality Theory*.
New York & London: Routledge. [1999 Doctoral dissertation, University of
Massachusetts, Amherst. Available on Rutgers Optimality Archive, ROA-
309.]
Alderete, John, Beckman, Jill, Benua, Laura, Gnanadesikan, Amalia, McCarthy,
John J., and Urbanczyk, Suzanne (1999) Reduplication with fixed segment-
ism. *Linguistic Inquiry* 30: 327–364. [Available on Rutgers Optimality
Archive, ROA-226.]
Ambros, Arne (1977) *Damascus Arabic*. Malibu, CA: Undena Publications.
Anderson, Stephen R. (1974) *The Organization of Phonology*. New York:
Academic Press.
Anderson, Stephen R. (1979) On the subsequent development of the 'Standard
Theory' in phonology. In Daniel A. Dinnsen (ed.) *Current Approaches to
Phonological Theory* 2–30. Bloomington, IN: Indiana University Press.
Angoujard, Jean-Pierre (1986) Les hiérarchies prosodiques en arabe. *Revue
québecoise de linguistique* 16: 11–38.
Aoun, Youssef (1979) Is the syllable or the supersyllable a constituent? *MIT
Working Papers in Linguistics* 1: 140–148.
Archangeli, Diana (1984) *Underspecification in Yawelmani Phonology and
Morphology*. Doctoral dissertation: Massachusetts Institute of Technology.
[Published 1988, Outstanding Dissertations in Linguistics Series, Garland,
New York.]
Archangeli, Diana (1985) Yokuts harmony: Evidence for coplanar representation
in nonlinear phonology. *Linguistic Inquiry* 16: 335–372.
Archangeli, Diana and Pulleyblank, Douglas (1994) *Grounded Phonology*.
Cambridge, MA: MIT Press.
Archangeli, Diana and Suzuki, Keiichiro (1996) Yokuts templates:
Correspondence to neither input nor output. In Brian Agbayani and Naomi
Harada (eds) *UCI Working Papers in Linguistics, Vol. 2: Proceedings of
the South Western Optimality Theory Workshop* 17–28. Irvine, CA: Irvine
Linguistics Students Association.
Archangeli, Diana and Suzuki, Keiichiro (1997) The Yokuts challenge. In Iggy
Roca (ed.) *Derivations and Constraints in Phonology* 197–226. Oxford:
Oxford University Press.
Bakovic, Eric (1999) Assimilation to the unmarked. In Jim Alexander, Na-Rae
Han, and Michelle Minnick Fox (eds) *University of Pennsylvania Working
Papers in Linguistics: Proceedings of the 24th Annual Penn Linguistics*

Colloquium. Philadelphia: Department of Linguistics, University of Pennsylvania. [Available on Rutgers Optimality Archive, ROA-340.]

Bakovic, Eric (2000) *Harmony, Dominance, and Control*. Doctoral dissertation. New Brunswick, NJ: Rutgers University. [Available on Rutgers Optimality Archive, ROA-360.]

Becker, Michael. (2006) CCamelOT – An implementation of OT-CC's GEN and EVAL in Perl. Handout of talk presented at Linguistic Society of America, 80th Annual Meeting, Albuquerque, New Mexico.

Beckman, Jill (1997) Positional faithfulness, positional neutralization, and Shona vowel harmony. *Phonology* 14: 1–46.

Beckman, Jill (1998) *Positional Faithfulness*. Doctoral dissertation. Amherst, MA: University of Massachusetts Amherst. [Available on Rutgers Optimality Archive, ROA-234.]

Beechey, Timothy (2006) A non-representational theory of geminate inalterability and integrity. Unpublished manuscript. Amherst, MA: University of Massachusetts Amherst.

Benua, Laura (1997) *Transderivational Identity: Phonological Relations between Words*. Doctoral dissertation. Amherst, MA: University of Massachusetts Amherst. [Available on Rutgers Optimality Archive, ROA-259. Published (2000) as *Phonological Relations Between Words*, New York: Garland.]

Bermúdez-Otero, Ricardo (1999) *Constraint Interaction in Language Change: Quantity in English and Germanic*. Doctoral dissertation. Manchester, UK: University of Manchester.

Bermúdez-Otero, Ricardo (2001) Underlying nonmoraic coda consonants, faithfulness, and sympathy. Unpublished manuscript. Manchester, England: University of Manchester. [Available at http://www.staff.ncl.ac.uk/r.bermudez-otero/DEP-mora.pdf.]

Bermúdez-Otero, Ricardo (2004) The acquisition of phonological opacity. Unpublished manuscript. Newcastle upon Tyne: University of Newcastle upon Tyne. [Available on Rutgers Optimality Archive, ROA-593.]

Bermúdez-Otero, Ricardo (forthcoming) *Stratal Optimality Theory*. Oxford: Oxford University Press.

Black, H. Andrew (1993) *Constraint-Ranked Derivation: A Serial Approach to Optimization*. Doctoral dissertation: University of California, Santa Cruz.

Blanc, Haim (1970) The Arabic dialect of the Negev Bedouins. In *Proceedings of the Israel Academy of Sciences and Humanities* 112–150. Jerusalem: Israel Academy of Sciences and Humanities.

Blevins, Juliette (1995) The syllable in phonological theory. In John A. Goldsmith (ed.) *The Handbook of Phonological Theory* 206–244. Cambridge, MA, and Oxford, UK: Blackwell.

Blevins, Juliette (2004) A reconsideration of Yokuts vowels. *International Journal of American Linguistics* 70: 33–51.

Boersma, Paul (1997) How we learn variation, optionality, and probability. *Proceedings of the Institute of Phonetic Sciences of the University of Amsterdam* 21: 43–58. [Available on Rutgers Optimality Archive, ROA-221.]

Boersma, Paul (1998) *Functional Phonology: Formalizing the Interaction Between Articulatory and Perceptual Drives*. The Hague: Holland Academic Graphics. [Doctoral dissertation, University of Amsterdam.]

Boersma, Paul and Hayes, Bruce (2001) Empirical tests of the gradual learning algorithm. *Linguistic Inquiry* 32: 45–86. [Available on Rutgers Optimality Archive, ROA-348.]

Booij, Geert (1996) Lexical phonology and the derivational residue. In Jacques Durand and Bernard Laks (eds) *Current Trends in Phonology: Models and Methods* 69–96. Salford, Manchester, UK: University of Salford.

Booij, Geert (1997) Non-derivational phonology meets lexical phonology. In Iggy Roca (ed.) *Derivations and Constraints in Phonology* 261–288. Oxford: Oxford University Press.

Borg, Alexander (1997) Maltese phonology. In Alan S. Kaye (ed.) *Phonologies of Asia and Africa* 245–285. Winona Lake, IN: Eisenbrauns.

Borowsky, Toni (1986) *Topics in the Lexical Phonology of English*. Doctoral dissertation. Amherst, MA: University of Massachusetts Amherst.

Brame, Michael (1972) On the abstractness of phonology: Maltese ʕ. In Michael Brame (ed.) *Contributions to Generative Phonology* 22–61. Austin: University of Texas Press.

Brame, Michael (1973) On stress assignment in two Arabic dialects. In Stephen R. Anderson and Paul Kiparsky (eds) *A Festschrift for Morris Halle* 14–25. New York: Holt, Reinhart and Winston.

Brame, Michael (1974) The cycle in phonology: Stress in Palestinian, Maltese and Spanish. *Linguistic Inquiry* 5: 39–60.

Bromberger, Sylvain and Halle, Morris (1989) Why phonology is different. *Linguistic Inquiry* 20: 51–70.

Bromberger, Sylvain and Halle, Morris (1997) The contents of phonological signs: A comparison between their use in derivational theories and in optimality theories. In Iggy Roca (ed.) *Derivations and Constraints in Phonology* 93–124. Oxford: Oxford University Press.

Broselow, Ellen (1980) Syllable structure in two Arabic dialects. *Studies in the Linguistic Sciences* 10: 13–24.

Broselow, Ellen (1982) On predicting the interaction of stress and epenthesis. *Glossa* 16: 115–132.

Broselow, Ellen (1992) Parametric variation in Arabic dialect phonology. In Ellen Broselow, Mushira Eid, and John J. McCarthy (eds) *Perspectives on Arabic Linguistics* 7–45. Amsterdam and Philadelphia: John Benjamins.

Broselow, Ellen, Chen, Su-I, and Huffman, Marie (1997) Syllable weight: Convergence of phonology and phonetics. *Phonology* 14: 47–82.

Burzio, Luigi (2002) Surface-to-surface morphology: When your representations turn into constraints. In Paul Boucher (ed.) *Many Morphologies* 142–177. Somerville, MA: Cascadilla Press. [Available on Rutgers Optimality Archive, ROA-341.]

Bye, Patrik (2001) *Virtual Phonology: Rule Sandwiching and Multiple Opacity in North Saami*. Doctoral dissertation. Tromsø, Norway: University of Tromso. [Available on Rutgers Optimality Archive, ROA-498.]

Bye, Patrik (2003) Opacity, transparency, and unification in the phonology of Tiberian Hebrew. In Makoto Kadowaki and Shigeto Kawahara (eds) *Proceedings of NELS 33* 475–494. Amherst, MA: GLSA. [Available at http://www.hum.uit.no/a/bye/Papers/hebrew.pdf.]

Campbell, Lyle (1973) *Extrinsic Order Lives*. Bloomington, IN: Indiana University Linguistics Club Publications.

Campos-Astorkiza, Rebeka (2004) Faith in moras: A revised approach to prosodic faithfulness. In Keir Moulton and Matthew Wolf (eds) *Proceedings of the North East Linguistics Society 34* 163–174. Amherst, MA: GLSA.

Cantineau, Jean (1939) Remarques sur les parlers sédentaires syro-libano-palestiniens. *Bulletin de la Societé de Linguistique de Paris* 40: 80–88.

Carpenter, Angela (2002) Noncontiguous metathesis and adjacency. In Angela Carpenter, Andries Coetzee, and Paul de Lacy (eds) *University of Massachusetts Occasional Papers in Linguistics 26: Papers in Optimality Theory II* 1–26. Amherst, MA: GLSA. [Available on Rutgers Optimality Archive, ROA-489.]

Casali, Roderic F. (1996) *Resolving Hiatus*. Doctoral dissertation. Los Angeles: UCLA. [Available on Rutgers Optimality Archive, ROA-215.]

Casali, Roderic F. (1997) Vowel elision in hiatus contexts: Which vowel goes? *Language* 73: 493–533.

Cassimjee, Farida and Kisseberth, Charles (1999) A conspiracy argument for Optimality Theory: Emakhuwa dialectology. In Jim Alexander, Na-Rae Han, and Michelle Minnick Fox (eds) *UPenn Working Papers in Linguistics 6(1)* 81–96. Philadelphia: Department of Linguistics, University of Pennsylvania.

Cathey, James E. and Demers, Richard A. (1970) On establishing linguistic universals: A case for in-depth synchronic analysis. *Language* 52: 611–630.

Causley, Trisha (1997) Identity and featural correspondence: The Athapaskan case. In Kiyomi Kusumoto (ed.) *Proceedings of the North East Linguistic Society 27* 93–105. Amherst, MA: GLSA Publications.

Causley, Trisha (1999) Faithfulness and contrast: The problem of coalescence. In Kimary N. Shahin, Susan J. Blake, and Eun-Sook Kim (eds) *The Proceedings of the West Coast Conference on Formal Linguistics 17* 117–131. Stanford, CA: CSLI Publications.

Chafe, Wallace (1968) The ordering of phonological rules. *International Journal of American Linguistics* 24: 115–136.

Chen, Matthew (1999) Directionality constraints on derivations? In Ben Hermans and Marc van Oostendorp (eds) *The Derivational Residue in Phonological Optimality Theory* 105–127. Amsterdam: John Benjamins. [Available on Rutgers Optimality Archive, ROA-453.]

Cho, Young-mee Yu (1995) Rule ordering and constraint interaction in OT. In *Proceedings of the Berkeley Linguistics Society 21* 336–350. Berkeley, CA: Berkeley Linguistics Society.

Cho, Young-mee Yu and King, Tracy Holloway (2003) Semisyllables and universal syllabification. In Caroline Féry and Ruben van de Vijver (eds) *The Syllable in Optimality Theory* 183–212. Cambridge: Cambridge University Press.

Chomsky, Noam (1964) *Current Issues in Linguistic Theory*. The Hague: Mouton.

Chomsky, Noam (1965) *Aspects of the Theory of Syntax*. Cambridge, MA: MIT Press.

Chomsky, Noam (1968) *Language and Mind*. New York: Harcourt Brace Jovanovich.

Chomsky, Noam (1995) *The Minimalist Program*. Cambridge, MA: MIT Press.

Chomsky, Noam and Halle, Morris (1968) *The Sound Pattern of English*. New York: Harper & Row.

Chung, Sandra (1983) Transderivational relationships in Chamorro phonology. *Language* 59: 35–66.

Clements, G. N. (1986) Syllabification and epenthesis in the Barra dialect of Gaelic. In Koen Bogers, Harry van der Hulst, and Maarten Mous (eds) *The Phonological Representation of Suprasegmentals* 317–336. Dordrecht: Foris.

Clements, G. N. (1990) The role of the sonority cycle in core syllabification. In John Kingston and Mary Beckman (eds) *Papers in Laboratory Phonology 1: Between the Grammar and Physics of Speech* 283–333. New York: Cambridge University Press.

Clements, G. N. (1991) Vowel height assimilation in Bantu languages. In K. Hubbard (ed.) *BLS 17S: Proceedings of the Special Session on African Language Structures* 25–64. Berkeley: Berkeley Linguistic Society.

Clements, G. N. (1997) Berber syllabification: Derivations or constraints? In Iggy Roca (ed.) *Derivations and Constraints in Phonology* 289–330. Oxford: Oxford University Press.

Clements, G. N. and Ford, K. C. (1979) Kikuyu tone shift and its synchronic consequences. *Linguistic Inquiry* 10: 179–210.

Clements, G. N. and Hume, Elizabeth (1995) The internal organization of speech sounds. In John A. Goldsmith (ed.) *The Handbook of Phonological Theory* 245–306. Cambridge, MA, and Oxford, UK: Blackwell.

Cohn, Abigail and McCarthy, John J. (1994/1998) Alignment and parallelism in Indonesian phonology. *Working Papers of the Cornell Phonetics Laboratory* 12: 53–137. [Available on Rutgers Optimality Archive, ROA-25.]

Cole, Jennifer S. and Kisseberth, Charles (1995) Restricting multi-level constraint evaluation: Opaque rule interaction in Yawelmani vowel harmony. Unpublished manuscript. Urbana, IL: University of Illinois. [Available on Rutgers Optimality Archive, ROA-98.]

Cowell, Mark (1965) *A Reference Grammar of Syrian Arabic*. Washington, DC: Georgetown University Press.

Crosswhite, Katherine (1998) Segmental vs. prosodic correspondence in Chamorro. *Phonology* 15: 281–316.

Crosswhite, Katherine (1999) *Vowel Reduction in Optimality Theory*. Doctoral dissertation. Los Angeles: UCLA.

Crosswhite, Katherine (2000a) The analysis of extreme vowel reduction. In Adam Albright and Taehong Cho (eds) *Papers in Phonology 4 [UCLA Working Papers in Linguistics 4]* 1–12. Los Angeles: Department of Linguistics, UCLA.

Crosswhite, Katherine (2000b) Sonority driven reduction. Unpublished manuscript. Rochester, NY: University of Rochester. [Available on Rutgers Optimality Archive, ROA-591.]

Das, Shyamal (2002) *Some Aspects of the Phonology of Tripura Bangla and Tripura Bangla English*. Doctoral dissertation. Hyderabad, India: Central Institute of English and Foreign Languages, University of Hyderabad.

Davis, Stuart (1995) Emphasis spread in Arabic and Grounded Phonology. *Linguistic Inquiry* 26: 465–498.

Davis, Stuart (1997a) The flowering of Optimality Theory: Ponapean nasal substitution and the problem of intermediate forms. Unpublished manuscript. Bloomington, IN: Indiana University.

Davis, Stuart (1997b) A sympathetic account of nasal substitution in Ponapean. In Rachel Walker, Motoko Katayama, and Daniel Karvonen (eds) *Phonology at Santa Cruz* 15–28. Santa Cruz, CA: Linguistics Research Center, University of California.

Davis, Stuart and Zawaydeh, Bushra (1997) Output configurations in phonology: Epenthesis and syncope in Cairene Arabic. In Stuart Davis (ed.) *Optimal Viewpoints* 45–67. Bloomington, IN: Indiana University Linguistics Club.

de Haas, Wim (1988) *A Formal Theory of Vowel Coalescence: A Case Study of Ancient Greek*. Dordrecht: Foris.

de Lacy, Paul (1998) Sympathetic stress. Unpublished manuscript. Amherst, MA: University of Massachusetts Amherst. [Available on Rutgers Optimality Archive, ROA-294.]

de Lacy, Paul (2002) *The Formal Expression of Markedness*. Doctoral dissertation. Amherst, MA: University of Massachusetts, Amherst. [Available on Rutgers Optimality Archive, ROA-542.]

Dell, François (1973) *Les règles et les sons*. Paris: Hermann, Collection Savoir.

Diem, Werner (1970) Die unreglemässigen Formen der 3. Person Feminin
    Singular Perfekt in den Dialekten der Sesshaften des syrisch-libanesisch-
    palästinischen Sprachgebietes. *Orbis* 19: 346–359.
Dinnsen, Daniel A., McGarrity, Laura W., O'Connor, Kathleen, and Swanson,
    Kim (1998) On the role of sympathy in acquisition. Unpublished manu-
    script. Bloomington, IN: Indiana University.
Donegan, Patricia J. and Stampe, David (1979) The study of natural phonology.
    In Daniel A. Dinnsen (ed.) *Current Approaches to Phonological Theory*
    126–173. Bloomington, IN: Indiana University Press.
Downing, Laura J., Hall, T. Alan, and Raffelsiefen, Renate (eds) (2005)
    Paradigms in Phonological Theory. Oxford: Oxford University Press.
Elenbaas, Nine and Kager, René (1999) Ternary rhythm and the Lapse con-
    straint. *Phonology* 16: 273–330.
Elfner, Emily (2006) Contrastive syllabification in Blackfoot. In Donald
    Baumer, David Montero, and Michael Scanlon (eds) *Proceedings of the
    25th West Coast Conference on Formal Linguistics* 141–149. Somerville,
    MA: Cascadilla Press.
Erwin, Wallace M. (1963) *A Short Reference Grammar of Iraqi Arabic*.
    Washington, DC: Georgetown University Press.
Farwaneh, Samira (1995) *Directionality Effects in Arabic Dialect Syllable
    Structure*. Doctoral dissertation. Salt Lake City, UT: University of Utah.
Féry, Caroline (2003) Onsets and nonmoraic syllables in German. In Caroline
    Féry and Ruben van de Vijver (eds) *The Syllable in Optimality Theory*
    213–237. Cambridge: Cambridge University Press.
Fischer, Wolfdietrich and Jastrow, Otto (eds) (1980) *Handbuch der Arabischen
    Dialekte*. Wiesbaden: Otto Harrassowitz.
Fitzgerald, Colleen M. (2002) Tohono O'odham stress in a single ranking.
    Phonology 19: 253–271.
Flemming, Edward (1995) *Auditory Representations in Phonology*. Doctoral
    dissertation. Los Angeles: UCLA.
Fodor, Jerry A., Bever, Thomas G., and Garrett, Merrill (1974) *The Psychology
    of Language*. New York: McGraw Hill.
Fukazawa, Haruka (1999) *Theoretical Implications of OCP Effects on Features
    in Optimality Theory*. Doctoral dissertation. College Park, MD: University
    of Maryland. [Available on Rutgers Optimality Archive, ROA-307.]
Fukazawa, Haruka and Miglio, Viola (1998) Restricting conjunction to
    constraint families. In Vida Samiian (ed.) *Proceedings of the Western
    Conference on Linguistics 9 (WECOL 96)* 102–117. Fresno, CA:
    Department of Linguistics, California State University, Fresno.
Gafos, Adamantios (1998) Eliminating long-distance consonantal spreading.
    Natural Language and Linguistic Theory 16: 223–278.
Gafos, Adamantios (1999) *The Articulatory Basis of Locality in Phonology*.
    New York: Garland.
Gafos, Adamantios and Lombardi, Linda (1999) Consonant transparency and
    vowel echo. In Pius N. Tamanji, Mako Hirotani, and Nancy Hall (eds)

Proceedings of the North East Linguistic Society 29, vol. 2: Papers from the Poster Sessions 81–95. Amherst, MA: GLSA Publications.

Gnanadesikan, Amalia (1997) *Phonology with Ternary Scales*. Doctoral dissertation. Amherst, MA: University of Massachusetts at Amherst. [Available on Rutgers Optimality Archive, ROA-195.]

Gnanadesikan, Amalia (2004) Markedness and faithfulness constraints in child phonology. In René Kager, Joe Pater, and Wim Zonneveld (eds) *Constraints in Phonological Acquisition* 73–108. Cambridge: Cambridge University Press. [Originally circulated in 1995. Available on Rutgers Optimality Archive, ROA-67.]

Goldrick, Matthew (2000) Turbid output representations and the unity of opacity. In Masako Hirotani (ed.) *Proceedings of the North East Linguistics Society 30* 231–246. Amherst, MA: GLSA Publications.

Goldrick, Matthew and Smolensky, Paul (1998) Opacity = turbidity + myopia? Unpublished manuscript. Baltimore, MD: Johns Hopkins University. [Handout annotated as 'Draft of October 11, 1998'.]

Goldsmith, John (1976a) *Autosegmental Phonology*. Doctoral dissertation. Cambridge, MA: MIT. [Published by Garland Press, New York, 1979.]

Goldsmith, John (1976b) An overview of autosegmental phonology. *Linguistic Analysis* 2: 23–68.

Goldsmith, John (1993a) Harmonic phonology. In John Goldsmith (ed.) *The Last Phonological Rule: Reflections on Constraints and Derivations* 21–60. Chicago: University of Chicago Press.

Goldsmith, John (1993b) Introduction. In John Goldsmith (ed.) *The Last Phonological Rule: Reflections on Constraints and Derivations* 1–20. Chicago: University of Chicago Press.

Goldsmith, John (1996) Tone in Mituku: How a floating tone nailed down an intermediate level. In Jacques Durand and Bernard Laks (eds) *Current Trends in Phonology: Models and Methods* 267–280. Manchester, England: European Studies Research Institute, University of Salford.

Gordon, Matthew (1996) Balto-Fennic-Sámi consonant gradation as fortition. In Chai-Shune Hsu (ed.) *UCLA Working Papers in Phonology 1* 107–124. Los Angeles: Department of Linguistics, UCLA.

Gordon, Matthew (1999) *Syllable Weight: Phonetics, Phonology, and Typology*. Doctoral dissertation. Los Angeles, CA: UCLA.

Gordon, Matthew (2003) The puzzle of onset-sensitive stress: A perceptually-driven approach. In Gina Garding and Mimu Tsujimura (eds) *WCCFL 22: Proceedings of the 22nd West Coast Conference on Formal Linguistics* 217–230. Somerville, MA: Cascadilla Press.

Gouskova, Maria (2003) *Deriving Economy: Syncope in Optimality Theory*. Doctoral dissertation. Amherst, MA: University of Massachusetts Amherst. [Available on Rutgers Optimality Archive, ROA-610.]

Green, Antony Dubach (2004) Opacity in Tiberian Hebrew: Morphology, not phonology. *ZAS Papers in Linguistics* 37 (December): 37–70. [Papers in phonetics and phonology, edited by S. Fuchs and S. Hamann. Available on Rutgers Optimality Archive, ROA-703.]

Grimshaw, Jane (1994) Minimal projection and clause structure. In Barbara
Lust, Margarita Suñer, and John Whitman (eds) *Syntactic Theory and
First Language Acquisition: Cross-Linguistic Perspectives, vol. I: Heads,
Projections, and Learnability* 75–83. Hillsdale, NJ: Lawrence Erlbaum.

Grotzfeld, Heinz (1965) *Syrisch-Arabische Grammatik*. Wiesbaden:
O. Harrassowitz.

Guerssel, Mohammed (1977) Constraints on phonological rules. *Linguistic
Analysis* 3: 267–305.

Gussmann, Edmund (1976) Recoverable derivations and phonological change.
Lingua 40: 281–303.

Haddad, Ghassan (1984) *Problems and Issues in the Phonology of Lebanese
Arabic*. Doctoral dissertation. Urbana, IL: University of Illinois.

Hagstrom, Paul (1997) Contextual metrical invisibility. In Benjamin Bruening
(ed.) *PF: Papers at the Interface [=MIT Working Papers in Linguistics
30]* 113–181. Cambridge, MA: Department of Linguistics and Philosophy,
MIT. [Available at http://www.bu.edu/linguistics/UG/hagstrom/papers/CMI-
MITWPL.pdf.]

Hale, Kenneth (1973) Deep-surface canonical disparities in relation to analysis
and change: An Australian example. In Thomas Sebeok (ed.) *Current Trends
in Linguistics* 401–458. The Hague: Mouton.

Hale, Mark and Kissock, Madelyn (1998) The phonology-syntax interface
in Rotuman. In Matthew Pearson (ed.) *Recent Papers in Austronesian
Linguistics: Proceedings of the Third and Fourth Meetings of the
Austronesian Formal Linguistics Society, UCLA Occasional Papers in
Linguistics #21* 115–128. Los Angeles: Department of Linguistics,UCLA.

Hale, Mark, Kissock, Madelyn, and Reiss, Charles (1998) Output-output cor-
respondence in Optimality Theory. In Emily Curtis, James Lyle, and Gabriel
Webster (eds) *The Proceedings of the West Coast Conference on Formal
Linguistics 16* 223–236. Stanford, CA: CSLI Publications. [Available on
Rutgers Optimality Archive, ROA-202.]

Hall, Nancy (2003) *Gestures and Segments: Vowel Intrusion as Overlap*.
Doctoral dissertation. Amherst, MA: University of Massachusetts, Amherst.

Halle, Morris and Idsardi, William (1997) *r*, hypercorrection, and the Elsewhere
Condition. In Iggy Roca (ed.) *Derivations and Constraints in Phonology*
331–348. Oxford: Clarendon Press.

Harries, Lyndon (1950) *A Grammar of Mwera*. Johannesburg: Witwatersrand
University Press. [Bantu Grammatical Archives 1.]

Harrikari, Heli (1999) The inalterability of long vowels in Finnish. Handout
from GLOW, Nanzan University, Nagoya, Japan.

Harris, Zellig (1946) From morpheme to utterance. *Language* 22: 161–183.

Hayes, Bruce (1986) Inalterability in CV phonology. *Language* 62: 321–351.

Hayes, Bruce (1987) A revised parametric metrical theory. In Joyce McDonough
and Bernadette Plunkett (eds) *Proceedings of the North East Linguistic
Society 17* 274–289. Amherst: GLSA Publications.

Hayes, Bruce (1989) Compensatory lengthening in moraic phonology. *Linguistic Inquiry* 20: 253–306.

Hayes, Bruce (1990) Precompiled phrasal phonology. In Sharon Inkelas and Draga Zec (eds) *The Phonology-Syntax Connection* 85–108. Chicago: University of Chicago Press.

Hayes, Bruce (1995) *Metrical Stress Theory: Principles and Case Studies.* Chicago: The University of Chicago Press.

Hermans, Ben and van Oostendorp, Marc (eds) (1999) *The Derivational Residue in Phonological Optimality Theory.* Amsterdam: John Benjamins.

Herzallah, Rukayyah (1990) *Aspects of Palestinian Arabic Phonology: A Nonlinear Approach.* Doctoral dissertation: Cornell University. [Distributed as Working Papers of the Cornell Phonetics Laboratory No. 4.]

Hewitt, Mark and Crowhurst, Megan (1996) Conjunctive constraints and templates in Optimality Theory. In Jill Beckman (ed.) *Proceedings of the North East Linguistic Society 26* 101–116. Amherst, MA: GLSA Publications.

Hockett, Charles F. (1973) Yokuts as testing-ground for linguistic methods. *International Journal of American Linguistics* 39: 63–79.

Hogg, Richard M. (1978) The Duke of York gambit: A variation. *Lingua* 44: 255–266.

Hooper [Bybee], Joan (1976) *An Introduction to Natural Generative Phonology.* New York: Academic Press.

Hooper [Bybee], Joan (1979) Substantive principles in natural generative phonology. In Daniel Dinnsen (ed.) *Current Approaches to Phonological Theory* 106–125. Bloomington: Indiana University Press.

Horwood, Graham (2002) Precedence faithfulness governs morpheme position. In Line Mikkelsen and Christopher Potts (eds) *Proceedings of the 21st West Coast Conference on Formal Linguistics* 166–179. Cambridge, MA: Cascadilla Press. [Available on Rutgers Optimality Archive, ROA-527.]

Horwood, Graham (2004) *Order without Chaos: Relational Faithfulness and Position of Exponence in Optimality Theory.* Doctoral dissertation. New Brunswick, NJ: Rutgers University.

Howe, Darin and Pulleyblank, Douglas (2004) Harmonic scales as faithfulness. *Canadian Journal of Linguistics* 49: 1–49. [Available at http://www.fp.ucalgary.ca/howed/PerceptualFaith.pdf.]

Humbert, Helga (1995) *Phonological Segments: Their Structure and Behavior.* The Hague: Holland Academic Graphics. [Doctoral dissertation, University of Leiden.]

Hume, Elizabeth (1998) Metathesis in phonological theory: The case of Leti. *Lingua* 104: 147–186. [Available on Rutgers Optimality Archive, ROA-180.]

Hume, Elizabeth (2001) Metathesis: Formal and functional considerations. In Elizabeth Hume, Norval Smith, and Jeroen Van de Weijer (eds) *Surface Syllable Structure and Segment Sequencing* 1–25. Leiden: Holland Institute of Linguistics (HIL). [Available at http://www.ling.ohio-state.edu/~Eehume/papers/hume_metathesisS5.pdf.]

Hyman, Larry (1985) *A Theory of Phonological Weight*. Dordrecht: Foris.

Hyman, Larry (1988) Underspecification and vowel height transfer in Esimbi. *Phonology* 5: 255–273.

Hyman, Larry (1993) Problems for rule ordering in phonology: Two Bantu test cases. In John Goldsmith (ed.) *The Last Phonological Rule: Reflections on Constraints and Derivations* 195–222. Chicago: University of Chicago Press.

Idsardi, William (1997) Sympathy creates chaos. Unpublished manuscript. Newark, DE: University of Delaware. [Available at http://www.ling.udel.edu/idsardi/work/1997sympathy.pdf.]

Idsardi, William (1998) Tiberian Hebrew spirantization and phonological derivations. *Linguistic Inquiry* 29: 37–73.

Ingham, Bruce (1982) *Northeast Arabian Dialects*. London: Kegan Paul International.

Inkelas, Sharon (1989) *Prosodic Constituency in the Lexicon*. Doctoral dissertation. Stanford, CA: Stanford University. [Published 1990, Outstanding Dissertations in Linguistics Series, Garland Press, New York.]

Inkelas, Sharon and Orgun, C. Orhan (1995) Level ordering and economy in the lexical phonology of Turkish. *Language* 71: 763–793.

Irshied, Omar (1984) *The Phonology of Bani-Hassan Arabic, a Bedouin Jordanian dialect*. Doctoral dissertation. Champaign, IL: University of Illinois at Champaign-Urbana.

Irshied, Omar and Kenstowicz, Michael (1984) Some phonological rules of Bani-Hassan Arabic, a Bedouin dialect. *Studies in the Linguistic Sciences* 14: 109–147.

Ito, Junko (1986) *Syllable Theory in Prosodic Phonology*. Doctoral dissertation: University of Massachusetts Amherst. [Published 1988. Outstanding Dissertations in Linguistics series. New York: Garland.]

Ito, Junko (1989) A prosodic theory of epenthesis. *Natural Language and Linguistic Theory* 7: 217–259.

Ito, Junko and Mester, Armin (1986) The phonology of voicing in Japanese: Theoretical consequences for morphological accessibility. *Linguistic Inquiry* 17: 49–73.

Ito, Junko and Mester, Armin (1997a) Featural sympathy: Feeding and counterfeeding interactions in Japanese. In Rachel Walker, Motoko Katayama, and Daniel Karvonen (eds) *Phonology at Santa Cruz* 29–36. Santa Cruz, CA: Linguistics Research Center, University of California.

Ito, Junko and Mester, Armin (1997b) Sympathy theory and German truncations. In Viola Miglio and Bruce Morén (eds) *University of Maryland Working Papers in Linguistics 5. Selected Phonology Papers from Hopkins Optimality Theory Workshop 1997 / University of Maryland Mayfest 1997* 117–139. [Available on Rutgers Optimality Archive, ROA-211.]

Ito, Junko and Mester, Armin (1998) German coda conditions: Sympathy meets freedom of the input. Handout from The Syllable: Typology and Theory, Tuebingen, Germany.

Ito, Junko and Mester, Armin (1999) Realignment. In René Kager, Harry van der Hulst, and Wim Zonneveld (eds) *The Prosody-Morphology Interface* 188–217. Cambridge: Cambridge University Press.

Ito, Junko and Mester, Armin (2001) Structure preservation and stratal opacity in German. In Linda Lombardi (ed.) *Segmental Phonology in Optimality Theory* 261–295. Cambridge: Cambridge University Press.

Ito, Junko and Mester, Armin (2003a) *Japanese Morphophonemics: Markedness and Word Structure*. Cambridge, MA: MIT Press.

Ito, Junko and Mester, Armin (2003b) Lexical and postlexical phonology in Optimality Theory: Evidence from Japanese. *Linguistische Berichte* Sonderheft 11: Resolving conflicts in grammars: 183–207. [Available at http://people.ucsc.edu/~ito/PAPERS/lexpostlex.pdf.]

Ito, Junko and Mester, Armin (2003c) On the sources of opacity in OT: Coda processes in German. In Caroline Féry and Ruben van de Vijver (eds) *The Syllable in Optimality Theory* 271–303. Cambridge: Cambridge University Press. [Available on Rutgers Optimality Archive, ROA-347.]

Iverson, Gregory K. (1974) *Ordering Constraints in Phonology*. Doctoral dissertation: University of Minnesota.

Iverson, Gregory K. (1976) A guide to sanguine relationships. In Andreas Koutsoudas (ed.) *The Application and Ordering of Grammatical Rules* 22–35. The Hague: Mouton.

Iverson, Gregory K. (1995) Rule ordering. In John A. Goldsmith (ed.) *The Handbook of Phonological Theory* 609–614. Cambridge, MA, and Oxford, UK: Blackwell.

Jensen, John (1995) Constraints and opaque interactions. *Cahiers linguistiques d'Ottawa* 23: 1–9.

Jesney, Karen (2005) *Chain Shift in Phonological Acquisition*. MA Thesis. Calgary, Alberta: University of Calgary.

Johnson, C. Douglas (1979) Opaque stress in Palestinian. *Lingua* 49: 153–168.

Johnstone, T. M. (1967a) Aspects of syllabication in the spoken Arabic of `Anaiza. *Bulletin of the School of Oriental and African Studies* 30(1): 1–16.

Johnstone, T. M. (1967b) *Eastern Arabian dialect studies*. Oxford: Oxford University Press.

Joos, Martin (1942) A phonological dilemma in Canadian English. *Language* 18: 141–144.

Joos, Martin (ed.) (1957) *Readings in Linguistics I*. Chicago and London: University of Chicago Press.

Jun, Jongho (1999) Generalized sympathy. In Pius N. Tamanji, Mako Hirotani, and Nancy Hall (eds) *Proceedings of the North East Linguistic Society 29* 121–135. Amherst, MA: GLSA Publications.

Kager, René (1993) Alternatives to the iambic-trochaic law. *Natural Language and Linguistic Theory* 11: 381–432.

Kager, René (1997) Rhythmic vowel deletion in Optimality Theory. In Iggy Roca (ed.) *Derivations and Constraints in Phonology* 463–499. Oxford: Oxford University Press.

Kager, René (1999a) *Optimality Theory*. Cambridge: Cambridge University Press.

Kager, René (1999b) Surface opacity of metrical structure in Optimality Theory. In Ben Hermans and Marc van Oostendorp (eds) *The Derivational Residue in Phonological Optimality Theory* 207–245. Amsterdam: John Benjamins.

Kager, René. (2001) Rhythmic directionality by positional licensing. Handout of talk presented at Fifth HIL Phonology Conference (HILP 5), University of Potsdam. [Available on Rutgers Optimality Archive, ROA-514.]

Kahn, Daniel (1976) *Syllable-based Generalizations in English Phonology*. Doctoral dissertation. Cambridge, MA: MIT. [Published by Garland Press, New York, 1980.]

Kaisse, Ellen M. and Hargus, Sharon (1993a) Introduction. In Sharon Hargus and Ellen M. Kaisse (eds) *Studies in Lexical Phonology* 1–19. San Diego: Academic Press.

Kaisse, Ellen M. and Hargus, Sharon (eds) (1993b) *Studies in Lexical Phonology*. San Diego: Academic Press.

Kaisse, Ellen M. and Shaw, Patricia (1985) On the theory of lexical phonology. *Phonology* 2: 1–30.

Kaneko, Ikuyo and Kawahara, Shigeto (2002) Positional faithfulness theory and the emergence of the unmarked: The case of Kagoshima Japanese. *ICU English Studies* 5: 18–36.

Karvonen, Daniel and Sherman [Ussishkin], Adam (1997) Sympathy, opacity, and u-umlaut in Icelandic. In Rachel Walker, Motoko Katayama, and Daniel Karvonen (eds) *Phonology at Santa Cruz* 37–48. Santa Cruz, CA: Linguistics Research Center, University of California.

Karvonen, Daniel and Sherman [Ussishkin], Adam (1998) Opacity in Icelandic revisited: a Sympathy account. In Pius N. Tamanji and Kiyomi Kusumoto (eds) *Proceedings of the North East Linguistic Society 28* 189–201. Amherst, MA: GLSA Publications.

Katayama, Motoko (1998) *Optimality Theory and Japanese Loanword Phonology*. Doctoral Dissertation: University of California, Santa Cruz.

Kaye, Jonathan (1974) Opacity and recoverability in phonology. *Canadian Journal of Linguistics* 19: 134–149.

Kaye, Jonathan (1975) A functional explanation of rule ordering in phonology. In *Papers from the Parasession on Functionalism* 244–252. Chicago, IL: Chicago Linguistic Society.

Keer, Edward (1999) *Geminates, the OCP, and the Nature of CON*. Doctoral dissertation. New Brunswick, NJ: Rutgers University. [Available on Rutgers Optimality Archive, ROA-350.]

Kenstowicz, Michael. (1981a) The metrical structure of Arabic accent. Handout of talk presented at UCLA-USC Conference on Nonlinear Phonology, Lake Arrowhead, CA.

Kenstowicz, Michael (1981b) Vowel harmony in Palestinian Arabic. *Linguistics* 19: 449–465.

Kenstowicz, Michael (1983) Parametric variation and accent in the Arabic dialects. In A. Chukerman, M. Marks, and J. F. Richardson (eds) *Papers from CLS 19* 205–213. Chicago: Chicago Linguistic Society.

Kenstowicz, Michael (1986) Notes on syllable structure in three Arabic dialects. *Revue québecoise de linguistique* 16: 101–128.

Kenstowicz, Michael (1994) Syllabification in Chukchee: A constraints-based analysis. In Alice Davison, Nicole Maier, Glaucia Silva, and Wan Su Yan (eds) *Proceedings of the Formal Linguistics Society of Mid-America 4* 160–181. Iowa City: Department of Linguistics, University of Iowa. [Available on Rutgers Optimality Archive, ROA-30.]

Kenstowicz, Michael (1995) Cyclic vs. non-cyclic constraint evaluation. *Phonology* 12: 397–436. [Available on Rutgers Optimality Archive, ROA-31.]

Kenstowicz, Michael (1996a) Base-identity and uniform exponence: Alternatives to cyclicity. In Jacques Durand and Bernard Laks (eds) *Current Trends in Phonology: Models and Methods* 363–393. Paris-X and Salford: University of Salford Publications. [Available on Rutgers Optimality Archive, ROA-103.]

Kenstowicz, Michael (1996b) Quality-sensitive stress. *Rivista di Linguistica* 9: 157–187.

Kenstowicz, Michael and Kisseberth, Charles (1971) Unmarked bleeding orders. *Studies in the Linguistic Sciences* 1: 8–28.

Kenstowicz, Michael and Kisseberth, Charles (1977) *Topics in Phonological Theory*. New York: Academic Press.

Kenstowicz, Michael and Kisseberth, Charles (1979) *Generative Phonology: Description and Theory*. New York: Academic Press.

Kikuchi, Seiichiro (1999) Opacity and transparency in Spanish plurals: A sympathetic approach. In *On'in Kenkyu [Phonological Studies]* 61–68. Tokyo: Kaitakusha. [Edited by Nihon On'inron Gakkai (The Phonological Society of Japan).]

Kiparsky, Paul (1968) Linguistic universals and linguistic change. In Emmon Bach and Robert Harms (eds) *Universals in Linguistic Theory* 170–202. New York: Holt, Rinehart and Winston.

Kiparsky, Paul (1971) Historical linguistics. In W. O. Dingwall (ed.) *A Survey of Linguistic Science* 576–642. College Park, MD: University of Maryland Linguistics Program.

Kiparsky, Paul (1973) Phonological representations. In O. Fujimura (ed.) *Three Dimensions of Linguistic Theory* 3–136. Tokyo: TEC.

Kiparsky, Paul (1976) Abstractness, opacity, and global rules. In Andreas Koutsoudas (ed.) *The Application and Ordering of Phonological Rules* 160–184. The Hague: Mouton.

Kiparsky, Paul (1982) Lexical phonology and morphology. In I. S. Yang (ed.) *Linguistics in the Morning Calm* 3–91. Seoul: Hanshin.

Kiparsky, Paul (1983) Word formation and the lexicon. In F. Ingemann (ed.) *Proceedings of the Mid-America Linguistics Conference* 3–29. Lawrence: University of Kansas.

Kiparsky, Paul (1984) On the lexical phonology of Icelandic. In C. C. Elert, I. Johansson, and E. Stangert (eds) *Nordic prosody III* 135–164. Umeå: University of Umeå.

Kiparsky, Paul (1985) Some consequences of Lexical Phonology. *Phonology* 2: 85–138.

Kiparsky, Paul (1993) Blocking in non-derived environments. In Sharon Hargus and Ellen Kaisse (eds) *Studies in Lexical Phonology* 277–313. San Diego: Academic Press.

Kiparsky, Paul (1997) LP and OT. Handout from LSA Summer Linguistic Institute, Cornell University.

Kiparsky, Paul (2000) Opacity and cyclicity. *The Linguistic Review* 17: 351–367.

Kiparsky, Paul. (2001) Stratal OT or sympathy? Handout of talk presented at University of Massachusetts, Amherst, MA.

Kiparsky, Paul (2003) Syllables and moras in Arabic. In Caroline Féry and Ruben van de Vijver (eds) *The Syllable in Optimality Theory* 147–182. Cambridge: Cambridge University Press.

Kiparsky, Paul (to appear) *Paradigmatic Effects*. Stanford, CA: CSLI Publications.

Kirchner, Robert (1996) Synchronic chain shifts in Optimality Theory. *Linguistic Inquiry* 27: 341–350. [Available on Rutgers Optimality Archive, ROA-66.]

Kirchner, Robert (1997) Contrastiveness and faithfulness. *Phonology* 14: 83–111. [Available on Rutgers Optimality Archive, ROA-51.]

Kisseberth, Charles (1969) On the abstractness of phonology: The evidence from Yawelmani. *Papers in Linguistics* 1: 248–282.

Kisseberth, Charles (1970) On the functional unity of phonological rules. *Linguistic Inquiry* 1: 291–306.

Kisseberth, Charles (1973) Is rule ordering necessary in phonology? In Braj B. Kachru, Robert B. Lees, Yakov Malkiel, Angelina Pietrangeli, and Sol Saporta (eds) *Issues in Linguistics: Papers in Honor of Henry and Renée Kahane* 418–441. Urbana, IL: University of Illinois Press.

Kisseberth, Charles (1976) The interaction of phonological rules and the polarity of language. In Andreas Koutsoudas (ed.) *The Application and Ordering of Phonological Rules* 41–54. The Hague: Mouton.

Klokeid, Terry (1976) *Topics in Lardil Grammar*. Doctoral dissertation. Cambridge, MA: MIT.

Koontz-Garboden, Andrew J. (2003) Tiberian Hebrew spirantization and related phenomena in stratal OT. Unpublished manuscript. Stanford, CA: Stanford University. [Available on Rutgers Optimality Archive, ROA-607.]

Koutsoudas, Andreas (1976) Unordered rule hypotheses. In Andreas Koutsoudas (ed.) *The Application and Ordering of Grammatical Rules* 1–21. The Hague: Mouton.

Koutsoudas, Andreas, Sanders, Gerald, and Noll, Craig (1974) On the application of phonological rules. *Language* 50: 1–28.

Kurisu, Kazutaka (2001) *The Phonology of Morpheme Realization*. Doctoral dissertation. Santa Cruz, CA: University of California, Santa Cruz. [Available on Rutgers Optimality Archive, ROA-490.]

Kuroda, S.-Y. (1967) *Yawelmani Phonology*. Cambridge, MA: MIT Press.

Laferriere, Martha (1975) Rule exceptions, functionalism, and language change. *Canadian Journal of Linguistics* 20: 161–182.

Lakoff, George (1993) Cognitive phonology. In John Goldsmith (ed.) *The Last Phonological Rule: Reflections on Constraints and Derivations* 117–145. Chicago: University of Chicago Press.

Lamontagne, Greg and Rice, Keren (1995) A correspondence account of coalescence. In Jill Beckman, Laura Walsh Dickey, and Suzanne Urbanczyk (eds) *University of Massachusetts Occasional Papers in Linguistics 18* 211–224. Amherst, MA: GLSA Publications.

Lee, Minkyung (1999) A case of sympathy in Javanese affixation. In Karen Baertsch and Daniel A. Dinnsen (eds) *Indiana University Working Papers in Linguistics I* 31–36. Bloomington, IN: Indiana University Linguistics Club Publications.

Lehiste, Ilse (1970) *Suprasegmentals*. Cambridge, MA: MIT Press.

Levi, Susannah V. (2000) Modern Hebrew: A challenge for sympathy. *University of Washington Working Papers in Linguistics* 19: 1–14. [Available on Rutgers Optimality Archive, ROA-758.]

Liberman, Mark (1975) *The Intonational System of English*. Doctoral dissertation. Cambridge, MA: MIT. [Distributed by Indiana University Linguistics Club Publications.]

Liberman, Mark and Prince, Alan (1977) On stress and linguistic rhythm. *Linguistic Inquiry* 8: 249–336.

Lindblom, Björn (1978) Final lengthening in speech and music. In E. Gårding, G. Bruce, and R. Bannert (eds) *Nordic Prosody: Papers from a Symposium* 85–101. Malmö: Department of Linguistics and Phonetics, Lund University.

Lombardi, Linda (1998) Evidence for MaxFeature constraints from Japanese. In Haruka Fukazawa, Frida Morelli, Caro Struijke, and Yi-Ching Su (eds) *University of Maryland Working Papers in Linguistics*. College Park, MD: Department of Linguistics, University of Maryland. [Available on Rutgers Optimality Archive, ROA-247.]

Lombardi, Linda (2001) Why Place and Voice are different: Constraint-specific alternations in Optimality Theory. In Linda Lombardi (ed.) *Segmental Phonology in Optimality Theory: Constraints and Representations* 13–45. Cambridge: Cambridge University Press. [Available (1995) on Rutgers Optimality Archive, ROA-105.]

Lowenstamm, Jean and Kaye, Jonathan (1986) Compensatory lengthening in Tiberian Hebrew. In L. Wetzels and E. Sezer (eds) *Studies in Compensatory Lengthening* 97–146. Dordrecht: Foris.

Łubowicz, Anna (2002) Derived environment effects in Optimality Theory. *Lingua* 112: 243–280. [Available on Rutgers Optimality Archive, ROA-103.]

Łubowicz, Anna (2003) *Contrast Preservation in Phonological Mappings*. Doctoral dissertation. Amherst, MA: University of Massachusetts Amherst. [Available on Rutgers Optimality Archive, ROA-554.]

Łubowicz, Anna (2006) Locality of conjunction. In John Alderete, Chung-hye Han, and Alexei Kochetov (eds) *Proceedings of the 24th West Coast Conference on Formal Linguistics* 254–262. Somerville, MA: Cascadilla Press.

Malone, Joseph L. (1993) *Tiberian Hebrew Phonology*. Winona Lake, IN: Eisenbrauns.

McCarthy, John J. (1979) *Formal Problems in Semitic Phonology and Morphology*. Doctoral dissertation. Cambridge, MA: MIT. [Published by Garland Press, New York, 1985.]

McCarthy, John J. (1980) A note on the accentuation of Damascene Arabic. *Studies in the Linguistic Sciences* 10: 77–98.

McCarthy, John J. (1981) A prosodic theory of nonconcatenative morphology. *Linguistic Inquiry* 12: 373–418.

McCarthy, John J. (1986) OCP Effects: Gemination and antigemination. *Linguistic Inquiry* 17: 207–263.

McCarthy, John J. (1988) Feature geometry and dependency: A review. *Phonetica* 43: 84–108.

McCarthy, John J. (1991) Semitic gutturals and distinctive feature theory. In Mushira Eid and Bernard Comrie (eds) *Perspectives on Arabic Linguistics* 63–91. Philadelphia: John Benjamins.

McCarthy, John J. (1993a) A case of surface constraint violation. *Canadian Journal of Linguistics* 38: 169–195.

McCarthy, John J. (1993b) Containment, consistency, and alignment. Handout from Rutgers Optimality Workshop I, New Brunswick, NJ.

McCarthy, John J. (1994a) On coronal 'transparency'. Handout of talk presented at TREND, Santa Cruz, CA. [Available at http://people.umass.edu/jjmccart/coronal_transparency.pdf.]

McCarthy, John J. (1994b) The phonetics and phonology of Semitic pharyn-geals. In Patricia Keating (ed.) *Phonological Structure and Phonetic Form:*

Papers in Laboratory Phonology III 191–233. Cambridge: Cambridge University Press.

McCarthy, John J. (1996) Remarks on phonological opacity in Optimality Theory. In Jacqueline Lecarme, Jean Lowenstamm, and Ur Shlonsky (eds) *Studies in Afroasiatic Grammar: Papers from the Second Conference on Afroasiatic Linguistics, Sophia Antipolis, 1994* 215–243. The Hague: Holland Academic Graphics.

McCarthy, John J. (1999) Sympathy and phonological opacity. *Phonology* 16: 331–399.

McCarthy, John J. (2000a) Harmonic serialism and parallelism. In Masako Hirotani (ed.) *Proceedings of the North East Linguistics Society 30* 501–524. Amherst, MA: GLSA Publications. [Available at http://people.umass.edu/~jjmccart/.]

McCarthy, John J. (2000b) The prosody of phase in Rotuman. *Natural Language and Linguistic Theory* 18: 147–197.

McCarthy, John J. (2002a) Comparative markedness [long version]. In Angela Carpenter, Andries Coetzee, and Paul de Lacy (eds) *University of Massachusetts Occasional Papers in Linguistics 26: Papers in Optimality Theory II* 171–246. Amherst, MA: GLSA. [Available on Rutgers Optimality Archive, ROA-489.]

McCarthy, John J. (2002b) *A Thematic Guide to Optimality Theory*. Cambridge: Cambridge University Press.

McCarthy, John J. (2003a) Comparative markedness. *Theoretical Linguistics* 29: 1–51.

McCarthy, John J. (2003b) OT constraints are categorical. *Phonology* 20: 75–138. [Available at http://people.umass.edu/jjmccart/categorical.pdf.]

McCarthy, John J. (2003c) Sympathy, cumulativity, and the Duke-of-York gambit. In Caroline Féry and Ruben van de Vijver (eds) *The Syllable in Optimality Theory* 23–76. Cambridge: Cambridge University Press.

McCarthy, John J. (2003d) What does comparative markedness explain, what should it explain, and how? *Theoretical Linguistics* 29: 141–155.

McCarthy, John J. (2005a) The length of stem-final vowels in Colloquial Arabic. In Mohammad T. Alhawary and Elabbas Benmamoun (eds) *Perspectives on Arabic Linguistics XVII-XVIII: Papers from the Seventeenth and Eighteenth Annual Symposia on Arabic Linguistics* 1–26. Amsterdam: Benjamins. [Available on Rutgers Optimality Archive, ROA-616.]

McCarthy, John J. (2005b) Taking a free ride in morphophonemic learning. *Catalan Journal of Linguistics*. [Special issue on phonology in morphology edited by Maria-Rosa Lloret and Jesús Jiménez. Available on Rutgers Optimality Archive, ROA-683.]

McCarthy, John J. (2007a) Restraint of analysis. In Sylvia Blaho, Patrik Bye, and Martin Kraemer (eds) *Freedom of Analysis*. The Hague: Mouton.

McCarthy, John J. (2007b) Slouching toward optimality: Coda reduction in OT-CC. *Phonological Studies (Journal of the Phonological Society of Japan)* 7.

McCarthy, John J. and Prince, Alan (1986/1996) Prosodic Morphology 1986. Report. New Brunswick, NJ: Rutgers University Center for Cognitive Science. [Available at http://ruccs.rutgers.edu/pub/papers/pm86all.pdf.]

McCarthy, John J. and Prince, Alan (1990a) Foot and word in prosodic morphology: The Arabic broken plural. *Natural Language and Linguistic Theory* 8: 209–283.

McCarthy, John J. and Prince, Alan (1990b) Prosodic morphology and templatic morphology. In Mushira Eid and John J. McCarthy (eds) *Perspectives on Arabic linguistics II: Papers from the Second Annual Symposium on Arabic Linguistics* 1–54. Amsterdam: John Benjamins.

McCarthy, John J. and Prince, Alan (1993a) Generalized Alignment. In Geert Booij and Jaap van Marle (eds) *Yearbook of Morphology* 79–153. Dordrecht: Kluwer. [Available on Rutgers Optimality Archive, ROA-7.]

McCarthy, John J. and Prince, Alan (1993b) Prosodic Morphology: Constraint Interaction and Satisfaction. Report. New Brunswick, NJ: Rutgers University Center for Cognitive Science. [Available on Rutgers Optimality Archive, ROA-482.]

McCarthy, John J. and Prince, Alan (1994) The emergence of the unmarked: Optimality in prosodic morphology. In Mercè Gonzàlez (ed.) *Proceedings of the North East Linguistic Society 24* 333–379. Amherst, MA: GLSA Publications. [Available on the Rutgers Optimality Archive, ROA-13.]

McCarthy, John J. and Prince, Alan (1995) Faithfulness and reduplicative identity. In Jill Beckman, Laura Walsh Dickey, and Suzanne Urbanczyk (eds) *University of Massachusetts Occasional Papers in Linguistics 18* 249–384. Amherst, MA: GLSA Publications. [Available on Rutgers Optimality Archive, ROA-103.]

McCarthy, John J. and Prince, Alan (1999) Faithfulness and identity in Prosodic Morphology. In René Kager, Harry van der Hulst, and Wim Zonneveld (eds) *The Prosody-Morphology Interface* 218–309. Cambridge: Cambridge University Press.

McGarrity, Laura Wilbur (1999) A sympathy account of multiple opacity in Wintu. In Karen Baertsch and Daniel A. Dinnsen (eds) *Indiana University Working Papers in Linguistics I* 93–107. Bloomington, IN: Indiana University Linguistics Club Publications.

McMahon, April (2000) *Chance, Change, and Optimality*. Oxford: Oxford University Press.

McRobbie, Zita (1999) *Quantity in the Skolt Lappish (Saami) Language: An Acoustic Analysis*. Bloomington, IN: Indiana University Research Institute for Inner Asian Studies.

Merchant, Jason (1997) Sympathetic devoicing and continuancy in Catalan. In Rachel Walker, Motoko Katayama, and Daniel Karvonen (eds) *Phonology at Santa Cruz* 57–62. Santa Cruz, CA: Linguistics Research Center, University of California.

Michelson, Karin (1988) *A Comparative Study of Lake Iroquoian Accent*. Dordrecht: Kluwer.

Mielke, Jeffrey, Hume, Elizabeth, and Armstrong, Michael (2003) Looking through opacity. *Theoretical Linguistics* 29 123–139.

Mitchell, T. F. (1960) Prominence and syllabication in Arabic. *Bulletin of the School of Oriental and African Studies* 23: 369–389.

Mohanan, K. P. (1982) *Lexical Phonology*. Doctoral dissertation. Cambridge, MA: MIT. [Distributed by Indiana University Linguistics Club Publications.]

Morén, Bruce (1999) *Distinctiveness, Coercion and Sonority: A Unified Theory of Weight*. Doctoral dissertation. College Park, MD: University of Maryland. [Available on Rutgers Optimality Archive, ROA-346.]

Moreton, Elliott (2003) Non-computable functions in Optimality Theory. In John J. McCarthy (ed.) *Optimality Theory in Phonology: A Reader* 141–163. Malden, MA, and Oxford, UK: Blackwell. [Available on Rutgers Optimality Archive, ROA-364.]

Moreton, Elliott and Smolensky, Paul (2002) Typological consequences of local constraint conjunction. In Line Mikkelsen and Christopher Potts (eds) *Proceedings of the 21st West Coast Conference on Formal Linguistics* 306–319. Cambridge, MA: Cascadilla Press. [Available on Rutgers Optimality Archive, ROA-525.]

Myers, Scott (1987) Vowel shortening in English. *Natural Language and Linguistic Theory* 5: 485–518.

Myers, Scott (1991a) Persistent rules. *Linguistic Inquiry* 22: 315–344.

Myers, Scott (1991b) Structure preservation and the Strong Domain Hypothesis. *Linguistic Inquiry* 22: 379–385.

Myers, Scott (1997) OCP effects in Optimality Theory. *Natural Language and Linguistic Theory* 15: 847–892.

Nespor, Marina and Vogel, Irene (1986) *Prosodic Phonology*. Dordrecht: Foris.

Newman, Stanley (1944) *Yokuts Language of California*. New York: Viking Fund.

Ní Chiosáin, Máire and Padgett, Jaye (2001) Markedness, segment realization, and locality in spreading. In Linda Lombardi (ed.) *Segmental Phonology in Optimality Theory: Constraints and Representations* 111–156. New York: Cambridge University Press. [Available on Rutgers Optimality Archive, ROA-503.]

Norton, Russell J. (2003) *Derivational Phonology and Optimality Phonology: Formal Comparison and Synthesis*. Doctoral dissertation. Colchester, Essex: University of Essex. [Available on Rutgers Optimality Archive, ROA-613.]

Noske, Roland (1984) Syllabification and syllable changing processes in Yawelmani. In Harry van der Hulst and Norval Smith (eds) *Advances in Non-Linear Phonology* 335–362. Dordrecht: Foris.

Noyer, Rolf (1997) Attic Greek accentuation and intermediate derivational representations. In Iggy Roca (ed.) *Derivations and Constraints in Phonology* 501–528. Oxford: Oxford University Press.

Odden, David (1991) Vowel geometry. *Phonology* 8: 261–289.

Odden, David (1997) Epenthesis, minimality, and degenerate syllables in Zinza. Handout from The Third Mid-Continental Workshop on Phonology, Indiana University, Bloomington, IN.

Orgun, C. Orhan (1996a) Correspondence and identity constraints in two-level Optimality Theory. In Jose Camacho, Lina Choueiri, and Maki Watanabe (eds) *The Proceedings of the West Coast Conference on Formal Linguistics 14* 399–413. Stanford, CA: CSLI Publications. [Available on Rutgers Optimality Archive, ROA-62.]

Orgun, C. Orhan (1996b) *Sign-based Morphology and Phonology, with Special Attention to Optimality Theory*. Doctoral dissertation: University of California, Berkeley. [Available on Rutgers Optimality Archive, ROA-171.]

Padgett, Jaye (1995) Feature classes. In Jill Beckman, Laura Walsh Dickey, and Suzanne Urbanczyk (eds) *University of Massachusetts Occasional Papers in Linguistics 18* 385–420. Amherst, MA: GLSA Publications. [Available on Rutgers Optimality Archive, ROA-112.]

Padgett, Jaye (2002) Constraint conjunction versus grounded constraint subhierarchies in Optimality Theory. Unpublished manuscript. Santa Cruz, CA: University of California, Santa Cruz. [Available on Rutgers Optimality Archive, ROA-530.]

Padgett, Jaye (2003) Contrast and post-velar fronting in Russian. *Natural Language and Linguistic Theory* 21: 39–87.

Paradis, Carole (1988) On constraints and repair strategies. *The Linguistic Review* 6: 71–97.

Paradis, Carole (1997) Non-transparent constraint effects in Gere: From cycles to derivations. In Iggy Roca (ed.) *Derivations and Constraints in Phonology* 529–550. Oxford: Oxford University Press.

Parker, Steve (1998) Disjoint metrical tiers and positional markedness in Huariapano. Unpublished manuscript. Amherst, MA: University of Massachusetts Amherst.

Parkinson, Frederick (1992) The feature pharyngeal in Rwaili Arabic: A case for long distance multiple linking. In Elizabeth Hume (ed.) *The Ohio State University Working Papers in Linguistics*. Columbus, OH: Department of Linguistics, The Ohio State University. [Volume 41, Papers in Phonology.]

Pater, Joe (1996) *NC. In Jill Beckman (ed.) *Proceedings of the North East Linguistics Society 26* 227–239. Amherst, MA: GLSA Publications.

Pater, Joe (1999) Austronesian nasal substitution and other NC effects. In René Kager, Harry van der Hulst, and Wim Zonneveld (eds) *The Prosody-Morphology Interface* 310–343. Cambridge: Cambridge University Press. [Available on Rutgers Optimality Archive, ROA-160.]

Pater, Joe (2000) Nonuniformity in English secondary stress: The role of ranked and lexically specific constraints. *Phonology* 17: 237–274. [Available on Rutgers Optimality Archive, ROA-107.]

Payne, David L. (1981) *The Phonology and Morphology of Axininca Campa.* Arlington, TX: The Summer Institute of Linguistics and University of Texas at Arlington.

Piggott, G. L. (1992) Variability in feature dependency: The case of nasality. *Natural Language and Linguistic Theory* 10: 33–78.

Piggott, G. L. (1995) Epenthesis and syllable weight. *Natural Language and Linguistic Theory* 13: 283–326.

Piggott, G. L. and Singh, Rajendra (1985) The phonology of epenthetic segments. *Canadian Journal of Linguistics* 30: 415–451.

Poser, William (1982) Phonological representations and action-at-a-distance. In Harry van der Hulst and Norval Smith (eds) *The Structure of Phonological Representations* 121–158. Dordrecht: Foris.

Potter, Brian (1994) Serial optimality in Mohawk prosody. In Katharine Beals, Jeannette Denton, Robert Knippen, Lynette Melmar, Hisami Suzuki, and Erica Zeinfeld (eds) *Proceedings of the Thirtieth Annual Regional Meeting of the Chicago Linguistics Society* 347–361. Chicago, IL: Chicago Linguistics Society.

Prince, Alan (1975) *The Phonology and Morphology of Tiberian Hebrew.* Doctoral dissertation. Cambridge, MA: MIT.

Prince, Alan (1980) A metrical theory for Estonian quantity. *Linguistic Inquiry* 11: 511–562.

Prince, Alan (1983) Relating to the grid. *Linguistic Inquiry* 14: 19–100.

Prince, Alan (1987) Planes and copying. *Linguistic Inquiry* 18: 491–510.

Prince, Alan (1990) Quantitative consequences of rhythmic organization. In M. Ziolkowski, M. Noske, and K. Deaton (eds) *Parasession on the Syllable in Phonetics and Phonology* 355–398. Chicago: Chicago Linguistic Society.

Prince, Alan (1996) A letter from Alan Prince. *Glot International* 6(2).

Prince, Alan. (1997) Paninian relations. Handout of talk presented at University of Massachusetts Amherst, Amherst, MA.

Prince, Alan (2002) Arguing optimality. In Angela Carpenter, Andries Coetzee, and Paul de Lacy (eds) *Papers in Optimality Theory II (= University of Massachusetts Occasional Papers 26)* 269–304. Amherst, MA: GLSA. [Available on Rutgers Optimality Archive, ROA-562.]

Prince, Alan and Smolensky, Paul (2004) *Optimality Theory: Constraint Interaction in Generative Grammar.* Malden, MA, and Oxford, UK: Blackwell. [Revision of 1993 technical report, Rutgers University Center for Cognitive Science. Available on Rutgers Optimality Archive, ROA-537.]

Prochazka, Theodore (1988) *Saudi Arabian dialects.* London: Kegan Paul International.

Pulleyblank, Douglas (1998) Yoruba vowel patterns: Deriving asymmetries by the tension between opposing constraints. Unpublished manuscript. Vancouver, BC: University of British Columbia.

Pullum, Geoffrey (1976) The Duke of York gambit. *Journal of Linguistics* 12: 83–102.

Roca, Iggy (ed.) (1997a) *Derivations and Constraints in Phonology.* Oxford: Oxford University Press.

Roca, Iggy (1997b) Derivations or constraints, or derivations and constraints? In Iggy Roca (ed.) *Derivations and Constraints in Phonology* 3–42. Oxford: Oxford University Press.

Rosenthall, Sam (1994) *Vowel/Glide Alternation in a Theory of Constraint Interaction*. Doctoral dissertation. Amherst, MA: University of Massachusetts Amherst. [Available on Rutgers Optimality Archive, ROA-126.]

Rubach, Jerzy (1997) Extrasyllabic consonants in Polish: Derivational Optimality Theory. In Iggy Roca (ed.) *Derivations and Constraints in Phonology* 551–582. Oxford: Oxford University Press.

Rubach, Jerzy (2000) Glide and glottal stop insertion in Slavic languages: A DOT analysis. *Linguistic Inquiry* 31: 271–317.

Sanders, Nathan (1997) On sympathetic correspondence. In Rachel Walker, Motoko Katayama, and Daniel Karvonen (eds) *Phonology at Santa Cruz* 91–102. Santa Cruz, CA: Linguistics Research Center, University of California.

Sanders, Nathan (2002) Preserving synchronic parallelism: Diachrony and opacity in Polish. In *CLS 37–1: The Main Session* 501–516. Chicago: Chicago Linguistic Society.

Sanders, Nathan (2003) *Opacity and Sound Change in the Polish Lexicon*. Doctoral dissertation: University of California, Santa Cruz. [Available at http://wso.williams.edu/~nsanders/diss.html.]

Sapir, Edward and Swadesh, Morris (1978) *Nootka Texts: Tales and Ethnological Narratives, with Grammatical Notes and Lexical Material*. New York: AMS Press.

Schane, Sanford (1968) *French Phonology and Morphology*. Cambridge, MA: MIT Press.

Schane, Sanford (1974) How abstract is abstract? In Anthony Bruck, Robert A. Fox, and Michael W. LaGaly (eds) *Papers from the Parasession on Natural Phonology* 297–317. Chicago: Chicago Linguistic Society.

Scobbie, James, Coleman, John, and Bird, Steven (1996) Key aspects of Declarative Phonology. In Jacques Durand and Bernard Laks (eds) *Current Trends in Phonology: Models and Methods* 685–709. Manchester, England: European Studies Research Institute, University of Salford. [Available at http://www.phon.ox.ac.uk/~jcoleman/scob962.pdf.]

Selkirk, Elisabeth (1980a) Prosodic domains in phonology: Sanskrit revisited. In Mark Aronoff and M.-L. Kean (eds) *Juncture* 107–129. Saratoga, CA: Anma Libri.

Selkirk, Elisabeth (1980b) The role of prosodic categories in English word stress. *Linguistic Inquiry* 11: 563–605.

Selkirk, Elisabeth (1981a) Epenthesis and degenerate syllables in Cairene Arabic. In Hagit Borer and Joseph Aoun (eds) *Theoretical Issues in the Grammar of the Semitic Languages (MIT Working Papers in Linguistics 3)* 111–140. Cambridge, MA: Department of Linguistics and Philosophy, MIT.

Selkirk, Elisabeth (1981b) On the nature of phonological representation. In J. Anderson, J. Laver, and T. Meyers (eds) *The Cognitive Representation of Speech* 379–388. Amsterdam: North Holland.

Selkirk, Elisabeth (1982a) The syllable. In Harry van der Hulst and Norval Smith (eds) *The Structure of Phonological Representations* 337–383. Dordrecht: Foris.

Selkirk, Elisabeth (1982b) *The Syntax of Words*. Cambridge, MA: MIT Press.

Selkirk, Elisabeth (1996) The prosodic structure of function words. In James L. Morgan and Katherine Demuth (eds) *Signal to Syntax: Bootstrapping from Speech to Grammar in Early Acquisition* 187–214. Mahwah, NJ: Lawrence Erlbaum Associates.

Sezer, Engin (1985) An autosegmental analysis of compensatory lengthening in Turkish. In Leo Wetzels and Engin Sezer (eds) *Studies in Compensatory Lengthening* 227–250. Dordrecht: Foris.

Shaw, Patricia (1980) *Dakota Phonology and Morphology*. New York: Garland.

Sherer, Tim (1994) *Prosodic Phonotactics*. Doctoral dissertation. Amherst, MA: University of Massachusetts Amherst.

Smith, Jennifer (2002) *Phonological Augmentation in Prominent Positions*. Doctoral dissertation. Amherst, MA: University of Massachusetts Amherst.

Smolensky, Paul. (1995) On the structure of the constraint component Con of UG. Handout of talk presented at UCLA, Los Angeles, CA. [Available on Rutgers Optimality Archive, ROA-86.]

Sommerstein, Alan (1973) *The Sound Pattern of Ancient Greek*. Oxford: Blackwell.

Spring, Cari (1990) *Implications of Axininca Campa for Prosodic Morphology and Reduplication*. Doctoral dissertation. Tucson, AZ: University of Arizona.

Sprouse, Ronald (1997) A case for enriched inputs. Handout from TREND, Berkeley, CA.

Sprouse, Ronald (1998) Encriched input sets as a source of opacity in OT. Handout from GLOW, Tilburg.

Stahlke, Herbert. (1976) Segment sequences and segmental fusion. *Studies in African Linguistics* 7: 44–63.

Stallcup, Kenneth L. (1980) Noun classes in Esimbi. In *Noun Classes in the Grassfields Bantu Borderland* 139–153. Los Angeles: Dept. of Linguistics, University of Southern California. [*Southern California Occasional Papers in Linguistics (SCOPIL)* 8.]

Steriade, Donca (1986) Yokuts and the vowel plane. *Linguistic Inquiry* 17: 129–146.

Steriade, Donca (1997) Lexical conservatism and its analysis. Unpublished manuscript. Los Angeles: UCLA. [Available at http://www.linguistics.ucla.edu/people/steriade/papers/Korea_lexical_conservatism.pdf.]

Steriade, Donca (1999a) Alternatives to syllable-based accounts of consonantal phonotactics. In Osamu Fujimura, Brian Joseph, and B. Palek (eds)

Proceedings of the 1998 Linguistics and Phonetics Conference 205–242. Prague: Karolinum Press. [Available at http://www.linguistics.ucla.edu/people/steriade/papers/Alternatives_to_Syllables.pdf.]

Steriade, Donca (1999b) Lexical conservatism in French adjectival liaison. In J.-Marc Authier, Barbara Bullock, and Lisa Reid (eds) *Formal Perspectives on Romance Linguistics* 243–270. Amsterdam: John Benjamins.

Tesar, Bruce (1995a) *Computational Optimality Theory*. Doctoral dissertation. Boulder, CO: University of Colorado. [Available on Rutgers Optimality Archive.]

Tesar, Bruce (1995b) Computing Optimal Forms in Optimality Theory: Basic Syllabification. Report. Boulder, Co: Department of Computer Science, University of Colorado. [Available on Rutgers Optimality Archive.]

Tesar, Bruce and Smolensky, Paul (1998) Learnability in Optimality Theory. *Linguistic Inquiry* 29: 229–268. [Available on Rutgers Optimality Archive, ROA-155.]

Tesar, Bruce and Smolensky, Paul (2000) *Learnability in Optimality Theory*. Cambridge, MA: MIT Press.

Tranel, Bernard (1999) Optional schwa deletion: On syllable economy in French. In Jean-Marc Authier, Barbara E. Bullock, and Lisa A. Reed (eds) *Formal Perspectives on Romance Linguistics: Selected papers from the 28th Linguistic Symposium on Romance Languages (LSRL XXVIII), University Park, 16–19 April 1998* 271–288. Amsterdam: Benjamins.

Truckenbrodt, Hubert (2002) Variation in p-phrasing in Bengali. *Linguistic Variation Yearbook* 2: 259–303.

van der Hulst, Harry (1989) Atoms of segmental structure: Components, gestures and dependency. *Phonology* 6: 253–284.

Vaux, Bert (to appear) The appendix. In Eric Raimy and Charles Cairns (eds) *Contemporary Views on Architecture and Representations in Phononological Theory*. Cambridge, MA: MIT Press. [Available at http://web.gc.cuny.edu/Linguistics/events/phonology_symposium/appendix.doc.]

Vennemann, Theo (1972) Phonological uniqueness in natural generative grammar. *Glossa* 6: 105–116.

Vennemann, Theo (1974) Phonological concreteness in natural generative grammar. In Roger W. Shuy and C.-J. Bailey (eds) *Towards Tomorrow's Linguistics*. Washington, DC: Georgetown University Press.

Walker, Rachel (1997) Faith and markedness in Esimbi feature transfer. In Rachel Walker, Motoko Katayama, and Dan Karvonen (eds) *Phonology at Santa Cruz* 103–115. Santa Cruz, CA: Linguistics Research Center, UC Santa Cruz.

Walker, Rachel (1998) *Nasalization, Neutral Segments, and Opacity Effects*. Doctoral dissertation. Santa Cruz, CA: University of California, Santa Cruz. [Available on Rutgers Optimality Archive, ROA-405.]

Walker, Rachel (2001) Positional markedness in vowel harmony. In Caroline Féry, Antony Dubach Green, and Ruben van de Vijver (eds) *Proceedings of*

HILP 5 212–232. Potsdam, Germany: University of Potsdam. [Linguistics at Potsdam 12. http://www-rcf.usc.edu/~rwalker/HILP5.pdf.]

Walker, Rachel (2003) Reinterpreting transparency in nasal harmony. In Jeroen van de Weijer, Vincent J. van Heuven, and Harry van der Hulst (eds) *The Phonological Spectrum, Part I: Segmental Structure* 37–72. Amsterdam: John Benjamins. [Available on Rutgers Optimality Archive, ROA-306.]

Wetzels, Leo and Sezer, Engin (eds) (1986) *Studies in Compensatory Lengthening*. Dordrecht: Foris.

Wheeler, Deirdre and Touretzky, David (1993) A connectionist implementation of cognitive phonology. In John Goldsmith (ed.) *The Last Phonological Rule: Reflections on Constraints and Derivations* 146–172. Chicago: University of Chicago Press.

Wiese, Richard (2001) The structure of the German vocabulary: Edge marking of categories and functional considerations. *Linguistics* 39: 95–115.

Wilbur, Laura (1998) Convergent sympathy. Handout from Linguistic Society of America annual meeting.

Wilkinson, Karina (1988) Prosodic structure and Lardil phonology. *Linguistic Inquiry* 19: 325–334.

Wilson, Colin (2000) *Targeted Constraints: An Approach to Contextual Neutralization in Optimality Theory*. Doctoral dissertation. Baltimore, MD: Johns Hopkins University.

Wilson, Colin (2003) Unbounded spreading in OT (or, Unbounded spreading is local spreading iterated unboundedly). Handout from SWOT 8, Tucson, AZ.

Wilson, Colin (2004) Analyzing unbounded spreading with constraints: Marks, targets, and derivations. Unpublished manuscript. Los Angeles: UCLA.

Yu, Alan C. L. (2000) Stress assignment in Tohono O'odham. *Phonology* 17: 117–135.

Zec, Draga (1995) Sonority constraints on syllable structure. *Phonology* 12: 85–129.

Zoll, Cheryl (1993) Directionless syllabification and ghosts in Yawelmani. Unpublished manuscript. Berkeley, CA: University of California. [Available on Rutgers Optimality Archive, ROA-28.]

Zoll, Cheryl (1998) *Parsing Below the Segment in a Constraint-based Framework*. Stanford, CA: CSLI Publications. [1996 Doctoral dissertation, University of California, Berkeley. Available on Rutgers Optimality Archive, ROA-143.]

Zoll, Cheryl (2004) Positional asymmetries and licensing. In John J. McCarthy (ed.) *Optimality Theory in Phonology: A Reader* 365–378. Malden, MA, and Oxford, UK: Blackwell.

Index

Page numbers in bold indicate the primary discussion of a topic. Constraints are listed here only if they are particularly relevant or important.

CPSIA information can be obtained
at www.ICGtesting.com
Printed in the USA
JSHW011207270623
43765JS00001B/6